FREE Test Taking Tips Video/DVD Offer

To better serve you, we created videos covering test taking tips that we want to give you for FREE. **These videos cover world-class tips that will help you succeed on your test.**

We just ask that you send us feedback about this product. Please let us know what you thought about it—whether good, bad, or indifferent.

To get your **FREE videos**, you can use the QR code below or email freevideos@studyguideteam.com with "Free Videos" in the subject line and the following information in the body of the email:

a. The title of your product

b. Your product rating on a scale of 1-5, with 5 being the highest

c. Your feedback about the product

If you have any questions or concerns, please don't hesitate to contact us at info@studyguideteam.com.

Thank you!

EMT Study Guide 2024-2025

3 Practice Tests and NREMT Prep Book

[7th Edition]

Lydia Morrison

Written and edited by TPB Publishing.

ISBN 13: 9781637751879

Table of Contents

Welcome **1**

FREE Videos/DVD OFFER 1

Quick Overview **2**

Test-Taking Strategies **3**

Introduction to the EMT Exam **7**

Study Prep Plan for the EMT Exam **9**

Airway, Respiration, and Ventilation **13**

Practice Quiz 37

Answer Explanations 38

Cardiology and Resuscitation **39**

Practice Questions 50

Answer Explanations 51

Trauma **52**

Practice Quiz 83

Answer Explanations 84

Medical, Obstetrics, and Gynecology **85**

Practice Questions 108

Answer Explanations 109

Operations **110**

Practice Quiz 127

Answer Explanations 128

EMT Practice Test #1 **129**

Answer Explanations #1 .... *150*

EMT Practice Test #2 .... *165*

Answer Explanations #2 .... *165*

EMT Practice Test #3 .... *199*

Answer Explanations #3 .... *220*

Index *233*

Welcome

Dear Reader,

Welcome to your new Test Prep Books study guide! We are pleased that you chose us to help you prepare for your exam. There are many study options to choose from, and we appreciate you choosing us. Studying can be a daunting task, but we have designed a smart, effective study guide to help prepare you for what lies ahead.

Whether you're a parent helping your child learn and grow, a high school student working hard to get into your dream college, or a nursing student studying for a complex exam, we want to help give you the tools you need to succeed. We hope this study guide gives you the skills and the confidence to thrive, and we can't thank you enough for allowing us to be part of your journey.

In an effort to continue to improve our products, we welcome feedback from our customers. We look forward to hearing from you. Suggestions, success stories, and criticisms can all be communicated by emailing us at info@studyguideteam.com.

Sincerely,
Test Prep Books Team

FREE Videos/DVD OFFER

Doing well on your exam requires both knowing the test content and understanding how to use that knowledge to do well on the test. We offer completely FREE test taking tip videos. **These videos cover world-class tips that you can use to succeed on your test.**

To get your **FREE videos**, you can use the QR code below or email freevideos@studyguideteam.com with "Free Videos" in the subject line and the following information in the body of the email:

a. The title of your product
b. Your product rating on a scale of 1-5, with 5 being the highest
c. Your feedback about the product

If you have any questions or concerns, please don't hesitate to contact us at info@studyguideteam.com.

Quick Overview

As you draw closer to taking your exam, effective preparation becomes more and more important. Thankfully, you have this study guide to help you get ready. Use this guide to help keep your studying on track and refer to it often.

This study guide contains several key sections that will help you be successful on your exam. The guide contains tips for what you should do the night before and the day of the test. Also included are test-taking tips. Knowing the right information is not always enough. Many well-prepared test takers struggle with exams. These tips will help equip you to accurately read, assess, and answer test questions.

A large part of the guide is devoted to showing you what content to expect on the exam and to helping you better understand that content. In this guide are practice test questions so that you can see how well you have grasped the content. Then, answer explanations are provided so that you can understand why you missed certain questions.

Don't try to cram the night before you take your exam. This is not a wise strategy for a few reasons. First, your retention of the information will be low. Your time would be better used by reviewing information you already know rather than trying to learn a lot of new information. Second, you will likely become stressed as you try to gain a large amount of knowledge in a short amount of time. Third, you will be depriving yourself of sleep. So be sure to go to bed at a reasonable time the night before. Being well-rested helps you focus and remain calm.

Be sure to eat a substantial breakfast the morning of the exam. If you are taking the exam in the afternoon, be sure to have a good lunch as well. Being hungry is distracting and can make it difficult to focus. You have hopefully spent lots of time preparing for the exam. Don't let an empty stomach get in the way of success!

When travelling to the testing center, leave earlier than needed. That way, you have a buffer in case you experience any delays. This will help you remain calm and will keep you from missing your appointment time at the testing center.

Be sure to pace yourself during the exam. Don't try to rush through the exam. There is no need to risk performing poorly on the exam just so you can leave the testing center early. Allow yourself to use all of the allotted time if needed.

Remain positive while taking the exam even if you feel like you are performing poorly. Thinking about the content you should have mastered will not help you perform better on the exam.

Once the exam is complete, take some time to relax. Even if you feel that you need to take the exam again, you will be well served by some down time before you begin studying again. It's often easier to convince yourself to study if you know that it will come with a reward!

Test-Taking Strategies

1. Predicting the Answer

When you feel confident in your preparation for a multiple-choice test, try predicting the answer before reading the answer choices. This is especially useful on questions that test objective factual knowledge. By predicting the answer before reading the available choices, you eliminate the possibility that you will be distracted or led astray by an incorrect answer choice. You will feel more confident in your selection if you read the question, predict the answer, and then find your prediction among the answer choices. After using this strategy, be sure to still read all of the answer choices carefully and completely. If you feel unprepared, you should not attempt to predict the answers. This would be a waste of time and an opportunity for your mind to wander in the wrong direction.

2. Reading the Whole Question

Too often, test takers scan a multiple-choice question, recognize a few familiar words, and immediately jump to the answer choices. Test authors are aware of this common impatience, and they will sometimes prey upon it. For instance, a test author might subtly turn the question into a negative, or he or she might redirect the focus of the question right at the end. The only way to avoid falling into these traps is to read the entirety of the question carefully before reading the answer choices.

3. Looking for Wrong Answers

Long and complicated multiple-choice questions can be intimidating. One way to simplify a difficult multiple-choice question is to eliminate all of the answer choices that are clearly wrong. In most sets of answers, there will be at least one selection that can be dismissed right away. If the test is administered on paper, the test taker could draw a line through it to indicate that it may be ignored; otherwise, the test taker will have to perform this operation mentally or on scratch paper. In either case, once the obviously incorrect answers have been eliminated, the remaining choices may be considered. Sometimes identifying the clearly wrong answers will give the test taker some information about the correct answer. For instance, if one of the remaining answer choices is a direct opposite of one of the eliminated answer choices, it may well be the correct answer. The opposite of obviously wrong is obviously right! Of course, this is not always the case. Some answers are obviously incorrect simply because they are irrelevant to the question being asked. Still, identifying and eliminating some incorrect answer choices is a good way to simplify a multiple-choice question.

4. Don't Overanalyze

Anxious test takers often overanalyze questions. When you are nervous, your brain will often run wild, causing you to make associations and discover clues that don't actually exist. If you feel that this may be a problem for you, do whatever you can to slow down during the test. Try taking a deep breath or counting to ten. As you read and consider the question, restrict yourself to the particular words used by the author. Avoid thought tangents about what the author *really* meant, or what he or she was *trying* to say. The only things that matter on a multiple-choice test are the words that are actually in the question. You must avoid reading too much into a multiple-choice question, or supposing that the writer meant something other than what he or she wrote.

5. No Need for Panic

It is wise to learn as many strategies as possible before taking a multiple-choice test, but it is likely that you will come across a few questions for which you simply don't know the answer. In this situation, avoid panicking. Because most multiple-choice tests include dozens of questions, the relative value of a single wrong answer is small. As much as possible, you should compartmentalize each question on a multiple-choice test. In other words, you should not allow your feelings about one question to affect your success on the others. When you find a question that you either don't understand or don't know how to answer, just take a deep breath and do your best. Read the entire question slowly and carefully. Try rephrasing the question a couple of different ways. Then, read all of the answer choices carefully. After eliminating obviously wrong answers, make a selection and move on to the next question.

6. Confusing Answer Choices

When working on a difficult multiple-choice question, there may be a tendency to focus on the answer choices that are the easiest to understand. Many people, whether consciously or not, gravitate to the answer choices that require the least concentration, knowledge, and memory. This is a mistake. When you come across an answer choice that is confusing, you should give it extra attention. A question might be confusing because you do not know the subject matter to which it refers. If this is the case, don't eliminate the answer before you have affirmatively settled on another. When you come across an answer choice of this type, set it aside as you look at the remaining choices. If you can confidently assert that one of the other choices is correct, you can leave the confusing answer aside. Otherwise, you will need to take a moment to try to better understand the confusing answer choice. Rephrasing is one way to tease out the sense of a confusing answer choice.

7. Your First Instinct

Many people struggle with multiple-choice tests because they overthink the questions. If you have studied sufficiently for the test, you should be prepared to trust your first instinct once you have carefully and completely read the question and all of the answer choices. There is a great deal of research suggesting that the mind can come to the correct conclusion very quickly once it has obtained all of the relevant information. At times, it may seem to you as if your intuition is working faster even than your reasoning mind. This may in fact be true. The knowledge you obtain while studying may be retrieved from your subconscious before you have a chance to work out the associations that support it. Verify your instinct by working out the reasons that it should be trusted.

8. Key Words

Many test takers struggle with multiple-choice questions because they have poor reading comprehension skills. Quickly reading and understanding a multiple-choice question requires a mixture of skill and experience. To help with this, try jotting down a few key words and phrases on a piece of scrap paper. Doing this concentrates the process of reading and forces the mind to weigh the relative

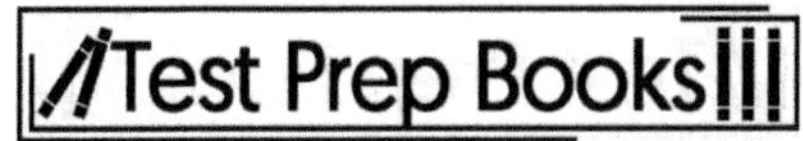

importance of the question's parts. In selecting words and phrases to write down, the test taker thinks about the question more deeply and carefully. This is especially true for multiple-choice questions that are preceded by a long prompt.

9. Subtle Negatives

One of the oldest tricks in the multiple-choice test writer's book is to subtly reverse the meaning of a question with a word like *not* or *except*. If you are not paying attention to each word in the question, you can easily be led astray by this trick. For instance, a common question format is, "Which of the following is...?" Obviously, if the question instead is, "Which of the following is not...?," then the answer will be quite different. Even worse, the test makers are aware of the potential for this mistake and will include one answer choice that would be correct if the question were not negated or reversed. A test taker who misses the reversal will find what he or she believes to be a correct answer and will be so confident that he or she will fail to reread the question and discover the original error. The only way to avoid this is to practice a wide variety of multiple-choice questions and to pay close attention to each and every word.

10. Reading Every Answer Choice

It may seem obvious, but you should always read every one of the answer choices! Too many test takers fall into the habit of scanning the question and assuming that they understand the question because they recognize a few key words. From there, they pick the first answer choice that answers the question they believe they have read. Test takers who read all of the answer choices might discover that one of the latter answer choices is actually *more* correct. Moreover, reading all of the answer choices can remind you of facts related to the question that can help you arrive at the correct answer. Sometimes, a misstatement or incorrect detail in one of the latter answer choices will trigger your memory of the subject and will enable you to find the right answer. Failing to read all of the answer choices is like not reading all of the items on a restaurant menu: you might miss out on the perfect choice.

11. Spot the Hedges

One of the keys to success on multiple-choice tests is paying close attention to every word. This is never truer than with words like *almost*, *most*, *some*, and *sometimes*. These words are called "hedges" because they indicate that a statement is not totally true or not true in every place and time. An absolute statement will contain no hedges, but in many subjects, the answers are not always straightforward or absolute. There are always exceptions to the rules in these subjects. For this reason, you should favor those multiple-choice questions that contain hedging language. The presence of qualifying words indicates that the author is taking special care with his or her words, which is certainly important when composing the right answer. After all, there are many ways to be wrong, but there is only one way to be right! For this reason, it is wise to avoid answers that are absolute when taking a multiple-choice test. An absolute answer is one that says things are either all one way or all another. They often include words like *every*, *always*, *best*, and *never*. If you are taking a multiple-choice test in a subject that doesn't lend itself to absolute answers, be on your guard if you see any of these words.

12. Long Answers

In many subject areas, the answers are not simple. As already mentioned, the right answer often requires hedges. Another common feature of the answers to a complex or subjective question are qualifying clauses, which are groups of words that subtly modify the meaning of the sentence. If the question or answer choice describes a rule to which there are exceptions or the subject matter is complicated, ambiguous, or confusing, the correct answer will require many words in order to be expressed clearly and accurately. In essence, you should not be deterred by answer choices that seem excessively long. Oftentimes, the author of the text will not be able to write the correct answer without offering some qualifications and modifications. Your job is to read the answer choices thoroughly and completely and to select the one that most accurately and precisely answers the question.

13. Restating to Understand

Sometimes, a question on a multiple-choice test is difficult not because of what it asks but because of how it is written. If this is the case, restate the question or answer choice in different words. This process serves a couple of important purposes. First, it forces you to concentrate on the core of the question. In order to rephrase the question accurately, you have to understand it well. Rephrasing the question will concentrate your mind on the key words and ideas. Second, it will present the information to your mind in a fresh way. This process may trigger your memory and render some useful scrap of information picked up while studying.

14. True Statements

Sometimes an answer choice will be true in itself, but it does not answer the question. This is one of the main reasons why it is essential to read the question carefully and completely before proceeding to the answer choices. Too often, test takers skip ahead to the answer choices and look for true statements. Having found one of these, they are content to select it without reference to the question above. The savvy test taker will always read the entire question before turning to the answer choices. Then, having settled on a correct answer choice, he or she will refer to the original question and ensure that the selected answer is relevant. The mistake of choosing a correct-but-irrelevant answer choice is especially common on questions related to specific pieces of objective knowledge.

15. No Patterns

One of the more dangerous ideas that circulates about multiple-choice tests is that the correct answers tend to fall into patterns. These erroneous ideas range from a belief that B and C are the most common right answers, to the idea that an unprepared test-taker should answer "A-B-A-C-A-D-A-B-A." It cannot be emphasized enough that pattern-seeking of this type is exactly the WRONG way to approach a multiple-choice test. To begin with, it is highly unlikely that the test maker will plot the correct answers according to some predetermined pattern. The questions are scrambled and delivered in a random order. Furthermore, even if the test maker was following a pattern in the assignation of correct answers, there is no reason why the test taker would know which pattern he or she was using. Any attempt to discern a pattern in the answer choices is a waste of time and a distraction from the real work of taking the test. A test taker would be much better served by extra preparation before the test than by reliance on a pattern in the answers.

Introduction to the EMT Exam

Function of the Test

The National Registry of Emergency Medical Technicians (NREMT) certifies EMTs that meet certain requirements. Among these requirements is that the candidate must pass the NREMT Cognitive Exam. Accordingly, the exam is typically taken by adults who wish to gain NREMT certification, and who have already completed a state-approved EMT course and a psychomotor exam.

EMT Cognitive Exam scores typically are only used as part of the NREMT certification process and not by employers or schools (other than the indirect use of considering the individual's certification status). The exam is used throughout the United States and across all jurisdictions therein.

Test Administration

All EMT Cognitive Exams are administered at Pearson VUE testing centers. The test may be taken at any Pearson VUE center at a date, time, and location convenient to the test taker.

Upon completing an approved EMS education program and meeting the other application requirements, individuals seeking certification are given three chances to pass the EMT Cognitive Exam. If the candidate does not pass on an attempt, he or she may apply to retest fifteen days after the failed attempt. If the candidate does not pass on any of the three attempts, he or she must complete an official remedial training program before applying to take the test again. If the individual completes the remedial training program but fails three more attempts, he or she must complete a state-approved education program all over in its entirety before applying for additional retesting attempts.

In compliance with the Americans with Disabilities Act, reasonable accommodations for individuals with documented disabilities are available for the EMT Cognitive Exam administration. Also, the Pearson VUE test centers at which the test is administered are ADA-compliant.

Test Format

The EMT Cognitive Exam is a Computer Adaptive Test, meaning that the computer program used for the test administration adjusts the difficulty of questions based on the test taker's performance up to that point on the test. On the EMT Cognitive Exam, once the testing software determines with 95% confidence that the test taker either does or does not meet the required standard, the test will end and the test taker will have passed or not passed, respectively. The maximum time allowed for the test is two hours, and the number of questions typically ranges between 70 and 120, depending on how quickly the algorithm reaches a result.

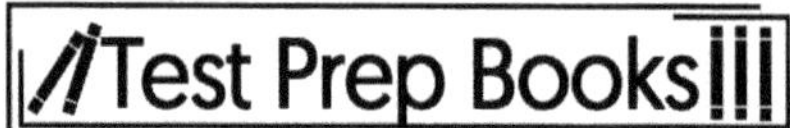

The exam is intended to cover the knowledge needed in all facets of work as an EMT. It is designed based on the National EMS Educational Standards, and not on any state-specific curriculum or material. A specific summary of test content follows:

Topic	Share of Exam	Adult / Pediatric Mix
Airway, Respiration, & Ventilation	18%-22%	85% Adult; 15% Pediatric
Cardiology & Resuscitation	20%-24%	85% Adult; 15% Pediatric
Trauma	14%-18%	85% Adult; 15% Pediatric
Medical; Obstetrics & Gynecology	27%-31%	85% Adult; 15% Pediatric
EMS Operations	10%-14%	N/A

Scoring

The test taker is not given a score, per se, but rather simply reaches a point where algorithms in the testing software determine with sufficient confidence that the test taker does or does not meet the required standard. Each question answered correctly adds to the algorithm's confidence that the test taker is qualified, while each incorrect response does the opposite.

Exam results are not available on the day of the test; instead, they are posted to the test taker's NREMT account about two business days after the exam is completed. Individuals may challenge the results of their EMT Cognitive Exam by requesting a manual exam review in writing within 30 days of completion of the exam and submitting a review fee.

Recent/Future Developments

Beginning in 2015, individuals whose applications are approved must complete the EMT Cognitive Exam within 90 days of receipt of the Authorization to Test. No other recent changes have been announced.

Study Prep Plan for the EMT Exam

1 **Schedule -** Use one of our study schedules below or come up with one of your own.

2 **Relax -** Test anxiety can hurt even the best students. There are many ways to reduce stress. Find the one that works best for you.

3 **Execute -** Once you have a good plan in place, be sure to stick to it.

One Week Study Schedule

Day 1	Airway, Respiration, and Ventilation
Day 2	Cardiology and Resuscitation
Day 3	Trauma
Day 4	Medical, Obstetrics, and Gynecology
Day 5	Operations
Day 6	Practice Test #1
Day 7	Take Your Exam!

Two Week Study Schedule

Day 1	Airway, Respiration, and Ventilation	Day 8	Hematology
Day 2	Respiratory Arrest	Day 9	Operations
Day 3	Cardiology and Resuscitation	Day 10	Communication at Scene of an Emergency
Day 4	Trauma	Day 11	Practice Test #1
Day 5	Soft Tissue Trauma	Day 12	Practice Test #2
Day 6	Differentiating Blunt from Penetrating MOI	Day 13	Practice Test #3
Day 7	Medical, Obstetrics, and Gynecology	Day 14	Take Your Exam!

One Month Study Schedule

Day 1	Airway, Respiration, and Ventilation	Day 11	Head, Neck, Face, and Spinal Trauma	Day 21	Communication at Scene of an Emergency
Day 2	Normal vs. Abnormal Breathing	Day 12	Differentiating Blunt from Penetrating MOI	Day 22	Consent
Day 3	Respiratory Failure	Day 13	Emergency Trauma Care	Day 23	Take a Break!
Day 4	Respiratory Arrest	Day 14	Medical, Obstetrics, and Gynecology	Day 24	Practice Test #1
Day 5	Venturi Masks	Day 15	Immunology (Allergic Reactions)	Day 25	Answer Explanations #1
Day 6	Cardiology and Resuscitation	Day 16	Endocrine Disorders	Day 26	Practice Test #2
Day 7	Hypotension/ Hypertension...	Day 17	Hematology	Day 27	Answer Explanations #2
Day 8	Trauma	Day 18	Gynecology and Obstetrics	Day 28	Practice Test #3
Day 9	General Assessment	Day 19	Operations	Day 29	Answer Explanations #3
Day 10	Soft Tissue Trauma	Day 20	Lighting	Day 30	Take Your Exam!

As you study for your test, we'd like to take the opportunity to remind you that you are capable of great things! With the right tools and dedication, you truly can do anything you set your mind to. The fact that you are holding this book right now shows how committed you are. In case no one has told you lately, you've got this! Our intention behind including this coloring page is to give you the chance to take some time to engage your creative side when you need a little brain-break from studying. As a company, we want to encourage people like you to achieve their dreams by providing good quality study materials for the tests and certifications that improve careers and change lives. As individuals, many of us have taken such tests in our careers, and we know how challenging this process can be. While we can't come alongside you and cheer you on personally, we can offer you the space to recall your purpose, reconnect with your passion, and refresh your brain through an artistic practice. We wish you every success, and happy studying!

Airway, Respiration, and Ventilation

Airway Management

Checking and managing a patient's airway to ensure adequate respiration is the first step in almost all medical emergencies. Without adequate respiration, brain damage or death can occur in under ten minutes. Respiratory distress can quickly escalate to respiratory failure. When oxygen cannot reach the heart, the entire cardiopulmonary system can fail, leading to cardiac arrest. The *"ABCs"* of first-responder treatment consist of *A: A*irway management (ensure the physical air passage is clear enough to allow for oxygenation and ventilation), *B: B*reathing (ensure the patient is breathing autonomously or with the help of oxygen therapy), and *C: C*irculation (ensure adequate blood circulation by monitoring the pulse, controlling bleeding, or performing CPR). Airway management consists of patient positioning, provider positioning, opening the airway, and suctioning.

Before beginning this process in either adult or pediatric patients, a physical assessment should be completed as time allows. This assessment may occur by the EMT, visually and by sound, without the patient even realizing it. The EMT should note the patient's work of breath (i.e. is the patient's breathing shallow or labored, is the patient grunting, wheezing, etc.), skin color and condition (i.e. pale, flushed, clammy, gray), and level of alertness. A patient that is overly lethargic and slow to respond likely is in serious danger. Obtaining respiratory rate, pulse rate, blood pressure, and blood oxygen levels is preferred. The Glasgow Coma Scale (GCS) provides EMTs with an indicator for how aggressive they should be in their interventions.

Glasgow Coma Scale

Behavior	Response	Score
Eye opening response	Spontaneously	**4**
	To speech	**3**
	To pain	**2**
	No response	**1**
Best verbal response	Oriented to time, place and person	**5**
	Confused	**4**
	Inappropriate words	**3**
	Incomprehensible sounds	**2**
	No response	**1**
Best motor response	Obeys commands	**6**
	Moves to localized pain	**5**
	Flexion withdrawal from pain	**4**
	Abnormal flexion (decorticate)	**3**
	Abnormal extension (decerebrate)	**2**
	No response	**1**
Total score	**Best response**	**15**
	Comatose client	**8 or less**
	Totally unresponsive	**3**

Adult Patients

Respiratory emergencies in adults are often due to an underlying chronic condition, such as heart disease, nerve disorders, or lung-specific pathologies. Acute conditions that cause respiratory injuries in adults include drug and/or alcohol overdose or lung trauma. While adult respiratory systems are fully developed, health factors such as obesity can affect how the steps of airway management are addressed and other disease conditions can alter the system's functioning capacity.

In the case of respiratory distress in an adult patient, airway management should proceed as follows:

1. Patient Positioning (assuming there is no risk to the patient's cervical spine)

Adult patients should be placed in the supine position with the oral, pharyngeal, and laryngeal axes aligned. To create this alignment, it is likely that padding will be needed under the back of the patient's head; the head needs to be approximately four inches off the ground. Obese patients will likely need a makeshift ramp under their shoulders that is high enough to align the patient's ear canal with their sternum. This type of neutral alignment is referred to as **sniffing position**; it increases air flow by decreasing resistance, and allows for ease of intubation, if needed. A 180-degree supine position can actually hinder airway management success. **Utilizing the Semi-Fowler's position**—a supine position of 30 to 45 degrees—is optimal with adult patients.

2. Provider Positioning

Ideally, at least three providers should be available to support the adult patient. One provider should be positioned at the top of the patient's head, while an assisting provider should be at the right side of the supine patient. The provider at the top of the patient's head maintains the patient's sniffing position, delivers bag valve mask (BVM) ventilation, and assists with CPR/AED processes, if needed. The provider at the right side of the supine patient assists with maintaining patient positioning, relaying any tubing material, and keeping an eye on the airway. The third provider is available for instances where extra handling may be needed, such as in transporting an obese patient, handling side effects of drug or alcohol use (such as loss of motor control or acts of violence) exhibited by the patient, or for rapidly deteriorating patients.

3. Opening the Airway

There are multiple ways to open the airway. The **head-tilt/chin-lift** method tips the head backward by placing one hand near the hairline and using the other hand to leverage the chin distally from the throat. This method is quick, reliable, and especially useful if an object is blocking the throat. This method should not be used if cervical spine injury is suspected.

The **jaw-thrust** method is an alternative, where the EMT places a hand on either side of the patient's face and cups the patient's jaws. The thumbs are placed on the patient's chin while the index and middle fingers are placed just below the temporal bone on the lower jaw. As the thumbs push the chin away, opening the mouth, the four fingers on the lower jaw push upward. This repositions the lower jaw so that the tongue is moved away from the opening of the throat. The EMT will need to hold the jaw in this position while any necessary intubation and/or ventilation occurs. The jaw-thrust was recommended as an alternative to the head-tilt/chin-lift method in instances where cervical spine injury was a concern, but recent studies show that it provides no benefit in this context and should not be considered a viable alternative. Rather, it is recommended to place the patient in the recovery position or use intubation if the cervical spine is at risk.

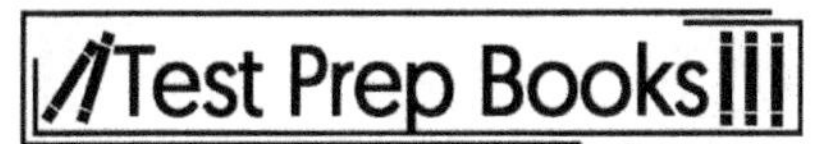

4. Suctioning
Suctioning refers to clearing any debris from the airway. It can be achieved by log-rolling the patient if vomiting or otherwise turning their head to the side, sweeping the patient's oral cavity with gloved fingers and removing any tangible debris, and through manual or motorized suction techniques. Patients with facial trauma, bleeding, the presence of mucus, or a gurgling sound in the throat will likely need tubal suctioning. Nasal suctioning is usually performed with a soft-tip catheter. For adult patients, suction pressure should be applied for no more than fifteen seconds at a time.

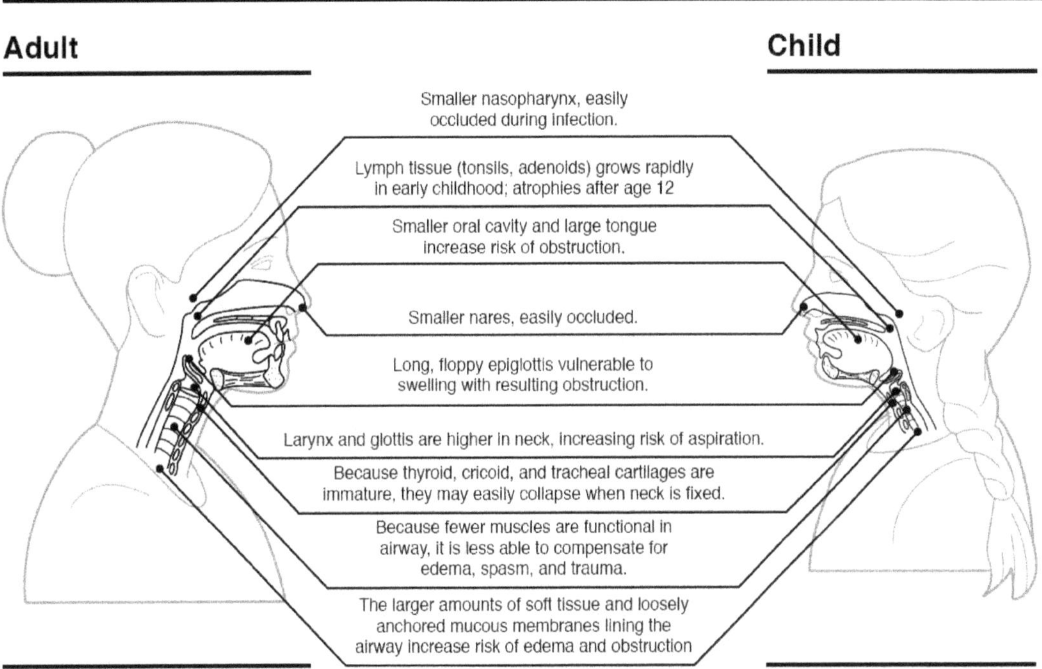

Pediatric Patients

Respiratory emergencies are the primary reason for pediatric hospital visits and the leading cause of non-congenital death in infants. They are the primary cause for cardiac arrest in children. Pediatric respiratory systems are in a rapid state of development from birth to age two, and many components remain much smaller in size until the child goes through puberty and reaches their full stature in early adulthood. For example, infants and young children primarily respire through the nose, yet the nostrils have a small circumference and are vulnerable to occlusion. The ratio of tongue size to the subglottic region is much smaller in children than in adults; this creates a narrower pathway in the anterior airway, which is also smaller and closer to the tongue. The anterior airway is also cone-shaped; the trachea is short. The physical nature of the oropharyngeal pathway makes it easier for children to choke on larger pieces of food, such as grapes, nuts, or sliced hot dogs, which is why healthcare providers recommend dicing such foods.

Pediatric patients also have less alveoli (the air sacs in the lungs in which the exchange of oxygen and carbon dioxide occurs). They also have less cartilage in the airway and softer rib cages, both contributing to a reduced mechanical ability for lung and chest expansion; breathing primarily occurs via the diaphragm. Finally, children have higher metabolic and oxygen consumption rates. Simply put, this means children require almost double the oxygen consumption of adults, yet the structures and components of the vascular system that assist in pulmonary processes are not yet fully developed. This makes pediatric patients especially vulnerable to respiratory obstructions or distress, and also requires a more detailed level of emergency care.

In the case of respiratory distress in a pediatric patient, airway management would differ from the adult patient as follows:

Patient Positioning (assuming there is no risk to the patient's cervical spine)

In young pediatric patients (three years old and younger), the child should be placed in a supine position with padding under their shoulders to create the sniffing position. In pediatric patients older than three, padding may also be needed under the back of the skull. Proper sniffing position is especially important in pediatric patients due to the large size of their heads, which remains disproportionally larger than their body size through a considerable part of childhood. In the supine position, the chin may be in a closer angle to the chest, effectively obstructing the airway further.

Provider Positioning

Ideally, at least two providers would be available to help the pediatric patient; compared to adult patients, it is unlikely that a pediatric patient would be too large or unruly that three EMTs would be absolutely necessary.

Opening the Airway

The airway can be opened through any method, but jaw-thrust and modified jaw-thrust are often most effective with pediatric patients. Especially with younger pediatric patients, it is important to minimize excessive head and neck movement. However, the pediatric patient's larger tongue size can cause an obstruction; this can be modified by the head-tilt/chin-lift process.

Suctioning

In pediatric patients, the placement and size of tubing (whether it is for suctioning or to provide ventilation) is important. The airway begins between the C3 and C4 vertebrae, so tubing does not need to be inserted as far as is necessary in an adult patient. The pediatric patient's epiglottis is larger and may cause obstruction, and the narrower airway makes it easier to irritate the vagal nerve, which can be innervated through the pharyngeal airway. This can result in bradycardia. Should any of these outcomes occur, they can usually be corrected with BVM ventilation or the use of atropine sulfate. In pediatric patients, suction pressure should be applied for no more than five seconds at a time.

Ventilation

In a medical context, **ventilation** is a component of the cardiopulmonary system. It refers to an inhalation of enough oxygenated air to support metabolic processes at the cellular level, and an exhalation complete enough to remove excessive carbon dioxide from cells and tissues. In a healthy person who is in a relaxed state, the diaphragm manages contractions responsible for the expansion and relaxation of the lungs. In a healthy person who requires more oxygen for functioning (such as in higher altitudes or during vigorous exercise), a number of chest, neck, abdominal, and pelvic muscles contract and relax to increase the rate of ventilation. Artificial ventilation may be required in cardiopulmonary emergencies when airway management techniques are unable to produce sufficient, autonomous

breathing in the patient. Adequate artificial ventilation should deliver full or partial tidal volume. Tidal volume should be approximately 10 milliliters of oxygen per kilogram of the patient's body mass.

Adult Patients

Artificial ventilation is commonly utilized in adult patients with a sudden lung injury; however, it is also a common intervention when the patient has a chronic underlying disease to which the acute respiratory event is secondary. For example, an adult patient with sleep apnea may experience a severe cardiovascular event, or a patient with alcoholism may experience apnea when intoxicated. Artificial ventilation can be created through positive pressure or negative pressure. Positive pressure ventilation is the most common type used in emergency settings; it involves creating pressure at the patient's airway to push air into the lungs. Negative pressure ventilation is virtually obsolete, but was commonly used before positive pressure ventilation was introduced in the 1950s.

Common methods of artificial ventilation all require a clear airway utilizing good airway management techniques to ensure successful ventilation. Placing the patient in a supine sniffing position is preferred. Common methods include:

Mouth-to-Mouth and Cardiopulmonary Resuscitation (CPR)

Most commonly recognized as a component of **CPR**, mouth-to-mouth resuscitation involves pressing one's mouth to the patient's mouth, forming a seal, and blowing air directly into the patient's mouth and lungs. It is the first line of defense for non-medical first responders or in instances where ventilation devices are not available. However, non-medical first responders are advised to perform mouth-to-mouth resuscitation with chest compressions. EMTs can deliver mouth-to-mouth resuscitation without chest compressions in cases where chest compressions are not needed. In general, high quality ventilation alone is preferred over CPR unless the patient is in cardiac arrest. If the patient is in cardiac arrest, chest compressions can help the heart deliver partially oxygenated blood to the brain and prevent brain damage or death until the heart can be restarted.

If the practitioner is unable to form a seal with the mouth, a seal can also be made with the nose. Referred to as mouth-to-nose resuscitation, this method can be used if the patient has lower facial injuries, if the patient has vomited, or if the rescuer does not have a barrier available. However, most EMTs will have some sort of barrier available to them. The simplest form is a plain pocket mask that covers the mouth and/or nose, which allows a rescuer to manually blow air in from their own mouth. More commonly utilized mask ventilators employ a bag that sources pressurized oxygen into the patient's lungs.

Finally, if the patient needs CPR, chest compressions are performed alongside ventilation at a rate of 100 to 120 compressions per minute. The area directly under the sternum is depressed approximately five to six centimeters by the heels of the rescuer's hands; this event equals one compression. If providing manual breathing, it should be performed in cycles as follows: 30 compressions are performed, then compressions stop while the rescuer delivers two breaths, and then another 30 compressions are performed.

Bag valve mask (BVM)

Also known as a manual resuscitator, the BVM is the most common ventilation method used in emergency airway management. It is an excellent intermediary ventilation technique when an advanced or long-term ventilation option is not yet available. It is preferable to any type of mouth-to-mouth, mouth-to-nose, or mouth-to-mask method. As its name states, the unit consists of a bag that is attached to an oxygen source on one end, and a pressure valve that connects to a mask for the patient on the other end. BVMs can be used when the airway is open and clear (normally referred to as a "patent airway"), in the instances of respiratory failure, and in instances where intubation is not possible.

The patient should be appropriately positioned; the patient's airway should be opened with an adjunct or laryngoscope, if necessary. The mask should be positioned over the patients nose and mouth; the rescuer should ensure that the mask is the appropriate size to create an adequate seal. The E-C technique should be utilized to hold the mask firmly in place: the thumbs are placed above the lips and the index finger over the chin, creating a C-shape; the remaining fingers are placed under the jaw in an E-shape. If another provide is unable to assist with the BVM, the E-C technique should be performed with just one hand while the other hand is used to compress the bag.

Adults should be ventilated at approximately eight to 12 breaths per minute, receiving approximately seven milliliters of oxygen per breath. This will result in a rate of approximately one bag squeeze every five seconds. Ventilation should be monitored with a pulse oximetry assessment due to higher risk of accidental hyperventilation with this method. The rescuer should note any abdominal distention, which indicates that air is flowing into the stomach. BVM ventilation will be more difficult in patients who are missing teeth, are over 57 years old, have jaw abnormalities, have thick facial hair, or are chronic snorers. BVMs should not be used for exceedingly prolonged periods of time.

Laryngeal Mask Airway (LMA)

The LMA is often an alternative to BVM ventilation, and is becoming more common in emergency settings when a more complicated airway issue is present, such as in cases where patients are unable to be positioned properly. It should not be used in patients with an upper airway obstruction. It should be avoided in patients who have already been on BVM ventilation, are in later stages of pregnancy, who have recently eaten, or who are obese. This ventilation technique greatly reduces the risk for gastric distention. These are best used in contexts where the patient is unconscious, as the device is relatively invasive; in operating rooms, this method requires anesthesia. The LMA is inserted into the patient's oral cavity along the palate into the hypopharynx, which isolates the trachea for concentrated air flow. These devices are often used in conjunction with tracheal tubes.

Demand Valves

These are able to provide 100% of oxygen and use high air pressure and high air flow rates. They are normally used with tracheal tubes.

Tracheal Tubes

This form of ventilating involves placing catheter tubing directly into the trachea that not only maintains the airway, but also ventilates. Endotracheal tubes are most common in emergency and critical care contexts. These thin tubes are inserted through the nose or mouth and guided directly into the trachea; a component of the tube can be inflated to fully seal the trachea. This prevents contamination from bodily fluids such as blood or gastric reflux, which are common obstacles in respiratory emergencies. When used with a demand valve, normal flow rates should be lowered if the need for CPR arises.

Transport

These are automatic ventilators that vary between high and low pressure. They provide consistent air flow at timed, constant pressures. These are useful in situations where the patient requires more care than just airway management and ventilation. If the patient is spontaneously breathing, automatic ventilators are able to adjust to accommodate and assist the patient.

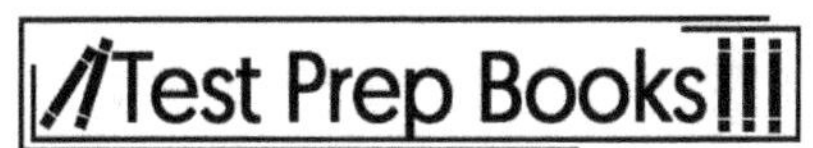

Pediatric Patients

In pediatric patients, the same ventilation techniques can be utilized but certain aspects of delivery will differ. These differences include:

Mouth-to-Mouth and Cardiopulmonary Resuscitation (CPR)

In pediatric patients, especially in those under one year of age, a mouth-to-nose seal should be formed, due to the small size and obligate nasal breathing preference demonstrated by infants. Chest compressions can often hinder progress. If they are absolutely necessary, they should be performed at a rate of 15 compressions per two breaths. Compressions are delivered below the sternum using the index and middle fingers.

Bag valve mask (BVM)

Airway adjuncts will likely need to be used with pediatric patients to maintain a patent airway, due to the size of the tongue and throat. Different masks are available for use with children and infants; they are more circular in nature. Bags are also smaller to reduce the risk of hyperventilation. Children should be ventilated at a rate of 16 to 20 breaths per minute. Infants should be ventilated at a rate of 20 to 30 breaths per minute.

Laryngeal Mask Airway (LMA)

As with BVMs, smaller mask sizes exist for pediatric patients, including neonates weighing at least two pounds.

Tracheal Tube

Pediatric patients rarely require the use of an inflated cuff to seal the trachea, as their tracheas are narrow enough to be sealed with a non-cuffed tube. Cuffed tubing may be beneficial if the patient is over eight years old. With all tubing, stabilizing the patients is important. With pediatric patients, however, it is especially vital, as small movements in tube placement can result in a host of undesired effects. Small tubal movements generally do not have the same far-reaching effects in adult patients. Pediatric patient tube size can quickly be estimated using the patient's smallest finger as a parallel. A more precise method to selecting tubing size is to add 16 to the child's age and divide that sum by 4.

Normal vs. Abnormal Breathing

Respiration processes and rate gradually change over the course of the lifespan. They also change in acute situations, such as with illness or trauma. Respiration rate is a common biomarker used to identify pathologies such as general pulmonary dysfunction (such as an obstruction, asthma, infection, or lung fluid), as well as more specific conditions like cancer, cardiovascular disease, cystic fibrosis, and even acute anxiety. Some instances of abnormal breathing are easily visible, such as a patient who is gasping or has discolored, bluish skin. Other instances may be less visible, but can easily be heard by placing a stethoscope over the patient's bare chest, back, and the space between the second and sixth intercostal muscles. A stethoscope can amplify sounds that indicate wheezing, a narrowing of the bronchial tubes, or stridor—a narrowing of the trachea. It can also be used to detect low- and high-pitched sounds in the lungs. A pulmonary function test measures the pace of inhalations and exhalations, as well as the volume of air intake and expulsion in a single breath.

Adult Patients

Normal resting respiration in healthy adults ranges from 12 to 16 breaths per minute. Elderly adults may breathe anywhere from 10 to 30 times per minute. Respiration rates outside of 12 to 25 breaths per minute for adults under 65-years-old is considered abnormal. Common abnormal respiratory conditions that may lead to an emergency situation include:

Apnea

This refers to temporary pauses in breath in which the lung volume stagnates. The musculature involved in respiration temporarily ceases function. Apnea can be caused by distress, laughing, trauma, or neurological disease. It is also a common sleep condition, in which a patient can stop breathing up to 30 times per hour. Without detection or treatment, sleep apnea can greatly tax the cardiovascular system and lead to cardiac events, due to the long periods of time without oxygen circulation. Sleep apnea is often an undetected condition.

Dyspnea

This refers to shortness of breath that may feel like tightness in the chest or impending suffocation. In emergency contexts, it can occur suddenly in patients facing cardiac events, trauma, hernias, asthma, pulmonary embolisms, pneumonia, extreme temperatures or altitudes, or from vigorous activity, especially if the patient is ill-prepared. Obese patients may feel **dyspnea** from mild or moderate activity, which does not necessarily lead to an emergency context. Patients with chronic respiratory, heart, or lung conditions—such as asthma, cardiomyopathy, or chronic obstructive pulmonary disease (COPD)—may also regularly experience bouts of dyspnea.

Hyperventilation

This refers to any context where there is more oxygen entering the blood than there is carbon dioxide being released. It is characterized by deep, often rapid, breathing lasting approximately half an hour. As a result, the patient might experience a pounding heartbeat, vertigo, numbness in the extremities, and chest tightness. Acute **hyperventilation** is often caused by anxiety, panic, or stress; it can often be managed by practicing slower breathing techniques (which may require coaching from someone other than the patient). Hyperventilation can also be caused by serious issues such as high blood glucose levels or aspirin overdoses. More serious acute cases may result in loss of consciousness, but this is relatively rare. Chronic hyperventilation is often associated with lung diseases such as emphysema or cancer. Supplemental oxygen may be needed. If a patient is hyperventilating they need to be seen by a physician and thus require transport to a medical facility.

Hypoxia

This refers to any instance where the body's tissues are receiving insufficient quantities of oxygen, due to dysfunction in any part of the process of transporting air from the nasal and oral orifices to the lungs to the tissues. Generalized **hypoxia** affects the body holistically; it is often seen in high altitude settings or in underwater resurfacing situations where the patient's body fails to adjust to the differences in air pressure. Generalized hypoxia is characterized by lightheadedness, nausea, heart palpitations, and fatigue. In severe cases, these symptoms precede more serious symptoms such as hallucinating, cyanosis, low blood pressure, and potentially, complete cardiac failure. There are both early and late signs of hypoxia. Early signs include anxiety, tachycardia, and restlessness. Late signs include cyanosis; weak, thready pulse; and changes in mental status. Localized hypoxia occurs when only certain tissues stop receiving adequate oxygen. This is characterized by cold, pale, and sometimes hard tissue. In severe cases, necrosis, especially gangrene, may present. Hypoxic patients should be provided with high-flow oxygen using a nonrebreathing mask. The same treatment can be administered to prevent hypoxemia.

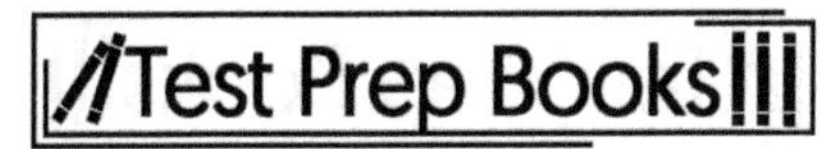

Hypoxemia

This specifically refers to hypoxic situations where blood oxygen content is insufficient. Any cardiovascular dysfunction or obstructions will cause some level of **hypoxemia**; these contexts can be triggered by neurological issues, such as strokes that affect the control centers in the brain that manage the frequency and depth at which the body respires. Hypoxemia is characterized by dyspnea, chest pain, abdominal pain and contractions, cyanosis, and chronic coughing.

Anoxemia

This refers to cases of extreme hypoxemia.

Hypercapnia/Hypercarbia

This refers to high levels of carbon dioxide in the blood, which results from poor carbon dioxide expulsion or low oxygen inhalation. When this occurs, the brain normally commands pulmonary responses leading to hyperventilation. If this doesn't occur, hypercapnia can be deadly. This condition is characterized by elevated blood pressure, flushed skin, twitching, excessive muscle contraction, confusion, lethargy, and headache. Severe cases may lead to convulsions.

Pediatric Patients

Normal resting respiration in healthy children changes as the child ages. Newborns to six-month-old infants will take between 30 to 60 breaths per minute. Six-month-old to 12-month-old infants will take between 24 to 30 breaths per minute. Children between the ages of one year and five years old will take between 20 to 30 breaths per minute. Children between the ages of six and twelve years old will display respiration rates similar to an adult, breathing between 12 and 20 times per minute. In newborns, infants, and toddlers, normal breathing can sound much different than that of an older child or adult. Coughing, choking, and whistling sounds can be normal at this age, but are concerning if they occur for successive and prolonged periods of time, are deep and raspy in nature, sound like a bark, or if the baby looks visibly distressed. Children with diagnosed asthma may know how to manage symptoms with an inhaler. However, if the child has severe wheezing, chest pain, feels flush or faint, cannot clear their throat, cannot stop coughing, or is unable to talk or stand, it is an emergency situation.

Signs of abnormal, and potentially dangerous, respiration problems include:

Hyperventilation

Over 60 breaths per minute is cause for concern. Bouts of rapid breathing, especially in newborns and infants, is common but usually doesn't exceed 40 breaths per minute. This can occur in overheated or stressed babies. Breathing rates greater than 40 breaths per minute may be due to fluid in the lungs or the beginning of pneumonia, which can be fatal at this young age. In older children, hyperventilation that seems to be occurring without the child engaging in physical exertion proportional to such effort is concerning.

Hypoxia

This condition may be seen in premature newborns, and is potentially life-threatening. If a baby is not receiving adequate air intake, he or she may exhibit flared nostrils, a depressed chest, and a bloated belly.

Hypercarbia/Hypercapnia

This condition is believed to be a contributing factor in sudden infant death syndrome (SIDS). Infants may rebreathe carbon dioxide (if they sleep on their stomach or under a blanket, for example) or may not have developed the reflex or neck strength to hyperventilate or turn their head in the context of hypercarbia.

Physical Changes

Bluish, pale, and cold skin and lips are a sign of an emergency. Any instance where a pediatric patient's chest and abdomen are not level with one another (one is depressed while the other is distended, similar to the angle of a seesaw) is also a sign of an emergency.

Respiratory Distress

Respiratory distress refers to any difficulty in breathing, even when adequate respiratory rates and tidal volume are present. This difficulty can be due to physiological or psychological reasons. Delivering oxygen in this situation prevents instances of respiratory distress from progressing further, often by relieving the burden of compensatory breathing by the patient.

Adult Patients

In all respiratory emergencies, the order of assessment for adult patients is as follows:

- Initial Assessment: Begins when the patient is in view. The rescuer should survey the environment for safety.
- Airway, Breathing, and Circulation (ABC) Assessment: The rescuer should determine if the patient seems to have adequate circulation (i.e., not experiencing a cardiac event), an open airway, and is breathing. If the patient is able to talk, the EMT should ask the patient if he or she feels hot, feverish, or clammy. Loss of consciousness, inability to breathe, and bluish skin require immediate attention to prevent a cardiac event.
- Assess Work of Breathing (WOB): The rescuer should notice the effort required for the patient to breathe. The inability to speak, lie flat, or maintain consciousness requires immediate attention. In emergency settings, EMTs should take special care with auscultation and assessing the details of distress. For example, a patient may have labored breathing, but noticing whether the patient is struggling to inhale or to exhale can guide the EMT to deliver the best intervention.

Other signs of respiratory distress in adults include:

- Bluish skin, lips, or nails
- Chest pain and tightness, often marked by the patient grabbing at their chest
- Elevated blood pressure
- Feelings of panic or anxiety
- Gasping, wheezing, and ragged sounding breaths
- Hyperventilation
- Rapid breathing
- Visibly labored breathing

Acute Respiratory Distress Syndrome (ARDS) refers to any condition where an injury of the lung prevents it from effectively functioning. Its onset is rapid, sometimes developing with hours. If untreated, it will quickly lead to lung failure. A wide array of causes can trigger ARDS. These include direct lung trauma such as the inhalation of poisonous or noxious vapors, drowning, pneumonia, aspiration, or infection

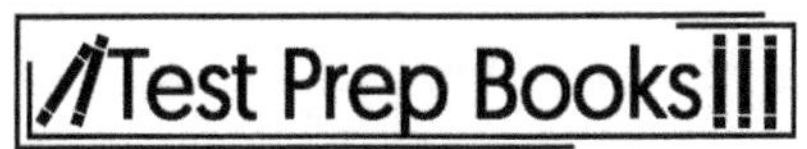

within the lung. These causes can also include indirect lung trauma such as heart failure, blunt force on the head, chest, or stomach, surgeries near the lungs (such as heart bypass surgeries), drug overdose, and sepsis.

It is important to note that these situations may not always lead to ARDS. ARDS is characterized by hyperventilation, a feeling of suffocation, and low blood oxygen levels. The condition is diagnosed through arterial blood gas tests, chest x-rays, or CT scans. It is treated by mechanical ventilation until the lungs heal, and usually requires that the patient receive tubal feeding and hydration until healing is complete. ARDS is a severe condition that often does not result in a complete recovery, with most patients experiencing some level of lung damage. Recovery is an ongoing process that usually takes months or years. Over 40% of ARDS patients succumb to the condition.

Pediatric Patients

In all respiratory emergencies, the order of assessment for pediatric patients is as follows:

Initial Assessment

Begins when the pediatric patient is in view. The rescuer must survey the environment for safety.

Pediatric Assessment Triangle (PAT)

This is a brief assessment lasting under sixty seconds, where the practitioner establishes a relationship (if possible) with the patient and notices any outward physical symptoms without ever touching the patient. The mnemonic TICLS covers the aspects that the practitioner should notice when conducting a PAT: Tone, Interactiveness, Consolability, Look/Gaze, Speech/Cry. Next, the EMT should notice the pediatric patient's breathing and whether it is labored or if any abnormal sounds are present, such as wheezing or gasping. Last, the rescuer should observe the pediatric patient's skin for pallor or mottling. Bluish- or grayish-tinged skin is a late stage of hypoxia in pediatric patients. The PAT is often the first reliable indicator of whether the pediatric patient's airway is open and patent.

Airway, Breathing, Circulation, Disability, Exposure (ABCDE) Assessment

This is a hands-on assessment performed sequentially as listed. First, the airway should be inspected and assessed to see whether it needs to be opened. Then, breathing is assessed. The EMT should count the respiratory rate for 30 seconds and listen to the lungs. Note that an elevated respiratory rate may be due to anxiety and panic that the child feels from the situation. A respiratory rate between 20 and 60 breaths is acceptable. Next, circulation is addressed by noting pulse rate, skin temperature, and blood pressure. Then, the rescuer should note whether any disabilities are present and determine the child's level of consciousness. This can be assessed using the AVPU scale, a descending scale that stands for Alert, responsive to Verbal stimuli, responsive to Painful stimuli, and Unresponsive. The assessment ends by assessing the child's body. This may require exposing the torso, arms, and legs; these should be assessed one part at a time and ideally with the assistance of a trusted caregiver, for the child's warmth and comfort.

Other signs of respiratory distress in pediatric patients include:

- A sunken chest
- Accelerated heart rate
- Cold, clammy, bluish or grayish tinted skin, lips, or nails
- Fatigue
- Flared nostrils

- Loud wheezing
- Rapid breathing
- Stridor
- Poor alertness and inability to focus

Additionally, pediatric patients in respiratory distress tend to lean the torso forward, often propping themselves up with their hands in front of them, to provide extra space for diaphragmatic movement. This is referred to as the tripod position. Consequently, pediatric patients assuming this posture should not be laid down in a prone or supine position. Patients might assume the sniffing position instead, with the head forward and chin and nose up as if sniffing the air.

Infant Respiratory Distress Syndrome (IRDS) is similar to ARDS in that it refers to a rapid onset of deteriorating respiratory function, but the condition relates to pediatric patients under the age of one. It usually occurs in premature newborns due to the lack of fully formed respiratory structures, which prevent complete inhalation and exhalation from occurring. IRDS is the leading cause of death in the first month of life. It is also treated by mechanical ventilation, and sometimes with the administration of glucocorticoids to speed up the infant's lung development. Without effective treatment, IRDS can lead to a collapsed lung, hemorrhage, sepsis, blindness, kidney failure, mental retardation, and/or cerebral palsy.

Respiratory Failure

Respiratory failure refers to any instance where one's respiratory system is unable to provide enough oxygen and remove enough carbon dioxide for the body's cells and tissues to perform life-sustaining metabolic processes. When a patient is in respiratory distress and is unable to compensate for the distress (either on their own or with emergency assistance), it usually leads to respiratory failure. The slowly decreasing levels of oxygen in the blood create a positive feedback loop that eventually diminishes the brain's ability to continue mechanisms—such as rapid breathing—that try to compensate for the lower oxygen levels.

Respiratory failure patients will either be in a state of hypoxemia (type I) or a state of hypercapnia (type II). Type I respiratory failure is more common. These failures are often caused by COPD, pneumonia, asthmatic attacks, pulmonary edemas or embolisms, ARDS, or pulmonary arterial hypertension. Type II respiratory failures are usually caused by COPD, asthmatic attacks, drug overdose, muscular disorders, head injuries, tetanus, or poliomyelitis. Respiratory failure can result from an acute condition (such as choking on a piece of food) or a chronic disease (such as a lung disorder). Acute respiratory failure comes on suddenly and is usually due to an obstruction or the presence of fluid in the alveoli. These types of respiratory failures are the most likely to lead to emergencies; without quick treatment, they can result in death. Chronic respiratory failure is usually the result of a permanently debilitating lung disease, such as emphysema. While this is a serious condition that usually requires continuous oxygen supplementation and lifestyle changes, it is relatively predictable and therefore less likely to suddenly escalate to a life-or-death situation.

Adult Patients

Signs of respiratory failure in adults are similar to those of respiratory distress and include:

- Anxiety
- Confusion
- Loss of consciousness

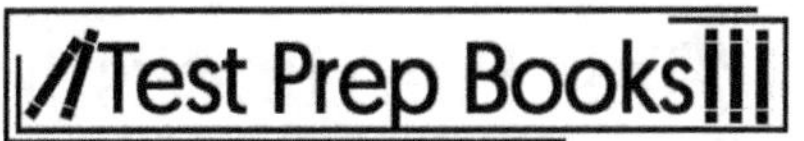

- Dyspnea
- Sleepiness
- Sweating

Adults with arterial blood oxygen tension lower than 60 mmHg are considered to be in a state of type I respiratory failure. Adults with arterial carbon dioxide tension higher than 50 mmHg are considered to be in a state of type II respiratory failure.

Pediatric Patients

Pediatric patients experiencing respiratory failure show signs similar to those of respiratory distress. These patients are inherently at a higher risk of respiratory distress progressing to respiratory failure. Premature infants, younger infants and toddlers, immunocompromised pediatric patients, and those with anatomic or physiological deficiencies are especially vulnerable. Pediatric patients with a history of chronic disease, especially congenital conditions, are also at an increased risk of respiratory failure. Pediatric patients experiencing respiratory failure will likely require extra airway support, such as through a nasopharyngeal or oropharyngeal airway, and intubation to maintain a patent airway.

After three weeks of age, infant arterial blood oxygen and carbon dioxide tension level requirements are approximately the same as an adult's.

Upper Airway Respiratory Emergencies

Upper airway respiratory emergencies refer to conditions affecting the nose, the nasal sinuses, and the pharynx. It is unlikely that the EMT will need to diagnose the exact condition causing the emergency, and many upper airway respiratory emergencies present in the same manner and require similar interventions.

The most common adult and pediatric upper airway respiratory emergencies are detailed below.

Adult

COPD

This is an umbrella condition that can refer to the presence of chronic bronchitis, emphysema, and/or other pulmonary diseases that all contribute to the progressive deterioration of the lungs' ability to breathe. It is most common in long-term smokers, but can also be caused by prolonged toxic inhalation (e.g., coal miners or factory workers that are frequently exposed to foreign elements in the air).

COPD is characterized by decreased elasticity of the airways and alveoli, deterioration of the walls of the alveoli, inflammation of the airways, and/or overproduction of mucus in the airways. It presents as productive, wet coughing, wheezing, chest tightness, and dyspnea. COPD patients may also have the appearance of a large, barrel chest due to the presence of trapped air in the lungs. COPD's onset is slow, so often the symptoms are initially attributed to something else, such as obesity or heart disease.

Mild and moderate COPD may be managed with anticholinergic bronchodilators (which decrease lung tissue inflammation and mucus production) and lifestyle changes, whereas severe COPD will require ongoing oxygen therapy (usually through a nasal cannula or mask) or a lung transplant. EMTs may be able to help administer prescription bronchodilators as part of the primary intervention process if working with such a patient. Supplemental oxygen should be delivered, but intubation and high flow techniques should be avoided, as they may further inflame the airway. Respiratory emergencies in patients with COPD may result from sudden lung failure, improper disease management, or complications from a common respiratory infection.

Chronic Bronchitis

Bronchitis, an inflammation of the bronchial membranes that can cause narrowing of the bronchioles, is considered chronic when a cough related to the condition (which may originally be diagnosed as an acute case) presents for at least three months within a two-year period. It may also be characterized by sputum. Swollen bronchioles or sputum independently can create an airway obstruction, but the presence of both together increases the risk of a respiratory emergency. In chronic bronchitis cases, the cells of the upper airway are more likely to become inflamed in response to common allergens or foreign bodies.

Emphysema

This condition is characterized by the breaking down of the alveolar walls. Once these structures degrade, the excess burden placed on the bronchioles causes them to collapse and obstruct the airway. This condition is irreversible.

Epiglottitis

This refers to inflammation of the **epiglottis** and the base of the tongue, which can cause swelling so severe that the airway can become blocked. This condition may start out as a simple respiratory infection or sore throat. Patients often drool excessively as the case becomes more severe. When it leads to epiglottitis that results in a respiratory emergency, primary emergency care should be simply to provide oxygen. In these cases, oxygen should be administered utilizing slower flow techniques, such as with slow bag valve mask ventilation. High flow techniques and manual examinations can further irritate the tongue and epiglottis, and lead to more swelling.

Foreign Body Airway Obstruction (FBAO)

Often characterized by choking, FBAO refers to any blockage in the airway caused by the presence of an unrecognized or unwanted entity. It often occurs when eating too quickly. Elderly patients with neurological disorders or dental problems are vulnerable to this issue. FBAO cases are often not complex situations, but can progress to critical conditions such as loss of consciousness and cardiac arrest within minutes. Mild cases may resolve themselves by involuntary coughing by the patient, but emergency services are often called when the case progresses past that point.

EMTs may attempt to ventilate using a BVM, but if ventilation interventions fail, back blows and abdominal thrusts should be delivered. Five back blows should be administered by hinging the patient's torso forward at the waist, supporting the patient's chest with one hand, and using the heel of the other hand to strike between the shoulder blades. These should be followed by five abdominal thrusts, where the hand on the patient's chest should be brought over the patient's navel. This hand should be made into a fist while the rescuer's opposite hand pushes the fist into the patient's abdominal wall, then upward. The back blows and abdominal thrusts should be stopped immediately if the foreign object becomes dislodged. If ventilation, back blows, and abdominal thrusts fail to improve the patient's condition, or if the patient becomes unconscious, a straight or curved blade laryngoscope can show whether the obstruction still exists in the airway. Forceps can be used to remove the obstruction if it is visible.

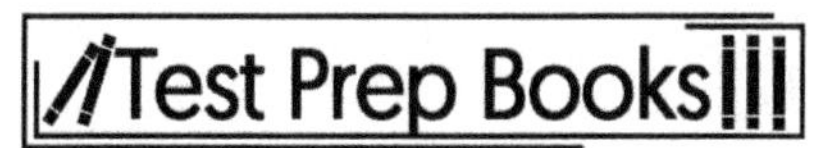

Pediatrics

Croup

Croup is a symptom of a pediatric respiratory infection. It is characterized by inflammation and swelling of the entire upper airway, including the larynx, trachea, and bronchioles. It is distinguished by a "barking" cough, due to the swollen larynx; this changes the vibration of the cough's sound as it passes. Most cases of croup are not serious, but if swelling is severe, it can result in an airway obstruction. In emergency cases, croup will need to be treated with humidified oxygen, possibly through intubation.

Bacterial Tracheitis

This refers to an infection of the trachea, which can result in excessive swelling, leading to airway obstruction, low blood pressure and cardiac arrest, sepsis, or pneumonia. It is extremely rare in adults. When it occurs, it tends to do so after a viral respiratory infection. In severe cases, intubation may be required.

FBAO

FBAO cases are most common in children under five years of age, as this demographic often puts items directly into their mouth or fails to chew foods completely. Some foods, such as hot dogs, popcorn, and nuts, can be hazardous to children in this age group as they can easily become lodged in the child's narrow airway. However, even well-supervised children can unintentionally swallow small items such as toy pieces, coins, beads, or hazardous foods. These cases should be oxygenated up to 100 percent. If ventilation does not help the patient, children under 12 months old should be given five back blows followed by five chest thrusts using the index and middle fingers. Children over 12 months should be given abdominal thrusts. Sweeping of the airway should only be conducted with a straight blade laryngoscope and forceps, removing the object with the forceps if it is visible. Otherwise, the foreign object could be lodged further.

Respiratory Arrest

Respiratory arrest refers to the complete cessation of breathing while the heart muscle is still able to function. However, a period of prolonged respiratory arrest will likely lead to a cardiac event. Respiratory arrest is characterized by imminent or presenting loss of consciousness.

Adult Patients

In adults, respiratory arrest is often caused by airway obstruction, neurological events (such as a stroke), drug abuse that inhibits nervous system functioning (such as opioid abuse, alcohol abuse, or sedative abuse), or weakness of the musculature involved in respiration (such as in cystic fibrosis patients). When respiratory arrest lasts longer than five minutes, irreversible brain damage and/or cardiac damage is likely.

Respiratory arrest is usually obvious as the patient has stopped visibly breathing and may be unconscious, but other symptoms include muscular retraction, cyanosis, choking (and potentially pointing toward the neck), and abnormal end-tidal volumes. Treatment includes clearing the airway and re-establishing breath through assisted ventilation. If cardiac treatment is also needed, chest compressions or defibrillation may also be utilized.

Pediatric Patients

In pediatric patients, respiratory arrest is most commonly caused by airway obstruction, especially in infants who are susceptible to nasal blockages. Infants are vulnerable to respiratory arrest without warning. This is attributed to the small size of the nostrils, the fact that infants are obligate nasal breathers for at least six months, and the cone shape of the trachea through pre-adolescence. Symptoms of respiratory arrest in the pediatric patient may include limp muscles, brachycardia, lack of chest and rib movement, and cyanosis. Treatment includes clearing the airway and re-establishing breath, usually through intubated ventilation. Cardiac arrest is highly correlated with respiratory arrest in pediatric patients. If cardiac treatment is needed, chest compressions should be administered immediately.

Lower Airway Respiratory Emergencies

The vocal cords are normally considered to be the physical marker distinguishing between the upper and lower airways. The conditions listed below are common emergency situations affecting the lower airway. As with upper airway respiratory emergencies, it is unlikely that an EMT will have to specifically diagnose these conditions; emergency treatments in these situations are similar, with oxygen administration serving as the primary course of medical care.

Adult

Asthma

Asthma is normally a chronic respiratory condition, and patients typically are aware of the diagnosis and the means to manage it (such as an inhaler). Occasionally, severe bouts of asthma do not respond to the patient's medication, which can lead to a respiratory emergency. These instances are normally acute and unpredictable, resulting from an external allergen. Adults may also experience emotional asthma, triggered by mental, emotional, or physical stress (such as job problems, a romantic breakup, or overexertion). Wheezing is normally present immediately in patients experiencing an asthma attack, as exhalation becomes a taxing process that can quickly lead to respiratory arrest. Wheezing, followed by an abrupt cessation of wheezing, is an extremely critical development, as this indicates that airflow into the bronchioles has ceased altogether. Even with oxygen supplementation, critically ill asthma patients may not reach adequate blood oxygen levels. Alert and engaged patients should receive CPAP ventilation; unconscious patients should receive slowly-administered BVM ventilation in order to prevent lung injury caused by excess air placement. Oxygen should be humidified.

Acute Pulmonary Edema

Most commonly seen in patients with congestive heart failure, **acute pulmonary edema** is caused by excessive fluid levels in the lungs that block oxygen and carbon dioxide exchange between the alveoli and the capillaries. Non-cardiac instances of acute pulmonary edema usually result from ARDS. CPAP ventilation provides a high enough flow pressure to force gas exchange, but should only be utilized if the patient is conscious, can follow commands, and is still breathing autonomously. Otherwise, a BVM should be used. Patients should be kept upright until hospitalized.

Cystic Fibrosis

This is a genetic disorder that affects multiple organs, but pulmonary failure is the most common emergency situation that tends to result from **cystic fibrosis**. This disease is characterized by excess mucus production. Patients often face repeated lung dysfunction, ranging from excess fluid in the lungs to tissue scarring. Consequently, emergencies can range from pulmonary obstruction cases to complete respiratory failure as the lungs gradually weaken over time.

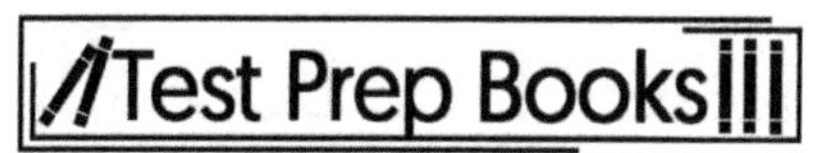

Toxic Inhalation

This is a broad term that refers to any instance of chemical, gaseous, or other noxious substance inhalation that hinders the lungs' ability to adequately respire and ventilate, or that structurally damages any physical component of the pulmonary system. The inhalation of toxins such as carbon monoxide, cyanide, and natural and/or industrial gases commonly results in the need for emergency services. Visibly hazardous events such as a home fire or chemical explosion can also result in the inhalation of noxious substances. However, even engaging in normally safe activities, such as painting or performing home repairs that require commonly used solvents or glues, can result in emergencies if they're performed in enclosed, small spaces without adequate ventilation.

The resulting consequences from toxic inhalation can vary. Carbon monoxide inhalation, for example, can quickly result in death since it is difficult to detect and also affects hemoglobin's ability to transport oxygen. Milder concentrations of inhaled toxins may result in less severe symptoms such as lightheadedness or nausea, which can alert an individual that a more serious condition is imminent. When providing care to patients affected by toxic inhalation, it is extremely crucial to assess the environment and ensure that EMTs are not exposed to harmful toxins, or that they have the proper safety equipment to deal with such an environment. Treatment for **toxic inhalation** normally involves delivering pure oxygen using a non-rebreather mask.

Pulmonary Embolism

This refers to the occurrence of a blockage in the pulmonary arteries. Although it is usually caused by a clot, it can also result from fat, fluid, or foreign objects in the artery. This blockage prevents adequate blood flow into the lungs. Severity of a **pulmonary embolism** depends on the size of the blockage; larger blockages will lead to highly visible signs of respiratory distress, such as sudden chest pain and dyspnea.

Pediatrics

Asthma

Pediatric patients differ from adults in asthmatic events in that their emergencies are almost always triggered by an external allergen or irritant. It is rare that a non-allergenic event (such as stress) causes an emergency asthmatic event in a pediatric patient. Most emergency cases occur in patients over two years old and will respond to epinephrine treatment.

Respiratory Syncytial Virus (RSV)

Pediatric patients are more vulnerable to viral infections leading to respiratory emergencies. **RSV** is a common, highly transmissible virus that causes inflammation of the lower airways and lungs. While many children experience only symptoms similar to the common cold, RSV in infants can progress to pneumonia. One common sign of RSV in infants is dehydration. The EMT can monitor the airway and breathing, provide supplemental humidified oxygen if needed, and transport the child to the hospital. ALS backup may be needed to provide IV fluids.

Bronchopulmonary Dysplasia

Bronchopulmonary dysplasia refers to a neonatal chronic lung disease, to which premature newborns are most susceptible because their bronchioles are not fully developed. As the newborn's lungs are not developed to fully handle this stress, the patient may experience lifelong respiratory problems, weakness, and infections.

Cystic Fibrosis

See "Cystic Fibrosis" under the Adults section above for a description of the disease. Note that the lifespan for those with this disease tends to be in the 30s, though often younger, so pediatric **cystic fibrosis** patients are common. Children with cystic fibrosis often have symptoms such as wheezing, sinus congestion, a chronic cough with thick mucus, and dyspnea. The EMT can provide suction and oxygen for a patient with cystic fibrosis.

When to Oxygenate and Ventilate

Knowing the appropriate time to deliver supplemental oxygen and assisted ventilation is a fundamental skill for EMTs. Delivering these practices too late can result in poor health outcomes for the patient, but delivering them too early, when they may not be necessary, can also cause patient discomfort and extreme complications. For example, a patient that is suffering from shortness of breath may not be experiencing a respiratory emergency at all, since shortness of breath can result from a number of physiological conditions. Delivering oxygen at a high flow rate during a serious cardiac event such as a myocardial infarction may actually injure the heart muscle. Over-oxygenating can also cause complications in obese patients. Monitoring oxygen saturation throughout the intervention and noticing the movement of the patient's chest and accessory muscles are ways to determine whether oxygen therapy and ventilation are appropriate for the situation. Oxygen therapy devices are attached to oxygen cylinders upon which flow rates and concentration levels can be adjusted by the EMT.

Adult Patients

The average healthy adult has a blood oxygen saturation level between 96% and 98%. In emergency situations, oxygen saturation levels below 94% should be noted, monitored, and may require oxygen therapy. Older adults often have blood oxygen saturation levels below 94%, as this tends to diminish slightly with age. If a patient's blood oxygen saturation level rapidly falls (normally marked by at least a 3% decrease over a 30- to 60-minute period), it likely indicates the need for oxygen therapy. Additionally, if the patient suddenly develops dyspnea that is visibly worsening, especially if they have a history of diabetes or kidney disease, oxygen therapy should be delivered.

The following devices are commonly used in emergency settings:

- **Nasal cannulas**: These deliver oxygen through tubal prongs placed directly into the nostrils at a flow rate ranging from 1 liter to 6 liters of oxygen per minute. This is a lower level oxygen concentration delivery system, delivering oxygen concentrations between 24% and 44%. They can be used in patients that are experiencing mild respiratory distress but are otherwise alert.

- **Non-rebreather masks**: This mask is placed over the patient's mouth and nose and delivers oxygen while transporting the patient's respired breath out of the device, so that it cannot be re-consumed. It is a higher flow and oxygen concentration device, delivering at a flow rate of 10 to 15 liters per minute and at a concentration of up to 90%. This is a good option for patients who are in critical, hypoxic conditions (blood oxygen levels of 90% or lower) but have the physical ability to breathe autonomously.

- **BVM**: This mask is similar to a non-rebreather mask—it is a one-way air flow mask placed over the mouth and nose, but oxygen delivery is controlled by a provider who squeezes an attached bag to release oxygen to the patient. It provides the highest oxygen flow rate, at 15 or more liters per minute, and also delivers oxygen at a concentration of 90% or more. This option is best for unconscious, non-breathing, and critically-hypoxic patients.

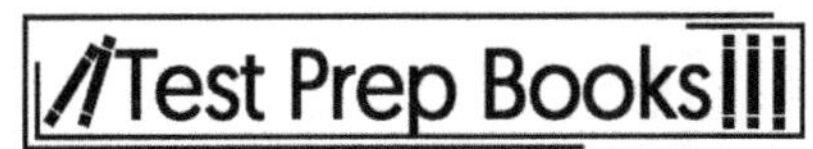

Pediatric Patients

The average healthy full-term newborn, infant, or child has a blood oxygen saturation level similar to an adult. It may be anywhere from 95% to 100%. Premature babies normally have blood oxygen saturation levels between 84% and 90%, which is considered moderately hypoxic and requires oxygen supplementation. However, providing oxygen therapy to a newborn should always be delivered at a lower flow and concentration rate. Over-oxygenating at this age can lead to blindness.

Older, conscious pediatric patients may be frightened by oxygen therapy devices or by having these devices near their faces. It is important to keep the pediatric patient calm to prevent the detrimental effects of anxiety from further exacerbating the respiratory emergency. If it seems unlikely that the pediatric patient will accept or maintain the placement of a nasal cannula or mask, a BVM can be gently waved over the patient's face, above the nose and mouth, so that the oxygen supply is available for the patient to inhale. This is called the **blow-by technique**.

Indications and Contraindications of Interventions

There are instances where the interventions that have been discussed in this section should and should not be used.

Manual Airway Management

- *Use of a nasal cannula:* This intervention is indicated in cases where blood oxygen saturation levels are low and when the patient is in a mild state of hypoxia. This intervention is contraindicated if the patient has nasal congestion or obstruction, has facial or nasal injuries, or is unwilling to wear or maintain the cannula.

- *Use of a non-rebreather mask*: This intervention is indicated in cases of moderate to severe hypoxia or respiratory distress. This intervention is contraindicated in patients vulnerable to hypercapnia, who have facial injuries, or who are unwilling or unable to wear and maintain the mask.

- *BVM ventilation*: This intervention is indicated in cases of respiratory failure, when intubation does not work or will not stay, and in cases where both high oxygen flow rate and high levels of oxygen concentration are needed. This intervention is contraindicated if the upper airway is blocked, if the EMT is inexperienced, if there is risk of aspiration or other fluid in the patient's mouth or airway, or if the patient is over 57 years of age, has a beard, is missing teeth, or has maxillofacial deformities.

- *Use of a rebreather masks*: This intervention is indicated in cases of mild hypoxia or respiratory distress where the patient is able to maintain their own breathing. This intervention is contraindicated in cases where the patient is vulnerable to hypercapnia, has fading or loss of consciousness, or is unwilling to wear or maintain the mask.

- *Use of tracheal tubing*: This intervention is indicated if the patient is experiencing a cardiac event, is unable to breathe autonomously, is unconscious, or is in a severely critical, traumatic condition. This intervention is contraindicated in cases where there is maxillofacial trauma, tracheal or pharyngeal blockages, or if there is a possibility that the patient has an injury to the cervical spine. Tracheal tubing may be necessary when spinal injury is present, in which case, the patient's head and neck should be completely stabilized and secured before placing the tube.

Suctioning

- **Endotracheal suctioning**: This type of suctioning is indicated when an artificial airway is in place and if fluid or other secretions are obstructing the tracheal pathway. This type of suctioning is contraindicated if it will aggravate the patient's condition; however, in a true emergency where endotracheal tubing is necessary, there will rarely be an actual contraindication due to the benefit of the endotracheal tubing procedure over the risk.

- **Nasotracheal and nasopharyngeal suctioning**: These types of suctioning are indicated when fluids or other obstructions (such as mucus, blood, food, etc.) are in the nasal-tracheal path or lower airway and cannot be otherwise removed. This type of suctioning is contraindicated if the patient has epiglottitis, croup, head or neck injury, is experiencing a cardiac event, or has trauma to the nasal area (including a bleeding nose).

- **Oropharyngeal suctioning**: This type of suctioning is indicated when fluid obstructs the oral cavity or the upper airway. This type of suctioning is contraindicated in the presence of maxillofacial trauma, if the patient is conscious and gagging, if the patient is able to cough, or if the patient has a foreign body obstruction.

Humidifiers

Humidifiers are used to moisten oxygen used in medical emergencies. They work by delivering sterile mist into the oxygen supply. Humidifiers are always used if oxygen therapy is delivered to the lower airway and/or is delivered through intubation. Humidifiers are often used when supplemental oxygen or oxygen therapy is delivered in arid climates, when the patient requires prolonged supplementation (usually meaning beyond a 24-hour period), or if the patient requests one. High flow oxygen supplementation can feel physically drying and uncomfortable, so EMTs may choose to humidify the oxygen in these instances if the patient is not able to request it.

Some types of respiratory emergencies, such as asthma, indicate oxygen humidification. For example, asthma emergencies should deliver humidified oxygen, as mucus plugs that are present may dry up during oxygen therapy, which can cause additional complications. Some studies have indicated that humidifiers do not increase patient comfort or airway moisture, and that alternative methods may work better for such purposes. These methods include using nasal cannulas with wider tubing (which decreases the pace of the air flow) and ensuring that the patient is sufficiently hydrated.

Humidifiers must be sterilized and dried after every use, as bacteria can easily grow in their warm, damp environments and infect patients.

Partial Rebreathers and Non-Rebreathers

A partial rebreather mask is a unique type of ventilation mask. Rather than allowing the patient's exhalations to completely pass out of the constructs of the mask, a partial rebreather mask stores a portion of the patient's exhalation in an attached bag. The patient "rebreathes" this air, and the flow of carbon dioxide serves to naturally stimulate the lungs. These may be used in less severe respiratory cases, and only when the patient is not at risk of hypercapnia.

Comparatively, a non-rebreather mask is only composed of a one-way flow path. It also consists of an attached bag that collects the contents of the patient's exhalation, but the bag is secured and carbon dioxide does not travel back to the patient. Emergency situations typically warrant the use of a non-

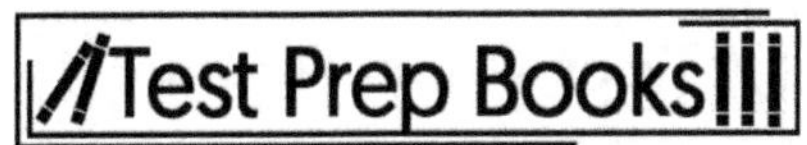

rebreather mask, as these are used to deliver high concentrations of oxygen in critical conditions such as bleeding and cardiac events, respiratory distress and arrest, shock, and trauma. Patients should be able to physically breathe on their own, but require a higher concentration of oxygen than what is naturally available to them.

Venturi Masks

The venturi mask is a high-flow oxygen delivery system that delivers calibrated levels of oxygen. This system mixes air present in the room with a concentration of pure oxygen; this concentration can be precisely calibrated. A venturi mask has holes on either side into which color-coded nozzles can be secured. Each nozzle will deliver a different concentration of oxygen. These can range between 24 and 60 percent, flowing at a rate ranging between four to 15 liters per minute. Venturi masks are typically used in patients with severe lung diseases, and are most commonly seen utilized in COPD patients. COPD patients will require an oxygen concentration delivery between 28 and 40 percent. Additionally, EMTs may choose to use venturi masks when the patient's respiratory ability cannot be gauged, as venturi masks will work exclusive of the patient's respiratory rates and tidal volumes, or when it appears the patient may be experiencing hypercapnia. Oxygen does not need to be humidified when it is delivered through a venturi mask.

Venturi Mask Specifications

Venturi valve colour	Inspired oxygen concentration (%)	Oxygen flow (l/min)	Total gas flow (l/min)
Blue	24	2 - 4	51 - 102
White	28	4 - 6	44 - 67
Yellow	35	8 - 10	45 - 65
Red	40	10 - 12	41 - 50
Green	60	12 - 15	24 - 30

Manually Triggered Ventilator (MTV) and Automatic Transport Ventilators (ATV)

MTVs are also referred to as flow-restricted, oxygen-powered ventilation devices. An MTV delivers oxygen, but has the ability to restrict flow speed. It must be attached to a pressurized oxygen source in order to work. It is important to maintain cricoid pressure when using an MTV due to the relatively high flow rate, which can cause abdominal distention and lung tissue damage if improperly monitored. MTVs deliver oxygen concentrations up to 100% at a rate of up to 40 liters per minute. These devices are contraindicated in patients that have chronic lung disease, chest injuries, or spine injuries.

ATVs are also powered by pressurized oxygen. They are quite similar to MTVs in function; the main difference is that ATVs are computerized. Ventilation rates can be pre-set and the EMT is able to perform other necessary tasks while monitoring the ATV. ATVs will adjust to the patient's respiratory rate and tidal volume. They are contraindicated in pediatric patients under age five, in situations where the patient experienced lung pressure issues (such as in scuba divers who ascend too quickly), and in patients with a pneumothorax.

Oral and Nasal Airways

Oral and nasal airways are external devices that assist with maintaining an open and patent patient airway. They are flexible and tube-shaped devices that come in a number of sizes in order to accommodate a range of patients.

Oral airways are sized based on the diagonal length of the patient's cheek, measuring from earlobe to mouth. After selecting an oral airway that is closest to this size, the provider will then open the patient's mouth, and slide the curved portion of the airway against the top palate. Once the airway makes contact with the throat, it must be rotated 180 degrees before sliding it into the throat. In a pediatric patient, the oral airway is rotated 90 degrees before sliding it into the throat. The EMT should ensure that the tongue is not blocking the path. In unconscious patients, an oral airway can be instrumental in keeping the tongue down, rather than blocking the upper airway.

Note that oral airways are contraindicated in conscious patients, as they require the patient to have no gag reflex, which is normally only achieved when the patient is unconscious. These devices are also contraindicated in patients with oral or maxillofacial trauma, or if the patient has a foreign body obstruction. If the patient does vomit, the airway will need to be removed, the patient's oral cavity and upper airway will need to be swept and suctioned, and a new, unused oral airway will need to be inserted as long as the victim has not regained consciousness.

Nasal airways are sized by measuring across the cheek the distance from the earlobe to the correlating nostril. They should be lubricated before use, then inserted against the bottom wall of the nostril. Nasal airways should slide in easily. If not, the other nostril should be used. Nasal airways should never be forced into place. These airways are contraindicated only in the event of skull, nasal, or facial trauma.

Note that these types of airways usually are associated with the need to suction, so once the airways are in place, EMTs should monitor patients for secretion build-up or other obstructions.

Pulse Oximetry

Pulse oximetry is a quick, easy, and cost-effective method of measuring and monitoring a patient's oxygen saturation levels. A pulse oximeter is comprised of a sensor that is attached to a small screen that displays its readings. The sensor detects oxygen saturated hemoglobin molecules using photo detection and delivers the reading as a percentage.

The sensor is normally placed on the patient's earlobe, fingertip, or other area where skin is relatively thin. Readings may be affected by bright lights in the area, poor perfusion, a hyperactive/flailing victim, nail polish, swelling of the sensor site, hypothermia, or if the patient is a smoker, has sickle cell disease, anemia, or carbon monoxide poisoning (due to these conditions' affect on hemoglobin). Pulse oximetry

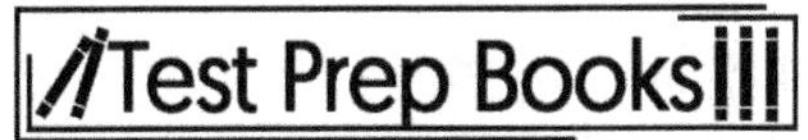

is not 100% accurate when compared to more invasive blood gas measurement techniques, but this tool is still extremely reliable when used to determine if a patient needs oxygen therapy. It is important to note that this method only deals with oxygenation and provides no indicators of ventilation.

Pulse oximetry is based off the oxygen-hemoglobin dissociation curve, which graphs the percentage of oxygen saturation against the arterial pressure of oxygen. As pressure rises, so do oxygen saturation levels. When oxygen saturation levels are low, as indicated by pulse oximetry readings, arterial pressure will also drop, indicating that hypoxic conditions can occur. The lowest functional limit of arterial pressure before respiratory problems occur is 60 mmHg, associated with 90% oxygen saturation levels.

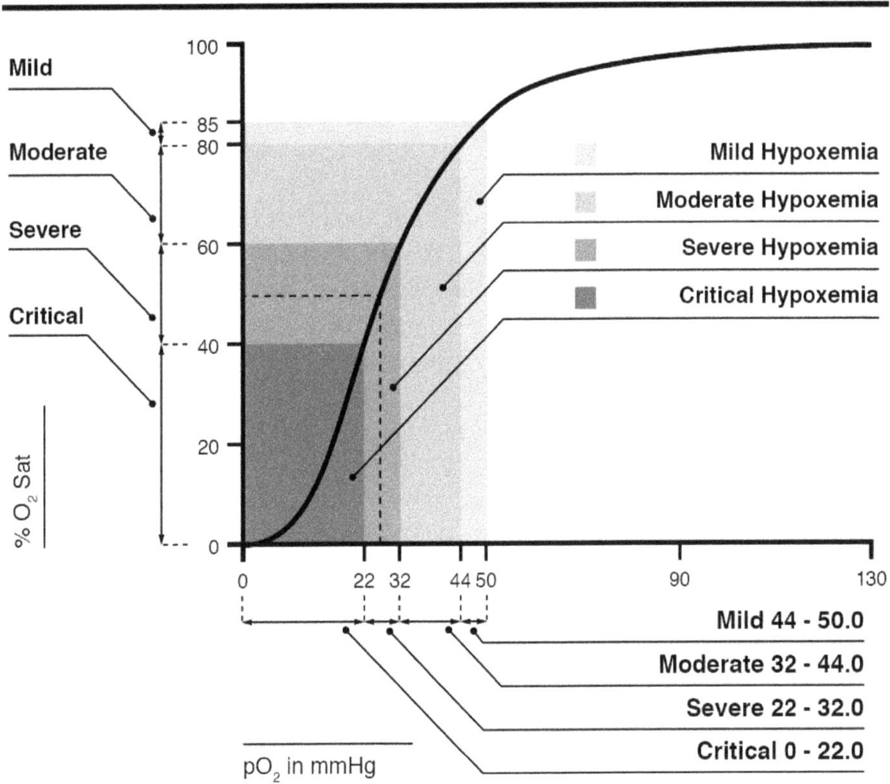

Blood Pressure

Blood pressure can be measured manually or automatically. Automatic readers are most commonly used. Blood pressure is affected by caffeine, stress, smoking, exercise performed just before measuring, temperature, a full bladder, and certain medications. Normal blood pressure is a systolic reading between 90 and 120, and a diastolic number between 60 and 80. The systolic pressure indicates how forcefully blood is traveling against arterial walls when the heart contracts, and the diastolic pressure indicates arterial blood force between heart beats (when the heart is at rest).

Manual

A manual blood pressure monitor utilizes a stethoscope, an arm cuff, and a manually-operated pressure gauge called a sphygmomanometer. With the stethoscope earpieces in, the EMT should find the brachial pulse (toward the inside of the elbow) using their index and middle fingers or the stethoscope. The head of the stethoscope should be placed over the pulse point, and the arm cuff should slide over the stethoscope head, just above the inside of the elbow. The cuff should be tightened to a snug fit. The pressure gauge is attached to a bulb with an airflow valve with a cap. The practitioner should tighten the cap completely before beginning the reading.

When ready, the practitioner should squeeze the bulb. With each squeeze, the cuff will tighten. The provider should keep squeezing the bulb until the gauge reads approximately 150 mmHg and the pulse is no longer audible. Pressure is then released by slowly opening the airway valve on the bulb. This will deflate the cuff and relieve pressure on the patient's arm. When the practitioner begins to hear the pulse again, the pressure reading should be noted as the systolic pressure (top number). As the cuff is further released, the sound of the patient's pulse will eventually no longer be audible. At this point, the pressure reading should again be noted and the value serves the diastolic pressure (bottom number).

Automatic

An automatic blood pressure monitor has a cuff that should be placed above the patient's elbow, then tightened to a snug fit. After powering on the device, the provider should wait until the screen reads "0". Then, the provider should press start, which will automatically inflate the cuff. The device should make an audible sound to indicate that the reading is complete or that there has been an error. It will show the reading or an error symbol on the monitor, then begin to deflate so that the practitioner can remove the cuff or redo the reading.

Practice Quiz

1. In the event of an untreated respiratory emergency, how quickly can the emergency result in brain damage or turn fatal?
    a. Within twelve minutes
    b. Within fifteen minutes
    c. Within ten minutes
    d. Immediately

2. The "ABCs" of first-responder treatment are an abbreviation referring to which order of operations?
    a. Airway management, Breathing, Circulation
    b. Access, Breathe, Continue
    c. Administer, Bypass, Call
    d. Airway management, Bypass, Cooperate

3. What is the primary benefit of placing an adult patient in the sniffing position?
    a. It inherently supports the ability for the patient to autonomously take in deep breaths through the nostrils.
    b. It aligns the oral, pharyngeal, and laryngeal axes, decreasing resistance in the airway and allowing for ease of intubation.
    c. It ensures that a cardiac event does not occur.
    d. It stabilizes the cervical spine to protect against injury.

4. What is the name for the sac-shaped structures in which carbon dioxide and oxygen exchange take place?
    a. Kidneys
    b. Medulla oblongata
    c. Alveoli
    d. Bronchioles

5. Which is the most common ventilation technique used in emergency management?
    a. Bag valve mask
    b. CPAP
    c. Negative pressure
    d. Mouth-to-mouth

See answers on the next page.

Answer Explanations

1. C: Although it may take longer, lack of oxygenated blood to the heart or to the brain can become fatal as soon as ten minutes from the start of the respiratory emergency. It is almost never immediate, though.

2. A: The rescuer should follow these steps when attending a respiratory emergency. They should make sure that the airway is open and patent, that the patient is breathing, and that adequate circulation is occurring. If not, those are the problems that need to be addressed immediately. The other options listed do not apply or make sense.

3. B: The sniffing position aligns these three axes in a way that best opens the airway. The sniffing position does not relate to the patient's ability to breathe through the nose, nor does it prevent an impending cardiac event from occurring. The sniffing position is often contraindicated in instances where the cervical spine is injured, as it actually destabilizes this area.

4. C: The alveoli are small sac-shaped structures at the end of the bronchioles where gas exchange takes place. The bronchioles are tubes through which air travels. The kidneys and medulla oblongata do not directly affect oxygen and carbon dioxide exchange.

5. A: The bag valve mask technique is the most common method of ventilation due to its ease of use and its ability to deliver high flow rates and high concentrations of oxygen. CPAP is often used in more complex cases. Mouth-to-mouth is typically used when equipment is not available, such as when a nonmedical bystander who has limited first aid experience is the first responder. Negative pressure ventilation is virtually obsolete at this time.

Cardiology and Resuscitation

Adult and Pediatric Cardiology and Resuscitation

Cardiology is a component of healthcare focused on the heart, including vascular systems associated with the heart (such as cardiac arteries and veins). **Cardiac arrest** refers to cessation of heart contraction due to a failure of the heart's internal electrical system. Healthcare providers who specialize in cardiology focus on preventive cardiovascular treatments, as well as managing and treating conditions such as cardiovascular disease, cardiac arrests, congenital cardiac and cardiovascular disorders, and cardiac traumas.

Adult and pediatric cardiology are two highly distinct fields, and providers are rarely interchangeable. This is due to the fact that the anatomy and physiology of adult and pediatric cardiovascular systems are different and require different interventions, even when experiencing the same condition (such as cardiac arrest). Most conditions and pathologies in adults differ significantly from the issues that present in pediatric patients.

Pediatric patients are more likely to present congenital heart conditions or respiratory issues that lead to a cardiac event. While adult resuscitative practices in emergency situations usually focus on immediately "jump starting" the heart through chest compressions or defibrillation, pediatric resuscitative practices often center first on correcting respiratory conditions to prevent or diminish the severity of cardiac events.

Cardiac System

The cardiac system's main component is the **heart**, a hollow muscle located in the middle of the chest with four chambers separated by thick walls. The thickest of these walls, the **septum**, runs vertically down the heart and separates it into left and right halves. In a healthy individual, blood cannot flow between these halves. This is important because the septum separates oxygenated from deoxygenated blood. Each half of the heart consists of a top chamber, called an **atrium**, and a bottom chamber, called a **ventricle**. The ventricles are responsible for pumping blood out of the heart. They receive blood from the two atria; in healthy individuals, blood only flows through one-way valves from the atria to the ventricles and cannot flow backward.

The heart works in tandem with the circulatory system; collectively, they are referred to as the **cardiovascular system**. The heart's primary purpose is to act as a pump for blood, moving it through a vast network of blood vessels. Two primary loops, originating from the heart, are responsible for the main circulation of blood through the body. The **pulmonary loop** pumps deoxygenated blood from the heart to the lungs and oxygenated blood from the lungs to the heart. The **systemic loop** takes oxygenated blood from the heart to various tissues throughout the rest of the body. The primary vessels that circulate blood are **veins** (which carry deoxygenated blood), **arteries** (which carry oxygenated blood), and **capillaries** (thin vessels that assist in carrying both types of blood to their final destination and are involved in gas and nutrient exchange at the tissue level).

When oxygenated blood enters the heart from the lungs, it first enters the left atrium and flows into the left ventricle through the **mitral valve**. The left ventricle pumps oxygen-rich blood through the **aortic valve** into the primary and largest artery, called the *aorta*. The aorta distributes blood to smaller connecting arteries, which transport the blood further away from the heart to capillaries that are able to deliver oxygenated blood directly to tissues that need it. As tissues use the oxygenated blood, deoxygenated blood is removed by capillaries that transport it to veins.

The two largest veins in the circulatory system are the **inferior vena cava**, which is the final collection point for deoxygenated blood from the lower extremities of the body, and the **superior vena cava**, which is the final collection point for deoxygenated blood from the upper extremities of the body. Both veins end in the right atrium, and the blood flows into the right ventricle through the **one-way tricuspid valve**. The right ventricle pumps deoxygenated blood back toward the lungs to become oxygenated. The blood then returns to the left atrium to begin the loop again. Both the left and right halves of the heart work simultaneously, so that oxygenated blood is distributed from the left ventricle to the rest of the body while deoxygenated blood is distributed from the right ventricle to the lungs with just a single cardiac contraction.

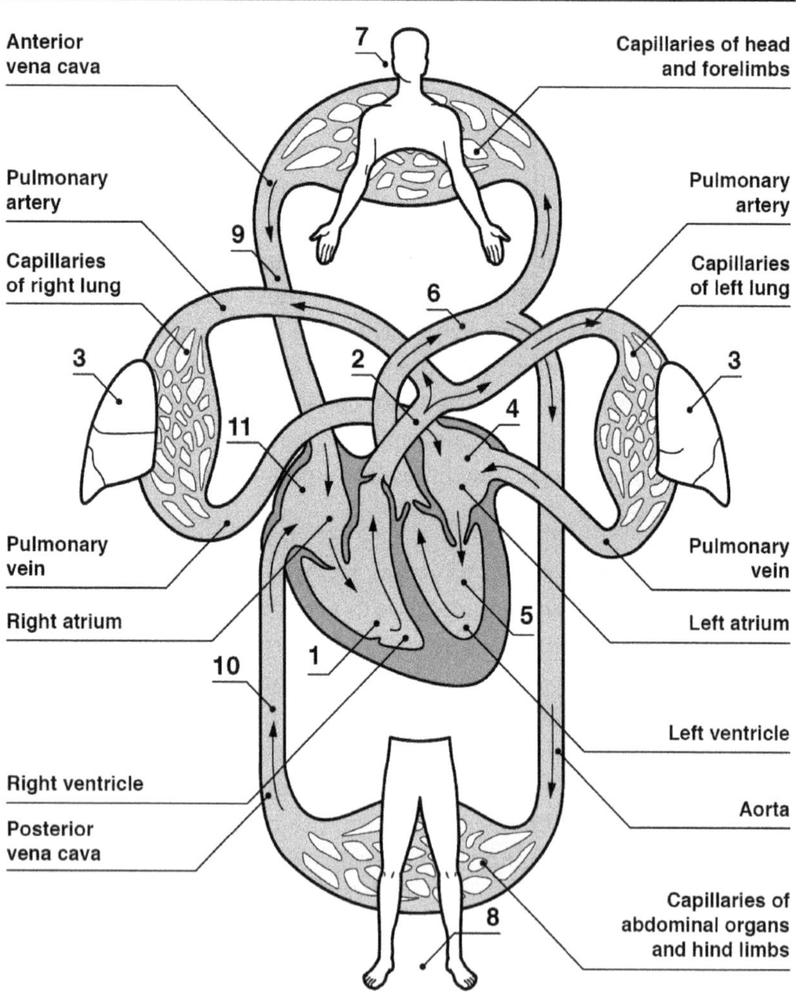

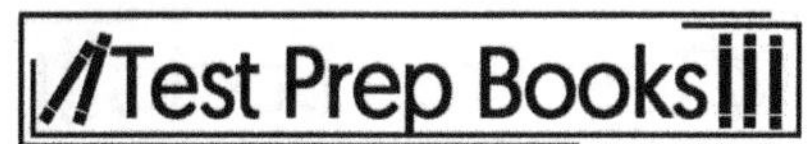

Blood Pressure

As mentioned, **blood pressure** refers to the force of blood exerted on the primary cardiovascular arteries as it is pumped through them. It is considered to be a vital sign; abnormally high or low blood pressure is often indicative of pathology. Blood pressure readings consist of two numbers: the systolic blood pressure written over the diastolic blood pressure. **Systolic blood pressure** refers to the pressure exerted on blood vessel walls when the heart contracts. **Diastolic blood pressure** refers to the pressure exerted on blood vessel walls when the heart relaxes between beats. Blood pressure is easily affected by sudden movement, caffeine or alcohol intake, stress, nervousness, smoking history, overall daily activity levels, and age. Sudden, unanticipated spikes or drops in blood pressure are usually indicative of a critical health status that should immediately be examined and treated. In emergency situations, blood pressure should be continuously monitored for this reason.

Assessing Normal versus Abnormal Cardiovascular Findings in a Patient

When called to the scene of an emergency, an initial cardiovascular assessment may be made by involving the patient or a relative. If possible, the patient's medical history should be obtained. Pediatric patients may have congenital heart defects. These most commonly include improper separation of the chambers (such as atrial septal or ventricular septal defects), improper arterial growth, or issues with the valves in the chambers. In adult patients, EMTs should look for cardiovascular risk factors such as previous heart attacks, strokes, hypertension, high cholesterol, smoker status, obesity, and current medications.

The patient may report abnormal chest sensations, such as pain, tightness, shortness of breath, a sensation of pressure over the rib cage, tingling or numbness in the jaw and back, or heaviness in the chest. Patients who are experiencing abnormal cardiovascular functioning, such as cardiac arrest, may also report digestive problems, hiccups, or stomach pain, as these areas are innervated by the same region responsible for the heart. They may also be able to provide a timeline of when symptoms began. Symptoms that should always be considered indicative of a critical cardiovascular event, even in the absence of chest pain, are nausea, vomiting, dizziness, and loss of motor control and strength. This is especially true in patients with a history of cardiovascular risk factors.

If the patient is unable to communicate appropriately with the **Emergency Medical Technician (EMT)** team, the EMT may need to rely solely on their own findings. The EMT should determine vital signs, including respiratory rate, temperature, heart rate, blood pressure, and appearance of skin. **Tachypnea**, an increased respiratory rate, and cold, greyish skin are both indicative of tissues not receiving enough oxygen, and may be present in patients suffering from stroke or embolisms. Flushed skin may be indicative of an irregular heart rate. Both abnormally high (**tachycardia**) and abnormally low (**bradycardia**) heart rates are indicative of abnormal cardiovascular functioning and often lead to cardiac arrest. Blood pressure often provides the most comprehensive indicator of the patient's overall health status. A high systolic blood pressure reading indicates that the left ventricle specifically is overcompensating, while a high diastolic blood pressure reading shows the blood vessel's elasticity and blockage. Abnormal blood pressure is linked to myocardial infarctions.

It is important to note the patient's overall health and the holistic context of the emergency when assessing vital signs. Endurance athletes, for example, naturally have lower heart rates, as do elderly patients. These do not necessarily mean these patients are suffering from bradycardia.

Chest Pain

Chest pain is a frightening experience, and therefore a common cause for summoning emergency care. However, the presence of chest pain can be attributed to several reasons, ranging from the quickly resolvable to the potentially fatal. For example, the pectoral muscles can be injured or strained during strenuous exercise or improper load bearing, and this can present as chest pain. This is a less urgent cause for concern than many other cases of chest pain and can usually be remedied with simple treatments like icing the affected area and administering over-the-counter pain relief medication.

Chest pain can also result from mental conditions such as high stress, anxiety, and panic attacks. In these instances, the patient may also report feeling unable to breathe properly and the sensation of a rapid heart rate. Patients typically make a full recovery in these cases once the stressor or panic trigger passes, and EMTs can assist in calming and soothing the patient, especially if the patient has a history of any such mental conditions. Because these symptoms are similar to that of serious cardiac events, it is important to rule out critical diagnoses such as cardiac arrest.

Cardiac ischemia is the result of no blood or oxygen reaching the heart, and can (but not always) result in chest pain referred to as **angina pectoris**. This is a temporary but painful experience, involving pressure across the chest, torso, arm, and/or back. It usually occurs acutely—triggered by exercise, excitement, or any other activity that causes an increase in heart rate. It may feel like the symptoms associated with a heart attack; the primary difference is that the symptoms do typically diminish without leading to any **tissue infarction** (an irreversible death of the tissues).

Cardiac ischemia is caused by blockages in the blood vessels (**atherosclerosis**) or hardened arteries (**arteriosclerosis**). Both conditions are the result of poor lifestyle behaviors, such as diets high in processed food, sedentary activity levels, and smoking. However, arteriosclerosis is also a natural byproduct of aging. Both conditions lead to a narrowing of the pathway through which blood can flow; when oxygenated blood is unable to reach the heart in time, cardiac ischemia may occur. Any instance of angina is indicative of cardiovascular disease or deterioration. It increases the risk for a more serious cardiac event. Therefore, if a patient appears to be in cardiac distress and has a history of angina or other cardiovascular events, it is an indicator that a critical intervention will be likely. Prolonged ischemia will likely result in cardiac arrest.

Silent cardiac ischemia, which doesn't present physical symptoms like angina, is common in women and diabetic patients. Over time, this weakens the heart and can lead to heart failure. Often, these patients do not realize they have any risk factors for heart failure and the cardiac event can come as an unfortunate surprise.

Cardiac Rhythm Disturbances

Cardiac rhythm is governed by cardiac muscle itself, which uses electrical conductivity to manage heart rate and chamber pressure. This electrical system is found in the right atrium and called the **sinoatrial node,** which signals to both atria to contract. The impulse then stimulates fibers in the ventricles to contract.

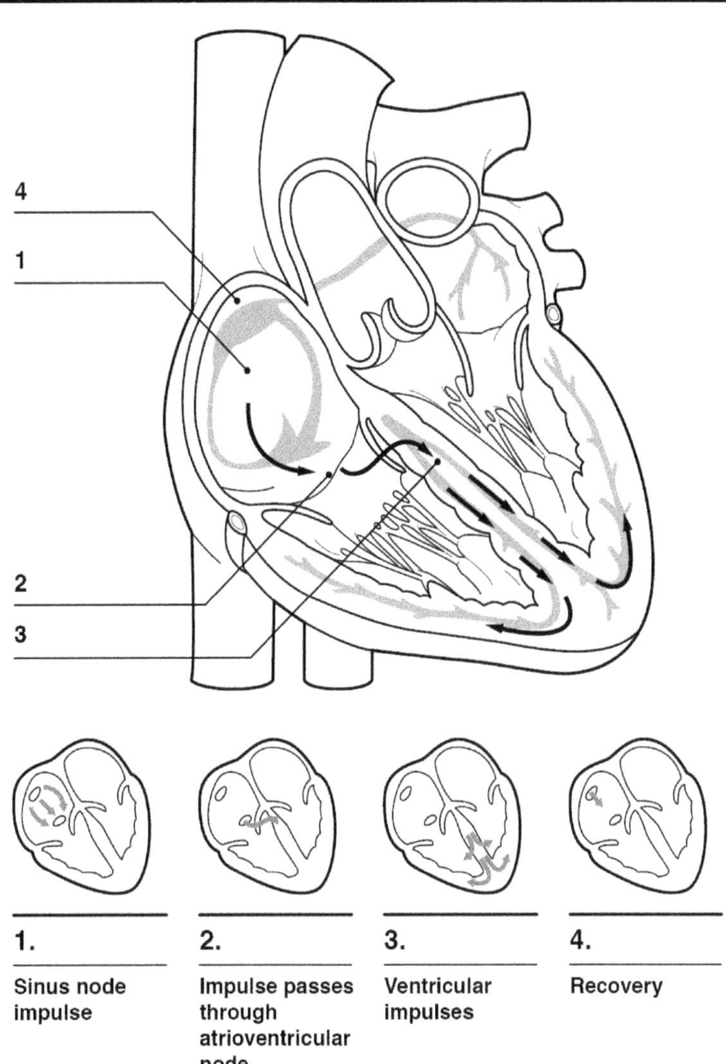

Disturbances to a healthy, normal cardiac rhythm are referred to as **arrhythmias**. These can be influenced by both congenital and lifestyle factors. Arrhythmias are characterized by fatigue, chest pain, inability to sweat, hot flashes, and dizziness. The most common congenital arrhythmia is **Wolff-Parkinson-White Syndrome**, a group of physical cardiac defects that lead to a disruption of how the heart's electrical signals function, consequently resulting in a dysfunctional heart rate and chamber pressure.

Several external and lifestyle factors can lead to arrhythmias. Some arrhythmias are temporary and not dangerous; for example, some people experience a brief increase in heart rate after drinking caffeinated beverages. Prolonged temporary arrhythmias, such as increased heart rate due to drug abuse, smoking, or constant exposure to high levels of cortisol can be extremely damaging to the heart muscle and its vascular network over time. These arrhythmias can slowly cause weakening of the heart and its vascular network. Heart attacks can also lead to permanent damage of the heart muscle; inactive or scarred areas of the heart disrupt electrical transmission as well.

Arrhythmias physiologically occur in a few different ways. Some affect the functioning of the atrial chambers. These are called **atrial fibrillation**, which is a dysfunction in certain muscle fibers in the atria that causes erratic atrial blood flow. Because the atria are mainly storage chambers for blood, this disruption can cause blood to flow to the ventricles in a disorderly manner. The result can be blood clots, because the blood does not move out of the chamber quickly enough. **Supraventricular tachycardia** refers to increased heart rate in the atrial chambers only, causing a differentiation between the pumping rates of the atria and the ventricles.

Ventricular fibrillation and **ventricular tachycardia** are similar dysfunctions to atrial fibrillation and supraventricular tachycardia, except they occur in the ventricles. They also lead to erratic blood flow and a disorganized, erratic, and fast-paced heart rate. These dysfunctions are most commonly treated with medication. If that does not work, the patient will usually receive an implanted pacemaker device. If surgery is necessary, the patient receives the Maze Procedure, which attempts to disrupt and reset the electrical pathways of the heart. Without proper management, arrhythmias often lead to cardiac arrest.

Cardiac Arrest

Cardiac arrest refers to cessation of heart contraction due to a failure of the heart's internal electrical system. In adults, cardiac arrest may come on without warning. In symptomatic patients, cardiac arrest is marked by chest pain, nausea, vomiting, tingling in the arm and back, and weakness. Patients quickly lose consciousness. For EMTs, a lack of a carotid pulse is the most obvious sign that a patient is in cardiac arrest. Without treatment, cardiac arrest usually becomes fatal in eight minutes or less.

In adult cases, cardiac arrest is most likely caused by **coronary artery disease**. Over time, coronary artery disease causes weakening of the left ventricle to the point where it can no longer pump. It can also block adequate amounts of blood flow to the heart, which disrupts the electrical signaling that allows the heart to pump in an orderly manner. Cardiac arrest can also result from inherited diseases that affect the heart's electrical system.

In pediatric patients, cardiac arrests are most likely due to respiratory complications. Pediatric patients are highly vulnerable to the effects from choking, drowning, neglect, and other respiratory complications, due to the smaller, less developed structure of their respiratory systems. Lack of oxygen quickly leads to cardiac arrest in this population. Additionally, congenital heart issues, traumas (such as infection at birth), and undetected disorders can lead to pediatric cardiac arrests.

For patients who are at especially high risk for cardiac arrest, or those patients who experience cardiac arrest and survive, almost all are treated with medication and some form of surgery. Some patients may receive an implantable cardioverter-defibrillator in their chest. This medical device monitors the heart and will internally defibrillate the heart if an arrhythmia is detected. Others who have high levels of

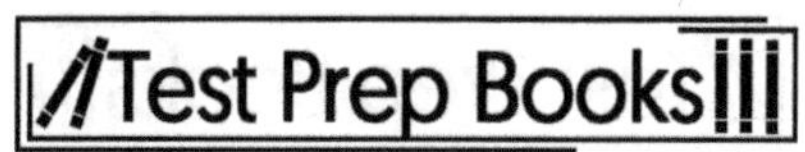

arterial blockage may undergo coronary angioplasty—a procedure that uses an inflated balloon to open blocked arteries, or a coronary bypass surgery, which reroutes blood flow away from blocked passages.

Stroke-Like Symptoms

A **stroke** results when a blood vessel in the brain becomes blocked or damaged, preventing oxygenated blood from reaching the brain. The risk factors for stroke include taking birth control pills, high cholesterol levels, diabetes, smoking, family history, sitting for long periods of time, and age. A stroke can result in damaged brain cells, leading to long-term loss of motor functions, thought processes, or speech. The specific effects of a stroke will depend on the location within the brain in which it occurred and the degree to which the brain tissue was damaged. It is important to ask patients or relatives how long their symptoms have lasted; treating strokes within three hours may provide the ability to reverse any damage and prevent long-term disability.

Strokes are characterized by an acute headache, numbness in the extremities, vision issues, slurring of speech, and muscle weakness, especially in the face and arms. Several conditions can mimic the symptoms of a stroke, and these conditions are especially common in the elderly. This can lead some patients to downplay the symptoms of an impending stroke, or even cause them to fail to realize that they have had a minor stroke. **Transient ischemic attacks** occur when a blood clot reduces blood flow (and thus oxygen supply) to the brain for a short period of time but then resolves. However, the symptoms can mimic that of a major stroke, although they do not last as long. These events increase the risk of suffering a major stroke. Some patients may "blank" for a few moments when having a minor stroke, and attribute it to forgetfulness or aging. More serious conditions that may cause stroke-like symptoms include migraines and seizures (which can both cause vision loss, speech problems, and muscle weakness), brain tumors, and **Bell's palsy**—a nerve condition that causes sudden, but temporary, paralysis.

Post-Resuscitation Care

Because patients who experience a cardiovascular event are often resuscitated before being admitted to the hospital, and because these patients are at increased risk of another event, post-resuscitation care is a crucial component of preventative care, increasing the patient's life expectancy, and eliminating or limiting cardiovascular and neurological damage. Post-resuscitation care encompasses aspects of monitoring and managing the patient's vitals, blood lipid and glucose panels, oxygenation and ventilation, and rehabilitation after discharge (to also include education for family and caregivers).

Patients who suffer cardiac arrest can benefit greatly from carefully administered therapeutic hypothermia, a practice which intends to reduce the patient's internal body temperature to between 89.6 degrees and 93.2 degrees Fahrenheit. This can be accomplished with ice packs, ice baths, or administering cold fluid through an infusion; the lowered body temperature may need to be maintained for up to 24 hours, depending on the patient and the context of the case. Because cardiac arrest prevents oxygenated blood from reaching the brain, the brain compensates by attempting to perform anaerobic metabolism. However, this causes cellular waste that leads to further oxygen depletion, which can make impending tissue damage worse.

Even if cardiac function is reestablished by the EMT team, any presence of necrotized (dead) brain or heart tissue will result in a flood of immune system activity, which may cause inflammation that the organ cannot handle. As the body's temperature is lowered, brain activity slows considerably. This effectively decreases metabolism, since it requires less oxygen, so it prevents the loop described from occurring, while still keeping the patient alive. This is a newer practice, and specific procedures are governed by the administrating hospital. Some organizations have not yet adopted this practice. Avoiding hyperthermia is of utmost importance when caring for a patient who has experienced a cardiovascular event.

Once the situation is stable, patients are rewarmed slowly and monitored for fluid loss, electrolyte imbalance, and vasodilation. At this point, it is likely that the patient will be suffering from electrolyte imbalance and abnormal glucose levels, both of which are deterrents to optimal recovery. Both should be consistently monitored through blood testing, because unconscious patients inherently mimic signs of poor electrolyte balance and hypoglycemia. Insulin and electrolyte fluid solutions will likely need to be administered.

Finally, patients may need consistent mechanical ventilation support. Rescuers will need to consistently monitor respiratory indicators such as respiratory rate and the extent to which the patient's breathing is labored. While patients who experience cardiac events are often unable to circulate oxygenated blood throughout their bodies, hyperventilating the patient can cause more harm than benefit. Arterial blood oxygen saturation is easily affected by changes in pressure, and hyperventilation can lead to vasoconstriction in the vessels serving the heart and the brain; counterintuitively, hyperventilation may actually lead to further oxygen depletion of these organs.

Assuming successful transport to a clinical setting and patient recovery, post-resuscitation best practices also focus on treatment of patients for the duration of their stay in the clinical setting. It further involves educating patients about the causes of their condition and how to prevent reoccurrences, and counseling patients' household members, caregivers, and friends in nurturing supportive lifestyle behaviors for the patient.

Hypotension/Hypertension from Cardiovascular Causes

A patient's blood pressure can provide a wealth of insight to the patient's overall health status. Normal blood pressure is a systolic reading of less than 120 mmHg and a diastolic reading of less than 80 mmHg (written as 120/80). A systolic reading of 140 mmHg or higher, or a diastolic reading of 90 or higher, is considered **hypertensive** (high blood pressure). Hypertension is considered the most dangerous risk factor for cardiovascular deaths, and can be a direct cause of heart failure, heart disease, and an enlarged heart. It is also the primary cause of at least 50 percent of stroke incidences.

Prolonged hypertension gradually damages blood vessels in two ways. First, the high force exerted on blood vessel walls damages their smooth inner lining and weakens the cellular structure. Second, the vessels dilate as the body compensates for the extra pressure and tries to lower it, but this dilation causes the vessels to lose their elasticity over time. As a result, they become hardened. Additionally, high blood pressure can be damaging to the cardiac muscle itself. When the vessels are unable to efficiently transport blood, the heart has to pump harder. This can cause a thickening of the left ventricle, which causes it to pump more inefficiently; or, the heart simply wears out to the point of failure. When the actual heart muscle is weakened or damaged, the patient may experience cardiac arrest or heart failure (due to the inability of the muscle to effectively contract), while damaged blood vessels can lead to a heart attack or stroke (due to the inability of oxygenated blood to reach these areas).

A number of factors can cause high blood pressure. Smoking, obesity, a sedentary lifestyle, a diet high in processed foods and trans fats, alcohol abuse, age, kidney disease, sleep apnea, genetics, and

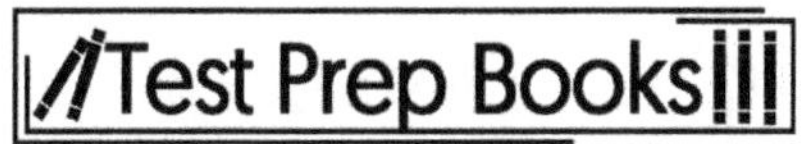

unmanaged stress are the most common causes for prolonged or chronic hypertension. Acute periods of hypertension may be caused by less harmful contexts such as temporary stress and vigorous exercise. However, hypertensive crises are situations when blood pressure suddenly spikes and does not return to an acceptable level. Patients who monitor their blood pressure at home are instructed to call emergency services if they receive a reading of 180/110. This often precedes a stroke or a cardiac event. It can result from ongoing cardiovascular degeneration or from a temporary event, such as overdosing on a stimulant drug. High blood pressure in pregnancy (**preeclampsia**) is usually an emergency that may require immediate bed rest or induction of labor.

Hypotension (low blood pressure) refers to a systolic reading under 90 mmHg and a diastolic reading under 60 mmHg. **Orthostatic hypotension** is a common, harmless drop in blood pressure that takes place when people quickly stand up. It is characterized by a few seconds of lightheadedness. Unless the patient feels prolonged symptoms such as lightheadedness, dizziness, nausea, or fainting, chronic hypotension is not necessarily as worrisome as chronic hypertension. Most hypotension readings are temporary, and can be due to something as simple as dehydration. Many endurance athletes have consistently lower blood pressures, and some medications, alcohol, sedative drugs, and diabetic complications (such as permanent nerve damage) can also cause hypotension. However, some acute instances of low blood pressure are an emergency. Severe blood pressure drops are also seen in instances of hemorrhage and shock. Decreases of blood pressure by more than 10 points is a red flag. In these situations, the patient is at risk of heart failure or cardiac arrest.

Shock

Shock refers to any context where the body is unable to circulate an adequate amount of blood to carry out essential physiological functions. It commonly occurs in emergencies of the cardiovascular system. **Cardiogenic shock** occurs as a result of direct cardiac muscle damage. It often presents due to heart attack or heart failure. **Hypovolemic shock** occurs as a result of heavy bleeding and overall low blood volume, which prevents adequate circulation from occurring. Shock patients will always exhibit low blood pressure. They may also present with cold, clammy, bluish skin; dehydration; shallow breathing; chest pain; and abnormal pulses. Patients in a state of severe shock may be unconscious. Shock patients will likely need to be treated with chest compressions if they aren't breathing and don't have a pulse, suctioning and mechanical ventilation, and/or defibrillation before or during transport. Pediatric patients under three months of age and all immunocompromised patients who appear to be in shock should be treated as septic.

Resuscitation

Cardiopulmonary resuscitation (CPR) addresses cardiac functioning, respiratory assistance, and circulatory issues. It is used in emergency situations where the patient is unresponsive and lacks a pulse or is experiencing agonal breathing. Though CPR employs chest compressions, it will not restart a heart in arrest or reset any presenting arrhythmias, but it may be able to affect electrical impulses in the heart in a way that will respond positively to external defibrillation. The goal of the procedure is to provide enough oxygen to the heart and the brain to prevent long-term damage, until the patient is able to receive more comprehensive treatment.

To administer CPR to adults, rescuers should make sure the environment is safe. Then, if possible, the patient should be laid in the supine position. Chest compressions—conducted by placing the hands on top of one another, interlacing the fingers together, positioning the heel of the bottom palm over the sternum, and pressing forcefully down about five centimeters in depth—should be conducted at a rate of one compression per half second. Airway management and appropriate assisted ventilation should also be employed, but proper chest compressions should take precedence if both cannot be conducted simultaneously.

In pediatric patients, however, airway management and ventilation are often more crucial than chest compressions. Because most pediatric cardiac events occur as a result of a respiratory issue, the respiratory issue should be addressed. Chest compressions can often cause more harm than good, especially if any objects are lodged in the airway. For children experiencing a cardiac event, an **automated external defibrillator (AED)** (rather than chest compressions) should be utilized as soon as possible. If an AED is not available, the heel of one hand should be used to deliver chest compressions at a rate of just under two per second. In pediatric patients under one year of age, just two fingers should be used to deliver chest compressions.

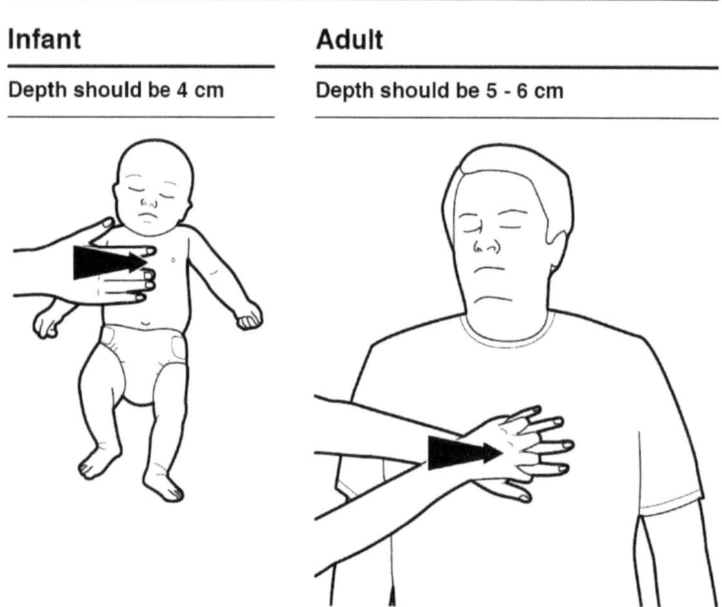

Automated External Defibrillators (AEDs)

An automated external defibrillator can play a crucial role in preventing cardiac arrest. Found as part of most first responder kits in places where large groups gather (such as community centers, restaurants, hotels, sports venues, entertainment venues, et cetera), AEDs are small, portable, and come with instructions that can be utilized effectively even by bystanders. The primary purpose of an AED is to detect ventricular cardiac arrhythmias and deliver electrical stimulation that resets a healthy cardiac rhythm. It will only work effectively on patients experiencing ventricular fibrillation or ventricular tachycardia. AEDs can be used on pulseless patients; however, they cannot provide any beneficial function to patients whose hearts are already in arrest and are not producing any electrical activity. Because AED treatment is limited to reestablishing ventricular cardiac rhythms only, cardiopulmonary resuscitation (CPR) may be required beforehand.

In addition to written instructions, AED devices provide audio instruction when powered on. The instructions will inform the user to expose the patient's chest (scissors are included in the kit, in case clothing needs to be cut), remove all metal objects (such as jewelry and undergarments with metal components), and shave visible hair (razors are included in the kit in case for this purpose). Sticky electrode pads, which come in adult and pediatric sizes, are adhered to the patient's chest, and the AED will detect if the patient can receive a shock. If so, the machine will instruct users to stand back, and it delivers shocks through the pads. Most models will administer additional shocks if needed or instruct the user to perform CPR (if shocks will not be of benefit). AEDs will also store data that can be provided to the hospital upon arrival.

AED devices should be regularly checked for proper functioning, battery strength, and expiration of parts.

Acting on Potential Cardiovascular Issues

There are a number of cardiovascular issues that can result in emergencies, and the first line of defense for each of them varies. Knowing distinct symptoms of cardiovascular emergencies can help responders quickly deliver the most effective intervention. Heart attacks are characterized by chest pain, pain in the shoulder, back, and neck, shortness of breath, and collapse. However, some patients (for example, many women) do not show any symptoms and simply collapse. If a heart attack is suspected, adult aspirin may be given. The patient should be placed in a comfortable position and may then require oxygenation, ventilation, and defibrillation. The rescuer should also prepare to provide chest compressions if the AED cannot detect an appropriate rhythm.

Arrhythmias may be the result of a congenital disease or an impending cardiac event due to coronary artery disease or drug abuse. Irregular heart rhythms may be characterized by flushed skin, anxiety, nausea, and vomiting. An abrupt change in blood pressure is also likely. If possible, it is important to first get the patient's medical history (such as if they have any diagnosed arrhythmias or an implanted pacemaker device) and an account of recent events, including when symptoms began. Oxygenation and ventilation should be provided and an AED should be at hand, as defibrillation may be needed. Again, the rescuer should be prepared to deliver chest compressions if the AED cannot detect an appropriate rhythm.

If the patient is experiencing heart failure, he or she may show low blood pressure and may have fluid in the lungs. Such patients may also experience high blood pressure that is unproductive, and may experience chest pain and shortness of breath. The patient should be placed in a comfortable position. However, if the patient is experiencing excessively high blood pressure, he or she should be placed in a seated position, if possible.

If a patient is in cardiac arrest and not exhibiting a pulse, the EMT should begin CPR and prepare to utilize the AED. Patients that are hemorrhaging or appear to be in some sort of shock should be treated with a focus on maintaining adequate blood oxygen saturation.

Practice Questions

1. What is the primary cause of cardiac emergencies in adult patients?
    a. Congenital issues
    b. Poor lifestyle behaviors
    c. Vegetarian diets
    d. Genetic predisposition

2. What is the primary cause of cardiac emergencies in pediatric patients?
    a. Congenital issues
    b. Poor lifestyle behaviors
    c. Vegetarian diets
    d. Genetic predisposition

3. If a patient appears to be experiencing a cardiac event and fluid can be heard in the lungs, what condition are they likely experiencing?
    a. A heart murmur
    b. A heart attack
    c. Heart failure
    d. A stroke

4. CPR and use of an AED is likely the first course of action that responders should take for which of the following patients?
    a. A young man who experienced chest pain and tingling in the arms before losing consciousness
    b. A middle-aged woman who is grabbing her chest, gasping for air, and has a slight greyish tinge to her skin
    c. A pregnant woman with an abnormally high blood pressure reading
    d. A young child who is gasping for air and has a slight greyish tinge to her skin

5. Silent cardiac ischemia is common in which demographic of patients?
    a. Pediatric patients
    b. Female patients
    c. Male patients
    d. Patients over the age of 65

See answers on the next page.

Answer Explanations

1. B: Most cardiac emergencies in adult patients result from poor lifestyle behaviors such as diets high in processed foods and trans fats, smoking, high stress, sedentary behaviors, and obesity. Congenital issues are more likely to cause cardiac emergencies in pediatric patients, especially newborns and infants. Genetic predisposition may cause some cardiac problems, but it is not the cause of most emergencies. Vegetarian diets are not positively correlated with cardiac emergencies.

2. A: Congenital issues are more likely to cause cardiac emergencies in pediatric patients, especially newborns and infants. Most cardiac emergencies in adult patients result from poor lifestyle behaviors. Genetic disposition may cause some cardiac problems, but they are not the cause of most emergencies. Vegetarian diets are not positively correlated with cardiac emergencies.

3. C: Fluid in the lungs, especially when heard in conjunction with low blood pressure, is primarily associated with heart failure. This occurs when the heart is unable to effectively pump blood out of the heart, so blood pools into the lungs. This situation does not occur with the other outcomes listed.

4. A: The young male is exhibiting symptoms of cardiac arrest. CPR and use of an AED is the first course of action for someone who is unresponsive and may be in cardiac arrest. The pregnant woman may require bed rest or induction of labor. The middle-aged woman and the young girl should not have CPR performed, or an AED used, while they are still conscious.

5. B: Female patients are most likely to experience silent cardiac ischemia— a cardiac event that exhibits no distinctive symptoms. Female patients, along with diabetic patients, are less likely to show the telltale signs of a cardiac event, such as chest pain or shortness of breath. They often may just feel tired or collapse.

Trauma

Adult and Pediatric Trauma

Trauma refers to the occurrence of any event where a transfer of energy causes a negative, intolerable effect on an individual's tissues, bones, or organs. Adult and pediatric trauma emergencies are categorized on a scale that ranges from Level 1 to Level 3. This distinction corresponds with the type of trauma center to which the patient should be transported. Along the continuum, Level 1 trauma centers have the ability to provide a wide range of high quality care at any time of the day, while Level 3 trauma centers may have fewer resources. Level 3 cases are typically ones where trauma was experienced, but the scope of the patient's case falls outside of the more severe requirements established for Level 1 and 2 parameters. Depending on the case, Level 3 admittances may later be transferred to a facility of another level. Treatment centers are often designated as serving adult or pediatric patients, although some centers do serve both populations. This distinction is important, as adult and pediatric interventions vary widely, and care providers are rarely interchangeable.

Multisystem Trauma

Trauma patients are characterized by physiological criteria including low systolic blood pressure, low respiratory rate, and a **Glasgow Coma Scale** (a neurological scoring test that determines a patient's level of consciousness) assessment of under 14. Anatomic indications may include amputation; two or more visible fractures; paralysis; any injury to the head, neck, torso, or pelvis; or a depressed chest (often indicative of broken ribs). **Multisystem trauma** refers to any instance where the patient has injuries affecting multiple systems of the body. It is considered one of the leading causes of death, and the number one cause of death in pediatric patients. Most traumatic incidents involve body or organ penetration (such as a bullet wound), toxic inhalation, poisoning, drowning, suffocating, explosions, or crushing from a heavy object. All of these situations can easily affect multiple systems in the body. Head traumas, spinal cord injuries, and aortic injuries are the primary causes of patient fatalities when multisystem trauma is present.

When EMT rescuers arrive at a scene involving a patient who likely suffered multisystem trauma (for example, in major vehicle accidents, which are the most common sites of multisystem trauma cases), their primary goal is to prevent further injury or decline of the live patient. While EMTs will follow usual protocols of addressing any immediate concerns (such as managing the patient's airway, ventilation, and oxygenation; managing symptoms of shock or hemorrhage; and stabilizing any skeletal injuries), it is vital that there is thorough and accurate communication with the receiving hospital in order to prepare the attending medical team. The ability of the EMT team to adequately stabilize the patient and communicate comprehensively with the receiving hospital is positively correlated with how well the patient recovers once in the hospital.

It is also important that the EMT team is aware of problems that can arise from certain traumatic injuries and prepares for the appropriate response. For example, a patient who experiences trauma near the heart is at an increased risk of also experiencing a cardiac event, so the EMT team should be prepared to manage that event. A patient who has lost a limb may be stabilized temporarily, but the potential volume of blood loss could cause symptoms of shock or heart failure. It is important that the EMT team is able to anticipate these changes and can quickly address various emergency situations, as

trauma cases can be unpredictable and volatile in terms of the chain of reactions that can occur within the patient.

Pediatric patients make up the majority of multisystem trauma cases. Almost any time a pediatric patient experiences a head injury, another system is likely to be affected, due to pediatric patients' skull anatomy and brain physiology. Behaviorally, pediatric patients of all ages are more likely than adults to make riskier decisions that increase their chances of experiencing trauma. Pediatric cases can be divided into three classes, where Class 1 multisystem traumas are the most critical and Class 3 multisystem traumas indicate that the patient was able to be stabilized by EMT services before being admitted to the receiving hospital; Class 2 multisystem traumas fall in the middle.

Relating the Mechanism of Injury to Injury Patterns

Different types of trauma correlate with different visible signs and physiological symptoms. Blunt force trauma and penetration traumas most commonly occur as a result of falls, crashes, or violence. The travelling speed before impact of the object that causes the trauma, the mass of the object that caused the trauma, and the distance at which the object that caused the trauma or the patient travelled (for example, in a fall or if being thrown in a collision), the location of the trauma, and any protective factors (such as the presence of an airbag) are all aspects that influence how severe the injury will be.

For example, if a patient wearing a seatbelt is travelling at a low speed in an average mid-sized sedan with functioning airbags runs off the road and hits a small tree, any trauma is likely to be much less severe than a motorcyclist who is not wearing a helmet, traveling at 80 miles per hour, and collides with an oncoming car going approximately the same speed. A patient who is forcefully hit in the head by an assailant is likely to experience more trauma to that area than a patient who slips and bumps their head against drywall.

In response to direct blunt force or penetration, most solid anatomical structures (such as bone) will shatter or crack. Other structures that are filled with air or fluid (such as the lungs, stomach, or blood vessels) will most likely burst or tear.

Vehicular accidents are one of the most common cases for which EMT services will be required. In these cases, knowing the specific way the crash occurred can provide EMTs with clues as to how injury patterns will present. Frontal impacts, where the patient's vehicle is hit head-on, most commonly result in injuries primarily on the upper half of the body (specifically, rib fractures, heart injuries, or aortic injuries) or primarily on the lower half of the body (specifically, pelvic fractures, or knee or hip dislocations). Lateral impacts, where the patient's vehicle is struck on the side, are likely to cause ruptures of organs in the torso area.

These impacts can also cause head, neck, and spinal injuries. Rear impacts, where the patient's vehicle is struck from behind, commonly result in spinal injuries that can range from minor to severe. Rolled vehicles can affect the occupants in unpredictable ways. Motorcycle accidents, however, involve different patterns. If a motorcycle is involved in a frontal accident, the patient is likely to have been ejected from the motorcycle. Depending on where the patient landed, or if he or she was hit by any other objects, the patient can be expected to have cervical spinal injuries, injuries to the organs in the torso, and broken bones. If the motorcycle is hit laterally, patients are likely to experience effects of crush-type injuries—where the area in question becomes compressed. Crush injuries can vary widely in severity, with symptoms ranging from mild bruising that can heal without medical intervention to tissue ischemia so severe that it necessitates amputation of the area.

Environmental Emergencies

Environmental emergencies refer to situations that occur as a result of what is occurring around the patient. Common instances of environmental emergencies include patients suffering from natural disasters, overheating or hypothermia, drowning and diving accidents, or animal or insect bites. In these instances, diligently surveying the scene upon arrival is crucial, as environmental emergencies can affect multiple people, including EMT personnel.

Natural disasters include somewhat unpredictable events like earthquakes, flooding, hurricanes, tsunamis, tornadoes, blizzards, and landslides. Hazards that result from natural disasters include things like noxious fumes, downed—yet live—electrical wires, fires, weakened residential and commercial structures, excessively hot or cold temperatures, and higher than normal instances of motor accidents.

EMT personnel may experience increased exposure to patients' bodily fluids (especially in instances where many injuries occurred simultaneously), and debris management to which they may not be accustomed. As always, EMT personnel should ensure that the scene and conditions are safe before they begin to treat patients. In natural disaster contexts, many large teams of EMTs can be expected to work with other rescue agencies (such as fire and police departments) to effectively help communities. Patient injuries and the necessary interventions can vary widely at the scene. For example, a community that has been hit by a tornado may have patients who need treatment for anything from superficial lacerations, to being struck by lightning, to serious crush injuries. Rescuers should anticipate this level of unpredictability.

When responding to a patient who is suffering from excess heat in some way—elevated body temperature not due to an internal fever, heat rash, heat exhaustion, etc.—such patients will likely need to be immediately cooled. This can be achieved by removing clothing, misting cool water on the patient, fanning the patient, placing cool rags on the patient's body, or administering cool fluids if the patient is able to take them. In severe cases, a water and electrolyte mix may be administered intravenously. Many overheated patients will need pressurized oxygen.

Patients suffering from excess cold should be removed from the source of cold. The patient should be undressed only if their clothing is wet. It is important to note whether the patient is experiencing a localized cold issue or general hypothermia. The area affected should be actively rewarmed only if there is a superficial injury and there is no chance that the area could be affected by the cold again. Otherwise, the area should simply be kept clean and sterile until the patient is admitted. Patients suffering from general hypothermia may need pressurized oxygen as well. The body temperature for mild hypothermia is 90 to 95 degrees Fahrenheit, 86 to 92 degrees for moderate hypothermia, and less than 86 degrees for severe hypothermia. When treating a patient with hypothermia, the intent is to keep the patient from losing any more heat. Warm, humidified oxygen can be delivered to help maintain internal temperature. After removing any wet clothing, blankets should be used to cover the patient, and then they should be transported to the hospital. Hypothermic patients should be handled lightly, since ventricular fibrillation could occur if they are handled too roughly.

Patients suffering from drowning or diving accidents will need a patent airway immediately, followed by cardiopulmonary resuscitation. Conscious patients should receive assisted ventilation.

Patients who have been attacked by an animal or insect should be kept calm. Ice and an antiseptic can be applied to the bite, and the area should be kept stationary. If possible, the animal or insect that caused the attack should be brought to the emergency department as well.

Secondary Assessment Related to Trauma Patients

The primary assessment of a trauma patient follows what is known as the **ABCDE approach**, which stands for Airway, Breathing, Circulation, Disability, Exposure. The goal of this approach is to notice and provide intervention for all conditions that could be considered life-threatening in a short-term period. The ABCDE approach is a systematic process that should be implemented upon contact with the patient (unless the patient appears to be in cardiac arrest), and thereafter at any periods of sudden deterioration (such as a spontaneous blood pressure drop or spike over 10 points).

The **secondary assessment** of a trauma patient takes place after the critical issues discovered from the primary assessments have been addressed and the patient has been relatively stabilized. Depending on the severity of the case, EMT personnel may not always reach the point of conducting a secondary assessment. It may take place later in the hospital by the patient's long-term medical team. These assessments, however, provide a great deal of information about the patient. Most deaths from trauma occur within three time frames: within minutes, within the hour (known as the **Golden Hour**, a period during which effective medical intervention is most likely to reduce or eliminate the possibility of a fatal outcome), or within days or weeks from the event.

If a patient has not succumbed to a traumatic event immediately, most responders will be intervening during the Golden Hour and all information that can be obtained about the patient will only serve to positively influence the patient's outcome. A secondary assessment may include gathering data about the patient's medical history; this information can come from the patient, bystanders, family or friends, or an electronic medical record. It should include items like potential allergies, previous or current medical conditions, and previous or current medications. Additionally, this inquiry can provide information about what led to the traumatic incident.

Next, the secondary assessment focuses on physical aspects of the patient. It includes taking and monitoring vital signs and examining the patient from head to toe. The head should be examined for bleeding from any orifices and any tenderness. The patient's pupils and general alertness of the eyes can provide insight to neurological issues. The neck should be examined for tenderness, but should otherwise be kept stable until admitted to the hospital, due to the inability to see the cervical spine without an x-ray.

The chest should be examined for any depressions or physical unevenness, and a stethoscope should be used to listen to the lungs and heart to note any arrhythmias or fluid buildup. Both the abdomen and the area running the length of the spinal column should be examined for distention, protrusions, and tenderness. Extremities should be examined for broken bones and ischemic tissues. Private areas should not be examined before hospital admittance unless there is visible bleeding or some other reason that warrants pre-hospital examination. It may be possible to conduct some functional exams at this time, including testing the patient's sensory awareness. All findings should be documented and reported to the admitting hospital.

Bleeding

A person **bleeds**, or **hemorrhages**, when an artery or a vein is either punctured or damaged. Bleeding must be controlled until the patient arrives at an emergency care facility. Patients who lose too much blood are at risk of death. Both adult and pediatric patients are treated for bleeding in the same manner. In cases of severe bleeding, vital signs should be assessed every five minutes and high-flow oxygen is usually indicated. It is important to document the approximate amount of blood loss and indicate the amount of time it took to lose that volume of blood.

In normal circumstances, a clot will form to close the area and bleeding will cease; however, there are times that the bleeding is so profuse that it must be addressed in the field. Bleeding can be either external or internal, and a patient may be bleeding externally and internally at the same time. The patient may be bleeding externally, through a break in the skin or through a body orifice, or may be bleeding internally, into an organ, a cavity, or in between tissues. An injury usually causes hemorrhage, but it may also occur as the result of an illness. **Hemophilia** and **von Willebrand's disease** can both cause the patient to suffer from bleeds. Severe bleeding can lead to hypovolemic shock, a condition that can be life-threatening.

Hypovolemic shock is a state of physical collapse and prostration caused by excessive blood loss, circulatory dysfunction, and inadequate tissue perfusion. If a patient loses approximately one-fifth of their total blood volume, then he or she may go into hypovolemic shock. Various conditions may cause hypovolemic shock, such as severe diarrhea, excessive perspiration, intestinal obstruction, acute pancreatitis, peritonitis, as well as severe burns, all of which can deplete body fluids. Symptoms of shock include rapid pulse; irritability; cool, clammy skin; lethargy; restlessness; and a pale appearance of the skin, or pallor.

When treating a patient who is in hypovolemic shock, the volume of blood and fluid must quickly be replaced. EMTs must determine where the bleeding originated and then control its flow. If the patient does not have a head injury, shock can be treated by raising the patient's legs 8-10 inches above the head so that the flow of blood is concentrated in the torso and toward the head. The heart, brain, and lungs are most affected by shock, and irreparable damage can occur to the patient in as little as 4-6 minutes. Excessive bleeding can be quite traumatic to the patient, so one of the goals for EMTs is to keep the patient calm so that the bleeding can be addressed quickly and efficiently. A non-rebreathing mask can be used to deliver high-flow oxygen, and suction should be performed as needed.

External Bleeding

External bleeding is bleeding that can be seen coming from an open wound on the skin or may come from an orifice, such as the ears, nose, mouth, or anus. Excessive external bleeding may present with symptoms such as cold and clammy skin, rapid and thready pulse, restlessness, thirst, drop in blood pressure, and a decrease of the level of consciousness. **Capillary bleeding** is the most common type of external bleeding. Scratches, minor cuts, and scrapes can cause capillary bleeding. **Venous bleeding** occurs when a vein is punctured or otherwise damaged and is characterized by slow leakage of dark red blood. **Arterial bleeding** is the most serious type of bleeding and this occurs when an artery is punctured or otherwise damaged. Spurts of bright red blood characterize arterial bleeding; the spurting is a result of the heart pumping blood through the arteries.

The primary way to stop external bleeding is to apply firm, steady pressure to the site from which it is occurring; this pressure can stop or slow the flow of blood. A pressure bandage is made from sterile or clean material, such as gauze. Once the pressure bandage is applied, it should not be removed, even to place additional bandaging to the wound. Instead, the new bandage should be placed over the one that is already in place. The bandages should be removed only upon arrival at the emergency care facility by the physician who is caring for the patient. If the pressure bandage is removed, bleeding may reoccur and make the situation worse.

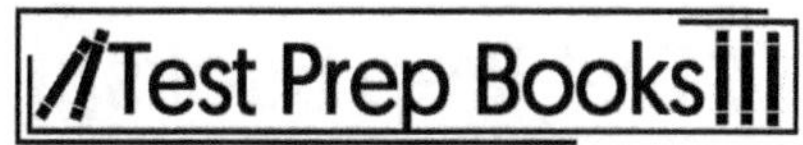

If the pressure bandage is not working, pressure can be applied to various parts of the body to slow the flow of blood. These places are called **pressure points** and are sites on the body where an artery is close to the skin. Once compressed, the blood flow is slowed to the area and is more easily controlled. Pressure points include the **temporal artery** in the middle of the scalp, the **brachial artery** in the inner side of the upper arm, the **radial artery** near the wrist, and the **femoral artery** in the leg. The bleeding may also be slowed by elevating the extremity above the heart. In correct order, bleeding should be addressed with direct pressure, then digital pressure, then the extremity should be elevated, and finally, a tourniquet can be used to control heavy, life-threatening bleeding.

A **tourniquet** is defined as a device used to stop the flow of blood through a vein or an artery, typically by compressing a limb with a cord or a tight bandage. A tourniquet is easily made by using a triangular bandage, rolling it longways into a 1-2-inch band that encircles the limb, and then tying it into a knot. Tourniquets should be applied 2-3 inches closer to the torso from the bleeding area. Tourniquets are effective in saving the patient's life if direct pressure and/or elevation does not control bleeding, especially if the patient is in a remote area and cannot get to an emergency care facility quickly. Tourniquets are wrapped tightly around the extremity and often knotted so that blood flow is controlled and lessened. If necessary, a second tourniquet can be applied closer to the torso than the first tourniquet. The time of application should be noted and the bleeding should be reassessed periodically.

Once the bleeding has slowed, direct pressure may be used to further control blood flow. The tourniquet should not be removed until the patient arrives at the emergency care facility and is under a physician's care. Tourniquets can cause permanent tissue damage, so they must not be used unless the patient is in danger of bleeding to death. Although using a tourniquet does not ensure that the limb will not be lost, it should be considered a last resort in the field.

Internal Bleeding

Internal bleeding is usually a medical emergency requiring rapid transport to the emergency care facility. A bruise is a contusion and indicates that bleeding has occurred between the layers of the skin. Internal bleeding may be caused by **blunt trauma**, which occurs when a patient collides with something at a high speed, or by **penetrating trauma**, which occurs when a foreign object penetrates the skin, such as gunshot wounds or stabbing injuries. If internal bleeding occurs in the brain, the patient may demonstrate symptoms of stroke, may enter a coma, and may die. Bruises on the neck, groin, or trunk may be symptomatic of severe internal bleeding, which may flow into the peritoneum or into the internal organs of the body, such as the liver, spleen, intestines, or kidneys.

Patients who have an internal bleed may exhibit symptoms such as nausea and vomiting; excessive thirst; cold, clammy skin; drop in blood pressure; and/or decreased consciousness. Additionally, they may experience bright red blood in the mouth, rectum, or other orifice. A coffee-ground appearance of vomitus and/or black, tarry stools called **melena** may appear. The patient may also experience dizziness or fainting (**syncope**) while sitting or standing or may experience orthostatic hypotension, which, as mentioned, is an abnormal decrease in blood pressure when a patient stands up. Patients must be monitored using the ABC's of assessment until they are transported to the emergency care facility.

General Assessment

Once the EMT arrives at the scene, an assessment must be performed so that each injury can be sufficiently addressed. First, the EMT must assess whether the patient and EMT can be safe in the area where the patient was found. Then, the ABCDE mnemonic is used to assess the condition of the patient.

The patient is assessed as follows:

- A – Airway
- B – Breathing
- C – Circulation
- D – Disability
- E – Exposure

When assessing the airway, the EMT should look for the rise and fall of the chest. If the chest does not rise and fall consistent with a good **airway** and normal breathing, then the EMT must check for breath sounds by **auscultation**, which can indicate that the patient is **breathing**. It is possible that some type of obstruction is preventing normal breathing in the patient. When assessing **circulation**, the radial and/or femoral pulse should be detected. Skin color is also important when assessing circulation; for example, a patient whose skin feels cool and/or clammy may be going into shock. **Disability** includes assessment of the pupils, their size, and their reactivity. The EMT should then disrobe the patient to look for injuries. During this **exposure** portion of the assessment, the EMT should search for bleeding or other wounds.

The ABCDE assessment is the first assessment performed upon the patient. Once the initial ABCDE assessment is completed, the EMT should conduct the secondary assessment, beginning with the head, and working downward toward the feet. When performing a secondary assessment of young children, the EMT should proceed from toe to head; older children are assessed in the same way that adults are, from head to toe.

Chest Trauma

According to the Centers for Disease Control and Prevention, trauma is the leading cause of death for individuals between the ages of 1-44. **Chest trauma** can result from an accident, or may be the result of a puncture wound. **Blunt trauma** is a serious injury that is caused by a blunt object or a collision with a blunt surface. Because the chest cavity houses several vital organs, such as the heart and lungs, injury to this area can be life-threatening. Patients may suffer chest trauma because of broken bones, such as fractures of the ribs or the sternum. The clavicle is the most common broken bone seen in pediatric and adult patients.

The seven upper ribs are called **true ribs**, while the lower five ribs are called **false ribs**, because they do not connect to the sternum. A **flail chest** exists when the patient has three or more fractured ribs in two or more places; the mortality rate for a patient with a flail chest is high because injuries may exist that are not readily seen. The **sternum**, or breast bone, is often broken when patients have open heart surgery. The sternum consists of three bones, including the manubrium, the body of the sternum, and the xiphoid process.

Chest trauma presents as a variety of different conditions. For instance, **atelectasis**, or the collapse of lung tissue, can occur because of **crepitus**, which is the grating of bone upon bone. Respiratory or diaphragmatic splinting are causes of complications from broken ribs.

Several types of chest sounds can be heard upon auscultation, including stridor, wheezing, crackles, and rhonchi. **Stridor** is usually heard upon inspiration but may occur during exhaling, and is characterized by a high-pitched breath sound, often because of an obstruction in the airway. Stridor can be heard without a stethoscope. **Wheezing** can be mild, moderate, or severe, and is a whistling sound most often heard during exhalation; this breath sound is commonly present in patients with asthma. **Crackles** are

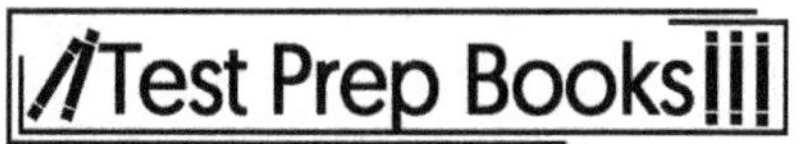

defined as short rattling or crackling sounds that may be indicative of emphysema. **Rhonchi** are low-pitched sounds heard in conditions such as pneumonia, when there are thick secretions that hinder normal breathing.

Several other conditions can interfere with the normal operation of the heart and/or lungs. **Pericardial tamponade** occurs when tears in the chambers of the heart begin to leak and the blood fills the thoracic cavity, causing the patient to die from bleeding. **Beck's triad** consists of three symptoms that indicate pericardial tamponade, including muffled heart sounds, hypotension, and elevated central venous pressure. This elevated pressure distinguishes pericardial tamponade from hemorrhagic shock. Other symptoms of pericardial tamponade include respiratory distress and tachycardia. The patient may experience pulsus paradoxus, in which the systolic blood pressure is less than 10-15 mmHg during inspiration. Pericardial tamponade is always a medical emergency. If the bleeding is not quickly stopped, the patient is likely to die.

Myocardial contusions and myocardial ruptures are additional injuries to the chest area. A **myocardial contusion** is a bruise to the muscle of the heart that often happens during a car accident. A **myocardial rupture** is usually fatal; it occurs when there is enough force to lacerate or tear the wall of the atria or ventricles. An **aortic rupture** is a condition in which the aorta tears or is ripped open. Like the myocardial rupture, aortic rupture is often fatal because the aorta is the largest artery in the body. Because so much blood is lost from wound, the patient will rarely recover.

A **pneumothorax** is defined as the presence of air or gas in the cavity between the lungs and the chest wall. This condition can cause a lung to collapse, and can be either open or closed. An **open pneumothorax** can be the result of a ruptured emphysematous vesicle on the surface of a lung, an open chest wound that allows air inside, or a severe case of coughing; some happen without any apparent reason. An open pneumothorax often produces a sucking or gurgling sound. A **closed pneumothorax** indicates that air is present in the pleural space. This type of injury may be caused by broken ribs or may occur without broken bones.

A **tension pneumothorax** occurs when air that has entered the thoracic cavity cannot get out. This condition can cause death quickly if it is not recognized soon enough to treat. The EMT can provide high-flow oxygen to avoid hypoxia. Added air will put pressure on the chest so this must be done cautiously. If possible, the EMT should make an early call ALS to perform chest decompression. Otherwise, the patient should be transported immediately to the hospital. A **hemothorax** is an accumulation of blood in the pleural space, while a **hemopneumothorax** is a combination of air and blood in the pleural space. Half of the patients who develop a hemothorax die within one hour of the injury.

Lung tissue in pediatric patients is fragile, and they have a smaller residual lung capacity. Because of this, **hypoxia**, which is a deficiency in the amount of oxygen at the tissue level, can develop quickly in the pediatric patient. The EMT should be prepared for respiratory failure if any of the following symptoms occur:

- Increased respiratory rate with signs of distress;
- Inadequate respiratory rate, especially with depressed mental status; and/or
- Cyanosis even while on oxygen.

Abdominal/Genitourinary Trauma

The abdominal cavity houses several vital organs, such as the liver, spleen, stomach, diaphragm, intestines, pancreas, kidneys, and appendix. Trauma to any of these organs can lead to death. Additionally, injury to one or more of these organs may not be recognized during the ABCDE assessment. Abdominal organs may be injured by compression or by shearing forces; **shearing forces** are unaligned forces pushing one part of the body in one direction and another part of the body in the opposite direction. Injuries to solid organs, such as the liver or spleen, can result in quick blood loss and the patient can bleed to death. Injuries to hollow organs, such as the stomach, intestines, or kidneys, may go unnoticed for a time and may produce infection, abscess, or sepsis.

Because the liver is a large organ and takes up a large amount of space in the abdomen, trauma to this area can pierce the liver and this can result in the patient's death. The **liver** filters blood from the digestive system and metabolizes drugs in the body. The **spleen** stores and filters blood, and helps to guard the body against infection. In children, as in adults, the liver and spleen are larger organs, but the child's liver and spleen are injured more often than those of the adult patient. The **retroperitoneal space** houses the **kidneys**, which function as filters that remove waste from the bloodstream. Patients who have a kidney or bladder infection may feel pain in the right and/or left hypochondriac regions of the body. The **bladder** and **urethra** are pelvic organs that can be damaged in car accidents, but may also be injured during a fall. A rupture of the bladder is more likely when the bladder is full at the time of the injury.

Signs and symptoms of abdominal trauma include pain and swelling in the abdominal area, back pain, chest pain, and painful urination. The patient may also experience signs of shock, or may exhibit signs of seatbelt restraint, such as bruising. When arriving on scene, the EMT should make note of any disarray in the vehicle or any obvious trauma at the scene. The patient may show signs of **peritonitis**, an inflammation of the peritoneum, which can be painful. **Grey Turner's sign**, which is characterized by bruising of the skin of the flanks or loin in acute hemorrhagic pancreatitis, is a strong sign of abdominal trauma. **Cullen's sign**, which is indicated by irregular hemorrhagic spots on the skin around the umbilicus, is also a sign of abdominal trauma.

Evisceration is defined as the extrusion of the viscera outside of the body, which can happen during an accident, injury, or after surgery. The viscera are the soft internal organs of the body, such as the intestines. If an evisceration happens prior to transporting a patient to a hospital, the wound should be covered with a sterile gauze that it slightly moist. As in other bleeding injuries, the gauze should not be removed once soaked through; instead, the EMT should add additional sterile gauze on top of the first application and continue to apply pressure to slow or stop the bleeding.

Orthopedic Trauma

The human body contains 206 bones, and is made of other types of tissue, including nerves, vessels, ligaments, joints, muscles, and tendons. The human body comprises two types of skeletons—the axial skeleton and the appendicular skeleton. The **axial skeleton** includes the skull, hyoid bone, thoracic cage, and vertebral column. The **appendicular skeleton** is made up of the upper and lower extremities and the girdles, which attach the extremities to the rest of the body. The skeleton and muscles work together to move the body and maintain an upright posture. Several types of muscle are found throughout the body, including cardiac, smooth, and skeletal. Skeletal muscle is the most common type of muscle found in the body.

Fractures are breaks in the continuity of a bone or cartilage and can be open or closed, as well as complete or incomplete. An **open fracture** exists when a protruding bone or other object causes a soft tissue injury. **Closed fractures** are breaks that have not penetrated the skin. A **greenstick fracture** is one that is broken on one side of the bone and intact on the other side. A **transverse fracture** occurs at right angles to the long axis of the bone. A fracture is said to be **comminuted** when it is splintered into pieces, while a **spiral fracture** is twisted, affecting the length of the bone as opposed to the width. **Oblique fractures** are neither parallel nor at a right angle to a specific or implied line. At the ends of the long bones sit the **epiphyseal plates**; fractures involving the epiphyseal plates are common childhood breaks. As children get older, hormones thicken the cartilage in long bones and they become harder and less susceptible to breaks.

Bones that are broken are often secured by a splint until the patient is under the care of a physician at a hospital or trauma center. **Splints** are used to immobilize an injury and can also decrease pain, bleeding, and contamination at the site of the injury. Soft or formable splints can be made into a variety of shapes to secure the injured body part. Rigid splints cannot be changed; for example, a board or plastic splint is not easily manipulated and can usually be classified as a rigid splint. **Traction splints** are designed to stabilize fractures in the middle of the femur. The traction splint is a temporary fix that will stabilize the fracture and will help to align the break until the patient arrives at an emergency care center and is under the care of a physician.

Most of the support of the chest wall in children comes from muscles, and because of this, infants and children have higher oxygen consumption rates and tire more quickly than older children and adults. The chest wall also offers less protection than in older children and adults. The EMT must pay close attention to the possibility of traumatic injury, and should provide full immobilization of the injury, especially when the patient is a young child. Additionally, when performing a secondary assessment on children, the assessment should proceed from head to toe in older children and from toe to head in younger children.

Sprains involve a twist of a ligament that causes pain and swelling, but not dislocation. Sprains are diagnosed by severity, beginning with a first-degree sprain, which results in minimal swelling; second- and third-degree sprains are progressively more serious. The ligaments in third-degree sprains are completely torn. A **strain** is the resulting injury that affects a muscle or tendon after overexertion or overextension. Because bones are softer in pediatric patients, possible sprains and strains should be treated as if they were actual fractures.

Shoulder injuries often happen in older adults, especially geriatric patients, whose bones are more brittle. Some injuries, such as **rotator cuff tendon injuries**, can be acute or chronic, and often happen because of a fall onto an outstretched arm. Although this is a common reflex, it is not wise to stretch the arm outward to lessen the effects of a fall, and this can make the injury worse.

Elbow and forearm injuries are common among children and athletes, and both injuries can be managed by using a splint and elevating and applying ice over the injured area for twenty minutes on, and then twenty minutes off.

Hand and finger injuries may be the result of sports, exercise, work-related injuries, and/or violence; these areas of the body should also be splinted, iced, and elevated, whenever possible. Injuries are usually more severe in the lower extremities because there is often a greater force used in the creation of the injury. These injuries are often accompanied by significant blood loss and are more difficult to manage because they can inhibit walking or moving about.

Joints can be dislocated; dislocations happen to the shoulders, elbows, hips, knees, fingers, and ankles, most often. Hip injuries are common among geriatric patients, and many die within one year of suffering the injury, often due to pneumonia, thromboembolism, and/or infection.

Patients with **musculoskeletal injuries** can be placed into one of four following classes:

- Life- or limb-threatening injuries or conditions, including life- or limb-threatening musculoskeletal trauma
- Other life- or limb-threatening vascular injuries and only simple musculoskeletal trauma
- No other life- or limb-threatening injuries but with life- or limb-threatening musculoskeletal trauma
- Isolated injuries that are neither life- nor limb-threatening

Patients who have **femoral injuries** are in danger of losing so much blood that even lightning-fast efforts cannot fix. Fractures in the femoral area can cause the broken bones to rub together, and contractions in the leg increase the patient's pain level. Swelling in the area is probable, so the leg needs to be immobilized and the patient should be watched for signs of shock. If dictated by local protocols, a **pneumatic antishock garment (PASG)** should be used to immobilize the injury. It should be noted that a femoral injury in children younger than four years old is often an indicator of child abuse, and should be reported to the appropriate authorities.

Knee, patellar, tibial, and fibular injuries should be immobilized with a rigid or formable splint, iced, and elevated, if possible. Finger and toe (**phalangeal**) injuries can be aided by "buddy splinting," which is done by taping the injured finger or toe to an adjacent one. These injuries should also be iced and elevated.

Fractures heal in several stages, depending upon the size and the severity of the injury. First, a hematoma forms at the site of the fracture, and then scar tissue forms. A **hematoma** is a collection of extravasated blood that has escaped from the vessel into the tissue and then is trapped in the tissues of the skin or in an organ, resulting from trauma or incomplete hemostasis after surgery. **Osteoblasts**, or immature bone cells and cartilage cells, form on the fracture site. Last, immature bone cells grow and mature. Most small fractures heal in a matter of weeks, while larger fractures, especially those in the legs, can take months to heal. Even small fractures in the hands may cause pain for years after the site has healed.

Soft Tissue Trauma

Soft tissue trauma (or **surface trauma**) may be obvious to the eye or may exist underneath the skin, sometimes without any bruising or contusions that would alert an EMT to the injury. A **contusion**, or bruise, does not disrupt the continuity of the skin; instead, the patient or EMT may notice bruising or other discoloration, swelling, and pain. The largest organ in the body is the **skin**—a layered covering that consists of the **outer epidermis**, **inner dermis**, and a deep layer of fibrous tissue called the **hypodermis**, which exists beneath the dermis. The skin includes openings of sweat and sebaceous glands and serves as the body's primary defensive structure. The epidermis is made up of thin epithelial tissue and has five layers. These layers include the outermost stratum corneum, the stratum lucidum, the stratum granulosum, the stratum spinosum, and the innermost layer—the stratum basale. The outermost layer comprises many layers of dead skin cells, which contain keratin. **Keratin** is a sulfur-containing fibrous

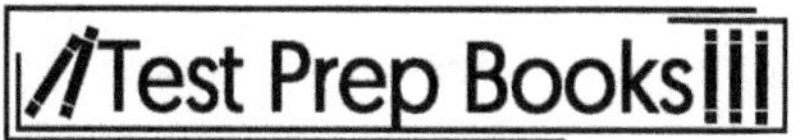

protein that forms the chemical basis of epidermal tissues, such as hair and nails. **Melanin** is the pigment in the skin that gives it color.

The **dermis** is the vascular, thick layer of skin that lies beneath the epidermis and contains elastic fibers, lymph vessels, blood vessels, connective tissue, as well as motor and sensory nerve endings. The dermis also contains an extracellular matrix composed of proteoglycans and glycoproteins along with collagen and elastin fibers. **Collagen** is a protein and is the major component of connective tissue that gives the skin strength and flexibility. Skin helps to protect the body from bacterial infections and to maintain fluid balance. The blood vessels in the dermis help to regulate body temperature, while its nerve tissue promotes responses to stimuli such as heat, cold, pain, and touch. The dermis also helps to cushion the body from stressors and strains. The hypodermis lies beneath the dermis and serves several functions; for instance, it provides further cushioning and insulation for the body. It also supports and protects organs and other structures underneath.

When an injury happens to the body, bleeding may occur; **hemostasis** is the stoppage of blood flow or the stoppage of bleeding, often by use of a hemostatic agent or drug. Four separate functions occur during hemostasis. First, during **vasoconstriction**, vasomotor action narrows blood vessels' lumens, which slows the flow of blood. Platelets then form at the site of the injury; **platelets** are minute, colorless, anucleate biconcave disks of cytoplasm that are released from bone, then adhere to other platelets and damaged epithelium. The platelets are then called **thrombocytes**. The third process is that of **coagulation**, which is the change from blood in liquid form to a thickened solid. This is commonly known as **blood clotting**. Finally, the platelets stick to the injured vessels, and collagen and other secretions create a seal over the injured vessels called a **platelet plug**. Coagulation is a quick process. When a blood vessel is damaged, prothrombin activator works to change prothrombin to **thrombin**, which is an enzyme that forms fibrin threads, and those threads form the clot.

The Inflammation Process

Soft tissue or surface trauma can interfere with the normal physiological functions of the body by way of inflammatory and/or vascular responses, which are an important part of the body's ability to heal. An **inflammatory response** is a tissue reaction to injury or an antigen that may include pain, swelling, itching, redness, heat, and/or loss of function. The response may involve dilation of blood vessels and leakage of fluid, which causes swelling, and the release of plasma proteases and vasoactive amines, such as histamine. **Histamine** is a chemical that may promote a vascular response. A **vascular response** usually happens after cellular injury and there is a dilation of the surrounding arterioles, venules, and capillaries. **Hyperemia**, which is an engorgement of blood in an organ or in surrounding areas, is the increase in pressure and capillary permeability that causes fluid to leak from the vessels into the interstitial space. Thus, the fluid produced by this leakage is called **interstitial fluid** and it often creates redness and swelling, and the skin may feel warm to the touch.

The inflammation process is a local response to cellular injury that is marked by capillary dilatation, leukocytic infiltration, redness, heat, pain swelling, and often loss of function. The body attempts to remain in a state of **homeostasis**, which means that it tries to maintain a relatively constant condition in the internal environment while continuously interacting with, and adjusting to, changes originating within or outside of the body system. Although it may be logical to think when applying this theory that the goal of the body is to stay the same, the reality is that the body is not in a static or fixed state; it is a state of continuous motion, adaptation, and/or change in response to the stimuli in the environment. **Equilibrium** is a state of chemical balance in the body, reached when the tissues contain the proper proportions of various salts and water.

During this process, **leukocytes**, which are white blood cells, rush to the infected or inflamed area of the body to fight off infection. The metabolic processes of tissues during healing, as well as the movement of lymphocytes, macrophages, and granulocytes, cause the skin to take on a red appearance and feel warm to the touch.

The Wound Healing Process and Scar Formation

A **wound** is defined as any physical injury involving a break in the skin, usually caused by an act or accident (rather than by a disease), such as a chest wound, gunshot wound, or puncture wound. At the point of healing, **scar tissue**, which is also known as **cicatrix**, forms as an avascular, pale, contracted tissue, and feels firm. The area around the scar is notably red and soft. Not all wounds heal at the same rate, and some are impeded by the patient's medical condition, drug use, and various other anatomical factors.

However, some wounds heal within a few days and do not leave any sort of scar. As mentioned, various medical conditions and diseases can affect the timing of healing, such as advanced age, diabetes, malnutrition, liver failure, severe alcoholism, cardiovascular disease, and peripheral vascular disease. While the EMT is in the field with the patient, a wound history should be made and kept within the patient's medical record. The EMT should record the approximate time of the injury, where it occurred, the mechanism of the injury and likelihood of any associated injuries, approximate blood loss, and level of pain felt by the patient, as well as information about the patient's most recent tetanus immunization.

Some people develop keloids or hypertrophic scarring, both of which are abnormal scar formations. **Keloids** (sometimes spelled **cheloids**) occur when there is an excessive growth of collagenous scar tissue that extends beyond the borders of the original wounds. **Hypertrophic scars** are formed from an excessive formation of new tissue in the healing of a wound.

Several types of wounds need closure, including wounds over joints or other tension areas, gaping wounds, and skin tears. A soft tissue wound can be considered open or closed. **Open wounds** include bites, abrasions, lacerations, punctures, and avulsions. Crush injuries, contusions, hematomas, and amputations are all types of **closed wounds**.

Open Wounds

Patients may receive bites from humans, animals, or insects, and various diseases can be spread through a bite wound. Bites are usually superficial, but they can involve structures deep within the body, including muscles and bones. The patient may experience complications from bite wounds such as abscesses, cellulitis, hepatitis B, and tetanus. All bites should be evaluated and treated by a physician.

An **abrasion** is defined as the scraping or rubbing away of the surface of the skin by friction. Abrasions may be the result of trauma or of some type of treatment, such as debridement following a burn. Abrasions should be kept clean and dry to help prevent infection.

Lacerations are wounds produced by tearing body tissue and often result in a great deal of bleeding. They can occur at the surface of the skin, but can also happen within the body when an organ is compressed or moved out of place by an external or internal force, such as a blow that does not break the skin. Surgery is usually necessary to repair an injury severe enough to wound internal organs.

Puncture wounds are usually made by sharp, pointed objects. Such wounds can be quite deep and can interrupt the normal continuity and function of involved organs. The patient may arrive at the emergency care center with the object that caused the wound still lodged in place; the attending

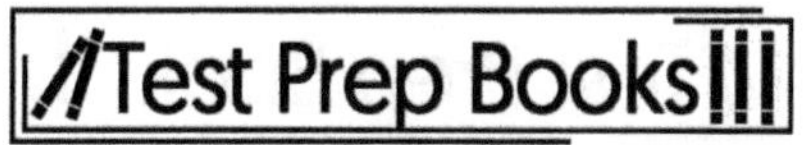

physician should determine the best way to remove the object and repair the wound. Items that cause puncture wounds should never be removed in the field by the EMT. Patients are usually given antibiotics after the injury is repaired to help avoid subsequent infection. If infection remains after treatment, it is possible that there is a retained foreign object in the patient's body.

An **avulsion** is defined as the forcible tearing away of a body part by trauma. This type of injury often happens when the patient is working with industrial equipment. Avulsed fingers, toes, limbs, or other separated tissues should be saved and taken to the emergency department or trauma center with the patient. If possible, the body part should be placed in a plastic bag with ice so that it can remain as clean and preserved as possible. A **degloving injury** is a type of avulsion that happens when soft tissues down to the bone—including the neurovascular bundles and sometimes tendons—are peeled off of the body part. Degloving injuries happen most often to appendages but can also happen when the hair is caught or entangled in machinery, which causes a scalp avulsion.

Closed Wounds

A **crush injury** is defined as a break in the external surface of the body due to a severe force applied against the tissues. Crushing injuries can be severe and life-threatening, and may present with symptoms such as the destruction of both muscle and bone tissue, hemorrhage, and fluid loss, which can lead to hypovolemic shock, hematuria, renal failure, and/or coma. The patient with a crush injury may have ruptured an organ, suffered a major fracture, and might experience hemorrhagic shock, even if the skin over the injury remains intact. A patient can die quite quickly if the crush injury is serious enough. Crush injuries are often seen in car accidents, industrial accidents, and in injuries that happen during war.

Crush syndrome, although rare, is a life-threatening, severe condition caused by extensive crushing trauma. It is characterized by destruction of muscle and bone tissue, hemorrhage, and fluid loss, resulting in hypovolemic shock, hematuria, renal failure, and coma. The patient experiencing crush syndrome needs intensive care with close monitoring of all vital functions, as well as administration of fluids, electrolytes, antibiotics, analgesia, and oxygen.

Although the patient with a crush injury may appear to be stable for a while, complications will occur once the patient is removed from the trapping environment that caused the injury. First, blood rich in oxygen returns to the body part that has been crushed. This is called **reperfusion**, defined as the restoration of blood flow to an area that was temporarily ischemic. This process can lead to shock, because it reduces the circulation of blood throughout the body. Second, the oxygen-rich blood moves back through the body and waste products and toxic substances are circulated throughout the body systems, which causes **metabolic acidosis**; this is a condition in which excess acid is added to the body fluids or bicarbonate is lost from them.

This process results in:

- **Hyperkalemia**: a greater than normal amount of potassium in the blood;
- **Hypocalcemia**: a deficiency of calcium in the blood serum;
- **Hyperphosphatemia**: a low phosphorus level in the blood; and/or
- **Hyperuricemia**: abnormally elevated levels of uric acid in the blood.

The third complication that can occur when a patient has a crushing injury is the release of myoglobin from damaged muscle cells in the injury area, which is filtered through the kidneys. This process can cause acute renal failure.

Compartment syndrome is a surgical emergency and can be a complication of a crush injury; symptoms may begin within a few hours of the injury or may appear up to forty-eight hours afterward. The most common causes of compartment syndrome, in addition to crushing injury, include tibial fractures, forearm fractures, hemorrhage, constrictive casts, prolonged limb compression, and burns. This condition results from elevated pressures within a confined muscle compartment, most commonly in the leg and forearm.

The Five P's of compartment syndrome include pain, paresthesia, pallor, paralysis, and pulselessness; however, the patient may not have all five of these symptoms, yet he or she can still have compartment syndrome. The patient will likely complain of severe pain and may also experience nerve dysfunction. The compartment is often firm, swollen, and tender when palpitated. Normal compartment pressure is less than 10 mmHg. The **delta pressure**, which is the diastolic blood pressure minus the tissue pressure, is the best predictor of irreversible muscle damage. Compartment syndrome is diagnosed when the delta pressure is ≤ 30 mmHg. The patient will likely undergo a surgical fasciotomy to correct this condition; until surgery, the affected limb should be placed at the level of the heart, supplemental oxygen should be administered, and constrictive casts or dressings should be removed.

Contusions are defined as injuries to tissues with skin discoloration without the breakage of skin; contusions are often called bruises. In these injuries, blood from broken vessels leaks into the surrounding tissues. The patient usually experiences swelling, pain, tenderness, and discoloration. These symptoms may be reduced by applying ice immediately after the injury.

As mentioned, a **hematoma** is a collection of extravasated blood trapped in the tissues of the skin or an organ resulting from trauma. At first, there is bleeding into the space containing the hematoma, but if space is limited, the pressure of the blood flow slows and eventually stops. The hematoma can often be felt and may be quite painful. If necessary, hematomas can be drained once the patient reaches the emergency care center, but precautions must be taken for infection.

An **amputation** happens when a patient experiences complete or partial loss of a limb. This may happen during an accident or may be medically necessary due to the progression of a disease in a limb. Bleeding must be controlled after an amputation because it can be extensive, and vital signs must be monitored continuously. The wound should be bandaged with additional dressings placed on top of previous bandages once they are soaked. A tourniquet may be used to help the bleeding to slow or stop.

Head, Neck, Face, and Spinal Trauma

Head

Head injuries to the scalp, skull, and/or brain can be dangerous and can cause mental impairment and permanent disability. Head injuries may be caused by vehicle accidents, participation in sports, home accidents, industrial accidents, intentional violent acts, and falls. When an object hits or penetrates the head, the patient is said to have a **direct injury**. When acceleration and/or deceleration forces result in the movement of the brain within the skull, the patient is said to have an **indirect injury**. Head injuries can also be open, such as bleeding wounds, or closed, with no visible signs of injury present. The EMT should follow criteria for spinal immobilization. All patients with head trauma should be quickly assessed and the EMT may assume that the patient has a spinal injury until examination and diagnostic procedures at the emergency care center have ruled out such injury.

Patients may have soft tissue injuries, concussions, skull fractures, and traumatic brain injury, as well as other types of head trauma, all of which must be carefully monitored by the EMT until the patient is

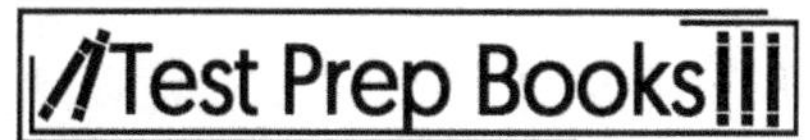

placed under the care of an attending physician. Head injuries are usually traumatic to the patient because the brain is such a vital organ; it is possible that some injuries to the brain may not be properly diagnosed for months or years because the symptoms can be quite subtle in nature. The EMT should be reassuring to the patient and keep them as calm as possible.

The internal and external carotid arteries and their branches provide the blood supply to the face; because of this vascularity, head injuries may bleed profusely, adding to the patient's anxiety. It is important that a clear airway is maintained in the event of a head injury, which may mean that suction should be used to ensure that the patient can breathe. Obstructions—such as broken teeth, dentures, and foreign objects—must be carefully removed so that the airway remains clear.

There are many signs and symptoms of head injury, including:

- Inability to wake the patient
- Short-term memory loss
- Loss of consciousness
- Dizziness
- Confusion
- Very high blood pressure
- Persistent headache
- Dilation of pupils
- Slurred speech
- Loss of coordination
- Convulsions
- Seizures
- Agitation or restlessness
- Inability to concentrate
- Ringing in the ears

Not all head injuries result in symptoms, and closed head injuries can be much more serious than those that are open. The EMT must determine and document the mechanism of injury as well as the events that led up to the injury, in addition to all symptoms. Patients with a head injury may vomit, and if this happens, the airway must be cleared immediately. The EMT must continually assess the patient for the need for spinal immobilization, and monitor the patient's vital signs and level of responsiveness every fifteen minutes when the patient is stable, and every five minutes if unstable.

Concussions

A **concussion** is defined as a head injury that results from violent jarring or shaking; it alters the way that the brain functions, although its effects may be temporary. Concussions are classified in three different grades, each with specific symptoms. **Grade 1 concussions** result in no loss of consciousness, temporary confusion, and the symptoms clear within fifteen minutes of the injury. **Grade 2 concussions** also result in no loss of consciousness and temporary confusion is present, but the symptoms last longer than fifteen minutes. **Grade 3 concussions** result in loss of consciousness for any length of time. Permanent brain injury may occur in the patient with a grade 2 or grade 3 concussion. Concussions are a type of **diffuse injury**, and are the most common types of brain injury; these are injuries in which the **neural processes (axons)** prevent the nerves from communicating with each other. Situations in which the patient gets worse after a concussion are cause to further evaluate the patient for more serious head injuries, such as those caused by contusion or hemorrhage.

Two types of amnesia may accompany concussions. Retrograde amnesia is a loss of memory of events or information that happened before the injury. Anterograde amnesia is a loss of ability to create new memories after the injury.

There are many signs and symptoms of concussion, including:

- Combativeness
- Temporary visual problems
- Issues with equilibrium
- Changes in vital signs
- Coordination problems
- Dizziness
- Fatigue
- Slurred speech
- Nausea and/or vomiting
- Headache
- Ringing in the ears
- Delayed response to questions

It may be difficult to diagnose concussions in infant or toddler patients because they are unable to communicate their symptoms. In addition to the symptoms experienced by adults with concussions, infants and toddlers may cry excessively, and seem dazed, irritable, or listless. Anyone who suffers a head injury should see a physician.

Moderate and Severe Diffuse Axonal Injuries

A patient with a **moderate diffuse axonal injury** will initially be unconscious and will experience confusion and amnesia of the injury event. Patients may also have difficulty concentrating, and be anxious and/or moody. They should be reassessed frequently for levels of consciousness. **Severe diffuse axonal injury** is the most severe form of brain injury, involving severe mechanical shearing of many axons in both cerebral hemispheres extending to the brain stem.

Skull Fractures

Several types of skull fractures are possible with a head injury, including those that are linear, depressed, basilar, and open vault. The EMT must continually consider the possibility of spinal injury while assessing the patient, so care must be taken when moving the patient during examination and treatment in the field. Several complications may occur with skull fractures, such as infection, cranial nerve injury, and underlying brain injuries.

Linear fractures are defined as those that resemble a line and do not displace the bone tissue. About 80 percent of skull fractures are linear. Most linear fractures do not involve a laceration, but infection is possible if a laceration is present. **Depressed fractures** are those in which fragments of bone are depressed below the normal surface of the skull.

Basilar fractures occur when the mandible condyles perforate the base of the skull; more commonly, this occurs when a linear fracture extends into the floor of the anterior and middle fossae. If a patient is bleeding from the ears or nose, gauze can be used for a halo test. If a lighter colored halo of fluid appears around the blood on the gauze, cerebrospinal fluid is present, which indicates that there is a skull fracture.

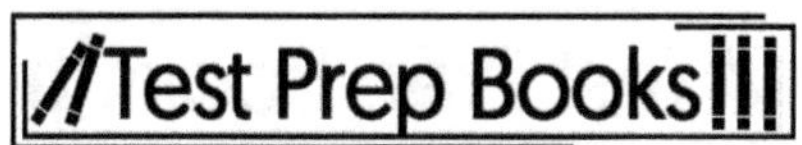

Several symptoms of basilar fractures exist, including:

- **Battle's sign**, which is ecchymosis over the mastoid process resulting from a temporal bone fracture
- **Ecchymosis** of one or both orbits, commonly called raccoon's eyes, resulting from fracture of the base of the sphenoid sinus
- **Cerebrospinal fluid leakage**, which can cause meningitis
- **Hemotympanum**, which is blood behind the tympanic membrane caused by fractures of the temporal bone

Battle's sign and raccoon's eyes are rarely seen in the emergency care center unless the bruising comes from an earlier injury. **Open vault fractures** are often the result of a small object striking the head at a high speed and are common with scalp lacerations.

Traumatic Brain Injuries

A **traumatic brain injury (TBI)** occurs when sudden trauma damages the brain. There are two categories of TBI: primary brain injuries and secondary brain injuries. Direct trauma to the brain causes a **primary brain injury**, while intracellular and extracellular derangements cause a **secondary brain injury**. Derangements, such as hypoxia and hypercapnia, are defined as an organ or part not functioning properly due to dislodged or injured parts. The severity of injury can be measured using the Glasgow Coma Scale (GCS) and is classified as mild, moderate, or severe; it can be further classified focal or diffuse. Contact usually causes **focal injuries**, such as skull fractures and brain hemorrhage, and such issues are often detectable to the naked eye. **Diffuse injuries** are those that are usually caused by acceleration/deceleration forces, but can also be from meningitis and hypoxia. They involve larger or more widespread brain regions, often with microscopic levels of damage, making them often more difficult to detect or define. Falls are the leading cause of traumatic brain injuries in both adults and children. Vehicle accidents and sports injuries are also common causes of traumatic brain injury.

The EMT should watch for signs and symptoms of a traumatic brain injury, and determine the mechanism and time of injury. The EMT should note any periods of unconsciousness that the patient experiences and how long they last, mental status, seizure activity, verbalization problems, and the patient's ability to move the extremities. The EMT should remember that patients may be confused and may not remember the events leading up to and during the injury. Information may need to be collected from family and/or friends who are present to determine the patient's medical history, drugs that the patient takes on a regular or an as-needed basis, and drugs and/or alcohol that the patient may have taken leading up to the injury.

Traumatic brain injury may occur in infants, whose responsiveness may be reduced. The infant may experience asymmetry in the pupils and/or face, as well as abnormalities in the motor function of the extremities.

Other signs and symptoms of traumatic brain injury in infants include:

- Lethargy
- Vomiting
- Seizures
- Bradycardia
- Decreased sucking reflex
- Apnea

Older children who experience traumatic brain injury may experience:

- Nausea
- Vomiting
- Headache
- Visual changes
- Hypertension
- Motor weakness
- Bradycardia
- Respiratory distress

An **Acquired brain injury (ABI)** occurs at the cellular level and is most often associated with pressure on the brain. It can be the result of a growth or tumor, or the result of neurological illness, such as a stroke. Like traumatic brain injuries, acquired brain injuries disrupt the brain's normal functioning. An ABI happens after birth and is not related to a congenital or a degenerative disease.

Focal Injuries

Focal injuries are defined as specific, grossly observable brain lesions. These injuries can result from contusions, edema, ischemia, and hemorrhage. Focal injuries occur in one region of the brain.

When the brain is bruised, producing a structural change in brain tissue, the patient usually has a **cerebral contusion**, which can result in more serious deficits and abnormalities than concussions. Local damage that occurs at the site of impact is called **coup**, and an injury that occurs at a site opposite the side of impact is called **contrecoup**. The patient may lose consciousness if the brain stem is contused. Patients who are comatose after such injury may experience prolonged comatose states. Usually, cerebral contusions heal on their own, although the length of time to heal may vary and the level of improvement may differ from patient to patient. Most patients who die from head injuries are shown to have cerebral contusions during the autopsy.

Cerebral edema is the swelling of brain tissue and can lead to increases in **intracranial pressure (ICP).** ICP can prevent blood from flowing into the brain, depriving it of the oxygen it needs to function. Swelling is a serious matter because the excess fluid has nowhere to go in the limited spaces inside the brain. This condition may be treated with medications, removal of small amounts of fluid from the brain, and/or surgery.

Ischemia is defined as an inadequate blood supply to an organ or a part of the body and can be chronic or acute. When the brain is not getting enough oxygen, the resulting condition is called **brain hypoxia**. While this is always a serious condition, depending upon the length of time that the patient has been without oxygen, it may be treated by just placing the patient on oxygen therapy. Ischemia can be caused

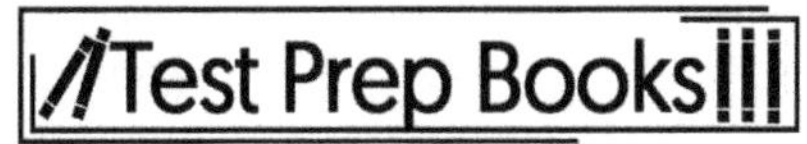

by choking, drowning, cardiac arrest, carbon monoxide poisoning, and stroke, among other conditions. The brain can survive for approximately six minutes after the heart stops beating.

Brain hemorrhage, also called **intracranial** or **intracerebral hemorrhage**, is bleeding in or around the brain. There are several causes of brain hemorrhage. Hypertension is the most common cause of this condition; therefore, it is important that hypertensive patients take their blood pressure medication exactly as prescribed. Over time, the walls of vessels can weaken, which can lead to rupture and bleeding. **Aneurysms**, which are defined as sacs or weak spots in the walls of arteries, veins, or the heart, may also cause brain hemorrhage. **Arteriovenous malformation (AVM)**, which is a tangle of abnormal blood vessels connecting arteries and veins, may cause bleeding in the brain, although it is a rare disorder and is usually congenital. Smoking and drug abuse, especially that of cocaine, can also lead to bleeding in the brain. The symptoms of brain hemorrhage depend upon what part of the brain is involved; they may come on abruptly and worsen quickly or may progress slowly over hours or days. Types of brain hemorrhages are usually classified based upon their location; these types include cerebral, epidural, subdural, and subarachnoid hematomas.

Cerebral hematoma, most commonly found in the frontal or temporal lobes of the brain, can be caused by deceleration, increased intracranial pressure, and/or skull fractures. Symptoms can include headache; weakness, tingling, or paralysis on one side of the body; balance and/or coordination problems; lethargy; and confusion. Cerebral hematoma symptoms can appear suddenly and the patient can deteriorate quickly.

An **epidural hematoma** takes place between the cranium and the dura mater, and although it is a serious condition, injury to the brain may not be severe. Patients who experience an epidural hematoma often have a temporary loss of consciousness followed by a lucid period. While half of the patients with this type of hematoma do not recover consciousness, the other half do recover and their neurological status returns to normal; however, recovery will differ from patient to patient.

Patients who are at risk for a **subdural hematoma** include those who have clotting deficiencies, hemophiliacs, and older adults. This hematoma is usually associated with the veins that bridge the subdural space, and it normally occurs between the dura mater and the surface of the brain in the subdural space. The lapse of time between injury and onset of symptoms determines the classification of subdural hematomas. An acute subdural hematoma is one in which the symptoms appear within twenty-four hours. A subacute subdural hematoma is symptomatic between two and ten days, and one that is symptomatic after two weeks is considered chronic.

A **subarachnoid hematoma** refers to bleeding into the cerebrospinal fluid. The most common symptom of a subarachnoid hematoma is a sudden, severe headache that begins in one area and then spreads, becoming dull and throbbing. Causes include trauma, rupture of an aneurysm, or arteriovenous abnormality. The patient may have a brief period of unconsciousness, and severe subarachnoid hematoma may result in continued unconsciousness, coma, and death. Permanent brain damage is common with this type of hematoma.

Neck

The **neck** is the main structure of support of the skull; injuries to this area of the body may involve soft tissue, bone structures, or both. Three zones separate the sections of the neck and are divided horizontally in the human body. Several structures, such as the trachea, esophagus, jugular vein, and carotid artery, are found in more than one zone. Zone I includes the base of the neck, from the sternal notch to the top of the clavicles or the cricoid cartilage. The highest rate of mortality is seen in Zone I, because of the major thoracic and vascular structures that are located there, such as the jugular vein, esophagus, trachea, and cervical spine. Zone II extends from the clavicles or the cricoid cartilage to the angle of the mandible; this section of the neck contains many of the same structures as Zone I, such as the carotid artery, jugular vein, esophagus, trachea, and cervical spine. Zone III is the section of the neck above the angle of the mandible, and contains the carotid artery, salivary glands, and pharynx.

The neck and its structures may be injured from:

- Violence
- Sports
- Horseback riding accidents
- Diving or other water-related activities
- Stabbings
- Hangings
- Strangulation
- Industrial accidents
- Vehicle accidents
- Blows to the neck

The EMT should remember that injuries to the neck area may result in restriction of the patient's airway, so continual assessment of neck injuries is indicated. The most commonly injured parts of the neck are blood vessels; if they are severed and bleeding is not controlled, the patient may die from excessive blood loss, which is called **exsanguination**. Intubation can help stabilize damaged areas of the neck, provide ventilatory support, and protect the airway. However, airway procedures that involve entry through the neck should be avoided; in most cases, a bag-mask device will provide adequate ventilation for the patient. The EMT should assume that a cervical spine injury is present when the patient has a neck injury.

Face

Facial injuries may be to the soft tissues or may be a result of fractures. Vascularity in the face can cause injuries to look quite serious. Life-threatening injuries in this area are possible, although rare. The facial bones can remain intact under tremendous stress; however, facial fractures may allow absorption of the force from blunt trauma.

Symptoms of facial fractures include:

- Crepitus
- Ecchymosis
- Pain or numbness
- Swelling
- Asymmetry of cheek bone or nasal septum
- Limited movement of the eyes or jaw
- Dental malocclusion

Nasal fractures are the most common facial fractures, followed by mandible fractures.

Le Fort fractures were first described in 1901 as three different patterns that occur in midface fractures. **Le Fort I fractures**, which are horizontal, are found in the region from the maxilla to the nasal fossa. **Le Fort II fractures** are usually triangular, and involve the nasal bones and medial orbits. **Le Fort III**

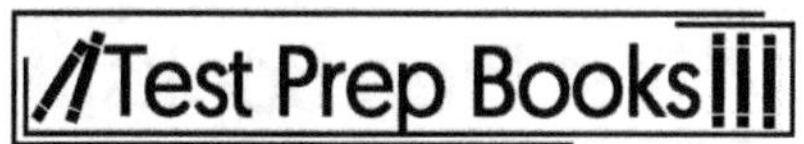

fractures are more complex than the other two fracture types, and involve separation of the facial bones from the cranial bones. Symptoms of midfacial fractures include an unstable maxilla, nasal flattening, lengthened appearance of the face, and leakage of cerebrospinal fluid from the nose. Patients with Le Fort fractures are hospitalized because of the risk of serious airway issues and the difficulty of correct placement of nasogastric or nasotracheal tubes.

The cranium and maxilla are both supported by the **zygoma**, more commonly known as the **cheek bone**. This bone also articulates with the frontal and temporal bones, as well as the maxilla. Symptoms of **zygomatic fracture** include a flattened cheek area and numbness of the cheek and nasal area. This type of fracture is often seen in combination with orbital fractures.

Eyes

A fracture of the floor and medial walls of the ocular orbit is called a **blowout fracture**, and is usually caused by a blunt object, such as a fist, ball, or rock. It occurs when an object of greater diameter than the orbital rim strikes the globe of the eye and the soft tissue around it. This places pressure on the orbital floor, and if fracture results, the orbital contents may be pushed into the maxillary sinus. Symptoms of **blowout fractures** include swelling, **double vision (diplopia)**, restricted movement of the eye, impaired extraocular movements, and **epistaxis** (nosebleed). Orbital fractures are commonly associated with other facial injuries.

Numerous parts of the eye can be damaged from trauma, including the conjunctiva, iris, cornea, pupillary sphincter, lens, retina, optic nerve, and other intraocular or intraorbital structures.

Injuries to the eyes should be evaluated by a physician in the emergency department or trauma center. Patients may complain of foreign bodies in the eyes, and when this is suspected, the EMT should inspect the inner surface of the upper and lower eyes. If an object is present, it should be removed, using gentle irrigation with sterile water or normal saline. Other injuries to the eye include vitreous hemorrhage and dislocation of the lens; the EMT should control any bleeding with gentle pressure and protect the eye with a metal shield or cardboard cup.

The patient may have a **corneal abrasion**, which is a scratch to the surface of the cornea of the eye. Symptoms of a corneal abrasion include pain, sensation of a foreign body, light sensitivity, and excessive tearing. Patients with contusion injuries experience pain and light sensitivity, along with traumatic dilation or constriction of the pupil. If blood is present in the aqueous fluid in the anterior chamber of the eye, the patient may be experiencing **traumatic hyphema**. There are numerous causes of hyphema, including blunt trauma, sports injuries, missiles, and projectiles, as well as physical abuse. The EMT should use a double patch on the eye to prevent movement, which can cause further aggravation of the injury.

A normal pupil will constrict when exposed to light and dilate when exposed to darkness. **Mydriasis** is defined as the dilation of the pupil of the eye. Abnormal pupillary responses are common after trauma, and are most often caused by direct trauma to the pupillary sphincter muscle. The pupils in their normal state should be black, round, and of equal size. Pupil abnormalities may be caused by drug use, previous surgical procedures, cataracts, and other causes. Patients with fixed and dilated pupils are usually given a poor prognosis, because the symptom usually indicates damage to the third cranial nerve and/or the upper brain stem or brain stem ischemia. The optic nerve and/or globe may also be damaged if the patient shows abnormal response in pupillary dilation. By instructing the patient to follow an object, such as a finger or pen, the EMT can assess and document abnormalities.

Nose

The nasal bones are fragile and easily broken; nasal fractures are the most commonly broken bones on the face. It takes twice the force to fracture the zygoma compared to the force required to fracture the nose. Many injuries to the nasal area consist of severe swelling and epistaxis, but do not result in broken bones. Physicians sometimes wait several days before treating nasal fractures to allow the body to heal on its own; however, many patients will express concern about deformity and disfigurement where the nose is concerned and they may want to consult with a reconstructive specialist.

For nontrauma patients with nosebleeds, the EMT should have the patient calmly sit down and lean the body and head slightly forward to prevent blood flow into the throat, which can cause nausea and vomiting. A damp washcloth or clean tissue can be used to apply gentle pressure to the nasal area, pinching the soft part of the nose together for at least five minutes. If the bleeding has not stopped at that point, it should be pinched together for another ten minutes. After fifteen to twenty minutes of direct pressure, the nose should stop bleeding, but if the bleeding continues, the patient should be taken to the emergency department or trauma center. If there is heavy bleeding from the nose, this could indicate a cervical spine injury. The patient needs to be kept in the position they are in if the airway can be managed in that position.

Spine

The spinal column is made up of 33 vertebrae which are divided into 5 sections; there are 7 cervical, 12 thoracic, 5 lumbar, 5 sacral, and 4 coccygeal vertebrae. **Cervical vertebrae** are the "joint above" when splinting, and the **sacrum** is the "joint below" in splinting. The **spinal cord** is found inside the **spinal canal** and is encased in the **vertebral foramen** and protected by the **spinal column**. Nerve roots from the **spinal cord** emerge from the spinal canal through the vertebral foramen and then travel throughout the body. **Ascending nerve tracts** carry messages from the body up the spinal cord and to the brain. **Descending nerve tracts** carry impulses from the brain through the spinal cord and down to various parts of the body. There are 31 pairs of spinal nerves that all originate from the spinal cord.

The EMT must determine the **mechanism of injury (MOI)** when evaluating a possible spinal cord injury. A positive classification of injury means that forces or impact during the injury suggest that there is a potential spinal injury. A negative classification of injury means that forces or impact during the injury do not suggest a potential spinal injury. If the EMT is uncertain about the forces or impact, the patient's injury should be classified as uncertain.

Once EMTs arrive at the scene and check for patient safety, they should complete an initial assessment. At this point, the EMT may determine that **spinal immobilization** is necessary. Once spinal immobilization has begun, it must be completed. **Extrication** is the process of removing a person from an entrapment, such as a vehicle, after an accident. Extrication or cervical collar application starts the immobilization process. Manual stabilization does not start the immobilization process. If the EMT decides that spinal immobilization is not indicated, he or she must document the reasons that support this decision; for example, an alert adult patient who has had a vehicle accident, can communicate, and has no complaints of injury, would likely not meet the criteria for spinal immobilization.

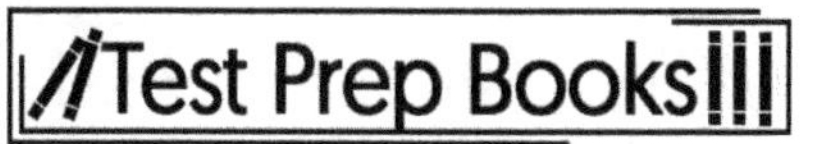

Spinal Immobilization Criteria

Spinal injury should be suspected if the blunt mechanism of injury is present and should be treated if one of the following criteria is present:

- Altered mental status for any reason, including alcohol or drug intoxication
- Complaint of neck and/or spine tenderness or pain
- Weakness, tingling, or numbness in the trunk or extremities at any time since the injury
- Deformity of the spine not present prior to the incident
- Distracting injury or circumstances that may lead to an unreliable physical exam or history

If the EMT has any doubt about a patient's injuries, spinal injury should be suspected and immobilization should be initiated. A combination of loading and rotational forces is a common mechanism of injury for spinal injuries. When one or more cervical vertebrae are dislocated and forced into the spinal canal, the result is often a spinal cord injury.

Axial loading is defined as the application of weight or force along the course of the long axis of the body; for example, a diver who hits his head on the bottom surface of a pool can incur a compression fracture or crushed vertebral body without a spinal cord injury. Flexion, hyperextension, and hyperrotation can cause fractures, as well as muscle and ligament injuries. **Lateral bending** occurs when sudden lateral impact moves the torso sideways. This type of injury can occur when a car crashes into the driver's side door or in contact sports. Intentional or unintentional hangings are examples of distraction injuries. Blunt and penetrating trauma and/or electrical injury can also cause spinal cord injuries.

Reassessment of Trauma Patients

Trauma patients should continuously be reassessed using the ABCDE method. Because traumatic injuries are often so severe and need immediate intervention, initial assessments of the patient's condition may change as time progresses. Traumatic injuries can cause a cascade of other effects that only appear over time, and regular assessments assist in catching these changes before they progress. Additionally, continuous assessments can catch conditions that may have previously been missed altogether. Some reports indicate that up to 10 percent of traumatic injuries are not caught by the primary assessment.

In general, EMT personnel can expect to reassess trauma patients anywhere from every five to ten minutes, depending on the severity of the case. In addition to continuing to abide by the ABCDE method, EMT personnel are expected to monitor the patient's vital signs, examine how interventions in place are affecting the patient and adjust accordingly, and note if other conditions are presenting. Conditions that require further examination or immediate intervention include sudden drops or spikes in any of the vital signs (blood pressure, temperature, pulse, and respiration rate), or if any new complaints are verbalized by the patient.

Reassessments can also help EMTs determine the best timing for procedures. Some procedures that are critical to survival may need to be done on site, but any procedure that can be performed during transport to the hospital should not be done on site. Transferring the patient to the appropriate trauma center in a timely fashion is the priority.

Differentiating Blunt from Penetrating MOI

As mentioned, blunt and penetrating traumas can cause similar patterns of injury, but they are different forms of trauma. The main difference is that blunt force traumas make contact with a larger surface area, while penetrating traumas usually have only one single point of initial contact (which can ultimately cause a wider spread of injuries). For example, two patients can experience brain injuries—one who experienced a blow to the skull (blunt force trauma), and one who experienced a gunshot wound to the head (penetrating trauma). Although both affect the same organ, the method of contact is quite different.

Blunt traumas are not only caused by a blow from an object that comes toward the patient. They can also be caused by something dropping or falling on the patient or from a fall itself. Regardless, the impact of a blunt trauma is affected directly by the directional movement of the impact (whether it was head-on, from behind, a lateral hit, or a rotational hit), and the velocity with which the impact took place. Restraining devices can often minimize the effect of blunt traumas, as they greatly reduce the velocity of one of the objects involved (usually of the patient). Many (though not all) blunt traumas are highly visible externally and look aggravated to the naked eye, but there may be hidden injuries.

Penetrating traumas encompass forces that hit the patient in a single point and puncture tissues. In addition to gunshot wounds, other common penetrating traumas include knife stabbings, impacts from particles after an explosion, or impalements from larger objects (including examples where the patient falls onto a sharp object). As with blunt traumas, velocity plays a role in the severity of penetrating traumas. Particles or bullets that hit the body at a faster velocity cause greater localized trauma, while low velocity can cause larger surface area trauma. Additionally, most penetrating traumas cause more internal damage than external damage. A patient may not visibly look as though they are badly injured, but may have an array of deep internal damage (especially to organs or vessels that have been penetrated). These situations can quickly become fatal, especially if the wounds are located between the head and the thighs.

Connecting Obvious and Hidden Injuries

Hidden injuries often occur as a result of obvious injuries, but are not immediately visible or are not visible without the assistance of imaging machinery (such as x-rays, MRIs, or CT scans). Therefore, EMT personnel should never assume that a visible injury is the only condition that will require an intervention. More than likely, there will be additional related injuries that should be anticipated. For example, a pregnant patient may appear to have only experienced mild whiplash from a motor accident, but should always be transported to an emergency department to have the condition of her fetus examined and monitored. A patient with a gunshot wound to the torso may only have an entry wound and not an exit wound, indicating that the bullet is lodged somewhere in their body—potentially in an organ or in a bone, which can cause internal hemorrhage or paralysis as time passes. Facial traumas may correlate with sensory damage. Chest and abdomen traumas often correlate with cardiac or pulmonary events, or sepsis.

Traumatic brain injuries, especially, should be monitored for additional hidden conditions. While a brain injury may be evaluated as stable after intervention and treatment, the effects of brain injury can slowly present and gradually worsen over time. It is common for patients who experience a seemingly mild concussion to succumb to mortality a few hours or days later, even when patients report "feeling fine." Other neurological effects, such as memory loss or personality changes, may be attributed to other causes but are actually the direct result of a prior brain injury. These injuries often cause social and

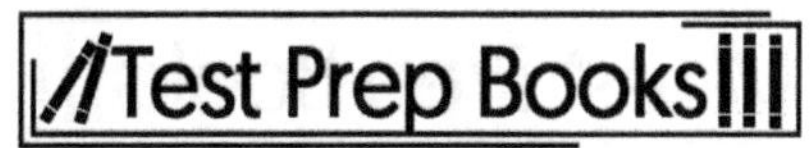

relationship problems when it appears that the patient's personality or intellect has suddenly changed. Unfortunately, many patients who experience head injuries (such as from sports or falls) do not always report it, especially if they don't notice any abnormal symptoms after the incident.

Managing Trauma

Care for a patient who has experienced a traumatic injury goes beyond pre-hospital and in-hospital treatment. It often requires guiding the patient and the patient's support system to understanding the traumatic experience (especially if it was one that was outside of the patient's control); coping with any temporary or permanent physical, emotional, and psychological changes that have resulted from the event; and possibly embarking on a new lifestyle. Many trauma survivors report feeling either unbearable physical or emotional pain or complete apathy; an inability to sleep, eat, or relax; increased anxiety and depression; and common flashbacks of the incident. Trauma survivors may also present changes in hormone and neurotransmitter concentrations and signaling. They are also at risk of exhibiting violence, substance abuse, and other self-destructive behaviors.

Managing these symptoms often requires behavioral-cognitive therapy (not just for the patient, but also for the patient's family and friends) that focuses on comprehending the event that took place, the patient's role in the event, understanding involuntary reactions that arise as a result, and how the patient's support system can best aid in the patient's recovery. These aspects may then be used to teach the patient how to frame the situation, understand their reactions, and implement healthy coping mechanisms that will best serve them in recovery. This type of therapy may be prescribed with other post-trauma care, such as physical rehabilitation. It is important that this educational and healing process begins while the patient is still in medical care, as many people will not voluntarily seek counseling once discharged from the hospital.

Emergency Trauma Care

Spinal Immobilization

Spinal immobilization refers to the practice of stabilizing the cervical, thoracic, and lumbar vertebrae so that the entire column of the spine is unable to move. The procedure is conducted using a stable collar around the cervical vertebrae, and/or a hard board that runs the full length of the patient's spine with the intention of retaining a neutral spinal alignment while in transport. The patient is bound to the board.

Collars that go around the cervical spine are best used on patients that experienced a traumatic, visible head or neck injury, or in patients who experienced an event that places them at a high risk of having trauma to the neck even if no symptoms are immediately showing (such as whiplash in a minor motor accident). Boards that are used in immobilization should not be used as the only method of stabilization in patients at risk of a cervical injury.

Spinal immobilization has a long history in the EMT industry, but recent studies indicate that it may not be an effective practice and that it may cause some degree of harm to most patients, including discomfort, respiratory obstacles, and neurological impingements. As a result, indications for when to use this procedure have shifted significantly. Rather than immobilizing the spine during any trauma case, and assuming the procedure cannot cause additional harm, it is vital for EMTs to make sure this technique is used only when the patient is presenting symptoms or at risk of having experienced a true spinal injury.

Seated Spinal Immobilization

Seated spinal immobilizations take place when a patient is conscious and injuries may be less severe (especially when there are no lower limb injuries), or if a patient must be moved from a seated position to the emergency vehicle or to a long board. Multiple EMT rescuers will be needed. Whenever possible, the rescuers should communicate their actions to the patient. This can also help the patient autonomously ensure that they do not make large movements with the head, neck, or back. One rescuer should support the patient in maintaining a neutral head and neck alignment to preserve the cervical spine, and another rescuer should place the cervical collar around the patient's neck. A short board—a plastic and rigid piece of support that goes the length of the head and torso—may be placed against the patient's head and back for extra support. X-shaped straps cross the patient's body, and an additional strap goes across the patient's upper chest and collar. There is also a strap that gets secured across the patient's forehead. This strap, along with the collar strap, should be secured last. Straps should be tightened to hold the board securely against the patient.

A **Kendrick extrication device** is also commonly used to employ seated spinal mobilizations *only* in contexts where the patient is not suffering from a life-threatening condition. It combines a flat board, a cervical support mechanism, and supportive head pads into a single device that is shaped like a board, which can easily be slid behind a seated patient. Secured straps cross the patient's body, and the device then wraps around the neck and torso of the patient before being secured. Rods placed within the device maintain the spine's neutral alignment. Again, the head should be secured last.

Long Board

Long boards are used in instances of severe spinal injury. They are usually made out of plastic and are rigid. They are large, but light. Patients can be immobilized onto a long board, usually with the assistance of a cervical collar, side padding to further assist with immobilization, and straps that attach to the board. Additionally, most boards can be used in conjunction with x-ray machines, allowing patients to remain stabilized during testing.

Patients that require long board immobilization should be moved by multiple rescuers onto the board in a logroll fashion, ensuring (before movement) that the patient's head will be completely on the board after placement. Rescuers should work together to ensure all regions of the patient's body (legs, pelvis, torso, neck, and head) move in quick synchronization and without misalignment, twisting, or sagging of any region. This precaution is taken to avoid further injury. Upon placement, small adjustments may be necessary to achieve spinal neutrality on the board. One rescuer should make the adjustments while other rescuers provide support to the patient's body and keep the board secured in place. Then, the patient should be strapped in across the torso, the pelvis (unless there is a pelvic or groin injury), and legs, if needed. During any form of board immobilization, the head should always be secured last.

In recent years, long boards have decreased in usage as the rigidity of the board can cause more harm than good for some patients. Alternatively, vacuum mattresses and extra padding on the long board can help alleviate the discomfort that comes with being immobilized. Many organizations recommend that EMT personnel avoid using a long board when the transport to the admitting hospital is long (over ten minutes), when the patient has gunshot wound related trauma above the waist, or when the patient has physical conditions that would present an obstacle (such as spinal scoliosis, spinal kyphosis or lordosis, late term pregnancy, obesity, etc.).

Extremity Splinting

Extremity splinting refers to a way of immobilizing the patient's limbs (rather than the spinal column). This technique is frequently needed in situations where the patient has a fractured arm or leg. When this is the case, it is quite visible, as limbs will often be at an abnormal angle and the patient will report and display a high degree of pain. The area may also be inflamed, tender, or swollen. In severe cases, the bone may have ripped through the skin, which may lead to excessive bleeding and shock if not quickly and adequately managed. The most likely scenarios requiring extremity splinting are closed and open fractures, although other, more complicated types of fractures may also be seen.

In cases where extremity splinting is needed, the EMT will likely use one or more rigid boards to stabilize the area. Before administering the splint, the rescuer should try to gather as much information as possible by asking the patient how the area feels, noting color and circulation of the area, if the patient is able to move the area, and if the patient is able to feel any sensation there. Sensory and musculoskeletal cues can indicate whether or not the patient has suffered spinal or nerve injury. The rescuer should try to realign the fracture before splinting, but in severe cases (or in cases where extreme pressure is felt), this may not be possible. Either way, nearby joints should also be splinted to assist with immobilization.

Some splints work in conjunction with a sling for extra support. For example, fractures in the arm are often supported with a sling across the upper body, in which the splinted limb rests during transport.

Traction Splinting

A **traction splint** is most commonly used with large bones where extremity splinting would not provide enough support. Traction splints are used to treat severe, single fractures, most commonly affecting the femur, but can also work with other bones in the hips or legs. Fractured femurs, especially, can cause a host of other issues, including blood loss and involuntary muscle contraction. These muscular contractions can cause the fractured pieces of the bone to move and overlap. A traction splint uses pressure to pull the overlapped pieces away from each other so that the bone can be splinted until treatment is available. If a large bone fracture is suspected, or if the area simply appears abnormal, it should be assumed to be fractured and should be treated with a traction splint.

A traditional traction splint utilizes the pelvis to work effectively. Therefore, broken pelvic bones and other fractures near the affected area are contraindications for using a traction splint. A **Hare traction splint** uses two rods on either side of the fracture, while a **Sager traction splint** uses only one rod against the fracture. One portion of the splint rests against the pelvis on the side of the fracture, and a strap loops around the foot on the side of the fracture. The metal rod supports the site of the fracture, and other straps cross over the leg and rod. The straps are tightened to create pressure that holds the rod in place against the fracture. This general blueprint has advanced considerably since its original inception in the late 1800s. Contemporary versions have both manual and automatic traction capabilities.

Smaller traction splints, called **dynamic traction splints**, work similarly but are intended to treat the small bones of the hand and fingers. These are typically not utilized in emergency situations.

Mechanical Patient Restraint

In some situations, patients will need to be restrained for appropriate care to be delivered. **Mechanical patient restraint** should be a last resort of conduct in emergency cases. Patients who are severely intoxicated or under the influence of substances, are experiencing an episode of psychosis or delusion, exhibiting contagious symptoms that could be life threatening to others, or otherwise threatening harm to themselves or others are examples of cases where mechanical restraint will likely be necessary, especially if verbal negotiation does not work. In situations like these, it becomes more important for the EMT to assess scene safety to ensure the patient is not in possession of, or otherwise able to access, items that could be used to harm rescuers. When working with pediatric patients, the parents or guardians should be the ones to provide restraint whenever possible.

When restraining a patient, it is important for the EMT to use the least amount of physical force necessary and to avoid additional harm or injury to the patient. The patient and their belongings should be treated with respect throughout the entire pre-hospital and transport process. Restraining the patient should not interfere with their ability to accept care. It is also important to note that patients experiencing a seizure should never be restrained, and that pregnant patients should not be restrained in a complete supine or complete prone position.

Additionally, detailed documentation is required any time a patient requires restraint during pre-hospital care. The guidelines for this documentation may vary by organization, but the documentation will typically require detailing what occurred, the nature of the emergency, why the patient needed to be restrained, how the patient was restrained, and any additional injuries that occurred. Laws dictating when patient restraint can be utilized also vary by state, so it is important for the EMT to know the established guidelines of the area where he or she works.

Tourniquets

Tourniquets are used to manage blood flow and circulation in a particular area, using external pressure. Their use is indicated in patients who are hemorrhaging, or at risk of hemorrhaging, due to major artery damage. Applying a tourniquet can save a patient's life or their affected limbs from amputation. Pediatric patients, especially, can benefit from tourniquet administration due to their small size and increased risk of rapidly bleeding out from traumatic injuries. If a medical tourniquet is not available, utilizing the cuff from an available blood pressure monitor is recommended. This should be used as a last resort, however.

Mass manufactured medical tourniquets are easy to use, can be established in under a minute, and can be administered by a single EMT rescuer. Tourniquets are placed close to the location of a wound, without being placed directly over it or near joints. The degree of tightness depends on the location of the wound and the width of the tourniquet. Once placed, the tourniquet should not be moved until the patient reaches the hospital and is in the care of its trauma team. The tourniquet should be monitored to ensure it has not loosened. Generally, tourniquets should not be left on longer than two hours, as irreversible tissue necrosis and nerve damage occurs within six hours.

Although the tourniquet is a life-saving device, the side effects are somewhat severe. The area affected tends to become irritated and deoxygenated, cellular pH levels become imbalanced, the risk of cellular edema increases, and nerve irritation is common. Therefore, removing the tourniquet comes with its own set of intervention protocols. Discharged patients may experience a phenomenon known as post-tourniquet syndrome, which can last anywhere from a few days to six months. This syndrome is characterized by paralysis, tremors, muscle dysfunction, and general weakness in the area where the tourniquet was placed.

MAST/PASG

Military Anti-Shock Trousers (MAST)/Pneumatic Anti-Shock Garments (PASG) are used to treat hemorrhaging patients and patients with pelvis injuries, with the intention of preventing the patient

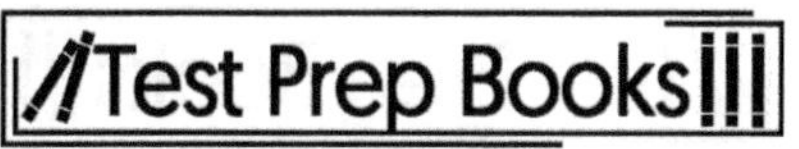

from going into shock or stabilizing the pelvis. Shaped like pants, they fit around the patient's lower half; the device can be wrapped onto the patient, slid onto the patient, or laid flat to where the patient can be placed into it. Sections are inflated to apply pressure to blood vessels (to stop excessive bleeding) or to stabilize broken bones, broken joints, or torn muscles. When used in hemorrhaging victims, the pressure from the device may return enough blood back into circulation to stabilize the patient until he or she is admitted to the hospital. They are best utilized in patients who have severe lower body bleeding injuries, such as a femoral artery wound. However, recent studies have shown that the amount of blood that recirculates from MAST/PASG application is about one-fourth of what was previously believed.

The use of MAST/PASG devices can present unpleasant side effects. The excess pressure on the torso can negatively affect the patient's breathing, as well as exacerbate injuries to the upper torso, chest, and lung area. While the compression offered by MAST/PASG devices can help reestablish and redirect blood flow in patients that are bleeding out (such as if a limb was severed), it can make internal hemorrhages worse to the point of expediting a fatal outcome. These devices should also not be used on any patients suffering a cardiac arrest or experiencing pulmonary edema. Additionally, it is important to note that removing MAST/PASG devices is a serious procedure that must be carefully monitored and managed. When the device is removed, blood pressure drastically falls and the body reacts as if it is quickly losing blood, so rescuers should avoid removing the device before the patient is admitted to the hospital, or should be prepared to stabilize the patient once more. The drawbacks of these devices leave them with minimal recommended use, instead favoring quickly transporting patients to a trauma center.

Cervical Collars

Cervical collars wrap around the cervical spine (vertebrae C1 to C7) to reduce or eliminate pain in the head and neck, and maintain neutral alignment down the cervical spine. They originally were used with the intention of immobilizing the spine, but this is actually not physically possible. Even in a cervical collar, the vertebrae of the cervical spine are able to move. However, the presence of the collar does remind patients to avoid large movements of the head and neck. Emergency services have switched to using soft cervical collars over rigid collars in recent decades. Soft cervical collars are flexible and fit specifically to the patient. They are less likely to restrict the airway, and are more comfortable for the patient. Additionally, they may be recommended by medical professionals for chronic or long-term neck issues. Some variations of these collars can even be bought at most pharmacies and drug stores; often people who have a history of neck and back problems will purchase them to manage temporary bouts of pain at home.

Rigid cervical collars are made of an inflexible plastic material. They were commonly used in emergency situations until recently; as of 2015, most emergency medical services prefer the use of a soft cervical collar in cases where the patient needs to limit spinal movement.

Though once considered a universal best practice in emergency contexts, using a rigid cervical collar has many limitations and can often harm patients (which ultimately led to the sharp decrease in their usage). Research showed that most patients experiencing an emergency did not actually face any risk of spinal injury; therefore, using a cervical collar was a waste of resources. In fact, many patients suffered more because the unnecessary cervical collar hindered the patient's ability to receive adequate assisted ventilation, as the hard-plastic material of the rigid cervical collars actually made it more difficult to maintain a patent airway and manage oxygen administration. Additionally, rigid cervical collars often place undue pressure on the cervical spinal cord and the arteries and veins that serve the head and neck. This, in turn, can cause neurological dysfunction and hazardous levels of intracranial blood pressure.

Consequently, it is recommended that the use of a rigid cervical collar is limited to cases of severe trauma, fracture, or dislocation of the head, neck, or spinal cord, rather than as a standard technique for any emergency situation.

Signs of definite spinal injury that would warrant the use of a cervical collar include paralysis; loss of normally voluntary functions (such as bladder control); numbness in the patient's extremities; muscle spasms; severe pain in the head, neck, upper back, or shoulders; uncontrollable movements; or poor neurological functioning.

Rapid Extrication

Rapid extrication refers to a technique where a patient is quickly moved from the scene of the trauma and stabilized onto a stretcher. It is a systematic process that is meant to keep vital areas of the patient's body—such as the head, neck, and pelvis—safe from additional trauma or stress while quickly preparing the patient for transport. It should be used in contexts where the scene is dangerous (such as due to an environmental hazard), the patient needs to be transported immediately (such as when suffering from catastrophic, life-threatening injuries), or the patient is in the way of other patients who need immediate care. It is most commonly used in motor vehicle accidents where the patient has to be removed from the vehicle in a seated position and ends in a supine position. Because this is a relatively fast process with multiple components, it requires a team of multiple EMT personnel to carry it out.

The technique begins by ensuring as much safety for the EMT personnel as possible. Although the scene may be safe, the process must move at a fast pace and precautions should be taken to ensure that neither the EMT personnel nor the patient will be harmed by environmental factors during rapid extrication. EMT personnel should also take the time to administer gloves, goggles, and any other self-protective barriers that should be used when handling a patient. One EMT team member should stand or crouch behind the patient and stabilize the patient's head and neck and maintain neutral alignment of the cervical spine.

If there is time, another EMT team member should perform a quick assessment of the patient's motor and sensory functions, and place a cervical collar, if needed. A third EMT team member should prepare the stretcher (or long board, if the situation warrants it). When it is time to move the patient to the stretcher, the first team member should support the patient's head and neck, the second team member should support the patient's torso and pelvis, and the third team member should support the patient's legs. Together, they should place the patient onto the long board in one motion while preserving the neutral alignment of the spine. All sensory and motor functions should be monitored while the patient is in transport.

Practice Quiz

1. Which demographic of patients makes up the majority of multisystem trauma cases?
   a. Adult
   b. Elderly (over age 70)
   c. Pediatric
   d. Immunocompromised

2. What is the primary difference between a Hare traction splint and a Sager traction splint?
   a. A Hare traction splint is a bipolar medical device, while a Sager traction splint is a unipolar traction device.
   b. A Hare traction splint is for adult patients, while a Sager traction splint is for pediatric patients.
   c. A Hare traction splint is for large lower limbs, while a Sager traction splint is for smaller upper bones, such as in the hand.
   d. A Hare traction splint is for rapid splinting, while a Sager traction splint takes more time to properly employ.

3. What is an advantage of modern-day tourniquets?
   a. They are simple, consisting of only sterile gauze.
   b. They can be effectively established by one person and in under one minute.
   c. They contain a built-in antibiotic dispensing unit and can be used for medical situations other than wound care.
   d. They can only be placed in hospital settings, which provide a more sterile environment.

4. An EMT team arrives at a scene where a male patient appears to have been stabbed and is bleeding moderately. As the team walks toward the patient, the patient holds one hand up and yells, slurring his words, "Don't come near me or I will attack!" The patient looks dazed and disoriented, but he glances around, and his eyes fall upon a small metal rod that is nearby. He begins to lunge toward it. What option is available to the EMT team at this point?
   a. The team should immediately leave the scene and let the patient fend for himself.
   b. The team should pull out any available items that could be used as weapons and prepare for self-defense actions.
   c. The team should attempt to restrain the patient, using established guidelines set by their geographic region and medical organization.
   d. The team should estimate the patient's body mass, and the EMT team leader should shoot the patient with an appropriately dosed tranquilizer dart.

5. Which emergency trauma practice has shifted greatly in indications and methodology in recent years?
   a. Spinal immobilization
   b. Extremity splinting
   c. Tourniquet application
   d. On-site amputation

See answers on the next page.

Answer Explanations

1. C: Pediatric patients are most susceptible to multisystem trauma, because their brains and bodies are still developing. A blow to the head or chest often results in the failure of other systems. While elderly and immunocompromised patients can suffer greatly in the event of multisystem trauma injuries, they do not make up the majority of cases.

2. A: A Hare traction splint utilizes two rods to support a broken limb, while a Sager traction splint utilizes a single rod. The other options are not accurate.

3. B: Modern tourniquets can be quickly administered in under a minute and by a single rescuer. Sterile gauze tourniquets are very antiquated. Modern tourniquets do not have built-in antibiotic dispensing and can be used in a wide variety of settings.

4. C: In this case, the EMT rescuers are allowed to restrain the patient due to the verbal and physical threats. They should follow guidelines that are established for them, and be sure to document the situation in its entirety as well. Patients should not be left to fend for themselves, fought, or tranquilized. In these cases, rescuers will need to work together to provide care to the best of their ability.

5. A: Spinal immobilization techniques have shifted from being accepted as a universal practice in most emergency cases, to requiring stringent indications before immobilizing a patient. This is due to many cases of spinal immobilization causing more patient harm than benefit. The other options do not apply.

Medical, Obstetrics, and Gynecology

Standard Assessment: Adult and Pediatric Patients

The primary goal of an Emergency Medical Technician (EMT) is to provide emergency on-site medical assistance and to transport a patient to a medical facility. Regardless of the emergency situation, all events require a standard assessment of the scene and patient before making any evaluations, attempted diagnoses, or treatments.

Upon arriving at the site of an emergency call, an EMT should do the following for both children and adults:

- Assess the situation, ensuring the scene is safe before proceeding.
- Maintain and support the patient's ABCs.
- Take the patient's vital signs: pulse, respiration rates, blood pressure, pulse oxygenation, pain level, and any other relevant measurements.
- Administer high-concentration oxygen via a non-rebreathing mask or a bag mask, if necessary.
- Determine appropriate interventions where local protocols allow, such as spinal stabilization, minimization of bleeding, epinephrine shots, CPR, etc.
- Obtain the patient's history regarding the current emergency by using the mnemonic *OPQRST*, either directly from the patient or, in the case of children, the patient's caretaker:
- *O*nset: Did the pain start gradually or suddenly? What was the patient doing when the pain started?
- *P*rovokes: What makes the pain better or worse?
- *Q*uality: Ask the patient to describe the pain; for example, sharp or dull?
- *R*adiates: Ask the patient to identify the area containing the most pain; then ask if the pain radiates to any other part of the body.
- *S*everity: Describe the pain on a scale from 1 to 10.
- *T*ime: When did the pain start?
- Obtain a SAMPLE history, either directly from the patient or, in the case of children, the patient's caretaker. SAMPLE is an acronym that stands for: *s*igns and symptoms, *a*llergies, *m*edications, *p*ast medical history, *l*ast oral intake, *e*vents leading up to the incident.
- If the situation is non-life-threatening, assess and evaluate the patient to determine the cause of the pain or illness.
- Prepare the patient for immediate transport to an appropriate medical facility.

Neurological Emergencies

There are several neurological conditions that are considered medical emergencies. In adults, the most severe are strokes and seizures. For children, seizures and headaches are of the utmost concern. Almost all neurological events result in an **altered mental status (AMS)**, or a change in behavior caused by a loss or interruption in brain function. AMS patients require immediate attention. Using the AVPU scale, the patient's level of consciousness should be the first thing assessed. The following list is a popular mnemonic (TIPS AEIOU) that describes the most common causes of AMS: *T*rauma, *I*nfection, *P*sychogenic causes, *S*eizure/syncope, *A*lcohol, *E*lectrolyte imbalance, *I*nsulin, *O*piates, *U*remia (kidney disease). Since AMS is a common symptom in diabetic emergencies, it's important to always check blood glucose levels when a patient is experiencing AMS.

Stroke

A **stroke** is caused by a blockage of blood to the brain that results in a loss of brain function. An **ischemic** stroke is caused by clots in the blood vessels within the brain, resulting in a restriction of blood flow and tissue death. A **hemorrhagic** stroke occurs when a blood vessel ruptures, causing a decrease in blood volume and flow as well as blood leakage into brain tissues. Strokes are most prevalent in adults, but they may occur in children who have certain diseases, such as sickle cell disease or congenital heart problems, which can cause strokes.

Symptoms of a stroke include: weakness or numbness in the face and limbs, particularly on one side of the body; difficulty speaking, understanding speech, or loss of speech (adults); loss of vision or dimming in one or both eyes; loss of balance or walking instability; and an intense headache with a sudden onset. Strokes can affect bodily functions including swallowing, making it important to check the airway in patients who are unresponsive. An oropharyngeal or nasopharyngeal airway may be needed as well as suctioning. If there's danger of secretions getting into the airway, the patient should be placed in the recovery position. Immediate transport of stroke patients to a hospital is necessary.

Seizures

A **seizure** is an electrical dysfunction of the neurological system that causes uncontrollable muscle movements and abnormal consciousness. Upon responding to a call involving a seizure, an EMT must determine in which part of the body the seizure began. The EMT must also make certain not to place anything in the patient's mouth to avoid both a biting and choking hazard. In adults, the most common type of seizure is a **generalized tonic-clonic seizure**. Symptoms include loss of consciousness followed by muscle rigidity and convulsion. It may also be accompanied by **tachycardia** (rapid heartbeat), sweating, and hyperventilation. In children, a **febrile seizure** is the most common type, caused by a high fever and resulting in a loss of consciousness followed by convulsions and muscle rigidity.

Headaches

A headache may be a sign of an underlying, life-threatening illness, so it's imperative to check for signs of stroke, meningitis, or a gaseous poisoning, such as from carbon monoxide. Severe headaches that occur suddenly, sometimes along with other symptoms such as a stiff neck, seizures, fever, vomiting, or altered mental status, could be life-threatening. It's also important to ensure the patient is comfortable and placed in a quiet environment with minimal lighting, and to transport the patient to the hospital.

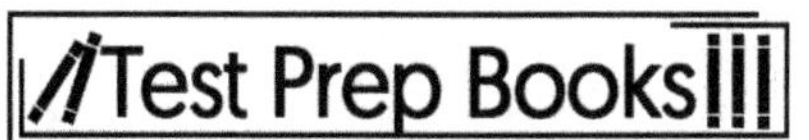

Abdominal Disorders

Most abdominal pain isn't the result of a life-threatening condition. It's important to be aware of what conditions could be life-threatening, however, especially in children. Upon first responding, an EMT is required to take patient vitals, support and maintain ABCs, assess body position and mental status, as well as identify the chief complaint and type of abdominal pain. Identifying the type of pain can help with a future diagnosis.

There are three primary types of abdominal pain. **Visceral pain**, or stimulation of an organ's nerve fibers caused by stretching of the organ's wall, is not localized and is often felt as a generalized dull ache. **Parietal (somatic) pain** is caused by irritation to the parietal peritoneal wall. The **peritoneum** is a serous membrane rich in nerves that lines the abdominal wall and protects the organs. Parietal pain is felt more locally and often described as sharp or stabbing. Finally, **referred pain** is a radiating pain felt somewhere other than the area that actually hurts. For example, a person experiencing irritation of the spleen may feel discomfort in their right shoulder.

In order to assess and identify the cause of abdominal pain, EMTs should have a basic understanding of abdominal anatomy.

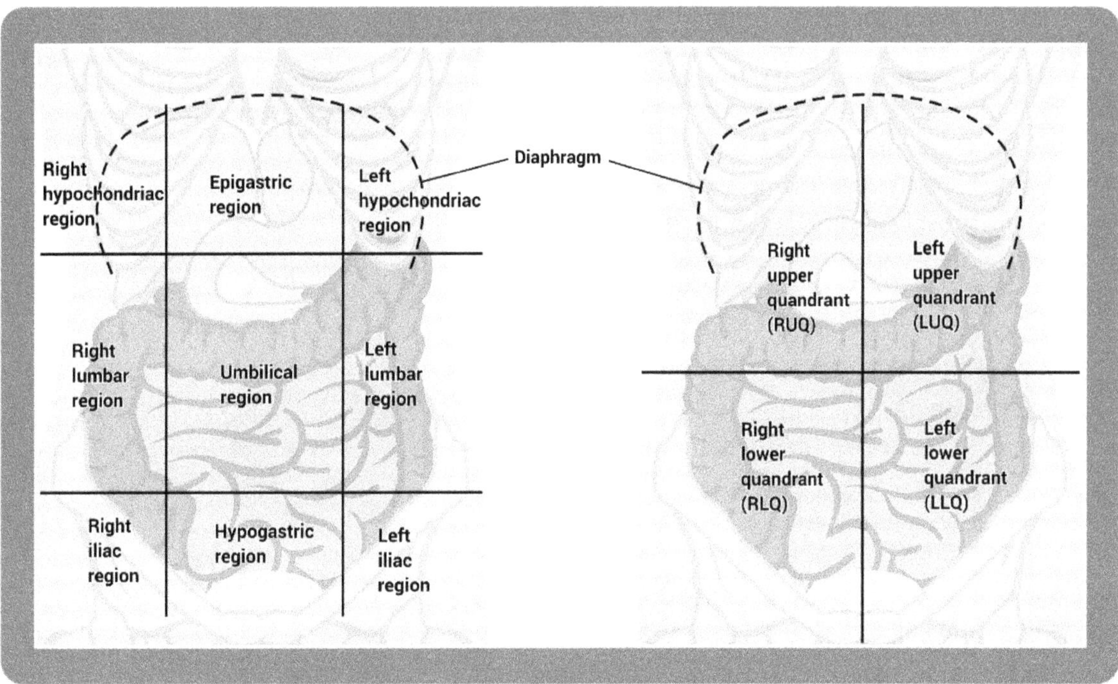

The abdomen is divided into four basic quadrants. Pain in any of these regions may originate in the organs associated with the respective quadrant.

Quadrant	Associated Organs
Right upper quadrant (RUQ)	Liver, gallbladder, and parts of the large intestine
Left upper quadrant (LUQ)	Stomach, spleen, pancreas, and part of the large intestine
Right lower quadrant (RLQ)	Appendix, small intestine, and (in women) fallopian tube and ovary
Left lower quadrant (LLQ)	Part of the small and large intestines, and (in women) the fallopian tube and ovary

Causes of Abdominal Pain

Abdominal pain is generally caused by irritation, stretching, or inflammation of an organ, as well as a decreased blood supply or a ruptured vessel.

The most common causes for abdominal pain in adults include:

- Abdominal aortic aneurysm: rupture of the aorta due to weakened arterial wall
- Appendicitis: inflammation of the appendix
- Bowel obstruction: blockage in the intestine
- Cholecystitis: inflammation of the gallbladder
- Constipation: decreased peristalsis leading to difficulty having bowel movements
- Cystitis: bladder infection
- Ectopic pregnancy: fetal implantation outside of uterus
- Esophagitis: inflammation of the esophagus
- Food poisoning
- Gas or air swallowing (most common in children)
- Kidney stones
- Pancreatitis: inflammation of the pancreas
- Peptic ulcer: erosion of the lining of the stomach
- Peritonitis: inflammation of the peritoneum
- Urinary tract infection

Assessing Abdominal Pain

Upon first responding to a call, it's imperative to determine whether the patient will need immediate medical attention; that is, determine if the patient is "sick" or "not sick." The patient is sick if they show signs of: **decreased perfusion**, i.e., decreased blood pressure, cold extremities, restlessness, confusion; **ischemic chest pain**, or complaints of crushing pressure in middle of chest; **pleuritic (respiratory) issues**, which present as shortness of breath, hyperventilation, etc.; and **signs of panic**, which must be present with other critical signs.

If the patient shows signs of illness, treatment should include supporting and maintaining ABCs, administering high-flow oxygen, placing the patient in supine position, monitoring vital signs, and

preparing for immediate transport to a medical facility. If the patient doesn't seem to be in any immediate danger, an EMT should perform an abdominal exam.

Performing an Abdominal Exam

To help determine the location and cause of pain, an EMT should perform an abdominal exam as outlined in the following procedure:

- Lay the patient in a supine position, facing up.
- Ask the patient to identify the location of the pain.
- Palpate the abdomen by pressing on the unaffected areas first. If the patient seems to be guarding, palpate the affected area *gently* after examining other areas. Palpation that is too hard or deep may result in organ rupture or perforation.
- Inspect the abdomen for distension, swelling, surgical scars, or changes in skin color.

If the cause of pain doesn't appear to be serious, treatment may consist of the following:

1. Placing the patient into a position of comfort
2. Administering a low-to-moderate flow of oxygen
3. Monitoring vital signs
4. Preparing the patient for transport, if necessary

Immunology (Allergic Reactions)

Immunology is the study of the immune system, which controls the physiological response to foreign invaders such as viruses, organisms, and bacteria. Immunologic emergencies consist of allergic reactions and **anaphylaxis**—an extreme and life-threatening allergic reaction. At least 1,000 Americans die each year due to such emergencies.

An **allergic reaction** is an exaggerated immune response to an external stimulus, which can present in the form of a bite, sting, or ingested or airborne particles. This stimulus then signals the immune system to release chemicals to combat the foreign invader, known as **histamines** and **leukotrienes**, both of which contribute to the allergic response. Allergic reactions may be mild, resulting in sneezing, watery eyes and nose, or hives, or the reactions may be severe, resulting in anaphylactic shock and respiratory failure.

Allergic reactions have five primary causes: medications, foods, insect stings or bites that inject venom (envenomation), chemicals (such as those in makeup or latex), and plants/animals (poison ivy, cat dander, pollen, dust, etc.).

Anaphylaxis affects multiple organs and, if left untreated, can cause rapid death. Signs and symptoms of anaphylaxis include: coughing and/or wheezing (high-pitched whistling); pain; itching; tightness in the chest; shortness of breath; difficulty breathing; and trouble swallowing. The patient may show neurological symptoms such as confusion, weakness, fainting, and dizziness. The patient's integumentary system may show symptoms such as hives or urticaria; rash; itchiness; pale skin; and swollen, itchy, or red skin, lips, eyes, and tongue. The patient may present with cardiological symptoms such as rapid heartbeat, a weak pulse, and low blood pressure. The patient may experience gastrointestinal symptoms such as nausea, vomiting, cramps, or diarrhea.

Epinephrine

Epinephrine reverses the effects of severe allergic reactions by causing vasoconstriction and hypertension. Application of epinephrine is necessary in severe and life-threatening allergic reactions, but it's essential for an EMT to know if local protocols allow an EMT to administer an epinephrine injection. The appropriate dosage of epinephrine is 0.15 milligrams for children under 66 pounds and 0.30 milligrams for adults.

Assessing an Immunologic Emergency

To properly assess and treat an immunological emergency, an EMT should follow these procedures:

- Assess the scene and environment to ensure it is safe (e.g., no bees are present) and take notice of the surroundings to determine the allergen (e.g., a giant beehive, food that may have triggered an allergy, etc.).

- Make a quick and primary assessment of the patient. Assess whether the patient is in danger of anaphylaxis. If a severe allergic reaction seems likely, call for advanced life support (ALS). Take and monitor vital signs.

- Initiate any necessary treatments. If the patient is unconscious, evaluate and treat ABCs. Administer high-flow oxygen and use basic life support or automated external defibrillator (AED) if their blood pressure or pulse is dangerously low. Maintain the normal body temperature of 98 degrees if hypothermia is detected. Place the patient in the supine position if anaphylaxis is suspected. If a stinger is still in place, swipe the stinger away with a hard object, such as a credit card, but do *not* remove the stinger with tweezers. If the patient is conscious, obtain their chief complaint, SAMPLE history, and OPQRST. Determine what, if any, interventions have already been performed, such as allergy medicine or epinephrine shots. In severe cases, an epinephrine injection is necessary to prevent anaphylactic shock. Depending on training, some EMTs may not be permitted to directly administer epinephrine, but they may be permitted to assist the patient in doing so. Patients who have a history of the allergy may already have a kit in their possession.

- Prepare the patient for transport, if necessary.

Infectious Disease

An **infectious disease** is a pathology caused by harmful organisms, such as bacteria, fungi, parasites, and viruses. Many infectious diseases are **communicable**, which means they can be transferred through touch, breathing, saliva, blood, and other bodily substances. The goal of an EMT is to properly care for and transport a patient with an infectious disease while keeping the disease contained via decontamination and other sterile practices. Infectious diseases that cannot be contained often lead to widespread infections of the population known as **epidemics** and **pandemics**. It's imperative that an EMT recognize the signs, symptoms, and mode of transmission of many infectious diseases in order to

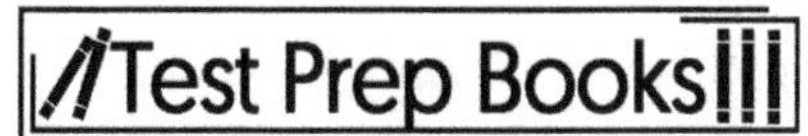

properly treat, contain, and protect themselves from it. The table below contains information on the most common infectious diseases.

Disease	Signs and Symptoms	Mode of Transmission
Meningitis (Inflammation of the meninges)	Fever Headache Severely stiff neck Kernig's sign (inability to extend leg) Brudzinski sign (hips and knees flex when neck is flexed)	Saliva (kissing, coughing, sneezing, etc.). Contaminated hands
Tuberculosis (Bacterial infection of the lungs)	Persistent cough Night sweats Fatigue Hemoptysis (coughing blood) Hoarseness of voice	Breathing airborne particles (coughing, sneezing, etc.).
Pneumonia (Inflammation of the lungs)	High fever Chills Pain in chest Expectorant cough Trouble breathing	Breathing airborne droplets (coughing, sneezing, etc.) Contaminated hands
Mononucleosis (Abnormal white blood cell count)	Sore throat Swollen lymph nodes Headache Muscle aches General malaise	Direct contact with saliva
Influenza (Viral infection of the lungs)	Fever Muscle aches Chills Respiratory problems	Breathing airborne droplets (coughing, sneezing, etc.) Contaminated hands
Hepatitis B (Inflammation of the liver)	Loss of appetite Jaundice Yellowing of the eyes Abdominal pain	Sharing needles
Hepatitis C (Inflammation of the liver)	Loss of appetite Jaundice Yellowing of the eyes Abdominal Pain	Blood-to-blood contact Sexual contact Blood transfusion Unsafe medical practices Mother to child

Disease	Signs and Symptoms	Mode of Transmission
Human Immunodeficiency Virus (HIV) (Destruction of the immune system)	Fever Fatigue Loss of appetite Recurrent infections Flu-like symptoms	Blood-to-blood contact Sexual contact Bodily fluids
Norovirus (Viral inflammation of stomach and intestines)	Diarrhea (watery) Nausea and vomiting Stomach pain Fever Weakness Body aches	Eating contaminated food Touching contaminated surfaces

Per the Occupational Health and Safety Administration (OHSA) and the Center for Disease Control and Prevention (CDC), EMTs are responsible for three primary concerns: to protect the health of the public, to manage outbreaks, and to prevent epidemics. These concerns are maintained by practicing proper hygiene, obtaining proper immunizations, wearing appropriate protective equipment, sterilizing the ambulance and medical equipment after use, and possibly undergoing quarantine. Each infectious disease has guidelines for managing it and caring for a patient. These guidelines are the same for both adults and children.

In order to comply with the above concerns, an EMT must be familiar with the cleaning routines associated with infectious diseases. To keep an ambulance and its equipment disinfected, a paramedic is required to appropriately dispose of medical waste, remove and appropriately discard used linens, wash and scrub any contaminated areas or surfaces, appropriately disinfect any equipment that cannot be discarded, and clean the stretcher (and any spills) with a germicidal-viricidal solution.

Assessing and Responding to an Infectious Emergency

When treating a patient with an infectious disease, EMTs must ensure they are wearing the appropriate personal protective equipment, generally in the form of disposable gloves and a protective mask. Other equipment, such as gowns, may be necessary depending on the illness. Once protective equipment has been applied, the patient's signs and symptoms must be assessed to determine the kind of illness. Protective equipment for the patient—usually a surgical mask—should be administered depending on the disease's mode of transmission. Having contained the disease as much as possible, an EMT may then maintain and support ABCs, take the patient's vital signs, assess the patient's mental status, and obtain SAMPLE and OPQRST histories. The patient should then be placed in a position of comfort, treated for dehydration, and prepared for transportation to a hospital. After the patient has been successfully delivered, the ambulance and equipment must be disinfected. All infectious disease incidents must be reported to the appropriate personnel.

Endocrine Disorders

The **endocrine system** is a collection of glands that secrete hormones. These hormones regulate countless physiological processes, including growth, metabolism, sexual reproduction, sleep, mood, and tissue development. Its primary function is to maintain **homeostasis**, which means keeping the body's internal condition stable. The endocrine system consists of the hypothalamus, pituitary gland, adrenal

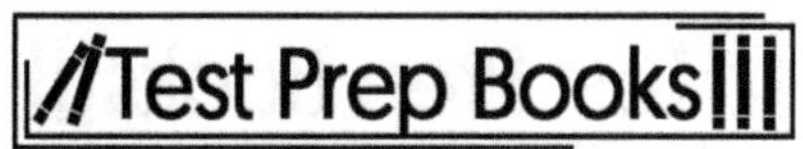

glands, thyroid and parathyroid glands, pancreas, and the ovaries in females and the testicles in males. Hormones secreted from these glands are released into the bloodstream and carried to the intended tissues and organs. Although the endocrine system and the nervous system are closely linked, while the nervous system acts rapidly, the endocrine system acts very slowly.

Major Endocrine Glands

Hypothalamus: A part of the brain, the hypothalamus connects the nervous system to the endocrine system via the pituitary gland. Although it is considered part of the nervous system, it plays a dual role in regulating endocrine organs.

Pituitary Gland: A pea-sized gland found at the bottom of the hypothalamus. It has two lobes, called the anterior and posterior lobes. It plays an important role in regulating the function of other endocrine glands. The hormones released control growth, blood pressure, certain functions of the sex organs, salt concentration of the kidneys, internal temperature regulation, and pain relief.

Thyroid Gland: This gland releases hormones, such as thyroxine, that are important for metabolism, growth and development, temperature regulation, and brain development during infancy and childhood. Thyroid hormones also monitor the amount of circulating calcium in the body.

Parathyroid Glands: These are four pea-sized glands located on the posterior surface of the thyroid. The main hormone secreted is called parathyroid hormone (PTH) and helps with the thyroid's regulation of calcium in the body.

Thymus Gland: The thymus is located in the chest cavity, embedded in connective tissue. It produces several hormones important for development and maintenance of normal immunological defenses. One hormone promotes the development and maturation of lymphocytes, which strengthens the immune system.

Adrenal Gland: One adrenal gland is attached to the top of each kidney. It produces adrenaline and is responsible for the "fight or flight" reactions in the face of danger or stress. The hormones epinephrine and norepinephrine cooperate to regulate states of arousal.

Pancreas: The pancreas is an organ that has both endocrine and exocrine functions. The endocrine functions are controlled by the pancreatic islets of Langerhans, which are groups of beta cells scattered throughout the gland that secrete insulin to lower blood sugar levels in the body. Neighboring alpha cells secrete glucagon to raise blood sugar.

Pineal Gland: The pineal gland secretes melatonin, a hormone derived from the neurotransmitter serotonin. Melatonin can slow the maturation of sperm, oocytes, and reproductive organs. It also regulates the body's circadian rhythm, which is the natural awake/asleep cycle. It also serves an important role in protecting the CNS tissues from neural toxins.

Testes and Ovaries: These glands secrete testosterone and estrogen, respectively, and are responsible for secondary sex characteristics, as well as reproduction.

Endocrine System Function

The endocrine system works primarily through **negative feedback loops**, meaning that the body senses changes in hormone levels within the bloodstream, and then releases hormones to oppose those changes. For example, when a person eats, their blood glucose rises, signaling the pancreas to release insulin, which causes glucose uptake in fat and muscle cells and effectively lowers blood glucose to normal levels.

Unlike exocrine glands, endocrine glands are ductless, meaning they secrete hormones directly into the bloodstream instead of through a duct. Exocrine glands include sweat glands, mammary glands, salivary glands, and the stomach and liver. The only endocrine gland that has an exocrine function is the pancreas, which secretes enzymes that break down the molecular components of food as well as secrete insulin and glucagon to control blood glucose levels.

Endocrine disorders are caused by an imbalance in the production of hormones and/or a complication in the body's ability to use the hormones produced. The most common endocrine emergencies, their signs and symptoms, and their treatments are discussed below.

Thyroid Disorders

Hyperthyroidism

Hyperthyroidism is caused by the overproduction of thyroid hormones (free T3 and T4), which causes a hyperactive metabolism. This can cause weight loss, increased appetite, heat intolerance, and weakness, as well as an enlarged thyroid gland, called a goiter. One endocrinological emergency related to hyperthyroidism is **thyrotoxic crisis**—a rare and potentially fatal emergency characterized by extremely high fever (106 °F or above), tachycardia, hypotension, irritability, delirium, coma, and nausea and/or vomiting. Emergency medical services are primarily supportive, so treating a patient with thyrotoxic crisis involves supporting and maintaining the ABCs and expediting patient transport to the hospital.

Hypothyroidism

The opposite of hyperthyroidism is hypothyroidism—the underproduction of thyroid hormone that causes a hypoactive metabolism, which may lead to weight gain or difficulty losing weight, fatigue, and mood swings. A **myxedema coma** is a hypothyroid-related emergency characterized by swelling of the skin and underlying tissues, making the skin appear waxy. Signs and symptoms include fatigue, lethargy, slowed mental function, cold intolerance, hypothermia, hypotension, and bradycardia. If left untreated, these symptoms can ultimately result in a coma. Treatment for a patient with myxedema involves supporting and closely monitoring ABCs (especially cardiac and pulmonary status), administering IV access but limiting fluids, assessing for other possible etiologies, and expediting patient transport to a hospital.

Adrenal Disorders

Addison's Disease

Addison's Disease is the inability of the adrenal cortex to produce **aldosterone** and **cortisol**, the hormones that govern the body's salt and water balance and help to fight stress and infections, respectively. Patients with Addison's Disease will experience **hyperkalemia** (too much potassium), darkening of the skin, **hypoglycemia** (low blood sugar), early-morning nausea, vomiting, and diarrhea, and possibly sudden cardiovascular collapse. Emergency medical services require the support and maintenance of the patient's ABCs, monitoring glucose levels, treating hypoglycemia if necessary, administering an IV for abundant fluids, and immediate transport to the hospital.

Cushing's Syndrome

Cushing's Syndrome occurs when the adrenal gland produces too much cortisol, which stimulates the pituitary gland to produce too much adrenocorticotropic hormone (ACTH). A patient with Cushing's may present with a "moon-faced" appearance, weight gain, and fat accumulation on the upper back (called a

"buffalo hump"), as well as in the shoulders (supraclavicular fat pad) and/or the abdomen. Patients may also experience slow healing of wounds, mood swings, skin changes (such as acne), difficulty concentrating or impaired memory, increased facial hair, and purplish abdominal striae. An EMT responding to a call for a patient with this disease will need to support and maintain the ABCs, obtain SAMPLE and OPQRST histories, prepare the patient for transport, and report any observations of Cushing's to the receiving faculty.

Pancreatic Disorders

Diabetes

Diabetes is characterized by the body's inability to metabolize glucose caused by an insufficient supply or utilization of **insulin**, which enables to body to absorb glucose. If the body cannot efficiently take in glucose in order to perform cellular respiration, the tissues will eventually waste away and become necrotic.

Diabetes is divided into two categories: **Type 1 (insulin-dependent)** and **Type 2 (non-insulin-dependent).** Type 1 diabetes occurs when the body's immune system destroys the pancreas' insulin-producing cells (called beta cells) in the islets of Langerhans. For this reason, it's considered an autoimmune disease. Because the body cannot produce insulin, injections of insulin are required over the patient's lifetime in order to control blood sugar. Also known as juvenile diabetes, patients are typically diagnosed in childhood or adolescence.

Type 2 diabetes is characterized by the body's inability to effectively respond to the insulin that it produces. This disease usually manifests in an adult's middle-age years (although it is occurring more frequently in younger and younger patients) as a result of sedentary lifestyle, a diet high in refined sugar, hereditary factors, and comorbidities such as high blood pressure and obesity. Treatment involves lifestyle changes such as healthy diet and exercise, and sometimes also a regime of medications that regulate the body's ability to produce and use insulin and control blood glucose.

Signs and symptoms of diabetes include frequent, plentiful urination (polyuria), increased thirst and frequent drinking (polydipsia), extreme hunger and excessive eating (polyphagia), bedwetting in children who usually don't urinate in their sleep, blurred vision, and fatigue. Children with diabetes typically experience seizures and dehydration.

Symptomatic hypoglycemia (low blood sugar) and **symptomatic hyperglycemia** (high blood sugar) are common emergencies associated with both types of diabetes. Although both conditions can cause altered mental status, a hypoglycemic patient may appear to be intoxicated since their level of consciousness may be depressed. The hypoglycemic patient's breathing may range from normal to rapid, their pulse rapid but weak, their skin may feel cold and clammy, and their blood pressure will be low. Patients experiencing hyperglycemia could have deep and rapid breathing with a rapid, weak, and thready pulse; dry, warm skin; and normal or low blood pressure. It's important to check the patient's blood glucose level. Patients with symptomatic hypoglycemia will need glucose, while hyperglycemic patients require insulin and fluids—provided by ALS or at the hospital—and rapid transport to the hospital. A serious complication of hyperglycemia is the development of cerebral edema. If there's any confusion about which condition the patient is experiencing, give glucose. Unconsciousness and the inability to swallow are the only contraindications to giving oral glucose.

A diabetic emergency known as **diabetic ketoacidosis (DKA)** or a hyperglycemic crisis is the most common type of endocrinological emergency to which an EMT will respond. DKA is a condition where the body uses fat and other sources for fuel instead of glucose, resulting in waste products that cause the blood to become acidic. A patient experiencing a hyperglycemic crisis will have fruity-smelling breath, deep and labored breathing (Kussmaul respirations), vomiting, abdominal pain, and even unconsciousness. The patient may have an emergency medical identification symbol on a bracelet that identifies him or her as a diabetic. An EMT responding to a DKA call can provide care by supporting and maintaining the ABCs, obtaining SAMPLE and OPQRST histories (especially diabetic history), and obtaining blood glucose level (and vital signs. The patient will need IV fluids and insulin, so immediate transport to a hospital is imperative for the patient's survival and recovery.

Psychiatric

A **psychiatric emergency** involves any psychiatric event in which the individual may harm themselves or others, including attempted suicide, depression, substance abuse, or violent behaviors. In general, there is very little hands-on treatment an EMT can perform. In most cases, a psychiatric emergency requires an EMT to call law enforcement and to restrain the individual. If restraint is necessary, the EMT should ensure that the police and at least four other people are present for legal purposes.

The following situations may be present in a psychiatric emergency:

- Agitated delirium: the patient is confused, disoriented, and possibly experiencing hallucinations. The patient may also present with restless activity with no known purpose.
- Organic brain syndrome: a temporary or permanent dysfunction of the brain that may be caused by a disruption of physiological activity, such as adequate blood to brain tissue.
- Functional disorder: dysfunction of organs with no known reason.

When analyzing a psychiatric emergency, an EMT should first assess the situation to be certain it is safe. If the patient is conscious, an EMT should also calmly identify themselves to the patient, and then identify any possible mechanisms of injury (MOI), such as head trauma. Finally, the EMT may perform standard emergency procedures, such as supporting and maintaining ABCs, taking vital signs, and SAMPLE and OPQRST histories. An EMT must be certain never to transport a psychiatric patient in the prone (face-down) position, as the patient may go into respiratory distress or cardiac arrest.

Toxicology

Toxicological emergencies are generally the result of poisonings and drug overdoses. EMTs must follow this very specific protocol:

Observe the Scene

Assess the situation, paying close attention to the surroundings to ensure there aren't signs of an airborne toxin (such as multiple unconscious or flailing victims) or any weapons. Identify the nature of illness (NOI), such as open alcohol bottles, syringes, empty containers, or strange odors. Determine if any/all patients are presenting with altered mental statuses, as patients may become unexpectedly violent.

Pre-Hospital Treatment

Maintain and support ABCs and vital signs and identify any life-threatening conditions. Obtain SAMPLE and OPQRST histories from the patient or their family members/friends. Perform a physical examination of the patient, with particular focus on the area of the body in which the toxin was exposed. If the event

was intentional, treat the situation as a psychiatric emergency in addition to a toxicological emergency. If the patient has taken a harmful or lethal dose of a suspected toxin, repeat vital signs every 5 minutes. Pay particular attention to the patient's breathing, as alcohol, opiates, and inhalants can depress the central nervous system and cause respiratory distress. Inhalants may also lead to seizures.

If the patient has ingested any poisons, it may be necessary to administer activated charcoal, bearing in mind that activated charcoal cannot be given to any patients with AMS. If the patient can have activated charcoal, shake the drink well then present it in a covered cup with a straw. The dose should be 12.5 to 20 g for children, and 25 to 50 g for adults. Take all containers, bottles, and labels from the scene to the receiving hospital for documentation and investigation. If the patient is suspected to have food poisoning, take the food to the receiving hospital.

Hematology

Hematology is the study, prevention, and treatment of blood-related disorders. Blood is composed of plasma and red blood cells and it carries countless physiological elements that maintain and protect the body, such as hormones, white blood cells, and platelets. Red blood cells also contain **hemoglobin**, the molecule that carries oxygen to tissues for cellular respiration. **Plasma** functions to suspend and transport these blood constituents and is composed of fluids, proteins, electrolytes, gases, and waste products. An essential hematological organ is the **spleen**, which is primarily responsible for the production and removal of red blood cells and the recycling of iron. It also serves as a blood reserve in cases of severe blood loss.

Emergencies and Pathophysiology

For an EMT, hematologic emergencies are rare and difficult to treat. The following emergencies outline the most common hematological diseases, their signs and symptoms, and treatment that an EMT can perform.

Sickle Cell Disease

Sickle cell disease is a genetic disorder that causes short-living (16 days) red blood cells to be sickle- or oblong-shaped—resulting in a deformation of hemoglobin that causes it to become a very poor carrier for oxygen. It may cause hypoxia, the rupture of blood vessels and spleen, and death. Children with sickle cell disease are most likely to die from infection. They are also at risk for ischemic stroke. It's most common in people of African or Mediterranean descent.

A sickle-cell emergency is caused by a blockage of blood to tissues and organs (**vaso-occlusive crisis**), a deficiency in red blood cell production (**aplastic crisis**), the rapid destruction of red blood cells (**hemolysis**), or an acute and painful enlargement of the spleen (**splenic sequestration crisis**). Signs and symptoms of a sickle-cell crisis include increased respiration, swelling of the digits, jaundice, signs of pneumonia, and priapism in male patients. Emergency medical services consist of supporting and maintaining ABCs, managing respiratory distress, obtaining SAMPLE and OPQRST histories, and preparing the patient for immediate transport. High-flow oxygen should be delivered at a rate of 12 to 15 L/min through a nonrebreathing mask if the patient is having trouble breathing or appears to have an AMS.

Clotting Disorders

A **clotting disorder** is a disease characterized by the body's inability to make sufficient proteins for **thrombosis**—the development of a clot to stop bleeding. There are two primary and opposing disorders;

thrombophilia is the body's tendency to develop random blood clots, and **hemophilia**, most common in males, is the inability to form blood clots when needed. Thrombophilia isn't common in pediatric patients and is treated with blood-thinning medications. **Deep vein thrombosis**, the formation of a blood clot in a deep vein, causes painful swelling and tenderness in one leg (generally the calf), warm skin, a deep ache in the clot area, and redness of the skin, particularly in the back of the leg below the knee.

Patients experiencing a hemophilic emergency may present with spontaneous and acute chronic bleeding, plentiful large and deep bruises, joint swelling and tenderness, and blood in the urine or stool. Emergency medical services consist of supporting and maintaining ABCs while noticing any signs of blood loss, bleeding of an unknown origin, and hypoxia. SAMPLE and OPQRST histories must be obtained and the patient must be transported to a hospital. If the patient has any signs of AMS or is having trouble breathing, administer high-flow oxygen using a nonrebreathing mask at a rate of 12 to 15 L/min.

Genitourinary (GU)/Renal

Genitourinary refers to the organs of the urinary and genital tracts. The renal, or urinary, tract consists of the kidneys, bladder, urethra, and ureters. The genital tract contains the organs of reproduction. For females, these are the vagina, uterus, fallopian tubes, and ovaries. For males, the organs are the testes, epididymis, vas deferens, prostate, penis, and seminal vesicles. The genital and urinary tracts are combined into a singular tract because they share a common origin and use the same pathways, such as the male urethra for sperm and urine excretion.

Comparison of the Female and Male Genitourinary Tracts

Female Genitourinary Tract

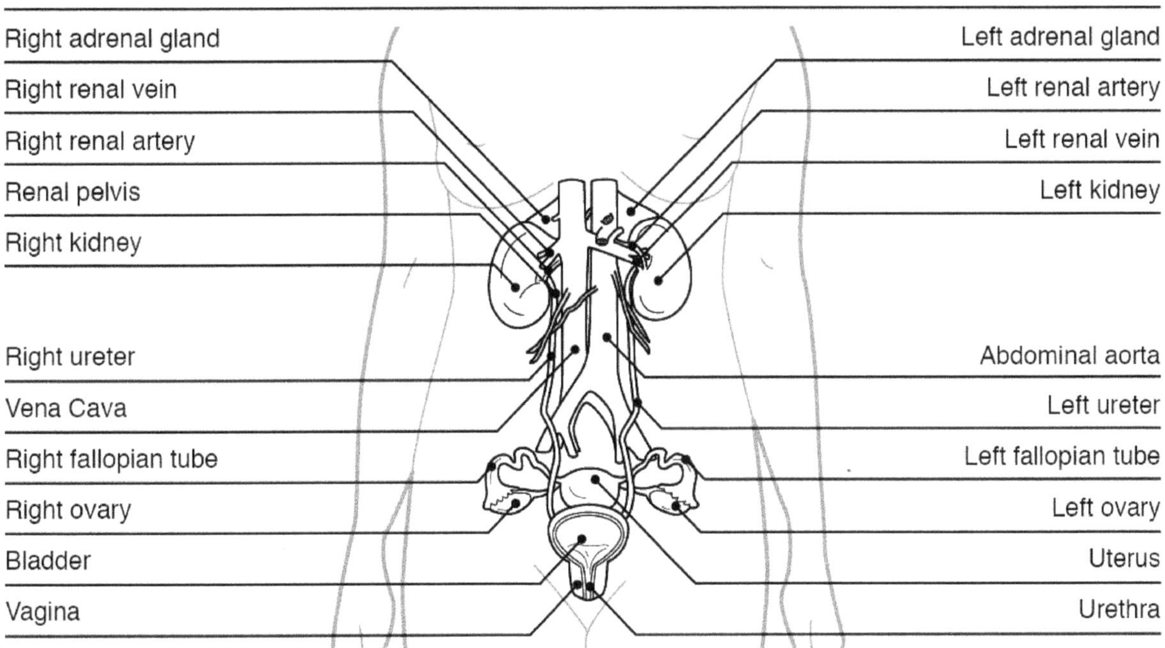

Male Genitourinary Tract

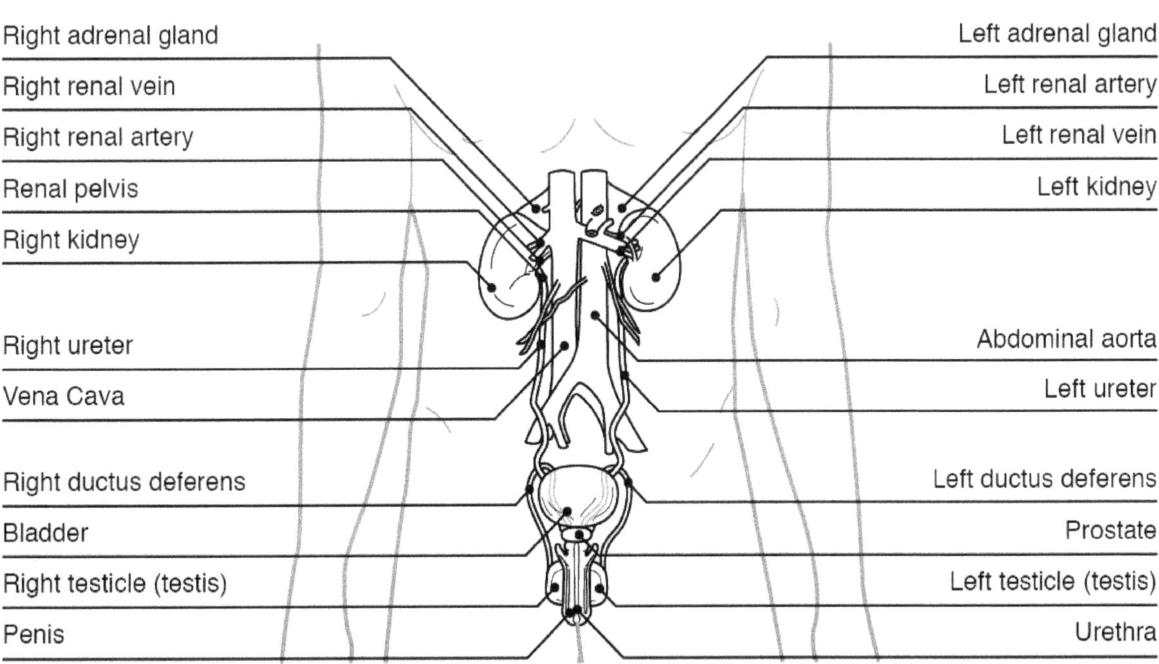

The function of the urinary system is to balance, filter, and regulate the body's levels of fluids, electrolytes, and metabolites, as well as eliminate waste and regulate blood volume, pressure, and acidity. In order to fully understand the potentially deadly emergencies of the genitourinary system, an EMT should know its anatomy and physiology.

Anatomy, Physiology, and Filtration Process of the Renal Tract

The **kidneys** are bean-shaped organs located on either side of the spinal column in the rear abdominal cavity within the retroperitoneal space. They are the organ involved in balancing electrolytes and water by filtering waste products from blood into urine. The **ureters** transport urine to the bladder. In a healthy individual, the kidneys receive anywhere from 12 to 30 percent of the body's systemic cardiac output.

The **nephrons** are the structural and functional units that act as filters and create urine. Each is composed of the **glomerulus**, the **glomerular (Bowman's) capsule**, the **proximal convoluted tubule**, the **loop of Henle**, and the **distal convoluted tubule**, which are illustrated in the following figure. A glomerulus is a cluster of capillaries that function as the main filter of blood that enters the kidney. The rate at which blood is filtered through the glomerulus is called the **glomerular filtration rate** (GFR). In the first step of filtration, blood moves from the **afferent arteriole** (the arteriole from the renal artery) into the capillaries of the glomerulus, causing the pressure to increase. As the pressure increases, fluid and solutes are forced from the glomerulus into the Bowman's capsule, a double-layered "cup" containing cells called **podocytes** that serve as filtration slits, allowing the filterable components of the blood to pass through the nephron.

Blood contains filterable and non-filterable components. Filterable components are water, nitrogenous waste, and nutrients. Non-filterable components—blood cells, platelets, and albumins—leave the glomerulus through the **efferent arteriole** (arteriole traveling away from the glomerulus). The filterable components form the glomerular filtrate, which passes through the various components of the nephron to eventually form urine.

After leaving the glomerulus, the filtrate passes through the proximal tubule into the loop of Henle, where water and electrolytes are reabsorbed. Following the loop of Henle, the filtrate enters the distal collecting duct (DCT) through the distal tubule. Antidiuretic hormone (ADH), secreted from the posterior pituitary gland, and aldosterone, secreted from the kidney, control the composition of the urine.

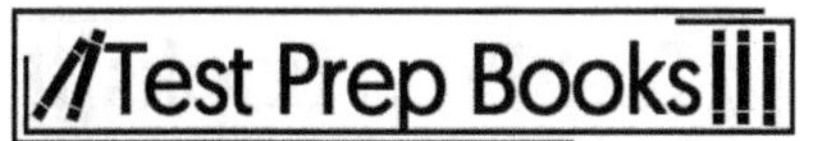

Aldosterone plays a key role in reabsorption of materials, and ADH contributes to water retention. Indeed, 99% of the filtrate is reabsorbed in the body, and the remaining 1% is released as urine.

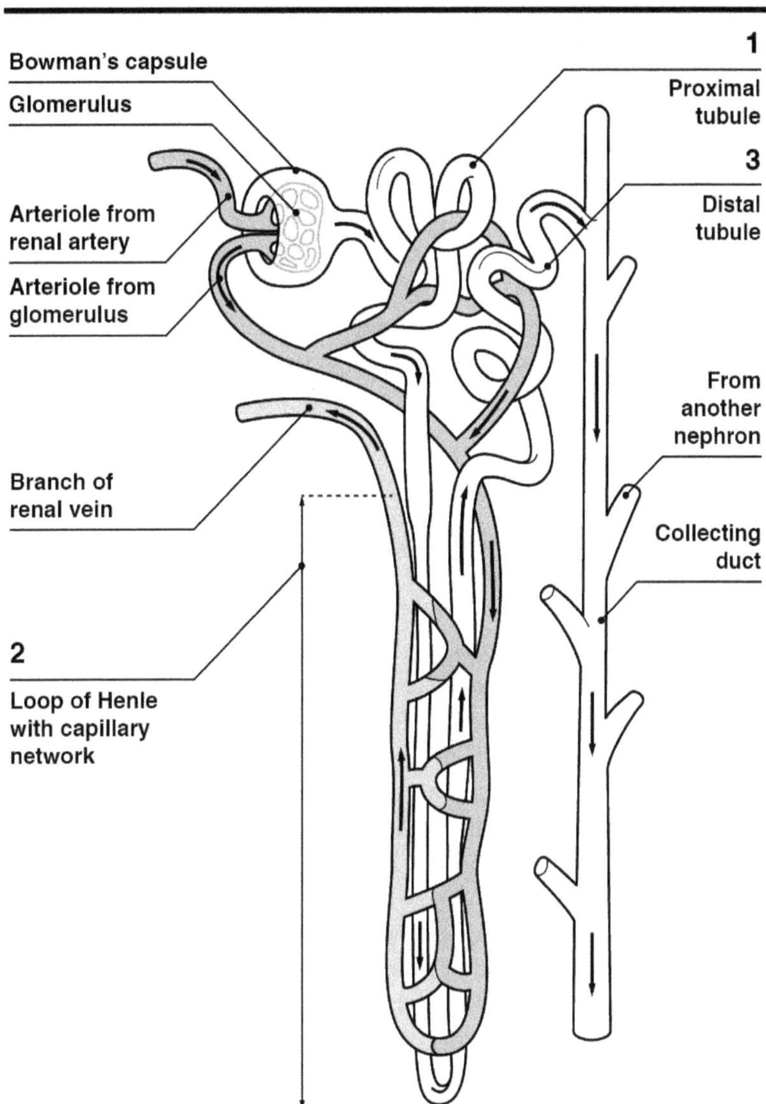

Once urine is formed, it enters the collecting ducts and passes through the calyces before proceeding to the renal pelvises and entering the ureters, which transport the urine to the bladder. The bladder holds urine until it's full. Signals from the brain prevent a person from urinating by contracting the external urinary sphincter until conditions to void are favorable.

Finally, once the external urinary sphincter is voluntarily relaxed, the urine enters the urethra—the final transport pathway for elimination.

Genitourinary Emergencies and Disorders

Genitourinary emergencies can be extremely dangerous if left untreated. The following list outlines the most common emergencies, their signs and symptoms, and the treatments an EMT can perform.

Urinary Tract Infections (UTI)

A UTI is an infection, usually within the urethra and bladder, that occurs when normal bacteria on the body's external surfaces, called **flora**, enter the urethra and multiply. Antibiotics are needed to kill the infection. Patients with a UTI may experience painful and frequent urination, or an urge to urinate when not necessary, as well as difficulty urinating. An EMT must support and maintain the patient's ABCs, take SAMPLE and OPQRST histories, and be prepared for the patient to experience nausea and vomiting. All patients should be transported to the hospital in a comfortable position.

Renal Calculi (Kidney Stones)

Kidney stones are solid crystalline masses that form in the renal pelvis of the kidney and become trapped anywhere along the urinary tract. They're created by an excess of insoluble salts and uric acid. A patient with kidney stones may present with severe pain in the side and back. This pain may spread to the lower abdomen and groin, causing a guarding of the abdomen, discolored urine, and symptoms of a UTI.

Acute Renal Failure (ARF)

Acute renal failure is characterized by a sudden decrease in filtration through the glomeruli of the nephron, causing toxins to accumulate in the blood. It occurs suddenly, usually over days or weeks. The condition is extremely dangerous and has a mortality rate of 50-80% in severe cases. If left untreated, it can lead to heart failure and metabolic acidosis. A patient experiencing ARF may present with a urine output of less than 500 mL/day (**oliguria**), complete cessation of urine production (**anuria**), as well as hypertension, tachycardia, pain and distention of the abdomen, altered mental status, and prolonged bleeding. Emergency medical services for ARF involve supporting and maintain ABCs, taking SAMPLE and OPQRST histories, placing the patient in the supine position, and preparing them for immediate transport to the hospital. Advanced life support (ALS) services may be required to provide IV fluids.

Chronic Renal Failure

Chronic renal failure is the progressive and irreversible loss of kidney function due to permanent damage to nephrons. Occurring over a period of months, CRF leads to the development of systemic complications that can cause death, including **uremia** (fluid, hormonal, and electrolyte imbalances), **azotemia** (abnormally high levels of blood nitrogen), pericarditis, and pulmonary edema. Signs and symptoms of CRF include an altered mental status, swelling of the feet and ankles, nausea and vomiting, hypotension, and tachycardia. Emergency medical care is similar to patients with ARF. Advanced life support (ALS) services may be needed to provide IV fluids to correct electrolyte imbalances.

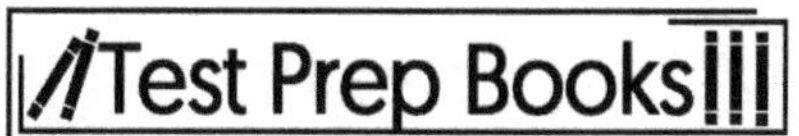

Gynecology and Obstetrics

Gynecology is the study, protection, and maintenance of female reproductive health. **Obstetrics** is the study of birth and delivery. These branches of medicine are confluent and are treated as one study by practicing physicians.

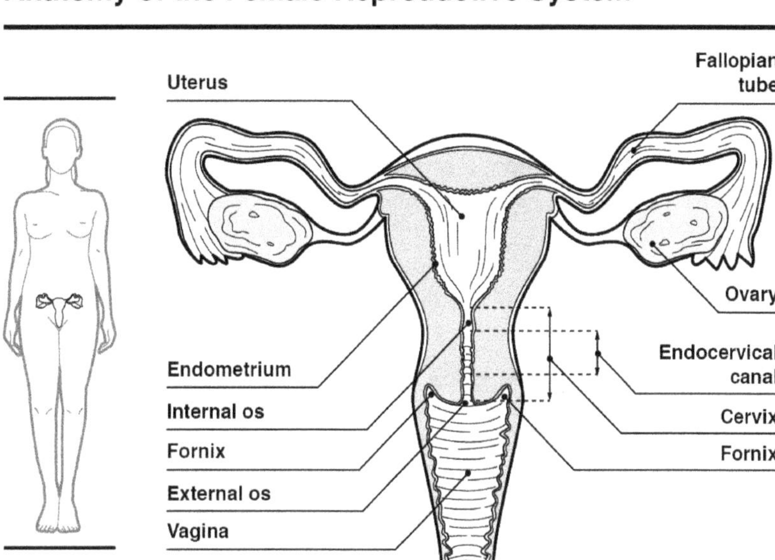

As with all diseases, it's helpful for an EMT to have a general understanding of female anatomy, which is illustrated above. The **vagina**, the canal involved in sexual intercourse and birth, is the opening at the bottom end of the birth canal and contains **Bartholin glands**, which secrete mucus to lubricate the vagina. The uterine opening to the birth canal is called the **cervix**. The **ovaries** are the primary female reproductive organs and are considered glands. They regulate the menstrual cycle and contain **follicles** that produce, at regular intervals, an **ovum** (egg), which, when fertilized by the sperm, eventually develops into a fetus. The **fallopian tubes** are vessels that transport the ovum to the **uterus** (the muscular organ that houses the embryo and contracts during labor), which is where fertilization takes place. There is one fallopian tube per ovary.

Gynecological emergencies can be fatal. If one is suspected, the most important thing an EMT can do is support and maintain the ABCs, and transport the patient to the hospital as quickly as possible. In addition to potential life-threatening diseases, a gynecological emergency call may include rape and sexual assault.

There is a specific protocol an EMT must perform regarding a woman's health, which is described below:

- Assess the scene: Determine if the scene is safe and if assistance is necessary. Identify the type of call (either a medical call or trauma call), the number of patients, and whether standard precautions have been taken. It's also important to note where the patient has been found. Identify the overall appearance of the patient. Note if she is conscious, if there are any obvious life threats, her emotional state, difficulty breathing, any signs of injury, and the position in which she was found.

- Protect and assess the patient: Ask any people not involved in the incident to leave the area to maintain the patient's privacy. Evaluate the patient's overall appearance, especially in the abdomen, noting any bruises, stretch marks, surgical scarring, swollen or distended abdomen, or needle tracks. Palpate the abdomen, starting at the quadrant farther from the pain. Expedite transport if the patient is bleeding, as this may be a sign of shock.

- Obtain medical history and details of the incident, if possible: Determine the MOI (mechanism of injury) or the NOI (nature of illness) and the patient's chief complaint. If the patient is bleeding excessively, be certain to obtain their gynecological history. Ask the patient if there is any possibility that she is pregnant and what kind of contraception she uses, if any. Inquire about the patient's obstetrics gravida, para, and abortion (GPA) history, including the number of times (if any) that the patient has been pregnant, given birth, and had an abortion, respectively.

- Treat the patient: If the patient is bleeding vaginally and there are signs of shock, treat it as shock. The patient may not show signs of shock, so it's important to check for a rapid or a weak pulse and skin that is sweaty, cool, or pale. Use sanitary pads externally to soak up blood, noting the number used. Place the patient in the supine position and administer oxygen. Place the patient on her left side if she is pregnant. Maintain and support ABCs. Prepare the patient for transport to the hospital. While en route, pay attention to the status of the patient by noting any improvement or decline, while consistently checking vitals.

Gynecological Emergencies

Ectopic Pregnancy

An ectopic pregnancy occurs when a fertilized oocyte (egg) is implanted outside of the uterus, typically within one of the fallopian tubes. It's extremely dangerous, as it may lead to rupture of the tube if not caught. Signs and symptoms of an ectopic pregnancy include generalized pain on one side of the abdomen, vaginal bleeding, a distended and swollen abdomen, and signs of shock. Ectopic pregnancy should be suspected if the woman reports a missed menstrual period and these signs are present. EMT care includes treating the patient for shock, supporting and maintaining ABCs, and transporting the patient on their left side (left lateral recumbent). It's also imperative never to give the patient anything by mouth and to keep the patient warm.

Pelvic Inflammatory Disease

Pelvic inflammatory disease (PID) is an inflammation of the fallopian tubes and the surrounding tissues of the pelvis, including the uterus and ovaries. It's the most common reason a woman will call for emergency medical services and is caused by organisms entering the uterus through the cervix. It occurs primarily in sexually active women, but may also be caused by the use of an intrauterine device (IUD). STDs are the main cause of PID, especially untreated chlamydia. PID is a serious condition that can lead to ovarian abscesses and scarring of the fallopian tubes, which can result in ectopic pregnancies. There's

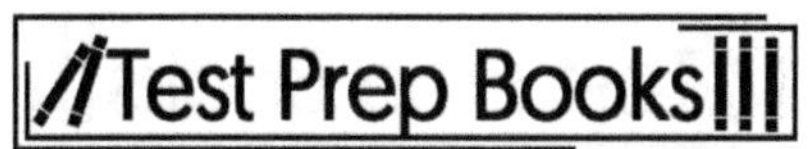

not much care that an EMT can administer for a patient that presents with PID, but an EMT can assess the patient and determine if there's abdominal pain during or after menstruation and if there are signs of peritoneal irritation. The EMT should also obtain SAMPLE and OPQRST histories and transport her comfortably and gently to a hospital.

Ovarian Cysts, Torsion, and Abscesses

An **ovarian** *cyst* is an extraordinarily painful condition caused by fluid-filled sacs on or within the ovary. If the cyst doesn't resolve, it may grow to a significant size and cause ovarian torsion, resulting in extreme lower abdominal pain that may present with nausea and vomiting. A **tubo-ovarian abscess** occurs when the fallopian tubes and ovaries are blocked by a large, infectious mass. Signs and symptoms of ovarian cysts may also include a dull, achy pain in the lower back and legs; breast tenderness; and painful menstruation.

If an ovarian cyst doesn't resolve, it may rupture. Signs and symptoms of a ruptured cyst include sharp pain in the lower abdomen, dizziness, weakness, and loss of consciousness. A patient with a tubo-ovarian abscess may present with severe abdominal pain, guarding of the abdomen, nausea and vomiting, fever, and abdominal distention. EMT care for an ovarian cyst and a tubo-ovarian abscess is the same as an ectopic pregnancy, while patients with ovarian torsion should be given an IV for pain medication and dehydration.

Sexually Transmitted Diseases

A sexually transmitted disease (STD) is a disease or infection transmitted through sexual contact. If a sexually transmitted disease is suspected, EMT treatment requires the administration of oxygen and an IV line, controlling any bleeding, and administering analgesics and antiemetics.

There are many kinds of STDs, the most common of which are listed below:

- **Bacterial vaginosis**: An overgrowth of bacteria in the vagina that may cause itching, burning, and a foul, "fishy" smell. If left untreated, it can lead to premature birth and PID. It's generally treated with metronidazole.

- **Chlamydia**: A disease caused by the **Chlamydia trachomatis** bacterium. Signs and symptoms include pain in the lower abdomen and back pain during intercourse, and/or bleeding between periods. It's also the STD most likely to cause PID.

- **Genital herpes**: An infection of the genitals, buttocks, or anal area characterized by sores and small red bumps that may blister. Herpes is caused by the herpes simplex virus and is divided into two categories based on the location: Type I is found on the lips and mouth, and Type II is found on the genitals.

- **Gonorrhea**: A disease acquired through the *Neisseria gonorrhoeae* bacterium. Signs and symptoms, which occur 2-10 days after exposure, may present as painful urination, burning or itching, and a yellowish or bloody vaginal discharge.

Sexual Assault

Sexual assault is any sexual activity that occurs without the consent of the recipient, the most common of which is rape, or forced sexual intercourse. An EMT should expect police involvement with sexual assault calls. When responding to a call, it's important to ask the patient if she would be more comfortable with a male or female EMT and to be cognizant of the patient's privacy, taking a very brief survey and history. It is *especially* important to preserve evidence, discouraging the patient from taking any actions that should undermine or destroy evidence. When assessing the patient, a paramedic must make a written observation her emotional state, the condition of her clothes, and any obvious injuries. It's imperative that an EMT remains nonjudgmental and compassionate.

Obstetric Emergencies

An obstetric emergency typically presents itself in the form of a field delivery. A **field delivery** means that an infant is birthed outside of a medical facility. If a field delivery seems inevitable, an EMT should wear the appropriate protective equipment, such as gloves, a gown, and eye protection. When assessing a patient in an obstetric emergency, an EMT will need to determine if the patient is in active labor or if delivery is certain. Signs of trauma or injury and observations of any drug paraphernalia or liquor bottles are necessary to ascertain the possibility of fetal alcohol syndrome.

Once the scene and patient have been assessed, an EMT may proceed to general supportive care, including maintaining and supporting ABCs, taking SAMPLE and OPQRST histories, and remaining alert for any signs of shock.

Labor/Normal Deliveries

Once labor has initiated, it cannot be prevented or slowed. A woman experiencing labor will present with a firm abdomen, a need to push or bear down, or crowning, which is when the head is visible at the opening of the vagina. An EMT should adhere to the following procedure for delivering a baby:

- Inform the patient that she will be giving birth outside of a hospital. Be calm and reassuring, protecting her privacy as much as possible. Someone should be watching the mother during the entire process.

- Place the patient in a comfortable position on a firm, flat surface on top of sterile sheets, supporting her head, neck, and back with pillows or blankets. She can have her feet flat on the surface/floor with her knees spread apart. She may be more comfortable on her side or in another position. Allow this if it is safe and the EMT can deliver the infant with the mother in this position.

- Constantly watch for crowning, as women who have given birth before may experience a speedy labor and delivery and their perineum can tear. Time the frequency and the length of the contractions. Once the head is crowning, put off transporting the patient until the infant is delivered. Transport to the hospital during delivery should only occur if the EMT is not confident in their ability to assist with delivering the baby.

- While wearing sterile gloves, be sure to suction the mouth and nose of the infant with a bulb syringe once it starts to emerge. Ensure that the umbilical cord isn't wrapped around the infant's neck, and guide the head downward to help the shoulders emerge. Be sure to carefully support the infant's body during the delivery; the body will be slippery.

- Once the neonate has fully emerged, dry the infant and keep it warm. Using a warm blanket, wrap the baby, making sure the top of the head is covered with only the face uncovered. Stimulate the newborn to breathe, if it isn't already, by positioning its head above its body, vigorously rubbing its back, buttocks, or feet. If breathing does not begin 15-30 seconds after delivery, or the infant's heart rate doesn't get above 60 beats per minute, administer 100% oxygen with a BVM. CPR must be performed by two EMTs using a 3:1 ratio of compressions to

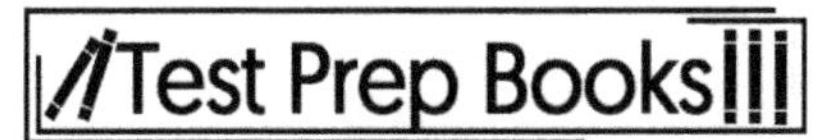

ventilation, with 120 total actions per minute. One EMT will provide ventilation, while the other will perform chest compressions using the hand-encircling technique. If infant death or stillbirth has occurred, do not attempt to resuscitate.

- After the newborn has been warmed, dry, and is breathing, place the infant on the mother's chest. Record the sex and the time of delivery. Obtain height, weight, and head circumference of the infant, if possible, as well as an APGAR score. Once the infant has been delivered, prepare to transport the patient, being alert for a possible need to deliver the placenta.

Labor/Abnormal Deliveries

Occasionally, an EMT may encounter an abnormal delivery. Some of these complications are life-threatening to the mother and the infant, and may result in the inability to deliver the child in the field, so patient transport must be rapid and careful.

If there's a fluid-filled sac instead of an infant's head at crowning, it is considered an unruptured amniotic sac. An EMT must puncture it by pinching and twisting the sac until fluid runs out, suctioning the nose and mouth as soon as the head emerges.

In a **breech delivery**, the buttocks of the baby are shown at crowning instead of the head, putting the infant at great risk of trauma. The EMT should call for advanced life support (ALS) and contact medical control. Breech deliveries are typically slow, allowing time for transport to the hospital. However, the baby must be delivered if the buttocks have already emerged from the vagina. The baby's buttocks and legs should spontaneously deliver, and the body must be supported. In order to keep the infant from suffocating, the EMT can make a "V" with their fingers and insert them into the vagina to create an airway. If a complete delivery doesn't occur, the EMT should transport the patient to the hospital immediately while holding their fingers in the vagina in order to ensure the baby is able to breathe until delivery is possible.

A **nuchal cord** occurs when the umbilical cord is wrapped around the newborn's throat, which can lead to strangling and suffocation. If the cord cannot be slipped over the head and shoulder, the EMT must clamp the cord in two places approximately two inches apart, make a cut between the clamps, unwrap the cord, and continue with delivery as usual.

Both **limb presentation** and **prolapse of the umbilical cord** require immediate transport to a hospital with the mother in a hips-up, head-down position. In the case of a prolapsed umbilical cord, her feet should be raised 6 to 12 inches and a pillow should be placed under her hips. If an arm, leg, or foot presents instead of the head, the EMT must cover the limb with a sterile towel. If the umbilical cord presents itself outside of the vagina before delivery, the umbilical cord should not be pushed back into the vagina, but instead, the infant's head should be gently pushed away from the cord, which should be covered with a sterile towel dampened with saline, and high-flow oxygen must be administered.

A **spontaneous abortion**, also known as a miscarriage, occurs when the fetus dies and is delivered before the 20th week of gestation. The EMT must maintain and support the mother's ABCs and prepare her for immediate transport to the hospital. If the patient is bleeding, treatment for shock may be expected. The EMT will need to cover the vagina with a sterile pad and collect any expulsions from the vagina, without ever pulling the tissue, while constantly monitoring the patient and taking serial vitals.

Practice Questions

1. Difficulty speaking, loss of speech, difficulty understanding speech, and weakness or numbness in the face and limbs, particularly on one side of the body, are signs and symptoms of which of the following emergencies?
   a. Seizures
   b. Hypothyroidism
   c. Stroke
   d. Cushing's syndrome

2. Which of the following procedures must an EMT perform at every emergency call?

   I. Support and maintain ABCs

   II. Attempt to obtain SAMPLE and OPQRST histories

   III. Treat for shock

   IV. Quickly apply a tourniquet

   a. Choice I only
   b. Choices I and II
   c. Choices I, II, and IV
   d. All of the above

3. A type of abdominal pain caused by stimulation of an organ's nerve fibers due to stretching of the organ's wall is referred to as which of the following?
   a. Visceral pain
   b. Parietal pain
   c. Referred pain
   d. Somatic pain

4. A 22-year-old male patient presents with pain in the lower-right quadrant of the abdomen. Which of the following is the likeliest cause of the pain?
   a. Kidney stones
   b. Food poisoning
   c. Appendicitis
   d. Urinary tract infection

5. Which of the following is NOT a step that should be followed when performing an abdominal exam?
   a. Ask the patient to identify the location of the pain.
   b. Lay the patient down in a prone position.
   c. Palpate the abdomen by pressing on the unaffected areas first.
   d. Inspect for changes in skin color.

See answers on the next page.

Answer Explanations

1. C: Stroke is caused by a loss of brain function, leading to difficulty speaking, loss of speech, difficulty understanding speech, and weakness or numbness in the face and limbs, particularly on one side of the body. Signs and symptoms of seizures include convulsions and muscle rigidity, so Choice *A* is false. Hypothyroidism is characterized by fatigue, lethargy, slow mental function, and waxy appearance, making Choice *B* incorrect. Cushing's syndrome is associated with weight gain and fat accumulation; therefore, Choice *D* is false.

2. B: An EMT must always check, support, and maintain a patient's airway, breathing, and circulation, as well as inquire about medical history and events leading to the emergency, making Choice *B* the correct answer. Not all emergency medical situations will result in shock, nor will a tourniquet always be necessary.

3. A: Visceral pain is caused by stimulation to an organ's nerve fibers due to stretching of the organ's wall, so Choice *A* is the correct answer. Parietal pain is caused by irritation to the parietal peritoneal wall, making Choice *B* false. Referred pain occurs when a radiating pain is felt elsewhere than the point of origin, so Choice *C* is also false. Somatic pain is caused by injury to the bones, muscles, skin, and connective tissues, making *D* incorrect as well.

4. C: The organs found in the lower-right quadrant of the abdomen are the appendix, small intestine, and female reproductive organs. Kidney stones are felt more in the back and side, as the kidneys are located in the retroperitoneal space, making Choice *A* false. Food poisoning is usually felt in the stomach and intestinal area and usually presents with nausea, vomiting, and diarrhea; therefore, Choice *B* is incorrect. The urinary bladder isn't found in the lower-right quadrant of the abdomen, so Choice *D* is incorrect. A key symptom of appendicitis is pain in the lower-right quadrant, making Choice *C* the correct answer.

5. B: The only way that an EMT can perform an abdominal exam is with the patient lying face up, known as supine position. Having the patient lie prone, or face down, makes an abdominal exam impossible, so Choice *B* is the correct answer. Every other choice is correct for the appropriate way to perform an abdominal exam.

Operations

Maintain Vehicle and Equipment Readiness

EMTs use a variety of vehicles to respond to an emergency, including fire engines, ambulances, and air transport. Some volunteer EMTs even utilize their personal vehicles. No matter the type, the vehicles must be fully functional and able to respond at a moment's notice. This readiness requires consistent and ongoing maintenance.

Communications Readiness

Radio equipment readiness is vital to the safety and operations of EMTs, so that they can communicate with each other and with the dispatching unit.

Equipment Readiness

Preparation entails ensuring that each vehicle is fully equipped with the designated proper inventory. Organizations use a daily ambulance inspection checklist to verify that the appropriate equipment, medications, and supplies are present. The checklist highlights items under the following categories:

- Airway management
- Suction
- Personal protection
- Patient assessment/diagnostic measurements
- Immobilization
- Cardiac management/care
- Obstetrics and gynecology
- Bleeding control and wound management
- Vehicle and receiving facility communication
- Medications
- Transport

The table below provides an example of the types of equipment and supplies needed for services. This list is not all inclusive and is only intended to provide a sample inventory of items.

Category	Equipment or Supply Examples
Airway Management	Pocket masks, bag valve masks, oxygen units, portable oxygen tanks
Suction	Wide bore tubing, bulb suction for infants with saline drops, suction aspirator
Personal Protection	Eye and face protection, disposable gloves, fluid resistant gowns or overalls, disposable biohazard bags for non-sharp waste bags
Patient Assessment/Diagnostic Measurements	Pulse oximeters for pediatric and adult patients, blood pressure cuffs in all sizes, patient care flashlights, scissors to cut clothing
Cardiac Management/Care	Defibrillator with age-appropriate pads

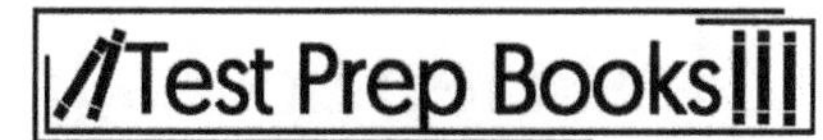

Category	Equipment or Supply Examples
Obstetrics and Gynecology	Sterile obstetrical kit that includes towels, 4x4 dressings, bulb suction, sterile gloves, cord clamps and ties, blanket, thermal absorbent blanket and head cover, heat-reflective material to cover infant
Bleeding Control and Wound Management	Sterile gauze in multiple sizes, gauze rolls, occlusive dressings, sterile water, hypoallergenic and regular adhesive tape
Vehicle and Receiving Facility Communication	Two-way radio frequency communication equipment
Medications	Approved medications such as activated charcoal, Acetaminophen, Albuterol, Aspirin, Diazepam, Epinephrine HCL, Fentanyl, Glucagon, IV electrolyte solutions, Nitroglycerin, Nitrous oxide, Oxytocin, and Sodium bicarbonate
Transport	Pillows, towels, sheets, blankets, stretchers, gurneys, stabilizing instruments
Immobilization	Backboards, cervical collars, head immobilizers, splints
Other Equipment	Continuous positive airway pressure (CPAP) equipment, nebulizer, advanced airways, intravenous (IV) solutions, fluid bag pole or roof hook

Standards and Guidelines

The **Occupational Safety and Health Administration (OSHA)** provides input for ambulance standards, and protects workers by ensuring their work environments are safe. Thus, along with the **National Institute for Occupational Safety and Health (NIOSH)**, they have equipment inventories that identify items such as those listed in the table above.

The **Commission on Accreditation of Ambulance Services (CAAS)** supports efforts to enhance the quality of patient care within the medical transportation system. This committee set many standards for the ambulance industry. Agencies with accreditation by CAAS meet a "gold standard" set by the ambulance service industry.

The agency or organization for which an EMT works will have a protocol that must be followed to ensure proper vehicle and equipment readiness. Additional guidelines may also exist for the city, county, or ambulance district regarding the medications, equipment, and supplies that an ambulance carries. Many of these guidelines require that vehicles remain ready for service and able to respond to the scene of an emergency at any given time.

Vehicle Maintenance

Vehicles should undergo regular cleaning to reduce the growth or spread of contaminants or communicable diseases. EMTs should utilize only approved solutions and practices to clean vehicle surfaces, such as floors and walls.

Next, all vehicles must have a vehicle safety and mechanical inspection. The table below provides a list of common areas that appear on the checklists for a ground ambulance vehicle inspection and mechanical inspection. A failure in any of these items could create problems in transporting patients and EMT staff during emergencies.

Item	Description
Engine	Ensure that it will start
Battery	Review the battery's charge status, fluid level, and connections
Sirens	Ensure that sirens are audible and functional
Transmission Fluid	Review the fluid level and condition
Power Steering Fluid	Review the fluid level, hose condition, and connections
Brakes	Individually assess the parking and vehicle brake systems to provide a review of fluid levels, condition, and any instance of leaks or wear
Tail Lights	Ensure both tail lights are operational
Headlights	Ensure all headlights are operational
Clearance Lights	Ensure all clearance lights are operational
Emergency Lights	Ensure emergency lights are functional and rotational
Horn	Ensure the vehicle and air horn are functioning correctly
Tires	Ensure all tires have even wear, adequate tread, and are properly inflated
Wheel Bearings	Ensure wheel bearings are properly adjusted and lubricated
Chassis Frame	Ensure vehicle components are secured to chassis frame, wiring is correctly installed, and all interfaces follow established regulatory guidelines for the style of vehicle in use
Suspension System	Check the shocks, springs, and stabilizer bars
Heating System	Ensure the heating system is functioning, particularly in cold climates
Air Conditioning System	Ensure the cooling system is functioning, especially in hot climates
Fuel Level	Ensure there is an adequate fuel supply
Drive	Ensure the vehicle is able to safely and adequately handle and travel roadways

Operating Emergency Vehicles

The emergency medical technician is responsible for operating emergency vehicles in response to emergency situations, as well as for assisting with non-emergency calls, including those calls seeking transport of patients from hospitals to their home. Non-emergency transportation may also include movement of patients from a local facility to a larger medical center or to a long-term rehab facility.

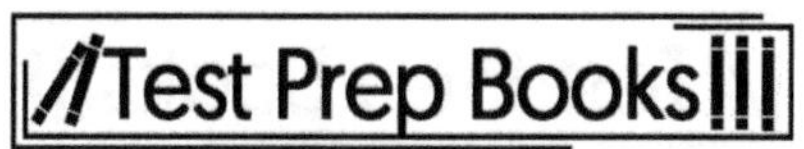

Emergency vehicles are at an increased risk for being involved in accidents. Common roadway distractions (i.e., cell phones, loud radios, other technology) directly impact how engaged other drivers are on the road and affect how other drivers respond to emergency vehicles. Additionally, many newer vehicles diminish roadway noise, including sirens, which also contributes to the risk that emergency vehicles face. Intersection collisions are among the most common types of crashes that ambulance drivers encounter. Accidents frequently occur when there are multiple-vehicle responses, as non-EMT drivers are not expecting a second or third emergency vehicle.

The inherent function of an emergency vehicle, which often involves traveling at high speeds along an unfamiliar route in a heavy vehicle, poses significant risks in itself. Establishing strategic routes, noting heavy traffic areas and heavy traffic times, and identifying the best route before departure can effectively reduce confusion or anxiety during travel. Driving makes up one component of teamwork among EMTs. The driver's focus should be on the road, while the team member riding in the passenger seat utilizes various forms of technology to assist with travel (i.e., GPS, phones, radio communication, or laptops). The passenger team member can use travel time to gain additional information about the emergency call from dispatch personnel. Drivers must follow the laws of the road to reduce the risk of creating another dangerous scenario. This effort includes maintaining a safe distance between the vehicle and other vehicles on the road and appropriately utilizing the vehicle's lights and sirens. This compliance also includes ensuring that the driver and passengers in the front and back of the vehicle always wear seatbelts.

Providing Scene Leadership

Scene safety is imperative during an emergency. Often, the EMT leader plays a crucial role in determining scene safety and how to proceed in safe and unsafe environments. Therefore, it is important to identify who will serve as lead EMT before arriving at the scene of an emergency. This essential step promotes efficiency and reduces the danger of miscommunication and errors.

The Lead EMT

The lead EMT will give direction at the scene, ensuring safety for the patient and the EMT team. Monitoring progress of multiple teams of emergency personnel may fall to the leader to manage. This also serves to organize and streamline vital actions that the EMT team takes when assisting the patient. When operating in a small team, the lead EMT may also be responsible for necessary procedures, such as conducting the patient assessment or interviewing witnesses. However, he or she may need to encourage collaboration and exchange of ideas at the scene while also carrying out life-sustaining operations, such as assisting with airway management.

Team Members

Team members should follow the direction of their leader, knowing that each member has a designated role in reducing further risk to the patient. Not only must each member perform their role with proficiency and efficiency, but each member must understand the importance of collaboration and coordination of their efforts with others who are responding to the scene.

During emergency calls, EMTs not only function as a member of a small team or a group of multiple EMT teams, but EMTs can also participate as team members who are supporting other emergency service responders.

EMTs must have an understanding of the roles of each responder at the scene. Other response agencies, including the police and fire departments, may arrive on the site in the case of an emergency. Collaboration is key during these instances.

Assessing the Scene

Upon arrival at the scene, EMTs must quickly assess the environment around them to determine if hazards exist that may create additional challenges for the patient or responders. Examples of hazards include:

- Downed power lines
- Fuel spills
- Chemical spills
- Individual(s) carrying weapons
- Traffic volume
- Signs of fighting
- Aggressive animals
- Darkness or unusual silence in a home

If a scene is not safe, EMTs do not have to initiate rescue actions on behalf of the patient until the environment is safe enough for them to enter. Next, the EMTs should look for indicators of what caused the emergency situation. For example, a patient next to a downed power line may indicate that the patient was electrocuted.

Scene Management

Scene management includes having the capacity to address multiple emergencies as they are unfolding in adverse conditions. EMTs must demonstrate organization and proactivity in swiftly establishing and sustaining scene safety, for rapid stabilization and transport of the patient. Upon arrival at the scene, after assessing their surroundings for any security risks that might impact both the patient and EMT staff, as noted above, EMTs must assess the number of patients requiring attention. Once additional help arrives, EMTs should not leave the scene until the lead EMT gives approval to exit. Leaving a scene before confirming a departure has been permitted can create risk for negligence or abandonment.

Positioning the Vehicle

The positioning of the vehicle at the scene has a significant role in how well EMTs can deliver patient care. Also, the positioning of the vehicle directly impacts the safety of the scene. Positioning vehicles in the emergency lane or on a blocked road supports scene safety. This practice allows for traffic to continue moving in other lanes at a slower pace and may allow for other emergency vehicles to easily arrive on the scene or exit the scene. The goal is to not hamper rescue or treatment efforts.

Sometimes, it may be necessary to utilize a vehicle as a barricade to protect EMT and other emergency personnel on the scene. Barricading is ideal if one is driving a larger vehicle, rather than a smaller one such as a van. The wheels of a vehicle should be in a position that allow for it to roll away from EMT personnel during a rescue event, should the vehicle be struck by traffic.

Emergency vehicles should always be visible to others approaching. Therefore, operators of emergency vehicles should select a convenient place to park—one that presents the least amount of danger or risk

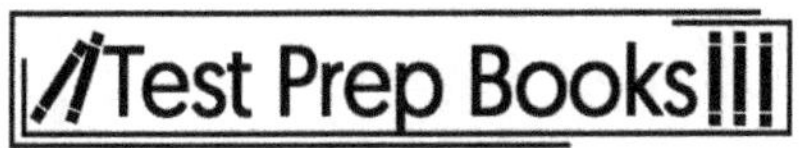

to others. Vehicles may require movement to another area. If the movement of a vehicle is required, it is necessary that the operator ensures the occupants are safe inside the vehicle. Once again, passengers must wear seatbelts.

Lighting

Caution is a must for EMT personnel when using headlights after sunset. Headlights facing oncoming traffic can blind the driver coming in the opposite direction and pose a risk for further injury. Also, some studies indicate that red revolving beacons may inadvertently attract intoxicated or exhausted drivers. It is recommended that headlights be shut off, and the amber rear-sealed beam blinkers be used to alert drivers that the vehicle is stopped.

Engaging Bystanders

During an emergency event, family, friends, witnesses, and other bystanders are often present. EMTs should show empathy, but also be careful to not break a patient's confidentiality or privacy while rendering care. EMTs may provide an explanation of what is happening, but must be mindful to not create privacy issues.

Violent Activity at Unsecured Scenes

Violence is a challenging problem that EMTs and other **emergency medical service (EMS)** personnel will likely encounter at some point. It is highly possible that an EMT may arrive at an active crime scene that the telecommunicator did not initially detect or identify. EMTs must report an active crime scene to the telecommunications center upon identification of this situation. EMTs should not remain at an active crime scene if the offender is still present, as this can pose a threat to their safety. Instead, EMTs should retreat from an unsafe scene until it is safe. Often, this requires collaboration with law enforcement teams. When possible and safe to do so, the EMT team should take the patient with them.

Crime Scenes and Preserving Evidence

EMTs should exercise caution and limit their disturbance of a crime scene, as their actions could compromise an active investigation by law enforcement. Adhering to this practice may mean a brief discussion with EMT personnel to determine how they will enter the crime scene and how many workers at a given time will assist in treating or removing the victim(s).

Hazardous Materials

EMTs will confront incidents in which a single hazardous substance or multiple hazardous materials are present. **The Institute of Hazardous Materials Management (IHMM)** defines **hazardous materials** as any biological, chemical, radiological, or physical agent that can potentially harm animals, humans, and the environment alone or in combination with another substance. OSHA generalizes this definition, identifying that a hazardous material consists of a chemical or substance that presents itself as a physical or health hazard. These substances are detrimental to an individual's health if released (e.g., as a result of spillage, leakage, pouring, emission, disposal, dumping, etc.).

EMTs' Involvement in Hazardous Events

Hazmat (hazardous material) events are dangerous and can impact both the victim and the EMTs arriving on the scene. There are instances in which the EMT will not know that there are hazardous materials in the area. An abundance of alertness and caution should be exercised in scenes where details of what caused the emergency are limited or unknown.

Motor Vehicle Accidents

Materials may be released before the arrival of EMTs, just as they are approaching the scene, or as care is taking place. An example of this is a response to a motor vehicle accident in which one of the vehicles involved is transporting hazardous materials.

Sick Person or Inexplicable Collapse

Initial reports may be vague, such as reporting that someone is sick or collapsed, without providing further details.

Suicide Attempts

EMTs may be at risk of exposure to hazardous materials during suicide attempts when carbon monoxide or gas asphyxiation may have been used by the victim.

Civil Disturbance

EMTs may have to respond to a civil disturbance in which hazardous materials were used, such as drugs or other chemicals. Signs of hazardous materials may not be obvious, or there may be a delay in reactions, or a secondary release.

Although some events will only impact a small group of people, other events will be widespread in nature, leading to a loss of multiple lives. Upon arrival at the scene, hazardous materials signs and vehicles should serve as a warning of the presence of a hazmat team.

EMTs are not necessarily expected to "manage" the hazardous event. They may, however, have an active role in notifying other people of the event and assisting in the overall control of the scene itself. EMS agencies have a responsibility to ensure staff has adequate training and can effectively engage other agencies that may arrive on the scene.

Role of the EMT at a Hazmat Event

First responders to a hazardous scene must complete basic, vital steps. The role of the EMT at a hazmat event is to complete the following tasks:

- Assess for environmental activities and the potential effect on patient care
- Assess the adequacy of available resources
- Notify the proper authorities

If the EMT is the only one on the scene upon discovering a hazardous material, proper notification of various authorities is essential. Necessary notifications include:

- Law enforcement
- Fire department
- Hazardous materials response personnel
- Public works
- Water and sewer department (for runoff)

Ideally, EMTs should park uphill from leaking hazards and one-hundred feet from wreckage. They should set the parking brake to reduce the risk for rollaway accidents involving the emergency vehicle.

Collaborative Operations with the Hazardous Materials Team

EMTs will process personnel who wear protective chemical clothing through medical evaluation before and after decontamination duties. Decontamination must occur to prevent the contamination of others beyond the scene. It is important to note that EMTs should not transport a patient without first ensuring decontamination has taken place. Isolation of the victim is critical until he or she undergoes an evaluation and is eligible for transport or release.

Zones of Operation for EMTs

EMTs operate within what is known as the **cold zone**—the space in which there is no contact with hazardous materials. The **warm zone** duties fall to those specialists capable of performing the decontamination procedure. Meanwhile, hazmat officials function within the actual **hot zone**.

An EMT's Role in a Hazardous Materials Emergency

Conditions that EMTs will commonly treat at the scene of a hazardous materials emergency include:

- Airway injuries related to thermal or chemical burns
- Poison ingestion
- Chemical and biological exposure
- Lacerations or punctures associated with projectiles
- Frostbite

EMT leadership means being able to react at a moment's notice, should the safety of the scene suddenly decline. The lead EMT's concern is not only for the safety of the patient, but also for the safety of other EMTs.

Standard Precautions

EMTs should follow standard patient precautions once the scene is secure. When working with patients, wearing gloves is essential, as doing so reduces the risk of spreading communicable diseases. Handwashing protocol also remains in place.

Protective eyewear may be necessary in cases where blood or other bodily fluids are present. A **high-efficiency particulate air filter (HEPA) mask** may also be an option if an EMT confronts a patient who is coughing, which can spread an airborne illness such as tuberculosis.

Finally, EMTs should maintain their personal immunization records and routine health examinations. This self-care contributes to the EMT's ability to remain healthy and able to work during emergency situations, and prevents patients from contracting disease from the responder.

Air Medical Service

Air medical service utilization takes place for medical, operational, and rescue reasons. If an EMT participates in supporting air medical transport, he or she should be familiar with the local protocol. For example, helicopter transports require the availability of a 100 × 100 foot area free of wires, trees, people, and other loose objects in order to land. This clearance must also be free of slopes with angles greater than eight degrees. Helicopters have very specific areas where it is safe to approach them, and therefore, EMTs should familiarize themselves with the danger areas of a helicopter, for instance, the tail rotor. The helicopter crew will direct patient loading, and EMT staff should follow the guidance of the helicopter crew during this operation.

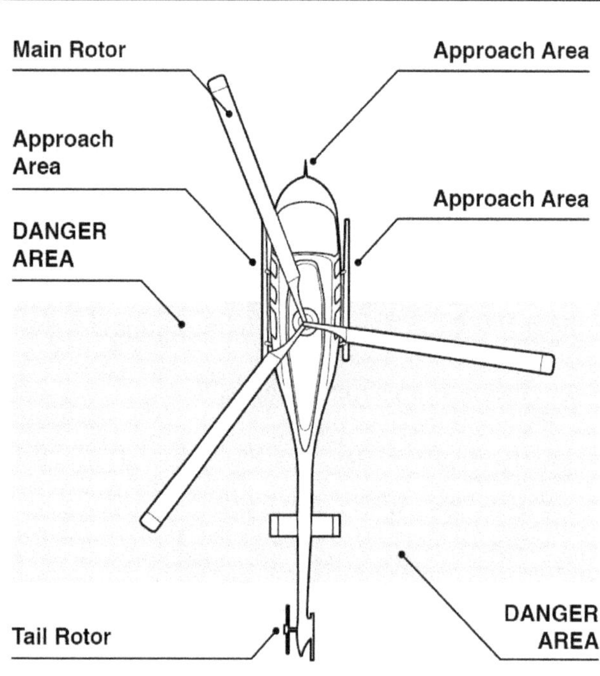

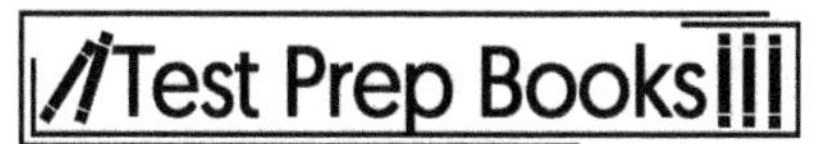

The following shows the proper way to approach a helicopter:

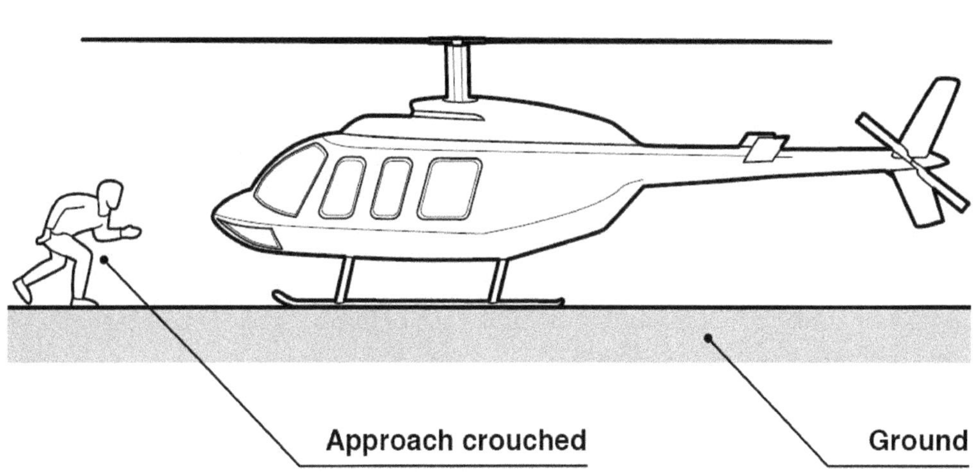

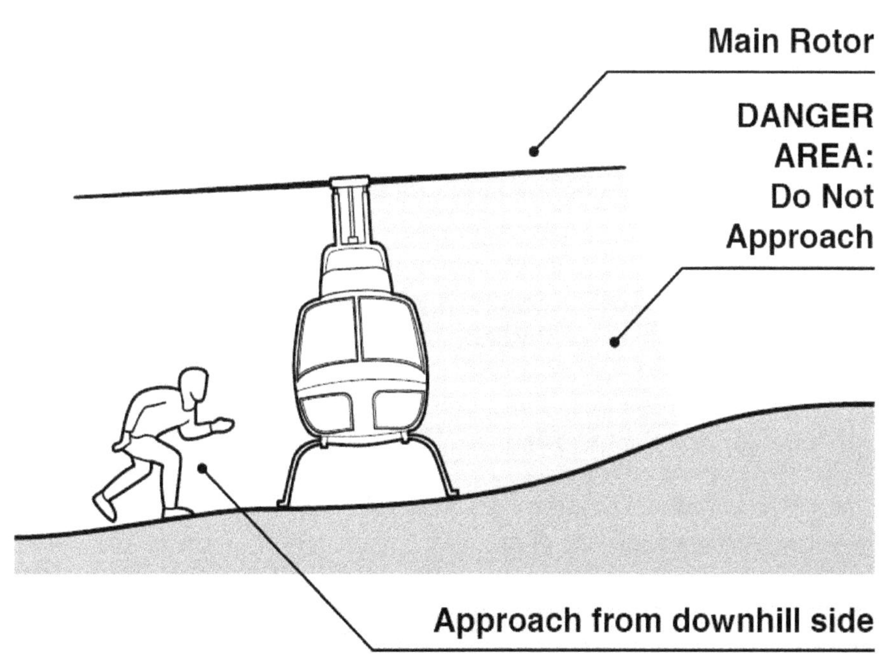

Communication at Scene of an Emergency

Emergency scenes can be chaotic in nature. Emergency responders must remain composed during an emergency so that they can effectively communicate with their team and the patient; they must also be able to carry out their tasks in an objective manner. There may also be bystanders, such as the victim's family, who might require emotional support from EMTs. Witnessing an accident or collapse can be a traumatizing experience for some people; therefore, EMTs should be prepared to wear many hats in these situations.

Rural Areas

Rural areas may present a challenge for EMS for a variety of reasons. For example, rural crews may encounter the difficulties of working with equipment that is old, may be unable to quickly reach the scene, or may be unable to gather adequate information about the scene before arrival. Communication may be further hampered due to dead spots along the route, which impact radio transmission, cell service, and other methods of gathering information. Each of these are challenges that EMTs must consider when supporting rural communities.

Resolving an Emergency Incident

The **National Association of Emergency Medical Technicians (NAEMT)** states that it is important to immediately report incidents as they occur, so as to reduce the risk of repetition in the future. Also, reporting mistakes as they happen can improve patient safety. Finally, communication about an incident reduces the risk for legal action by the affected party.

The Patient Safety Act

The **Patient Safety Act** provides EMS organizations and staff with the ability to gather information about safety events. The Patient Safety Act also allows and encourages EMS practitioners to voluntarily report safety incidents.

Providing Emotional Support

During the interview process following an emergency, it may be necessary for EMT staff to provide emotional support to family, friends, witnesses, or coworkers. In these instances, EMTs will have to demonstrate a level of empathy. EMTs should remember to take care of themselves as well, keeping an eye out for signs of stress and burnout. Everyone copes differently with stressful work environments. A physically, emotionally, and mentally healthy EMT is able to provide the best level of care for a patient in need.

Maintaining Medical/Legal Standards

It is expected that EMTs will adhere to guidelines of practice associated with their license and certifications, which mandate their scope of practice. Responders are expected to adhere to their state's standards (note that standards vary by state) to ensure adequate protection of the patient and the EMT. The **Medical Practice Act** permits medical directors or physicians to delegate certain procedures to EMS personnel. EMTs are held to a standard of care that dictates how someone with their training should perform, given a situation or circumstance, using similar equipment.

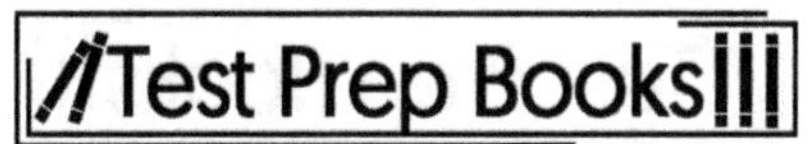

There are multiple organizations that contribute to establishing these standards of care, including:

- The American Heart Association (AHA)
- American Ambulance Association (AAA)
- National Association of Emergency Medical Technicians (NAEMT)
- State Department of Health
- Department of Transportation

Also, regional systems may dictate standards of care.

Avoiding Negligence

Negligence is the failure to demonstrate the care that a reasonably sensible individual would exhibit in a given situation. Failure of an EMT to adequately perform their duty may leave the responder open to a lawsuit. The table below provides a summary of types of negligence and descriptions of each.

Type of Negligence	Description
Simple (Ordinary) Negligence	Simple or ordinary negligence is not gross nor is it malicious in nature, but does define a failure to follow the ordinary care protocol
Gross Negligence	Gross negligence occurs when there is a complete disregard or concern for others' safety
Comparative Negligence	Comparative negligence occurs when the plaintiff is partially responsible for injuries to himself or herself
Criminal Negligence	Criminal negligence takes place when the deviation from the standard of care is so great that it leads to detrimental, often preventable, risk or death

To prove negligence, a patient must have evidence that demonstrates the obligation to care exists, a breach of duty regarding the standard of care occurred, an injury was the consequence, and that the breach of duty led to the injury:

- Duty to Act on Behalf of the Patient: Patients must establish that a necessary duty existed to provide care to the patient in a reasonable capacity.

- Breach in the Standard of Care: Patients must be able to show that there was a failure to act on their behalf at a reasonable level by the EMT; a standard of care was not met.

- An Injury Occurred: There must be evidence or a demonstration that there was an injury or tangible harm to the patient.

- The Breach Caused the Injury: Patients must demonstrate that the breach of duty was a direct cause of their injury. EMTs are at risk for accusations of abandonment or negligence if they terminate care without a patient's consent or without the establishment of continuing care from another resource.

Abandonment

Abandonment occurs when EMT professionals terminate patient engagement and services without an adequate reason. Transferring a patient's care to someone with fewer skills than the EMT, for example, is abandonment. Examples of abandonment include failure to transport a patient or transferring care to a less capable professional.

Libel

Libel is the defamation of someone's reputation—through written or other media forms—using false statements. During the documentation process, EMTs must ensure that their documentation remains objective in nature—that is, not subjective. Patient history and assessment findings are examples of objective findings. For example, documenting that someone "looks under the influence" could be categorized as subjective information and thus, as libel. The table below provides additional examples of libel.

Libelous Statements
Documentation of the following in a patient's chart, with libelous statements in boldface: "The patient continues to slur his words and **appears to be drunk."** **"The patient appears to be schizophrenic.** He kept yelling at EMT Jones each time he tried to apply a dressing to the right forearm." "Patient reported feeling dizzy and light-headed. **It was clear that she was faking these symptoms to get attention from her family."**

Slander

Slander is the verbal defamation of someone's name or character in which a false statement is made that may prove harmful to the individual's reputation or that of their family. It is rife with malicious intent and disregard for the damage that the false statements might cause. Slander qualifies as a tort or civil wrong, which can form the basis for a lawsuit.

Consent

EMTs must obtain **consent** from a competent adult or emancipated minor who is not classified by the courts as being medically incompetent to deliver care or to transport a patient to the hospital. Competent patients are lucid, able to understand instructions, follow commands, answer questions, and understand treatment recommendations. Also, a competent patient understands the consequences of their actions. Consent enables patients to formally make decisions about the care they are about to receive, as detailed in the table below.

Consent
Patients who grant consent understand:
The presence of injury and illness
Treatment recommendations
Potential benefits, risks, and dangers of treatment
Treatment alternatives
The potential adverse outcomes of refusing treatment or transport

Transporting a competent patient against their will to the hospital could lead to assault and battery charges against EMTs. **Assault** occurs when a person experiences fear of bodily harm without giving consent. **Battery** occurs with the unlawful touching of a person.

Implied Consent

Consent can be *implied* in those instances in which patients are not able to express their wants, such as when they are in an unconscious state. Failure to obtain consent prior to transport of a patient can create a liability, leaving an EMT at risk for accusations of kidnapping, false imprisonment, or bodily harm. Thus, EMTs must ensure and document that the patient is physically, emotionally, or mentally incapable of granting consent.

Reasonable Force

EMTs may use *reasonable force* to manage or control a disorderly or violent patient to prevent injury or harm to the patient, other EMT staff, or others on the scene. Excessive force creates the risk for lawsuits, therefore EMT staff must tread lightly when using force or restraints on combative patients.

Actual Consent (Informed or Expressed)

Actual consent, also known as *informed* or **expressed consent**, is consent that is given by an individual who is legally and mentally capable of making decisions pertaining to their health and well-being prior to treatment. The patient understands the extent of the care they are to receive, including the risks and benefits of the procedure. Patients do have the right to revoke their consent at any time during treatment or transport.

Involuntary Consent

Involuntary consent is the treatment of an adult against that patient's will and may take place only under the following conditions:

- A magistrate orders treatment
- A peace officer or corrections officer orders treatment for a patient under arrest or in custody

It is important to note that a competent adult who is under the custody of police does not lose the right to give consent or make their own decisions about medical treatment. Involuntary consent should only occur in the case of an emergency to save a life or limb.

Minors' Consent

Individuals under the age of 18 years of age are **minors**. They are not an **emancipated minor** (an adult) per the court. Parents, guardians, or other adults who have a close relation to the child may provide actual consent. Implied consent applies in those instances in which there is a life or limb threat, or any parental refusal of treatment. As with adults, mentally competent parents and guardians have the right to refuse care for their child. They, too, should receive information about the risks, benefits, treatments, and alternatives for care. If the parent or guardian still refuses care, EMTs must attempt to obtain their signature, or that of a witness, prior to leaving the scene.

Consent for Emancipated Minors

As noted above, emancipated minors are adults. Emancipated minors are persons under the age of 18 who are legally independent of any biological or non-biological guardians, therefore they can declare decisions about their health care without the input of another person. They may be married, pregnant, or a member of the armed forces who live independently without adult supervision. It is this qualification as an adult that gives them the right to give informed consent.

Withdrawing Consent

Competent adults may choose to **withdraw consent** for transport or treatment after care is underway. Their refusal of care, however, must be an informed refusal.

Refusal of Care or Transport

There is a chance that the patient may refuse care or transport. The EMT should assess if the individual refusing care is mentally and physically competent to make this decision and understands the possible significance of refusing care. It is within the rights of mentally competent adults to refuse treatment. The EMT must inform the patient of the risks, benefits, potential treatments, or alternatives. Finally, if the patient still refuses care, the EMT must document the refusal and obtain a signature from the patient or witness that validates the patient's refusal of care. If the patient refuses to sign the form, the EMT must also document this refusal. Should a patient refuse transport or care, EMTs may say one of the following statements (or something similar) to the patient:

- "You can call 911 at any time for assistance, should you change your mind."
- "If your symptoms worsen or you do not feel better, you can contact 911 for help. An ambulance will come to pick you up and take you to an emergency room."

Some patients may decide to accept only a portion of the treatment recommendation and refuse the remainder of the treatment plan. It is up to the EMT to discuss the risks that may accompany partial treatments, document the patient's refusal of the treatment, and obtain the signature of the patient or a witness. Witnesses can include law enforcement or other emergency service professionals who are present on the scene.

Good Samaritan Laws

Good Samaritan laws provide protection for those who perform an act in good faith to achieve a standard of care. This protection includes tending to those who are suffering from injury, illness, or who are in need of rescue. The intention of this law is to reduce the degree of fear of would-be rescuers who fear legal retaliation for unintentional injury or wrongful death that might result from a mistake while rendering care. The ideal candidates for these laws are those who do not have a duty to act on behalf of someone suffering from injury or at risk of death (such as a bystander or passerby).

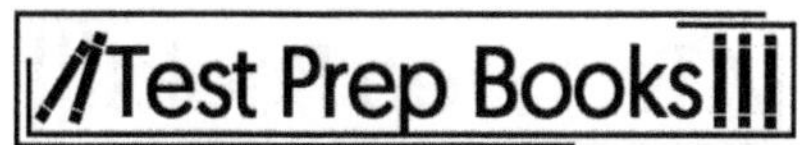

However, many states do have similar laws to provide legal protection for EMTs as well. Some states, like California, provide legal protection to all EMS providers who are acting under the scope of healthcare employment. Other states, like Virginia, provide additional legal protection to government, non-profit, and volunteer EMS personnel only. A number of states distinctly mention that this immunity is provided to responders who are acting without compensation, but are ambiguous regarding off-duty EMTs. Therefore, knowing the specific immunity laws (and noting the exact wording) for the state in which an EMT is licensed is important.

Confidentiality

Patient confidentiality promotes the security of a patient's medical and personal health information. The practice of **confidentiality** means that there is a protection in place that prevents the sharing or distribution of a patient's medical history, assessment findings, or treatment. **The Health Insurance Portability and Accountability Act (HIPAA)** requires medical professionals to protect the privacy of patients as it pertains to their medical treatment and other personal health information. Information exchange is limited strictly to those involved with the patient's care. HIPAA violations incur risk of civil and criminal penalties.

Patient confidentiality is vital. Confidentiality guarantees patient privacy and gives testimony to an EMT's professionalism. The release of patient information should only take place under the following conditions:

- To support continuity of care efforts
- To support law enforcement operations
- To fulfill a third-party billing requirement
- When under subpoena
- When patient consents to release information (patient signs consent)

EMTs are at risk for accusations of invasion of privacy if they release confidential information about a patient without legal justification.

Patients may review their records or request copies of their records. They also have the right to restrict who has access to their health records, thus requiring providers to communicate with them only (excluding the instances listed above).

Reporting Requirements

There are a few circumstances where a medical professional may share a patient's confidential information. Events that require reporting include the birth of a child, child abuse, elder abuse, sexual assault, injury due to felony, injuries that occur because of drugs, or death. Finally, EMTs may share patient information with emergency room staff such as nurses and doctors. EMTs must be careful to avoid accusations, by presenting information in an objective manner.

The table below provides a brief overview of the reporting requirements for different scenarios:

Situation	Actions
Crime Scene	EMTs should survey the scene, document what they observe, be careful to not disturb the scene, and report findings to law enforcement
Child Abuse	EMTs must report child abuse observations to law enforcement, treating physicians, and child protective services
Sexual Assaults	EMTs must report the assault to law enforcement, with the permission of the patient, and retain evidence
Death	EMTs should document their findings and contact the coroner and law enforcement without disturbing the scene

Inappropriate release of a patient's medical information can lead to a lawsuit against the EMT, under the category of libel or slander. EMTs found guilty must pay financial damages to the patient.

Professional Development

EMTs may participate in refresher courses to reinforce or update their skillset. Also, EMTs may pursue continuing education opportunities in a variety of settings, including online classrooms, local colleges, or universities. Continuing education courses are a wonderful way to build knowledge and keep up with the evolution of healthcare.

Practice Quiz

1. Which level of consent takes place if a patient is unconscious during delivery of care?
   a. Implied consent
   b. Expressed consent
   c. Actual consent
   d. Informed consent

2. When can a minor give consent for their own care?
   a. All minors under the age of 18 can give consent for their own care.
   b. Only emancipated minors can give consent for their own care.
   c. Only minors between the ages of 16 and 18 can give consent for their own care.
   d. Minors can only give consent for care in the presence of a guardian or parent.

3. An EMT who hands off care to someone with a lesser skillset or licensure level may be accused of which of the following?
   a. Assault
   b. Abandonment
   c. Exposure
   d. Desertion

4. If a competent patient refuses transport to the hospital and the EMT takes the injured party to the hospital against that person's will, the EMT is at risk for which of the following legal charges?

   I. Assault

   II. Battery

   III. Kidnapping

   a. Choice I only
   b. Choices I and III
   c. Choices II and III
   d. All of the above

5. Who can give consent for minors not emancipated by the court?

   I. Parents

   II. Guardians

   III. Adults who are close to the minor in relationship

   a. Choice I only
   b. Choice II only
   c. Choices I and II
   d. All of the above

See answers on the next page.

Answer Explanations

1. A: Implied consent is an acceptable form of consent for someone who is unconscious and unable to speak, or to sign a form granting consent to receive care or transport to a facility. Actual consent, which is also known as informed or expressed consent, is attainable from a patient who is alert, awake, knowledgeable, and mentally capable of making decisions.

2. B: An adult must be present to make decisions regarding a child's medical care unless the child is an emancipated minor. Emancipated minors are individuals under the age of 18 who are legally independent of any biological or non-biological guardians. Because of this, they can declare decisions about their health care without the input of another person.

3. B: EMTs should not release a patient to a lower level of care or to someone who is less skilled than they are because it may create risk for the patient and opens the EMT up to legal risks. The term for such an activity is abandonment because the EMT is leaving the patient with someone who more than likely will not be able to provide the same quality of care.

4. D: EMTs must be careful in transporting a patient to a medical treatment facility against their will or ignoring their refusal to receive care. This action is the equivalent of kidnapping, assault, and battery in the eyes of the law. Thus, all of these choices are correct.

5. D: Consent for minors should be given by a close adult relation, parent, or legal guardian of a minor. Minors or children under the age of 18 are not considered to be legally competent or capable of making decisions about their health care, and they need the guidance or influence of a capable adult who can make decisions on their behalf.

EMT Practice Test #1

1. You arrive at a scene where a worker has been struck by lightning. He is unresponsive and not breathing. CPR has been in progress by a bystander who is familiar with CPR. Your partner takes over chest compressions, and you look to facilitate airway management. While attempting to ventilate the patient with a BVM, you notice minimal to no chest rise. What would be the next appropriate action?
   a. Perform nasal intubation.
   b. Transport to the nearest trauma center without intervention.
   c. Reposition the patient's airway and form a better seal around the mouth.
   d. Wait for a few minutes to ensure the electrical charge has dissipated before starting CPR.

2. An EMT is called to the scene of a workplace accident. A 55-year-old male worker was operating heavy machinery when his hand got caught in the equipment, resulting in a partial amputation of two fingers. The patient is conscious and alert but is in significant pain and bleeding profusely from the amputated fingers. What is the most appropriate initial action for the EMT to take in this situation?
   a. Apply a tourniquet above the amputated fingers to control the bleeding.
   b. Apply direct pressure to the wound to control the bleeding.
   c. Elevate the patient's injured hand above the level of his heart.
   d. Place the amputated fingers in a plastic bag and immerse them in ice.

3. Jenny, an EMT, needs to deliver chest compressions to a ten-month-old infant. What is the appropriate hand placement for delivering compressions to this patient?
   a. Heel of one palm over the infant's sternum
   b. Hands stacked, fingers interlaced, with the heel of the bottom hand over the infant's sternum
   c. Two fingers over the infant's sternum
   d. None of the above because a ten-month-old infant should not receive chest compressions

4. A 3-year-old child is displaying signs of respiratory distress. Upon arrival at the scene, the EMT notes that the child is drooling, appears anxious, and is creating a high-pitched noise during inhalation. Which of the following actions should the EMT take?
   a. Perform a head-tilt/chin-lift maneuver to open the airway.
   b. Administer oral fluids to help relieve the child's throat discomfort.
   c. Administer oxygen and assist ventilations with a bag valve mask.
   d. Place the child in a supine position for easier assessment of the airway.

5. You respond to an adult female who states that while she was gardening, she felt a sharp pain to her forearm. She complains of severe pain and there is a puncture wound on her left forearm. The area is very swollen, warm, and painful to the touch. The patient doesn't complain of any shortness of breath or the feeling of her throat swelling, but she does say that it feels like she is losing feeling in her fingers. What is your course of action?
   a. Apply an air splint on the forearm to reduce swelling, then elevate the limb.
   b. Apply ice packs to sting area, then wrap forearm with compressive dressing and elevate the limb.
   c. Administer 0.30 mg of subcutaneous/intramuscular epinephrine via EpiPen.
   d. Immediately apply a tourniquet above the sting location, apply ice packs, and elevate the area.

6. An EMT arrives at a major motor vehicle accident and begins to assist an adult female who was an unrestrained passenger. The patient is alert, oriented, and denies any loss of consciousness, but she complains of lower extremity pain with some deformity to the leg. The patient also has head pain with a scalp laceration that is bleeding profusely, as well as painful respirations. What should the immediate next step be?
   a. Applying high-flow oxygen to assist with respirations
   b. Immobilizing the C-spine and keeping the patient still to prevent further injury
   c. Attempting to stop the bleeding of the scalp laceration with direct pressure and a sterile dressing
   d. Conducting an assessment of the lower extremity for potential fracture

7. When a patient is no longer appropriately ventilating and enters respiratory failure, what gas cannot be eliminated from their circulation correctly?
   a. Oxygen
   b. Carbon dioxide
   c. Methane
   d. Argon

8. A 10-year-old boy with a history of sickle cell disease is found lying on the ground, complaining of severe pain in his right arm. Upon assessment, his arm appears swollen, and he is holding it close to his body. What is the most likely cause for this patient's symptoms, and what is the immediate action that should be taken?
   a. The patient is experiencing acute compartment syndrome and requires application of ice to the arm, elevating the arm above heart level, and applying a compression bandage.
   b. The patient is experiencing sequestration crisis and requires immediate and expedited transport to the hospital.
   c. The patient has fractured his arm from osteoporosis. The arm needs to be splinted in the position found.
   d. The patient is experiencing a vaso-occlusive crisis and requires supplemental oxygen since circulation is impaired.

9. You are dispatched to answer a call for a possible ischemic stroke. Upon arrival, you perform your assessment, including the Cincinnati Stroke score. Upon completion, the patient has notable facial droop, arm drift, and slurred speech. The patient claims that their symptoms started six hours ago. Upon gathering their medical history, you discover that the patient takes Coumadin and aspirin, had an MI eight months ago, and had a stroke two years ago. Which of the following is NOT a contraindication for tPA administration for this patient?
   a. Prior MI
   b. Six hours since onset of symptoms
   c. Patient taking Coumadin
   d. Patient taking aspirin

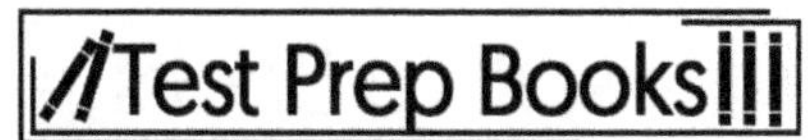

10. You are responding to a call for an adult male who appears confused and agitated. Upon arrival, you find a conscious adult male who witnesses said was seated and began to act confused. You come upon the patient, who is alert but confused and agitated. There does not appear to be any trauma. Suddenly, the patient starts to have a seizure. The patient's body stiffens, and he begins to convulse. What should you do to manage this seizing patient?

a. Restrain the patient's movements to prevent injuries during the seizure.
b. Position to maintain an open airway and protect him from choking.
c. Administer benzodiazepines to stop the seizure immediately.
d. Apply pressure to the patient's chest to stop the convulsions.

11. A patient was involved in a high-speed motor vehicle collision. He is unconscious, has snoring respirations, is without signs of hemorrhaging, and has a weak, rapid pulse. What is the most appropriate initial intervention?

a. Start chest compressions.
b. Insert an oropharyngeal airway.
c. Apply a cervical collar.
d. Administer high-flow oxygen.

12. You arrive on scene to a 23-year-old male patient who is warm to the touch and complaining of an unquenchable thirst. He states that he is a diabetic and his last oral intake was a day ago. He also states that he is constantly hungry but doesn't feel like eating and has been using the bathroom constantly. You check blood glucose level, and it registers 350 mg/dL. Which condition do you suspect and what is your plan of care?

a. The patient is suffering from hypoglycemia. Administer glucose if tolerated and transport at leisure.
b. The patient is suffering from hyperglycemia and requires insulin. Assist patient with insulin injection and transport immediately.
c. The patient is suffering from diabetic ketoacidosis (DKA). Allow the patient to drink clear fluids if able and transport him immediately.
d. The patient is suffering from hypothyroidism. Administer required high-flow oxygen and transport immediately.

13. An adolescent boy complains after a bicycle fall about pain in the groin area. What would NOT be a sign/symptom of testicular torsion?

a. Swelling and discoloration of the scrotum
b. Pain in the genital area radiating down the leg
c. Pain during urination
d. Blood in the urine

14. When transporting a patient that is actively undergoing chemotherapy treatment, what care must you take into consideration?

a. The patient is high risk and needs to be transported as quickly as possible.
b. The patient is highly contagious, and you should wear gloves, a gown, and goggles.
c. The patient is at risk of infection, and both the patient and the EMTs should be masked.
d. All linen that contacted the patient must be disposed of in a biohazard container, and any surfaces must be cleaned and sterilized.

15. You arrive at the scene where a patient has collapsed and is without a pulse. You notice that the patient has an implanted cardioverter-defibrillator (ICD). What is the appropriate action regarding the use of an ICD in this situation?
    a. Do not use the AED due to the presence of the ICD.
    b. Apply the AED pads as usual and follow the AED prompts.
    c. Remove the ICD before applying the AED pads.
    d. Place the AED pads directly over the ICD.

16. Tim and Tom are two EMTs treating a patient, Joe, who is in respiratory distress. Joe is conscious and can gesture to respond, but he is having trouble speaking, keeps rubbing the outside of his throat, has a hoarse voice, is drooling, and is hyperthermic. Tim and Tom hear stridor upon Joe's inspiration and suspect epiglottitis. What course of action is contraindicated in this case?
    a. Keeping the patient calm
    b. Requesting ALS intercept for possible emergent need for an advanced airway
    c. Monitoring Joe's pulse oximetry
    d. Manually sweeping the oral cavity before placing a tracheal tube

17. How frequently should EMTs assess vehicle readiness?

    I. Daily

    II. After emergency care is provided

    III. Only when there are visible issues

    a. Choice I only
    b. Choice II only
    c. Choice III only
    d. Choices I and II

18. You are called to a residence where a 6-month-old infant had a fall from a crib. Upon arrival, you find the infant conscious and crying inconsolably. The baby opens her eyes in response to your voice, but she is irritable and inconsolable. The infant pulls away and exhibits decerebrate posturing when you touch her extremities. What GCS score would you assign to this infant?
    a. GCS score of 8
    b. GCS score of 9
    c. GCS score of 10
    d. GCS score of 11

19. Which of the following protocols has been proven to be beneficial to post-cardiac arrest patients in their neurological recovery?
    a. Maintaining an SpO2 greater than 96%
    b. Targeted temperature management
    c. Ending tidal capnography monitoring
    d. Administration of catecholamine infusion

20. A patient presents with a sudden-onset, painful, swollen ankle after a twisting injury. No obvious deformity is seen. What is the most appropriate initial step in management?
   a. Applying heat
   b. Elevating the ankle and applying ice and a compression bandage
   c. Immobilizing with a plaster cast
   d. Administering antibiotics

21. You are dispatched to a residential address where a 2-year-old child is experiencing sudden abdominal pain, vomiting, and inconsolable crying. The parents state that they have been noticing "red jelly stool." Which of the following actions should you take first?
   a. Transport the child to a hospital immediately.
   b. Auscultate for bowel sounds.
   c. Administer over-the-counter pain medication.
   d. Administer IV fluids to correct fluid imbalance.

22. A 35-year-old male patient presents with blunt trauma to the chest. He is complaining of chest pain and shortness of breath. The first responder notes decreased breath sounds on the right side. En route to the hospital, the patient becomes diaphoretic, his breathing becomes more rapid and labored, his oxygen saturation decreases to 85%, and the first responder notes tracheal deviation and jugular vein distention. What should the EMT do first?
   a. Turn the patient on his side.
   b. Suction the patient's airway.
   c. Administer rescue breaths with a bag valve mask.
   d. Request ALS intercept.

23. Which of the following assessments is NOT part of the Cincinnati Prehospital Stroke Scale?
   a. Loss of visual acuity
   b. Arm drift
   c. Facial droop
   d. Abnormal speech

24. A 54-year-old male has complaints of severe back pain on his right side, just below his ribcage. He states that the pain is radiating to his groin, it burns when he urinates, and it looks like blood is in his urine. You notice that he is restless and cannot get into a comfortable position. What are your initial impression and actions?
   a. The patient is most likely suffering from a urinary tract infection. Apply ice to the groin area and transport with head elevated.
   b. The patient is most likely suffering from a urethral stricture. Restrict the urge to urinate and transport with knees flexed.
   c. The patient is suffering from a sexually transmitted infection. Encourage clear liquid intake and transport the patient on unaffected side with knees flexed.
   d. The patient is suffering from renal calculi. Encourage clear liquid intake, save the patient's urine, and transport in position of comfort.

25. A 30-year-old female presents with a blunt injury to her upper abdomen. She is complaining of abdominal pain. She only complains of abdominal pain radiating to her back and some nausea. Upon physical examination, her abdomen is rigid and tender with some bruising in the LUQ. What next step should the EMT take?
   a. Determine the patient's last oral intake.
   b. Begin shock prevention interventions.
   c. Check for potential back/spinal injury based on back pain.
   d. Auscultate bowel sounds.

26. A 28-year-old male is displaying erratic and aggressive behavior at a mall. He is seen to be shouting, pacing, and threatening other people. Which of the following should you do first?
   a. Attempt to subdue the patient to prevent harm to others.
   b. Maintain a safe distance and observe the scene until law enforcement arrives.
   c. Approach the individual and attempt to engage him verbally to calm him down.
   d. With the help of law enforcement, apply restraints to the patient's extremities.

27. An EMT is responding to a critical emergency call and has their ambulance sirens and lights activated. As the EMT driving the ambulance, how should they navigate through a red traffic light intersection?
   a. Slow down and proceed through the intersection without stopping since the siren is activated.
   b. Come to a complete stop, then proceed cautiously.
   c. Continue through the intersection at a normal speed, giving the right of way to other vehicles.
   d. Proceed through the intersection at a higher speed since the siren is activated.

28. You are dispatched to a skilled nursing facility to transport a patient to the ER who is *C. difficile* (*C. diff*) positive and in droplet precautions. What extra precautions must you take for this patient and yourself?
   a. Standard body substance isolation procedures
   b. Standard body substance isolation procedures and an N-95 mask for the patient if able to tolerate
   c. Gloves, mask, and gown protection
   d. Gloves, mask, and gown protection (isolation precautions) and your squad and equipment will need to be cleaned and sanitized before transporting your next patient

29. A one-month-old patient presents as cyanotic and is using accessory muscles to breathe. The patient's mother reports that the patient was recently diagnosed with RSV. The EMT notes excess mucus production to the nares. What should the EMT do first?
   a. Suction the nares.
   b. Call for ALS intercept.
   c. Start chest compressions.
   d. Blind-sweep the patient's mouth for foreign bodies.

30. Which of the following rhythms is NOT considered a perfusing cardiac rhythm?
   a. First-degree heart block
   b. Sinus tachycardia
   c. PEA
   d. A-fib

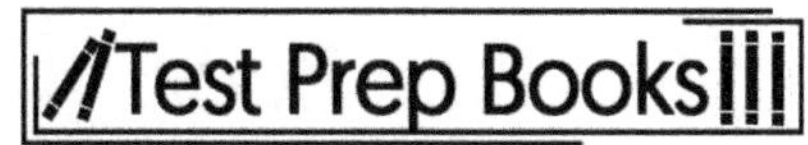

31. A patient has an open chest wound and presents with ashen skin, painful labored breathing, and obvious signs of air entering the thoracic cavity. Which immediate steps should be taken?
    a. Place a gloved hand over the open wound followed by an occlusive dressing.
    b. Apply a sterile gauze dressing held in place with bandages.
    c. Apply weight over the open wound to prevent paradoxical chest movements.
    d. Apply a hemostatic dressing.

32. A 56-year-old man presents complaining of midsternal chest tightness that started while he was seated and watching the news, about 20 minutes prior to ambulance arrival. His blood pressure is 165/76, oxygen saturation is 98 percent on room air, and respirations are 20 breaths per minute. First responders perform an EKG, which shows a regular rate of 75 beats per minute with some ST depression. The patient has no allergies, and his only reported medical history is high blood pressure. What should the EMT do first?
    a. Administer 324 mg of aspirin.
    b. Administer supplemental oxygen.
    c. Start CPR.
    d. Encourage the patient to take his blood pressure medication.

33. What is the first intervention for a patient who appears to be hyperventilating?
    a. Have the patient breathe into a paper bag.
    b. Administer oxygen by face mask.
    c. Tell the patient it's all in their head.
    d. Assist the patient with breathing exercises to slow their breathing.

34. CPR is in progress on a pediatric patient. Chest compressions are paused for a pulse check and for the AED (automated external defibrillator) to analyze the patient's heart rhythm. The patient has no palpable pulse, and the AED says that a shock is advised. What should the EMT do first?
    a. Hold chest compressions until the shock is administered.
    b. Question the parents to see if the patient ingested any caustic substances.
    c. Continue to check for a pulse until shock is administered.
    d. Continue chest compressions until the AED is charged and the patient is cleared.

35. Upon arriving at the scene of a call, an EMT notices a strong odor and several unconscious people on the ground. Which of the following emergencies has most likely occurred?
    a. A toxicological emergency
    b. A psychiatric emergency
    c. A hematological emergency
    d. An immunological emergency

36. You are dispatched to an adult male complaining of burning epigastric pain and nausea. The patient states he has a history of hypertension and GERD, and his gallbladder has been removed. He reports that his last oral intake was approximately 6 hours ago. His vital signs are BP 150/90, pulse 80, RR 14. His skin is warm and dry. What is your care for this patient?
    a. Administer high-flow oxygen, have the patient hold a baby aspirin under his tongue, and assist with morphine if available.
    b. Listen for bowel sounds, restrict oral intake, and transport in position of comfort.
    c. Listen for bowel sounds, encourage oral intake, and transport in position on patient's side.
    d. Apply alternating ice/heat compresses to affected area and transport in position of comfort.

37. You are transporting a pediatric patient with possible hypovolemia from persistent vomiting. Which of the following formulas should a clinician use to determine if the pediatric patient is hypotensive?
   a. $60 + \text{patient's age in years}$
   b. $70 + \text{patient's age in years}$
   c. $60 + 2 \times \text{age in years}$
   d. $70 + 2 \times \text{age in years}$

38. You respond to an elderly patient who has a loud, raspy cough, and you can see that the patient appears to be coughing and there appears to be bright, red blood on the tissue. You are told that he requires contact precautions. What precautions are necessary for this type of patient?
   a. Gloves, surgical mask, and goggles for you, and surgical mask for the patient if tolerated
   b. Gloves, mask, and gown protection (isolation precautions), and your squad and equipment will need to be cleaned and sanitized before transporting your next patient
   c. Gloves, mask, and gown protection
   d. Gloves and surgical mask for you, and surgical mask for the patient

39. Collin is an EMT who is part of a team that is transporting a car accident victim to the hospital. The patient is alert and oriented at the beginning of the call, but the patient slumps over and you notice no chest rise-and-fall, although they have a radial pulse. What immediate intervention should be performed?
   a. Place the patient on an NRB at 15 LPM.
   b. Place the patient in the lateral recumbent position to allow secretions to drain out.
   c. Perform a needle chest decompression.
   d. Insert a basic airway and begin delivering rescue breaths at a rate of 12 to 20 per minute.

40. You have been performing CPR on a patient in cardiac arrest when your partner tells you that he feels a carotid pulse at the next pulse check. After loading the patient into the ambulance, what might the EMT consider in the continuum of care?
   a. Targeted temperature management
   b. Any possible DNRs
   c. The patient's PaO_2
   d. Placement of a definitive airway

41. A patient has called 911 after having woken up with a severe headache and flushing to the face. The patient reports that he has been using a propane stove to heat his home. The patient is alert but somewhat confused. What should you do next?
   a. Insert a nasal airway and place the patient at 2–6 LPM via nasal cannula.
   b. Immediately remove the patient from the home and place the patient on a continuous positive airway pressure (CPAP) device.
   c. Immediately remove the patient from the home and apply high-flow oxygen via a non-rebreather mask.
   d. Provide nebulizer treatments via handheld nebulizer at 6 LPM.

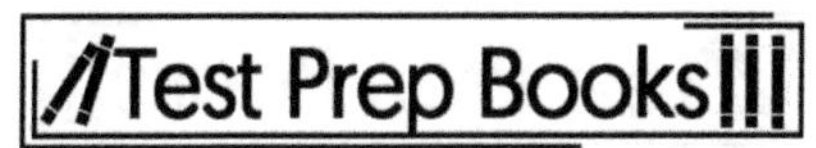

42. A patient was involved in a motorcycle collision and is complaining of severe pain in his right lower leg. The EMT notices a deformity, and the patient's foot is pale, cold, and extremely swollen. What next step should the EMT take?
    a. Attempt to align the leg to anatomical position.
    b. Check for distal pulses.
    c. Apply a traction splint.
    d. Remove constrictive clothing and attempt to place the leg on the level of the heart.

43. You are dispatched to a park where a pregnant woman who is in her third trimester is anxious and diaphoretic. She suddenly complains of shortness of breath and chest pain. What action should you take?
    a. Administer nitroglycerin for the woman's chest pain.
    b. Lay the woman on her left side to increase blood flow to the baby.
    c. Administer high-flow oxygen via non-rebreather mask to improve oxygenation.
    d. Place the woman in a semi-Fowler position to assist in breathing.

44. An adult approaches the ambulance appearing in distress. He is clasping at his throat with both hands. He is gasping and unable to form words or cough. The first responders see no signs of trauma. What should the EMT do first?
    a. Place an oropharyngeal airway (OPA).
    b. Give the patient something to drink.
    c. Dispatch ALS response.
    d. Perform the Heimlich maneuver.

45. An adult female presents with right-sided lower abdominal/pelvic pain that rates a 10/10. She states that the pain is sharp and stabbing, with some radiation down her lower back. She also complains of nausea and vomiting. She states there is no chance she is pregnant. What are your actions for this patient?
    a. Place a warm compress on the affected area, restrict the patient's oral intake, and transport in a position of comfort.
    b. Place a cold compress on the affected area, restrict the patient's oral intake, and transport in a position of comfort.
    c. Place a warm compress on the affected area, encourage oral intake of clear liquids, and transport in a position of comfort.
    d. Don't place any compress on the affected area, encourage oral intake of clear liquids, and transport in a position of comfort.

46. An elderly individual slipped and fell in his home and hit his head on the floor. Upon arrival, the EMT notes that the individual is conscious but disoriented and has a small scalp laceration. What action should the EMT take first?
    a. Perform a detailed neurological examination to determine any deficits.
    b. Slowly help the individual up and into a chair.
    c. Keep the individual lying down and stabilize his head and neck.
    d. Apply a sterile dressing to the scalp laceration to control the bleeding.

47. During pregnancy, which ominous sign should be aggressively treated in order to prevent further deterioration of the fetus and mother?
    a. O_2 saturation of 90%
    b. Preeclampsia
    c. Hypotension
    d. Tachycardia

48. You are dispatched to a respiratory distress call. When you arrive at the patient's house, you note a wife who runs to your ambulance and claims that her husband is allergic to peanuts and that he accidentally had a peanut butter snack. When you enter the house, you note a patient with angioedema, urticaria, stridor, and a distressed complexion. After completing your initial assessment and general impression, which treatment should be your first-line priority in order to stop the anaphylactic reaction?
    a. Provide the patient with 50 mg tablet of Benadryl.
    b. Suction the patient's airway to ensure no remains of peanut butter snack are still present.
    c. Use the patient's prescribed EpiPen.
    d. Monitor the patient's airway and expect to perform a surgical cricothyroidotomy.

49. You are transporting a patient after getting ROSC post-cardiac arrest. While ventilating the patient, what should be your target $ETCO_2$?
    a. 25-30
    b. 30-35
    c. 35-40
    d. 40-45

50. A 55-year-old female patient presents with a waxy and swollen appearance, fatigue, cold intolerance, hypothermia, hypotension, and bradycardia. The patient states she has a history of hypothyroidism. What care would be provided to this patient?
    a. Maintain and monitor patient's airway and breathing and provide heat compress to neck and groin area.
    b. Maintain and monitor patient's airway and breathing, cardiac output, and blood sugar levels. Provide the patient with a blanket.
    c. Check patient's blood sugar levels and adjust per patient's prescription if known.
    d. Monitor the patient's O_2 saturation and blood sugar levels and provide a blanket.

51. A 10-year-old child is involved in a bicycle accident and suffers from a head injury. The child is conscious but confused, has a laceration on their forehead, and is actively bleeding. What should be the EMT's immediate action?
    a. Applying direct pressure to the forehead laceration to control the bleeding
    b. Gently shaking the child to assess their level of responsiveness
    c. Removing the child's bicycle helmet to assess the head injury better
    d. Keeping the child lying flat on their back and maintaining spinal precautions

52. An 85-year-old patient presents as confused, febrile, sneezing, and coughing. His family reports that he has had a decreased appetite for the past few days. The patient's breathing appears labored and tachypneic, and the patient's oxygen saturation is 85% on room air. What should you do first?
    a. Listen to breath sounds to rule out respiratory infection.
    b. Administer high-flow supplemental oxygen via non-rebreather mask.
    c. Have the patient hold a baby aspirin under his tongue until it dissolves.
    d. Apply cool compress to forehead to relieve fever.

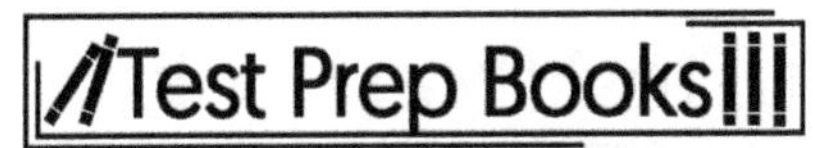

53. A 22-year-old male is lying supine and is not responsive to stimulus after a motor vehicle collision. You open his airway with a jaw-thrust maneuver due to facial trauma and determined that he is bradycardic and apneic. You attempt to ventilate the patient but are unsuccessful. What should you do?

   a. Perform a head-tilt/chin-lift maneuver and try to ventilate again.
   b. Begin chest compressions.
   c. Insert an NPA and attempt to ventilate.
   d. Insert an OPA and attempt to ventilate.

54. You respond to an adult female who states that she is a breast cancer patient who had a left breast mastectomy. What should be your question about her surgery and why?

   a. Ask her if she knows if her lymph nodes were removed. If they were, obtain blood pressure from the right arm only.
   b. Ask her if she knows if her lymph nodes were removed and when the surgery took place. If they were removed and the surgery was less than a year ago, blood pressure can be checked on either arm.
   c. Ask her if she knows if her lymph nodes were removed. If they were not, obtain blood pressure from the right arm only.
   d. Ask her if she knows if her lymph nodes were removed and when the surgery took place. If they were removed and the surgery was more than a year ago, blood pressure can be checked on either arm.

55. What type of fracture would be found in infants and toddlers but not usually in adults?

   a. Commuted
   b. Compound
   c. Spiral
   d. Greenstick

56. When performing chest compressions on a pediatric patient, what depth should be achieved to adequately perform CPR?

   a. $1\frac{1}{2}$ inches
   b. 2 inches
   c. 3 inches
   d. $\frac{1}{2}$ the depth of the chest

57. A 7-year-old patient presents with shortness of breath and labored breathing that includes the use of accessory muscles. The patient is alert and oriented, but is having difficulty speaking in complete sentences. Upon listening to lung sounds, the first responder hears expiratory wheezing. The patient's oxygen saturation is currently 95% on room air. What should the EMT do first?

   a. Administer the patient's prescribed nebulizer.
   b. Place the patient on supplemental oxygen via nasal cannula.
   c. Place the patient on supplemental oxygen via nonrebreather.
   d. Place the patient on CPAP.

58. An adult male is prescribed a new medication for his erectile dysfunction. He tried it for the first time and is now experiencing an erection that has lasted 6 hours. His penis is extremely swollen and painful, and it is difficult for him to urinate. What is your first action to take?
   a. Transport the patient immediately, as this is a life-threatening condition.
   b. Apply ice compresses to the affected area.
   c. Apply pneumatic pelvic immobilization device.
   d. Apply warm compresses to the affected area.

59. You are transporting an elderly male with advanced dementia for a scheduled dressing change. The nurses report that the patient is stable but becomes agitated at times, asking for his deceased wife and/or his children who live out of state. During transport, the patient becomes irritated with what is going on and calls for his wife. What do you do to try to help the patient become less irritated?
   a. Attempt noninvasive techniques like conversing with the patient, distraction, and redirection.
   b. Request that the nurse give the patient some anti-anxiety medications prior to loading the patient.
   c. Request law enforcement to place the patient in restraints.
   d. Verbally reprimand the patient for his behavior and reason with him.

60. Which of the following terms indicates a situation where there are too many patients, overburdening an EMS system?
   a. Mass casualty incident
   b. Multiple request incident
   c. TC3
   d. Multiple patient request

61. Janet, an EMT, is called to the home of an elderly woman who seems to live alone. Her neighbor stopped by and noticed that the woman seemed to be in distress. The woman is conscious but is having great difficulty speaking. While attempting to speak, she gasps and begins violently coughing. Her cough sounds wet. She frantically points to a stack of paper on her counter. Janet rifles through the papers and discovers the woman, named Susie, is 76 years old and was diagnosed with grade 2 COPD the previous week. There are also some over-the-counter cold and flu medications with the paperwork. Janet quickly measures Susie's oxygen saturation with her pulse oximeter, and it reads 87%. What should Janet do next?
   a. Place Susie in the sniffing position and suction out whatever is causing the wet cough.
   b. Call her supervisor.
   c. Immediately supplement the elderly woman's breathing with a BVM device.
   d. Keep Susie upright and prepare to administer oxygen by Venturi mask.

62. An EMT and their partner were performing CPR on a pediatric patient, and medical direction has instructed them to cease performing CPR. Which of the following should the EMS crew do in order to provide emotional support for the patient's mother?
   a. Tell the patient's mother that they are extremely sorry.
   b. Cover the patient with a blanket.
   c. Leave all interventions in place.
   d. Call the patient's father and tell him what happened.

63. A 70-year-old female patient presents with abdominal pain, nausea, and confusion. The patient's vitals are stable, her blood sugar is normal, she does not meet stroke assessment criteria, and she feels warm to the touch. What do you suspect and what actions do you take?
    a. The patient is potentially having a myocardial infarction (MI). Administer high-flow oxygen, a baby aspirin, and nitroglycerin if prescribed.
    b. The patient is experiencing gastrointestinal discomfort. Have the patient drink clear fluids and advance to crackers if tolerated.
    c. The patient is suffering from a urinary tract infection. Restrict any oral intake and obtain oral temperature.
    d. The patient is suffering from heat stroke. Remove any constrictive clothing and put ice packs on the neck, axillary, and groin areas.

64. How long after return of spontaneous circulation should targeted temperature management be performed for the post-cardiac arrest patient?
    a. Twenty-four hours
    b. Six hours
    c. Forty-eight hours
    d. Four hours

65. An EMT understands that a DNR order may be revoked or become invalid when:
    a. The patient is unconscious.
    b. The patient is elderly.
    c. The patient's medical condition improves significantly.
    d. The patient's healthcare provider changes.

66. You are dispatched to a residential address for a woman with complaints of severe lower abdominal pain and extensive vaginal bleeding. She is diaphoretic, and her color is pale. Her husband states that she is in her first trimester of pregnancy. What might she be experiencing and what are your actions?
    a. The patient is experiencing round ligament pain. Ask the patient to stretch her lower abdomen and place a warm compress on the affected area.
    b. The patient is experiencing an ectopic pregnancy. This is a potentially life-threatening condition, and the patient requires immediate transport.
    c. The patient is potentially having a miscarriage. Perform a vaginal exam and look for tissue parts and use pressure dressing to control bleeding.
    d. The patient is experiencing a placental abruption. Encourage oral fluid intake and transport the patient on her right side.

67. An EMT is responding to a motor vehicle collision. Upon arrival, they encounter an adult patient who was the driver of the vehicle. The patient is conscious but complaining of severe chest pain and difficulty breathing. The steering wheel has caused significant damage to the driver's side of the chest area. What is the most appropriate immediate action for the EMT to take in this situation?
    a. Administer pain medication to alleviate chest pain.
    b. Check for chest wounds.
    c. Immobilize the patient's chest with a chest binder.
    d. Provide high-flow oxygen through a non-rebreather mask.

68. Which of the following is the best way to help foster relations with the surrounding populace that an EMS crew responds to?
    a. Attending town hall meetings
    b. Providing mental health services to the community
    c. Giving tours of their ambulance rig
    d. Providing the best patient care

69. According to the American Heart Association, how often is it required to renew a BLS, ALS, or PALS card course?
    a. Every year
    b. Every two years
    c. Every five years
    d. Never because they are permanent cards

70. A 3-year-old child has ingested a household cleaning product. She is conscious and alert but is drooling and appears to be in pain. What is the most appropriate initial management?
    a. Administer activated charcoal.
    b. Induce vomiting.
    c. Dilute the substance by administering milk or water.
    d. Do not attempt to neutralize the substance and transport immediately.

71. When performing CPR on an adult, what is the correct way to ventilate a patient after an advanced airway is in place?
    a. 15:2 compressions to ventilations
    b. Every five compressions
    c. Every five to six seconds
    d. 30:2 compressions to ventilations

72. EMT Nick is working with a visibly inebriated patient that is drifting in and out of consciousness. The patient is sitting upright but will slump over for periods of ten to twelve seconds before returning to consciousness. The patient's oxygen saturation level just fell from 94% to 90%, and Nick is preparing to deliver supplemental oxygen. Nick notices the patient's tongue is causing an obstruction, especially when the patient drifts off. Which of the following actions is contraindicated in this situation?
    a. Placing a nasal cannula into the patient's nostrils.
    b. Keeping the patient upright in a tripod stance.
    c. Placing an oral airway into the patient's mouth to keep the tongue down.
    d. Talking to the patient in a calm, comforting voice.

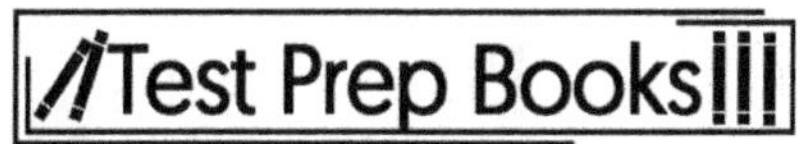

73. You are transporting an adult female who is paralyzed and has a tracheostomy tube. En route to the hospital, you hear her cough loudly, then she struggles to breathe. You do not see any chest rise as her face starts to turn red. She loses consciousness and is not breathing. Two rescue breaths do not produce any noticeable chest rise. What is your next step?
   a. Tilt her head back with head tilt/chin lift and attempt rescue breaths. If no chest rise, insert an oral airway and ventilate with bag valve mask.
   b. Check the trach tube for any obstruction, attempt rescue breaths through tube, suction tube and attempt rescue breaths again, and ventilate manually with bag valve mask.
   c. Open airway with jaw thrust and attempt rescue breaths. If no chest rise, insert an oral airway and ventilate with bag valve mask.
   d. Tilt her head back with head tilt/chin lift and attempt rescue breaths. If no chest rise, insert nasal airway and ventilate with bag valve mask.

74. First responders encounter a patient complaining of left-sided chest pain that is radiating to his left arm. The patient is diaphoretic and nauseous. A 12-lead EKG is completed, showing ST elevation. What should the EMT do first?
   a. Begin transport to a hospital with cardiac facilities.
   b. Defibrillate.
   c. Administer rescue breaths.
   d. Perform needle decompression.

75. An adult male is playing organized tackle football. While attempting to make a tackle, the patient is hit in the sternum with the crown of the opposing team member's helmet. It appears officials have immobilized the patient with his helmet on. An EMT arrives on the scene to find the player supine with a large bruise mid-chest with some deformity. The patient is alert but appears confused. His skin is cool and clammy to the touch. During the EMT's examination, the patient becomes unresponsive. There are no signs of respirations, and a pulse cannot be detected. What is the first immediate action to take?
   a. Doing a scapular pinch to ascertain if the patient is responsive to painful stimuli
   b. Opening the patient's airway with their helmet on using the jaw-thrust method and starting chest compressions
   c. Attempting to remove the patient's helmet to better open the airway and then beginning chest compressions
   d. Transporting immediately as the chest injury precludes chest compressions

76. You arrive on scene to find an adult male who was working on his car when his wrench slipped, and he lacerated his forearm. During your review of past medical history, he states that he was recently in the hospital for atrial fibrillation, and they gave him some "blood pills." The laceration appears superficial but is bleeding profusely. He has gone through multiple shop towels and the wound continues to ooze blood. The patient asks for a bandage. What should your actions be?
   a. Bandage the wound with sterile gauze and compression dressings and leave some extras for the patient and advise him to seek additional care if bleeding continues.
   b. Apply a hemostatic dressing and wrap with compression dressings.
   c. Bandage the wound with sterile gauze and compression dressing and apply supplemental pressure with additional dressings and/or pneumatic splint if appropriate.
   d. Bandage the wound with sterile gauze and compression dressings and apply pressure to brachial pressure point to reduce bleeding.

77. A patient is complaining of chest pain. Which of the following is NOT a contraindication for administering sublingual nitroglycerin?
    a. The patient took Viagra the night before.
    b. The patient's systolic blood pressure is <90.
    c. The patient has an allergy to nitroglycerin.
    d. The patient's systolic blood pressure is >100.

78. A 30-year-old patient is having an anaphylactic reaction due to an insect sting. The EMT's partner grabs the EpiPen from their scene bag and inquires about epinephrine and its effects on the body. The EMT should describe epinephrine as:
    a. A bronchodilator and vasoconstrictor
    b. A bronchoconstrictor and vasoconstrictor
    c. A bronchodilator and vasodilator
    d. A bronchoconstrictor and vasodilator

79. While responding to the aftermath of a tornado, an EMT's partner asks, "What is the primary responsibility of EMS providers during a community disaster drill?" What would be the correct response?
    a. To provide immediate medical care to simulated disaster victims
    b. To educate the community on emergency preparedness measures
    c. To evaluate the performance of other agencies and organizations
    d. To practice and refine response protocols and procedures

80. What is the primary responsibility of EMS providers in the staging area during a multi-casualty incident?
    a. To provide immediate medical care to critically injured patients
    b. To coordinate the transport of patients to the appropriate healthcare facilities
    c. To prepare for and await further assignment from incident command
    d. To document patient care and ensure accurate billing

81. An EMT is responding to a workplace accident. A 50-year-old male construction worker fell from a significant height and landed on his feet. He is conscious and alert, but he complains of excruciating back pain and is unable to move his legs. On assessment, the EMT notices a visible deformity in the middle of his spine. The patient's lower extremities are limp, and he has lost sensation and motor function below the waist. After immobilizing the patient for potential C-spinal injury, what should be the next concern?
    a. Obtaining a set of vital signs to determine the baseline
    b. Giving the patient high-flow oxygen via a non-rebreather mask
    c. Immobilizing the lumbar spine and supporting the lower extremities to prevent further injury
    d. Applying a compression device to immobilize the pelvic girdle and stabilize the hip

82. Which structure serves as the electrical stimulator of the cardiac muscle?
    a. The sinoatrial node
    b. The left ventricle
    c. The aorta
    d. The tricuspid valve

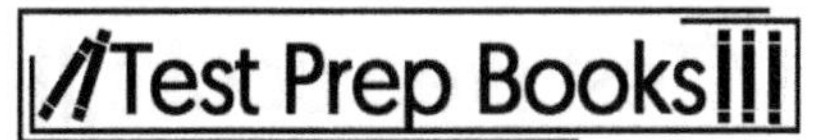

83. You arrive at a high school for a 15-year-old having intense cramping with an 8/10 pain. She states that she has been diagnosed with a menstrual issue and has had issues with her periods, but has not had pain this intense, especially in how abruptly it came on. What action should the EMT take?
    a. Provide emotional support.
    b. Administer over-the-counter pain medication.
    c. Monitor the patient for 15 minutes.
    d. Initiate transport to the hospital.

84. You are ventilating a patient, who was found down and not respirating, with a BVM and OPA. On your next breath, you feel increased resistance, and the patient starts coughing. What are your next steps to perform?
    a. Remove the OPA and provide supplemental oxygen.
    b. Call for ALS support to sedate the patient.
    c. Remove the OPA and insert an NPA.
    d. Provide back blows and abdominal thrusts.

85. How would an EMT attempt to open the airway for a patient with a suspected C-spine injury?
    a. Head-tilt/chin-lift method
    b. Insert an oral airway into the patient
    c. Jaw-thrust method
    d. Position the head and spine in natural supine position (neutral positioning)

86. You arrive to an adult male patient who tells you he is a multiple sclerosis (MS) patient and doesn't know if he is suffering a relapse or has had a stroke. He states that he has lost vision in his right eye, and he has lost use of his right arm and leg. He denies any trauma and says that during his last relapse he only had vision problems and not motor issues. How do you differentiate between the possible stroke vs. MS relapse?
    a. You don't. The treatments are relatively similar, so there is no need to differentiate.
    b. You immediately check for cranial nerve function by having the patient raise their eyebrows, smile, stick out their tongue, and follow a penlight without moving their head.
    c. You assess the patient's response to pain on both the affected and unaffected sides. Take note of the differences.
    d. You begin a cognitive assessment to see if the patient can answer basic questions (e.g., patient's name, today's date/month).

87. You and your partner have arrived on scene to a patient with no respiratory drive. Your partner places an OPA in the patient's mouth and you begin to provide positive pressure ventilations with attached oxygen. While ventilating, you are unable to get the patient's SpO2 to rise and you feel non-compliance as you ventilate. Application of what could help raise the patient's SpO2?
    a. End tidal capnography
    b. Nasal cannula set at 6 LPM flow rate
    c. PEEP valve
    d. CPAP or BiPAP

88. What is the primary responsibility of EMS providers in the rehabilitation area during a prolonged incident or response operation?
    a. To provide medical care to injured responders and victims
    b. To coordinate resources and logistics for response operations
    c. To monitor and assess the health and well-being of responders
    d. To document incident activities and maintain records

89. An EMT responds to an adult patient experiencing a sudden onset of right-sided weakness, left-sided facial drooping, and slurred speech. What would be the most appropriate course of action?
    a. Apply oxygen via nasal cannula and transport to the nearest hospital.
    b. Perform a glucose check.
    c. Administer aspirin and transport to the nearest hospital.
    d. Assist the patient into a comfortable position and assess vital signs.

90. A 7-year-old child has fallen from a tree and is complaining of severe pain in the right arm, which appears deformed. What is the most appropriate initial management of this injury?
    a. Applying a splint to the arm in the position found
    b. Attempting to reposition the arm to its normal anatomical position
    c. Administering pain medication before attempting any movement of the arm
    d. Immediately rushing the child to the hospital without any immobilization

91. A homeless man is found outdoors in freezing temperatures. The patient is conscious but shivering uncontrollably and is confused with slurred speech. You note cold, pale skin. What should your actions be?
    a. Give the patient warm beverages to raise body temperature.
    b. Remove any wet clothing and apply blankets, heated if available.
    c. Gently immerse the patient's hands and feet in warm water.
    d. Place hot compresses in neck, axillary, and groin areas.

92. You are dispatched to a patient at 0100 for chest discomfort. Upon arrival, you note a patient with Levine's sign that appears diaphoretic, tachypneic, and in distress. What is the term for chest pain that occurs at night?
    a. Kehr's angina
    b. Brudzinski's angina
    c. Chovec's angina
    d. Prinzmetal's angina

93. A patient is being transported to the hospital for hypoxia related to a recent pneumonia diagnosis. The patient is currently on 4 liters nasal cannula with an oxygen saturation of 94%. The patient starts to fall asleep and the first responder notices that the patient is breathing primarily through their mouth, rather than their nose. The patient's oxygen saturation decreases to 89% and does not significantly improve with an increase in supplemental oxygen, but improves when the patient wakes and breathes through their nose. What should the EMT do first?
    a. Place the patient on an oxygen mask.
    b. Keep the patient awake.
    c. Place the patient on CPAP.
    d. Place an NPA to maintain the nares if the patient falls asleep.

94. While the EMT is assessing a patient involved in a motor vehicle accident, the patient complains of chest pain and difficulty breathing. The patient is immobilized and has no other complaints. Upon physical assessment, the EMT notices a section of the flail chest with paroxysmal respirations. How does the EMT assist the patient with their breathing?
    a. Supplying the patient with high-flow oxygen via a non-rebreather and transporting supine
    b. Placing a weight (sandbag) on the flail section and transporting on the affected side if permissible
    c. Covering the section of the flail chest with an occlusive dressing and sterile bandages
    d. Supplying high-flow oxygen and transporting the patient in a seated, slightly forward position

95. A patient is being cared for by two EMTs. ALS has been dispatched but has not yet arrived. The patient is unconscious, and CPR is in progress. At pulse check, no pulse is felt, and the AED states that the patient is in asystole. What should the EMT do first?
    a. Defibrillate.
    b. Administer additional rescue breaths.
    c. Continue chest compressions.
    d. Insert an LMA.

96. An EMT arrives at the scene to find a 40-year-old female with a large laceration in the LRQ of her abdomen. She is conscious but confused and appears agitated. On assessment, the EMT notices moderate bleeding that appears controlled with direct pressure. The patient's blood pressure is 90/60 mmHg, heart rate is 120 bpm, and respiratory rate is 28 breaths per minute. What should be the first interventions?
    a. Administer high-flow oxygen, elevate her legs, apply continuous pressure on the wound, and commence rapid transport.
    b. Administer high-flow oxygen, give a baby aspirin under the tongue, and assist with nitro if the patient has it.
    c. Administer low-flow oxygen via nasal cannula, conduct a detailed physical assessment, and determine the patient's history.
    d. Administer high-flow oxygen, apply an occlusive dressing on the wound, and conduct a detailed physical assessment.

97. What is the primary responsibility of EMS providers during a hazardous materials incident?
    a. To decontaminate patients and the environment
    b. To provide immediate medical care to affected individuals
    c. To secure the scene and prevent further exposure
    d. To communicate with specialized hazmat response teams

98. You respond to a call for a 40-year-old female patient who was stung by a bee. Upon your arrival, the patient presents with difficulty breathing, swollen lips and eyes, tightness of chest, and dizziness. What is your first course of action?
    a. Immediately apply a tourniquet above the sting location, apply ice packs, and elevate the area.
    b. Administer 0.30 mg of IV epinephrine EpiPen.
    c. Administer 0.30 mg of subcutaneous/intramuscular epinephrine via EpiPen.
    d. Administer 0.15 mg of subcutaneous/intramuscular epinephrine via EpiPen.

99. A pregnant woman in her third trimester is in distress and experiencing sudden vaginal bleeding. She is conscious and her vitals are currently stable. What action should you take?
    a. Perform a vaginal examination.
    b. Move the patient to a seated position.
    c. Move the patient to her left side.
    d. Administer oxygen and encourage fluid intake.

100. What type of stroke is due to a thrombus (clot) occluding distal circulation for the vessels of the brain, causing tissue death?
    a. Hemorrhagic stroke
    b. Ischemic stroke
    c. TIA
    d. Myocardial infarction

101. As a patient enters respiratory failure, the patient's SpO2 will lower, and their CO_2 will start to rise significantly. Which of the following acid-base disorders would you see in this patient?
    a. Metabolic acidosis
    b. Metabolic alkalosis
    c. Respiratory alkalosis
    d. Respiratory acidosis

102. An EMT responds to a mass casualty incident and is responsible for tagging individuals at the scene. They come across an individual who has a laceration to their thigh. The individual is ambulatory, and their vital signs are stable. What tag should the EMT assign to this patient?
    a. Black tag
    b. Yellow tag
    c. Green tag
    d. Red tag

103. Which of the following is considered a shockable rhythm that can progress to cardiac arrest if not promptly treated?
    a. Sinus bradycardia
    b. Ventricular fibrillation
    c. Pulseless electrical activity (PEA)
    d. Asystole

104. A patient has a burn covering their entire right arm. Using the rule of nines, what percentage of their body is burned?
    a. 9%
    b. 18%
    c. 27%
    d. 36%

105. Upon reaching your unconscious patient and hearing snoring respirations, you decide to insert an NPA, or nasopharyngeal airway. What is the correct way to appropriately size an NPA?
    a. Corner of mouth to earlobe
    b. Nostril to tragus
    c. Nostril to lobe
    d. Corner of mouth to tragus

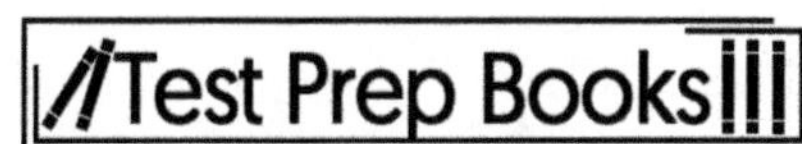

Answer Explanations #1

1. C: If a patient's chest does not rise with BVM ventilation, Choice *C,* repositioning the airway and ensuring a correct seal around the mouth, would be the best course of action. Choice *A* would not be within an EMT's scope of practice. Choice *B* is not the immediate priority in the absence of breathing or pulse. Choice *D* is a misconception; there's no need to wait, as the human body does not store the electrical charge.

2. B: In this scenario, the immediate priority is to control the bleeding to prevent further blood loss and maintain the patient's circulation. Applying direct pressure to the wound is the most appropriate initial action in this situation, as it helps to control the bleeding and stabilize the patient's condition. Applying a tourniquet above the amputated fingers, Choice *A*, is not warranted in this situation. Tourniquets are typically reserved for severe, life-threatening bleeding that cannot be controlled by other means (arterial bleeds, major venous, etc.). Elevating the hand, Choice *C*, may be useful in some cases, but direct pressure is the immediate priority to control the bleeding effectively. Placing the amputated fingers in a plastic bag and immersing them in ice, Choice *D*, is a good practice for preserving the amputated tissue. However, it should not be the initial priority.

3. C: Infants only require light pressure during chest compressions. Both full-hand options would provide too much pressure and could be dangerous for the infant.

4. C: The child is displaying signs of epiglottitis, a serious condition that occurs when the epiglottis in the throat becomes inflamed and swollen. This is typically caused by a bacterial infection. This condition can progress rapidly and lead to severe airway obstruction, which would make it a medical emergency. Maintaining adequate oxygenation and ventilation is the most important action to take in this scenario. Choice *A,* performing a head-tilt/chin-lift maneuver to open the airway, should not be done in cases of suspected epiglottitis because this may cause complete airway closure. Even though instincts might encourage EMTs to administer oral fluids, Choice *B*, this could actually make the child's symptoms worse and obstruct the airway further. A person with suspected epiglottitis should never be placed in a supine position, and their airway should not be assessed. Instead, the individual should be in an upright position to help facilitate breathing.

5. B: The patient appears to have suffered a sting from an unknown insect. The rapid swelling is from a histamine reaction. Left untreated, the pressure can cause loss of blood flow to the distal extremity. Application of ice and a compress dressing along with elevation will reduce the inflammation. Choice *A* would be inappropriate, as it would be extremely painful. The patient is not displaying signs of anaphylaxis, so Choice *C* would be inappropriate, and a tourniquet is not indicated for an insect bite, making Choice *D* incorrect.

6. B: Even though there is no mention of LOC, the fact that the patient was unrestrained should be the first clue to immobilize the C-spine. The forces a person encounters while unrestrained in a vehicle accident may not cause visible injuries, but the risk of C-spine fracture is greater for an unrestrained passenger. Choice *A* would not be appropriate as there are no signs of respiratory distress. Choice *C* may seem appropriate, but scalp wounds bleed profusely since the scalp is extremely vascular. While attention should not be delayed, it can wait until after the patient is immobilized. Choice *D* would be an issue that the EMT would pay attention to after the patient has been stabilized to prevent further injury.

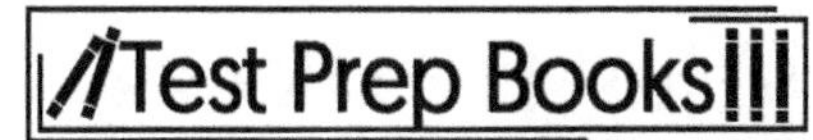

7. B: A biproduct of cellular respiration is carbon dioxide. When the body's energy and oxygen demands increase, there is an increase in carbonic acid, which breaks down into water and carbon dioxide. Carbon dioxide needs to be offloaded from circulation due to its slightly acidic nature. However, if carbon dioxide cannot be offloaded, it fills the hemoglobin and renders the blood unable to take on more oxygen.

8. D: The patient's symptoms suggest a vaso-occlusive, or pain, crisis. This occurs when sickle-shaped blood cells stick together in the vessels, blocking the flow of blood. As a result, this leads to severe pain and swelling in the area. The immediate action the EMT should take is to administer oxygen since blood flow is impaired. Choice *A*, compartment syndrome, occurs when there is increased pressure in a confined muscle compartment. When this occurs, there is impaired blood flow to the area and risk for tissue damage. For patients with compartment syndrome, it is important to seek immediate medical attention and immobilize the affected area. Choice *B*, sequestration crisis, is a complication where sickled cells become trapped in the spleen. As a result, the spleen is enlarged, and there is a high risk for cardiovascular compromise. Patients need to receive immediate medical attention in these scenarios. Choice *C* is incorrect, as there is no evidence of physical trauma to the arm. Splinting will be of no benefit to the patient.

9. D: There are many exclusion criteria for the administration of tPA, a thrombolytic therapy used to break down a clot in the brain's vasculature. Significant findings that do not allow for administration of tPA include the following: greater than 4.5 hours since onset of symptoms, patient on anticoagulant medication, and prior history of heart attack.

10. B: During a seizure, it's essential to protect the patient from potential harm while maintaining their airway. One position is on their side, commonly known as the recovery position. This position helps prevent aspiration of saliva or vomit and allows any secretions to drain out of the mouth, thus reducing the risk of choking. It also maintains a patent airway throughout the seizure. Restraining the patient's movements, Choice *A*, can lead to injuries or fractures or exacerbate the seizure activity. Administering benzodiazepines, Choice *C*, is not within the scope of EMT practice, as the administration of medications is typically reserved for higher-level medical professionals. Applying pressure to the patient's chest, Choice *D*, will not stop the convulsions and can cause harm to the patient.

11. B: In an unconscious patient with snoring respirations, the most appropriate initial intervention is to open the airway using an oropharyngeal airway. Snoring respirations indicate a partially obstructed airway, usually by the tongue. Chest compressions, Choice *A*, are not indicated unless the patient is pulseless. A cervical collar, Choice *C*, could be applied later once the airway is secured, but is not the most important step. Administering high-flow oxygen, Choice *D*, would not be effective if the airway is obstructed.

12. C: The telltale signs of diabetic ketoacidosis (DKA) are the three "polys": extreme thirst (polydipsia), extreme hunger (polyphagia), and frequent urination (polyuria). In addition, blood glucose levels over 250 mg/dL would indicate a patient in DKA. Care is mostly supportive, but transport should be immediate, as DKA can be life threatening if left untreated. Choice *A* is incorrect, as the patient is not suffering from hypoglycemia, even though they haven't eaten in a day. The patient's liver is metabolizing muscle tissue in place of food intake. Adding additional sugar would be detrimental. Choice *B* is incorrect, as hyperglycemia is blood glucose levels 100-250 mg/dL and is usually corrected with an insulin bolus in a hospital setting. Using the patient's insulin would not be indicated and would provide little benefit. Choice *D* is incorrect, as the patient is not suffering from hypothyroidism.

13. D: Testicular torsion occurs when a blood vessel twists upon itself, restricting blood flow to the affected area. Choices *A, B,* and *C* are all symptoms of a testicular torsion as the blood flow blockage will cause swelling and discoloration near the torsion with pain radiating down the leg. Choice *D* will not be a sign as the injury is not to the urinary system.

14. C: Chemotherapy attacks all fast-growing cells. While it will kill cancer cells, it will also kill beneficial cells. The patient's immune system is highly compromised while on chemotherapy. For the protection of the patient, all emergency responders that will be in contact with the patient should be masked, as should the patient. Actively being on chemotherapy does not require rapid transport unless a life-threatening condition exists, making Choice *A* incorrect. While the patient is at high risk of infection, they are not contagious, and full body protection is not required, nor is sterilization of surfaces that the patient came in contact with, making Choices *B* and *D* incorrect.

15. B: The appropriate action regarding the use of an AED in a patient with an ICD is to apply the AED pads as usual and follow the AED prompts. While it is important to avoid placing the AED pads directly over the ICD, the AED can still be used for rhythm analysis and delivering appropriate shocks, if necessary. The presence of the ICD should not prevent the use of the AED in providing potential life-saving interventions. Choices *A, C,* and *D* are not recommended actions according to the BLS guidelines.

16. D: Joe is showing symptoms of epiglottitis. A clinician should consider all differential diagnosis when treating airway disorders. Further aggravating or inserting a tube is likely to irritate the area further and may cause it to swell shut, leading to a complete obstruction. Tim and Tom should keep Joe calm, monitor his appearance, monitor his pulse oximetry, and request an ALS intercept as they attend to and transport him.

17. D: EMTs should ensure their vehicles are able and ready to respond to an emergency and transport an ill or injured patient. This ability to sustain a state of readiness requires a consistent schedule. Many organizations use an inventory checklist to ensure that consistent assessments take place.

18. B: The Glasgow Coma Scale (GCS) can be modified for infants and young children to assess their level of consciousness and neurological function. The pediatric GCS evaluates eye opening, verbal response, and motor response in a manner appropriate for infants. In this scenario, the patient would be rated as follows:

- Eye opening: The infant opens her eyes in response to your voice, which corresponds to a GCS score of 3.
- Verbal response: The infant is irritable and inconsolable, which corresponds to a GCS score of 4.
- Motor response: The infant exhibits decerebrate posturing, indicating a GCS score of 2.
- To calculate the total GCS score, add the scores from each component: 3 (eye opening) + 4 (verbal response) + 2 (motor response) = 9.

19. B: The use of targeted temperature management is implemented to reduce the metabolic demand of the brain and other organs to reduce the risk of damage after cardiac arrest. This protocol has been shown to reduce mortality and improve neurological function after times of low perfusion.

20. B: After an acute ankle injury, it's important to control swelling and pain. Remember, for acute minor soft-tissue injuries, RICE (Rest, Ice, Compression, Elevation) is the best course of action. Choice *A*

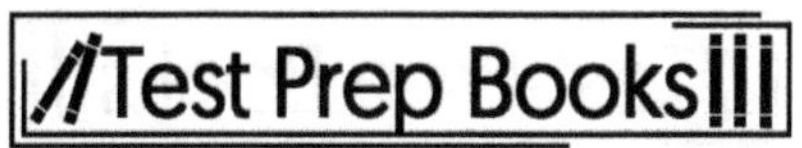

can increase inflammation in the early stages of injury. Choice *C* is premature without proper assessment and imaging to determine the extent of the injury. Choice *D* is not indicated unless an infection is suspected.

21. A: The child's symptoms are that of intussusception. Intussusception occurs when the intestines telescope or fold into another segment, which causes a blockage. It is usually seen in pediatric patients and presents with severe, sudden abdominal pain, vomiting, and blood and mucus in the stool. For general abdominal pain, bowel sounds may provide useful information, but the symptom of "red jelly stool" is a sign that this patient requires immediate transport, making Choice *B* incorrect. Choice *C*, administering over-the-counter pain medications, is not appropriate for suspected intussusception since treatment is done by healthcare professionals in a hospital. Although administering fluids may be necessary, it is not the first action to take, making Choice *D* incorrect.

22. D: The patient initially showed signs of a pneumothorax with decreased breath sounds on one side. The patient has now progressed to displaying signs of tension pneumothorax, which can cause the patient to decompensate into cardiac arrest if not treated quickly. Because of this risk, it is essential that the first responder quickly identifies the condition and intercepts with a provider capable of performing needle chest decompression. The other interventions listed will not decrease the pressure to the patient's thoracic cavity.

23. A: The Cincinnati Prehospital Stroke Scale is an assessment that can identify a possible stroke. The components of this assessment are arm drift, facial droop, and abnormal speech. Loss of visual acuity could be a symptom of a stroke, but it isn't a part of the essential Cincinnati Prehospital Stroke Scale.

24. D: Renal calculi, also known as kidney stones, cause patients to experience frequent and painful urination. They experience severe, colicky pain in the lower back or side that can radiate to the groin. The patient should be encouraged to urinate if able, and the collected urine should be given to hospital staff. If passed, the stone can be used to determine the cause of stone formation. Patients are usually best at determining the position of transport. Choice *A* is incorrect, as a urinary tract infection usually presents with a fever and the pain is usually in the groin/pubic area. Choice *B* is incorrect, as urethral stricture is a narrowing of the urethra, making urination difficult and not presenting as back pain. Choice *C* is incorrect, as a sexually transmitted disease does not normally present with blood in the urine and back pain.

25. B: The liver is the most injured organ in blunt abdominal trauma, and the location of pain and discoloration points to this. A liver laceration can cause significant internal bleeding, leading to a rigid and tender abdomen, and can lead to hypovolemic shock quickly. Choice *A* would be helpful later in the assessment but is not an immediate concern. The pain from a lacerated liver can present with pain to the back area, but the rigid abdomen should clue the EMT to potential liver injury; therefore, Choice *C* would not be appropriate. Choice *D* will be something to do, but a liver laceration may not cause any change to the patient's bowel sounds, and this can wait until later in the assessment, if time permits.

26. B: This individual is experiencing signs of agitation and potential aggression. The safety of the EMT and others is the priority in this situation, which is why maintaining a safe distance and observing the scene is the best action to take initially. Choice *A* is incorrect, as it puts you in danger. Choice *C* is incorrect. The EMT should not approach the individual to calm the individual down because this may escalate the situation and cause potential harm to others. Restraining the individual should only be done when there is an imminent threat to others, making Choice *D* incorrect.

27. C: When responding to a critical emergency call, it is vital to get there as soon and as safely as possible. This means continuing through an intersection at a normal speed, even if there is a red light. The EMT still must be mindful of other vehicles. Choice *A* is incorrect as not stopping can increase the risk of a collision. Choice *B,* completely stopping and then proceeding, is not appropriate; this is a critical emergency call, and it is important to get to the scene as soon as possible. Proceeding through the intersection at a higher speed since the siren and lights are activated can also increase the risk of collision, making Choice *D* incorrect.

28. D: *C. diff* is a highly contagious bacterial infection that causes colon inflammation, and the patient suffers from severe diarrhea. The bacteria can live for a prolonged time on surfaces, so the patient needs to be as isolated as possible. You need to protect yourself and anyone else who may be transported later by thoroughly washing your hands with soap and water and disposing of PPE and any linens used in an appropriate container. No other people should be allowed into the ambulance until it has been thoroughly cleaned and sanitized. Choices *A*, *B*, and *C* are not appropriate precautions.

29. A: Neonatal patients are obligate nose breathers until around two to six months of age. Because of this, excess mucus production can cause an emergent upper airway obstruction in these patients and suctioning is required. ALS will need to be involved, but this should occur after the patient's airway is clear. Chest compressions are not indicated since the patient is breathing and conscious. The EMT should never blind-sweep the patient's mouth in search of a foreign body, as this may cause increased obstruction.

30. C: When patients are in PEA (pulseless electrical activity), the electrical signal travels through the heart, but the mechanical part of the heart doesn't respond to the electricity. This means that no blood is being pumped.

31. A: An open chest wound can lead to a pneumothorax. A gloved hand will stop air from rushing in. This must be followed by an occlusive dressing because it prevents air from entering the chest cavity. Sterile gauze dressing, Choice *B*, would not provide the airtight seal that an occlusive dressing would. Choice *C* would be appropriate for a flail chest segment but not an open chest wound. Choice *D*, hemostatic dressings, are not indicated for chest wounds and do not provide the needed seal.

32. A: This patient is showing signs of acute coronary syndrome. Initial treatment for this condition is administration of aspirin, an antiplatelet medication, which can help decrease clot production. Supplemental oxygen may help for comfort; however, the patient currently has an adequate oxygen saturation, so this intervention is not required. CPR is not indicated, as the patient is alert and has a pulse. The EMT should not be advising the patient to take his blood pressure medication. Although his blood pressure is somewhat elevated, this could be due to a variety of factors (such as pain or acute stress), and this intervention requires advanced medical training to decide.

33. D: Hyperventilation can be caused by acute anxiety and by medical conditions. The first intervention is to assist the patient in attempting to slow their breathing rate. Breathing into a paper bag or oxygen mask may be dangerous for patients who are experiencing hyperventilation due to a medical condition, so this should not be done without medical direction. The EMT should never tell the patient that their symptoms are "all in their head," as this can increase anxiety and decrease trust in first responders and other medical professionals.

34. D: Breaks in chest compressions should be as short as possible. Therefore, chest compressions should continue while the AED is charging and resume immediately after the defibrillation is administered.

35. A: An emergency involving a strange odor and several unconscious people is indicative of airborne poisoning, making this a toxicological emergency. Psychiatric emergencies involve mentally unstable patients, hematological emergencies are blood-related emergencies, and immunological emergencies involve allergic reactions. Nothing within the question indicates mental instability or bleeding, and it is unlikely that multiple patients have the same allergy, so Choices *B*, *C*, and *D* are incorrect.

36. B: The patient is more than likely experiencing a flare-up of his GERD. His history of GERD and last oral intake being 6 hours ago are your clues. Excess stomach acid builds without any food intake. A GERD patient already has trouble keeping stomach acid out of the esophagus, and with excess acid this is exacerbated. While he presents with some potential cardiac issues, the stable vital signs and skin don't indicate a cardiac issue, making Choice *A* incorrect. Choice *C* would be incorrect because with any abdominal issue, you want to restrict oral intake until what is causing the pain can be determined. Applying compresses to the area will have little benefit to the patient, making Choice *D* incorrect.

37. D: When treating pediatric patients, body size and blood pressure are different depending on the patient's age. The formula $70 + 2 \times (\text{age in years})$ gives the clinician the ability to determine if the patient is hypotensive according to the relative size of the pediatric patient. For example, if the patient was 6 years old, the equation would read $70 + 2(6) = 82$. Anything under 82 for the systolic blood pressure would be considered hypotensive.

38. A: The patient presents with the sign of an upper respiratory infection, potentially tuberculosis. Droplets from the patient must encounter your mucous membranes (eye, nose, mouth) to cause infection. The droplets themselves do not pose a long-term risk of exposure on surfaces, so full gown is not required. Choices *B*, *C*, and *D* are not appropriate for contact precautions.

39. D: The patient still has a pulse, so rescue breathing is warranted. Supplemental oxygen is important to ensure perfusion, but it is not the immediate action needed. Placing the patient in the lateral recumbent position would not ventilate the patient. Performing a needle chest decompression is an advance practice skill that ALS personnel would need to administer.

40. A: After resuscitation, AHA recommends a targeted temperature management between 32 and 36 degrees Celsius. This temperature management has been proven to improve neurological outcomes in a post-ROSC (return of spontaneous circulation) patient. Placement of a definitive airway is important, but a clinician should remember to stay within their scope of practice.

41. C: This patient is exhibiting signs of carbon monoxide poisoning. The first line of treatment for a patient with suspected carbon monoxide poisoning is to exit the affected area and bring the patient out into the fresh air. The patient will require high-flow supplemental oxygen to prevent hypoxia. Choice *A* is incorrect, as a nasal airway may be indicated in a patient who is unconscious and unable to maintain their airway. A CPAP device is meant for patients in severe respiratory distress who are struggling to open their lungs, making Choice *B* incorrect. Choice *D* is incorrect, as nebulizer treatments are meant for treating COPD and asthma exacerbation.

42. D: Compartment syndrome is a severe medical condition where increased pressure inside the muscle compartments can hinder blood circulation, depriving nerve and muscle cells of essential oxygen and nutrients. Removing constrictive clothing and elevating the limb will help to reduce the pressure that is building. Choice *A* could cause additional harm to the patient. Choice *B* would not be appropriate as compartment syndrome usually occurs at pressures less than arterial pressure. Because of this, distal pulses can be present. The patient is complaining of lower leg pain, so this eliminates Choice *C* since a traction splint would be indicated for an upper leg fracture.

43. C: The woman is most likely experiencing a pulmonary embolism, a serious medical condition that can potentially lead to death. Pregnant women are at increased risk for developing blood clots due to alterations in blood clotting factors and increased pressure on the veins in their pelvis. Improving oxygenation is essential in this situation to maintain vital organ function. Choice *A*, administering nitroglycerin, is not appropriate. Even though nitroglycerin is used for angina and other chest pain-related conditions, it is contraindicated in pregnancy. Laying the woman on her left side is generally helpful during pregnancy to increase blood flow to the placenta and baby, but in this situation, the woman is in respiratory distress. Putting her in the left lying position could make her symptoms worse and decrease oxygenation, making Choice *B* incorrect. Choice *D* is also incorrect, as this position does not provide adequate support for blood flow. The woman should be sat up straight.

44. D: Clasping at one's throat, and possibly gasping (with no signs of trauma), is a hallmark sign of choking. The Heimlich maneuver should be performed to help remove the foreign body and open this patient's airway. Once the airway is opened, or if the Heimlich is unsuccessful and the patient is at risk of decompensating, then ALS should be dispatched to the scene. An OPA is contraindicated and may force the foreign body deeper into the trachea. Water is also contraindicated, as the patient may aspirate the water if he is choking on a foreign body.

45. A: With the patient denying any chance of pregnancy, you should be looking for a potential ovarian cyst. The patient will often complain of lower abdominal pain with radiation to the lower back that can be confused for kidney stones, but there is not any issue with urination for ovarian cysts. The care is limited to a warm compress to the affected area to alleviate some of the pain, restricting oral intake, and transporting in the most comfortable position for the patient. A cold compress is not going to provide much benefit to the patient, making Choice *B* incorrect. You want to restrict a patient's oral intake to prevent any accidental aspiration, making Choices *C* and *D* incorrect.

46. C: The most appropriate action to take is to keep the patient lying down and to stabilize his head and neck to prevent any potential movement that could cause further complications. Spinal immobilization is essential when head trauma is present until the cervical spine has been assessed and cleared. Choice *A* is incorrect as a detailed neurological examination is beyond the scope of pre-hospital care. The EMT should only perform a brief neurological assessment to determine any immediate concerns or signs of severe injury. Choice *B*, getting the individual up into a chair slowly, is also incorrect as this increases the risk of making the injury worse. Choice *D*, applying a sterile dressing to the laceration to control the bleeding, is an important action to take but should not come before immobilizing the head and neck.

47. C: Keeping in mind that pregnancy causes the amount of circulating blood and plasma to increase, hypotension in pregnancy can cause inadequate perfusion to the fetus. Utero-placental insufficiency can create an increased risk of spontaneous abortion or miscarriage.

48. C: While Benadryl and a surgical cricothyroidotomy would be possible with an ALS crew, an EMT should stay within their scope of practice. The most critical intervention would be to ensure that the patient doesn't enter shock and maintains an airway. Choice *C* uses epinephrine, which would cause

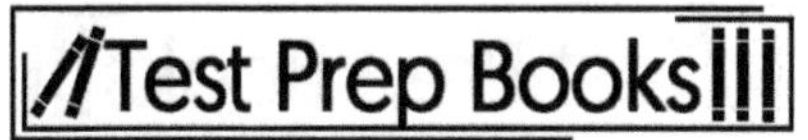

bronchodilation and vasoconstriction, temporarily helping the patient until he can be taken to the hospital.

49. C: In the AHA post-resuscitation algorithm, a patient's target $ETCO_2$ should be 35-40 mmHg. This is because the patient is in metabolic acidosis due to the patient being in anaerobic metabolism while in cardiac arrest. The goal is to "blow off" some of the excess carbon dioxide and thus also stabilize the patient's pH.

50. B: Hypothyroidism is caused by too little thyroid hormone, which regulates metabolism, causing a hypoactive metabolism and leading to a waxy and swollen appearance, cold intolerance, hypothermia, hypotension, and bradycardia. Most care is going to be supportive to the patient, as your options are limited. Choice *A* is incorrect because you would not want to put heat compresses since the patient's hypothermia is not environmentally related. Choice *C* is incorrect, as more than blood sugar needs to be monitored. Choice *D* is incorrect because O_2 saturations will provide you with some data, but not the most valuable data, and not the only information you need.

51. D: Keeping the child lying flat on their back and maintaining spinal precautions is the most appropriate immediate action in the case of a head injury with potential trauma. Maintaining spinal precautions helps minimize movement of the spine and reduces the risk of exacerbating any spinal cord injuries. Applying direct pressure to the forehead laceration, Choice *A*, may help control the bleeding, but it should not be the immediate priority when dealing with a head injury. Gently shaking the child, Choice *B*, is not recommended, as it could worsen any possible head or neck injuries. Removing the child's bicycle helmet, Choice *C*, should be avoided unless the helmet interferes with proper airway management.

52. B: The patient is hypoxic and requires supplemental oxygen to prevent further complications. Listening to breath sounds may be a useful assessment for further treatment, but the patient's need for improving his oxygen saturation is the highest priority, making Choice *A* incorrect. An aspirin may be helpful to decrease the patient's chest pain but, again, is of lower priority to treating hypoxia, making Choice *C* incorrect. Choice *D* is incorrect, as the patient's fever is the lowest priority now.

53. D: If a patient has facial trauma, a clinician should have a high degree of suspicion that the patient may have a basilar skull fracture and possible cervical fracture, which contraindicates *A* and *C*. The patient also has a pulse, so CPR is contraindicated. This only leaves Choice *D*, insert an OPA and attempt to ventilate.

54. A: The key question for any patient who underwent a mastectomy is to find out if the lymph nodes were removed. When the nodes are removed, the lymph system does not work as efficiently. Repeated blood pressure readings on the affected side can cause damage to the lymph system on that side and cause lymphedema. If lymph nodes have been removed, blood pressure readings should be taken on the unaffected side. Choices *B* and *D* are incorrect, as the nodes were removed, so the reading should be taken on the right arm. Choice *C* is incorrect because if the nodes were not removed, the increased risk of lymphedema is not present, so both arms can be used.

55. D: A greenstick fracture is characterized by an incomplete fracture where the bone is bent and thin slivers of bone separate from one end. Since a child's bones are still developing and not as rigid, this fracture is most often seen in children. The hardness of adult bone makes this type of fracture extremely uncommon in adults. Choice *A* is a fracture where the bone breaks into multiple pieces. Choice *B* is a fracture where the bone protrudes from the skin. Choice *C* is a fracture from a twisting force, and the fracture spirals around the bone. All three of the other types of fractures can be seen in children and adults.

56. B: For pediatric patients, the appropriate depth for chest compressions is at least 2 inches. If a provider does not reach this depth, perfusion will be inadequate for the rest of the body. Three inches is too deep for chest compressions, as is $\frac{1}{2}$ of the chest's depth.

57. A: This patient is showing signs of bronchoconstriction with wheezing and difficulty breathing. Nebulizers are the typical treatment for bronchoconstriction. The patient does not currently require supplemental oxygen. Therefore, a nasal cannula and nonrebreather are not indicated at this time. CPAP should not be administered to a pediatric patient without advanced medical directive, as it could cause barotrauma to the lungs.

58. A: Many of the medications for erectile dysfunction are derived from a blood-pressure-reducing medication. An erection lasting more than 4 hours is a life-threatening emergency. If the patient has other conditions, it can exacerbate the condition and the patient can suffer from permanent penile damage. Choices *B*, *C*, and *D* are all inappropriate.

59. A: Patients with advanced dementia can often become irritated when their normal daily routine is disrupted. Their memory is often fading, and they may not remember that family members have died or no longer live with them. The least invasive measure you can take is to try and converse in a low voice. Attempt to distract the patient with small talk, like asking about their favorite hobby or job they had. If it is safe, you can give a dementia patient a small task to distract them, like folding a towel. Choices *B*, *C*, and *D* are all inappropriate for a dementia patient.

60. A: An MCI or mass casualty incident is an incident where there is a high demand on EMS services due to the number and nature of patients. A good example of this would be a natural disaster or a multi-vehicle collision scene. There isn't a specific number of patients to meet this criterion, but when EMS becomes overburdened and unable to provide appropriate care to all injured personnel, it is considered an MCI.

61. D: Venturi masks are often the best course of action when treating COPD patients, and since Susie is able to sit upright, this will assist in keeping her airway open. If Susie is alert while upright, there is no need to place her in the sniffing position. There is not a vital need for Janet to call her supervisor, and bag-valve-mask ventilation would not be appropriate in this scenario.

62. C: While counterintuitive, leaving all interventions in place displays to the patient's parents that the EMS crew attempted to resuscitate the patient. If an EMT removed any interventions, it could give hope back to the parents and lengthen the grieving process. If there is ever a question of what to do next, medical control will give instructions on how the crew should proceed.

63. C: Elderly females often present with increased confusion when experiencing a urinary tract infection (UTI). This can quickly advance to sepsis if treated as a non-emergent condition. There is no evidence that suggests a cardiac issue. While it can't be ruled out, the present signs and symptoms don't indicate that MI interventions are warranted, making Choice *A* incorrect. The patient should not be given water in case of aspiration risk or of emergent invasive procedures that may be conducted at the hospital, making Choice *B* incorrect. The patient is not presenting with symptoms of heat stroke. The skin of a patient suffering heat stroke is considerably warmer than a febrile patient, making Choice *D* incorrect.

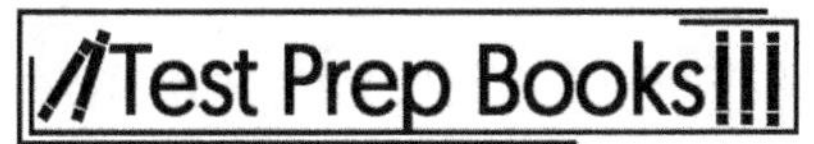

64. A: The American Heart Association suggests that targeted temperature management therapy should last twenty-four hours to preserve as much neurologic function as possible. The temperature should be between 32 and 36 degrees Celsius.

65. C: The only way that a DNR order may become revoked or invalid is when a patient's medical condition improves significantly, and they want to change their resuscitation status. Being unconscious does not invalidate a DNR order if the DNR reflects the patient's wishes, making Choice *A* incorrect. A person's age does not influence the validity of a DNR order, making Choice *B* incorrect. Choice *D* is also incorrect as the patient or their legal representative decides on DNR orders based on their medical wishes and condition. A DNR will follow a patient to their next provider.

66. B: The woman's signs are indicative of a possible ectopic pregnancy; she should be transported to the emergency room immediately. Choice *A* is incorrect, as round ligament pain, a common symptom in pregnancy, does not cause bleeding or signs of shock. Choice *C* is incorrect because although a miscarriage also presents with vaginal bleeding, signs of shock (such as diaphoresis) and severe abdominal pain are not common. Choice *D,* placental abruption, would present as painless vaginal bleeding, making this answer choice incorrect.

67. D: Providing high-flow oxygen through a non-rebreather mask helps support the patient's respiratory efforts and oxygen saturation. It is vital in cases of chest trauma and difficulty breathing to ensure an adequate oxygen supply to the body's tissues and organs. Administering pain medication, Choice *A*, may be necessary, but it should not be the immediate priority when dealing with potential chest trauma and difficulty breathing. Choice *B* is not an immediate action. The patient's breathing is the priority concern. Immobilizing the patient's chest with a chest binder, Choice *C*, may be helpful in certain cases, but it is not the immediate priority in this scenario. Always prioritize airway, breathing, and circulation (ABCs) in trauma situations.

68. D: While there are many ways EMS personnel can help foster relationships within the communities they serve, providing the best possible care to patients builds trust in their service. These relationships influence views on EMS and can impact the respect given to any EMS service.

69. B: The AHA or American Heart Association card courses are due to be recertified every two years. In order to perform EMS or EMT duties in any state, an EMT must have current card courses. The recertification process allows the AHA to update out-of-practice standards and ensure proficiency when performing each category.

70. D: In the case of ingestion of a potentially harmful substance, the most important step is to get the child to a healthcare facility as quickly as possible. Attempting to neutralize the substance at home can be dangerous and is not recommended. Administering activated charcoal, Choice *A*, or inducing vomiting, Choice *B*, can potentially cause more harm, especially if the substance is caustic. Diluting the substance with milk or water, Choice *C*, is also not recommended, as it can potentially spread the substance further into the digestive tract.

71. C: After an advanced airway is in place, a provider should initiate breaths at a rate of one breath for every five to six seconds. This is essentially normal rescue breathing as ventilations will no longer interrupt or interfere with compressions.

72. C: The patient is conscious, so placing an oral airway is contraindicated, as the patient's gag reflex is likely to prevent any benefit of the airway and may even cause the patient to vomit. In this case, since the patient is somewhat conscious with only mild hypoxia, a nasal cannula may work best. Keeping the patient upright and soothed/cooperative may be useful to providing care as well.

73. B: The presence of the tracheostomy tube renders opening the airway at the head useless. The point of ambient air for the patient is the tracheostomy tube. Just as you check the patient's mouth for an obstruction, you would do the same for the tube. Manual ventilation would be at the tube. Choices *A*, *C*, and *D* are all incorrect because, as mentioned, opening the airway at the mouth will not open the airway.

74. A: As soon as a clinician suspects a myocardial infarction, first responders should be in touch with the nearest cardiac hospital to ensure that interventions are initiated as early as possible. ST elevation is a sign of an ST elevation myocardial infarction (STEMI), which is caused by a severe blockage in heart vasculature. Defibrillation is only indicated in pulseless ventricular tachycardia and ventricular fibrillation. Rescue breaths would be indicated if the patient was not breathing sufficiently on his own. Needle decompression would be indicated if tension pneumothorax was suspected.

75. B: The patient's airway must be opened, but the helmet should stay in place. Removal of the helmet could make any potential C-spine injury worse. The facemask can be removed to better examine the airway. The airway should be opened with the jaw-thrust method. The patient requires chest compressions to stay alive. Choice *A* is not indicated as there are no signs of respiration, so the airway needs to be opened first. As stated above, the helmet should remain on, so Choice *C* would not be appropriate. While immediate transport should be made, Choice *D*, it does not preclude starting chest compressions.

76. C: A-Fib can cause the formation of clots within the heart. To prevent this, a patient is often prescribed anticoagulants to prevent clot formation. A side effect is this risk for increased bleeding. A minor cut for a healthy individual can be a medical emergency for someone on anticoagulants. While direct pressure would be the first intervention, often it is insufficient to control bleeding and requires further interventions. You should consider supplemental pressure where available to increase pressure. Simple bandaging and leaving extras for the patient would be inappropriate, as the patient would not know what to do for continued bleeding. Choice *B* would be inappropriate in this scenario, as hemostatic dressings are used for catastrophic bleeding. A pressure point is only to be used in an arterial bleed and would be inappropriate, making Choice *D* incorrect.

77. D: If the patient has a prescription for nitroglycerin, it is safe for them to take it for chest pain if they have a systolic blood pressure (SBP) of greater than 100. Nitroglycerin should not be given to anyone with an SBP of less than 90, as nitroglycerin can lower their blood pressure and put them into shock. Nitroglycerin is also contraindicated with phosphodiesterase inhibitors (such as Viagra) and for patients with an allergy to nitroglycerin.

78. A: Epinephrine is an alpha 1, beta 1, and beta 2 receptor agonist in the body. Alpha 1 receptors cause vasoconstriction. Beta 2 receptors cause bronchodilation. Because the patient is having an anaphylactic reaction, the patient's vessels have dilated and their bronchus has constricted. These symptoms are corrected by the administration of epinephrine.

79. D: During a community disaster drill, the primary responsibility of EMS providers is to practice and refine response protocols and procedures. While providing immediate medical care to simulated disaster victims, Choice *A*; educating the community, Choice *B*; and evaluating the performance of other

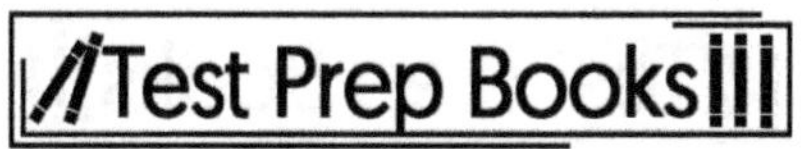

agencies and organizations, Choice *C*, are important, they are not the primary responsibility during the drill.

80. C: During a multi-casualty incident, the primary responsibility of EMS providers in the staging area is to prepare for and await further assignment from incident command. While providing immediate medical care, Choice *A*; coordinating patient transport, Choice *B*; and documenting patient care, Choice *D*, are important, they are not the primary responsibility in the staging area.

81. C: In this scenario, the patient experienced a fall from a significant height. The presence of excruciating back pain, a visible deformity in the middle of his spine, and the inability to move his legs are indicative of a possible lumbar spine compression fracture. The loss of sensation and motor function below the waist suggests a spinal cord injury at the level of the lumbar spine. Choice *C* will provide the most protection from additional injury. Choice *A* is important, but it can be obtained after the patient is sufficiently immobilized to prevent any further injury. While supplemental oxygen may be helpful, there is nothing to indicate the patient needs high-flow oxygen, so Choice *B* is incorrect. Choice *D* would not be indicated for a spinal fracture. Pneumatic compression devices are indicated for femur and pelvic fractures and would not prevent movement of the lower back.

82. A: The sinoatrial node is the primary stimulator of electrical activity in the heart. The other structures listed play a role in blood flow, but they do not deal with electrical stimulation.

83. D: Although the patient has been diagnosed with dysmenorrhea, or painful periods, the fact that this is sudden and more intense than usual warrants further investigation. She should be transported to the hospital for further testing and evaluation. Providing emotional support is important, but it is not the first action that should be taken, making Choice *A* incorrect. Administering pain medication may be helpful, but this should not be an action for you to take, making Choice *B* incorrect. Choice *C* is also incorrect, as simply monitoring the patient for 15 minutes does not address the acuity of her condition.

84. A: If the patient regains consciousness, the provider should pull the OPA out, assist in the re-oxygenation of the patient with supplemental O_2, and suction if needed. A patient maintaining their own airway and ventilations is the best outcome, and they should be assisted when possible.

85. C: The problem with opening an airway for a suspected C-spine patient arises from the need to keep the patient's head immobile. Choice *C* is the only maneuver to open the airway without moving the head. It can be used in helmeted patients after injury. Choices *A* and *B* require the patient's head to be moved. Choice *D*, neutral positioning, would be used to ensure an open airway in infants.

86. B: MS is a chronic immunological disorder that affects the patient's central and peripheral nervous system. It is a series of immunological attacks followed by periods of remission. The span between relapse and remission can vary between patients. Some have attacks weekly, while others go years without one. MS can present with any number of symptoms depending on where in the CNS the attack occurs. While MS can affect cranial nerves, it is highly uncommon—but a stroke will always affect the cranial nerves. Therefore, having a patient smile or raise their eyebrows may reveal facial droop or the inability to raise both eyebrows, which are telltale signs of a stroke. For a stroke patient, time is critical. Pharmacological treatments must be administered within a specific time, making Choice *A* incorrect. Choices *C* and *D* are not going to provide any useful information.

87. C: Choice *C*, PEEP, or positive end expiratory pressure, can help facilitate oxygenation by recuperating alveoli, which could raise the patient's SpO2. Capnography would be useful if you wanted to determine if cellular respiration was happening. A nasal cannula or CPAP/BiPAP would not help a patient in respiratory failure.

88. C: During a prolonged incident or response operation, the primary responsibility of EMS providers in the rehabilitation area is to monitor and assess the health and well-being of responders. While providing medical care to injured responders and victims, Choice *A*; coordinating resources and logistics for response operations, Choice *B*; and documenting incident activities and maintaining records, Choice *D*, are important, they are not the primary responsibility in the rehabilitation area.

89. A: This patient is experiencing a stroke. The most important action to take for this patient is to administer supplemental oxygen to encourage perfusion while transporting the patient to the nearest hospital for stroke assessment and care. Even though checking the patient's blood glucose level is important to rule out hypoglycemia, the patient's symptoms are indicative of a stroke, making Choice *B* incorrect. Choice *C* is incorrect because aspirin should not be administered for this patient until they are evaluated by a physician to determine whether the stroke is hemorrhagic or ischemic. Giving aspirin to patients having a hemorrhagic stroke can potentially worsen bleeding and provide further complications. Even though helping the patient into a more comfortable position and monitoring vital signs is important, this does not address the underlying stroke that the patient is experiencing, making Choice *D* incorrect.

90. A: In the case of a suspected fracture, it is important to immobilize the injury in the position found to prevent further damage. Attempting to reposition the arm, Choice *B*, could potentially cause more harm. While pain management is important, Choice *C* should not delay other necessary interventions. Rushing the child to the hospital without any immobilization, Choice *D*, could potentially cause further injury.

91. B: The patient's signs and symptoms indicate hypothermia. In cases of hypothermia, initial treatment should focus on preventing further heat loss and utilizing passive rewarming techniques. Passive rewarming includes removing wet clothing and covering the patient with warm blankets or clothing. This allows the body to regain its normal temperature slowly, avoiding any complications. Administering warm beverages might seem like a good idea, but the patient's swallowing ability may be compromised. Additionally, warm beverages do not provide effective rewarming of the core, making Choice *A* incorrect. Immersing the patient in warm water or aggressive active rewarming techniques using a heat source such as a heating compress could cause a patient to experience an arrhythmia, making Choices *C* and *D* incorrect.

92. D: Prinzmetal's angina is a type of chest pain that occurs at night, typically when the patient is asleep. The most notable impression is when a patient wakes up from a dead sleep with chest pain. This type of chest pain responds well to nitroglycerin and occurs due to a coronary artery spasm.

93. A: This patient appears to not be receiving enough supplemental oxygen because the method of administration does not match how he is breathing. Because of this, the first responder should perform Choice *A* and change to an oxygen mask, which will allow the patient to receive oxygen through both his nose and mouth. Keeping the patient awake may be an option, but since the patient has a known infection, rest is ideal whenever possible to aid in healing. CPAP and high-flow oxygen are not indicated since the patient is able to achieve an ideal oxygen saturation when the mechanism of delivery matches his breathing pattern.

94. B: The patient is having difficulty breathing because the section of the chest is moving opposite to the rest of the thorax, decreasing how much the lungs can inflate. A weight, like a sandbag, placed on the flail segment will stop the opposite movement and may provide some assistance to the patient. If possible, transport the patient on the affected side to help decrease flail section movement. Choice *A* is incorrect; while the patient may require supplemental oxygen, there is no indication that high flow is necessary. The patient should be transported on the affected side if possible. Choice *C* is incorrect; an occlusive dressing is used to prevent air from entering from an external wound and would not be indicated in this situation. Choice *D* is indicated for use when a person is having difficulty exhaling (e.g., COPD) and would not provide any assistance in this instance.

95. C: Asystole is not a shockable rhythm. Chest compressions should be continued until ALS arrives and can continue with advanced interventions. Rescue breaths should continue at a ratio of thirty compressions to two breaths. Additional breaths may cause too many pauses in chest compressions.

96. A: Hypovolemic shock occurs when there is a significant loss of blood or fluid from the circulatory system, leading to inadequate perfusion of vital organs and tissues. In this case, the patient's bleeding appears controlled, but her vital signs indicate potential internal bleeding. Choice *B* would be appropriate for potential cardiac issues. While hypovolemia can lead to cardiac issues, the priority is treating the patient for shock. Choice *C* would be appropriate for a superficial wound with stable vitals. Choice *D* would be appropriate for a sucking chest wound, but occlusive dressings would not be used in an abdominal wound.

97. B: During a hazardous materials incident, the primary responsibility of EMS providers is to provide immediate medical care to affected individuals. While decontaminating patients and the environment, Choice *A*; securing the scene and preventing further exposure, Choice *C*; and communicating with specialized hazmat response teams, Choice *D*, are important, they are not the primary responsibility of EMS providers during a hazardous materials incident.

98. C: Based on the description of the signs and symptoms, one can conclude that the patient is suffering from anaphylaxis, meaning that she will require a shot of epinephrine, making Choice *A* incorrect. Choice *B* is incorrect, as the injection of the EpiPen is not intravenous. The patient is 40 years old; she will need an adult dose of 0.30 mg of epinephrine, the correct adult dose; therefore, Choice *C* is the correct answer. Choice *D* is incorrect, because 0.15 mg is the dose for a pediatric patient.

99. C: Sudden bleeding in the third trimester of pregnancy is abnormal and can indicate placental abruption, an obstetric emergency. The EMT should move the woman to her left side to help improve venous blood flow to the heart and increase blood flow to the organs, specifically the placenta. The left lateral position allows for reduced pressure on the vena cava, which can help increase blood flow. Choice *A* is incorrect because a vaginal examination should be conducted by healthcare professionals in the hospital setting, not by an EMT. If the EMT performed a vaginal exam on this patient, it could cause further harm to both mother and baby. Choice *B* is incorrect, as having the woman sit up can increase bleeding and discomfort. Although administering oxygen and fluids is important to help with oxygenation and fluid balance, it is more important to ensure blood flow to the organs and placenta. Additionally, the amount of oral intake would be of little benefit. Therefore, Choice *D* is incorrect.

100. B: Ischemic strokes occur when a clot prevents blood circulation to the brain. These differ from hemorrhagic strokes, which occur due to bleeding in the brain that causes an oxygen deficit. A transient ischemic attack (TIA) is a "mini-stroke." Symptoms of TIAs resolve rather quickly and typically without deficit. Myocardial infarction is not a type of stroke.

101. D. Choice *D* demonstrates what acid-base balance the patient would be in. The patient would not be able to offload the carbon dioxide appropriately. This causes respiratory acidosis, which can lead to organ failure and subsequently death if left untreated.

102. C: A color-coded triage system is used in mass casualty incidents to help prioritize care based on the severity of injuries. A green tag is assigned for ambulatory patients with minor injuries and stable vital signs. These patients can wait for care as other individuals may need to be attended to first. A black tag is for an individual who has severe injuries and is unlikely to survive, making Choice *A* incorrect. Yellow tags, Choice *B*, are for patients who have non-life-threatening injuries but still require medical care. These individuals are stable and can wait longer to receive treatment. Examples of these sorts of injuries include fractures and burns. Choice *D* is incorrect as red tags are for patients with life-threatening injuries that require immediate medical attention to prevent death. Examples of these injuries include severe bleeding and compromised airways.

103. B: Ventricular fibrillation is a shockable rhythm that can lead to cardiac arrest. It is characterized by chaotic and irregular electrical activity, and defibrillation is used to try to restore a normal heart rhythm. Sinus bradycardia, pulseless electrical activity, and asystole are all non-shockable rhythms.

104. A: The rule of nines is a tool used in prehospital and emergency settings to estimate the total body surface area (TBSA) affected by a burn. According to this rule, each arm constitutes 9% of the total body surface area. Therefore, if a patient has a burn covering their entire right arm, it would be estimated that 9% of their body is burned. This is important for determining the severity of the burn and guiding treatment decisions, such as fluid resuscitation.

105. C: To appropriately measure an NPA, a clinician should measure it from the nostril to the earlobe. If an NPA is sized incorrectly, ventilation or respiration will not make it past the tongue and other back-of-the-throat obstructions.

EMT Practice Test #2

1. An adolescent male who suffered a fall from his skateboard presents with a partial avulsion on the left forearm with moderate bleeding. The patient is alert and oriented and denies any head trauma. There is no deformity to the affected arm, and the patient has good neurological and motor function. What would be the steps for treating the wound?
   a. Remove the flap of lacerated skin, cleanse the wound, and apply sterile bandages to control the bleeding.
   b. Cleanse the wound, put the flap of lacerated skin over the wound, and apply sterile bandages to control the bleeding.
   c. Apply a tourniquet above the wound site to control the bleeding, then cleanse the wound and apply sterile bandages.
   d. Cleanse the wound, put the flap of lacerated skin over the wound, and apply a hemostatic dressing with additional pressure dressings to control the bleeding.

2. What is the normal respiratory rate for an adult patient per minute?
   a. 12 to 24 breaths per minute
   b. 5 to 6 breaths per minute
   c. 10 to 18 breaths per minute
   d. 12 to 20 breaths per minute

3. What GCS score would you assign to a patient who is unconscious, makes incomprehensible sounds, and withdraws from painful stimuli?
   a. GCS score of 3
   b. GCS score of 5
   c. GCS score of 7
   d. GCS score of 9

4. A patient is being transported to the hospital for complaints of chest pain and tachycardia. The patient suddenly loses consciousness and lets out agonal breaths. The first responder is unable to palpate a pulse. What should the EMT do first?
   a. Administer naloxone
   b. Defibrillate
   c. Start CPR
   d. Dispatch ALS response

5. A patient has a gunshot wound to the thigh with active arterial bleeding. Direct pressure fails to control the bleeding. What is the next appropriate step?
   a. Apply a tourniquet above the wound.
   b. Apply a hemostatic dressing to the wound.
   c. Administer IV fluids to maintain blood pressure.
   d. Transport immediately without further attempts to control the bleeding.

6. Which of the following scales should be used when determining if a patient is having a stroke?
   a. Cincinnati Stroke Scale
   b. Indianapolis Stroke Score
   c. Minnesota Stroke Scale
   d. Massachusetts Stroke Score

7. A patient presents lethargic, not following commands, and smelling heavily of alcohol. The patient is breathing steadily and responds to painful stimuli. However, the patient falls back asleep shortly after the stimuli has stopped. The patient does have a gag reflex. The first responder notes that the patient has snoring respirations and an oxygen saturation at 89% on room air. What should the EMT do first?
   a. Place a nasopharyngeal airway (NPA).
   b. Place an oropharyngeal airway (OPA).
   c. Place the patient on a non-rebreather.
   d. Administer naloxone.

8. An EMT is dispatched to a factory where a worker has accidentally spilled a chemical on their left hand and arm. The EMT notices that the skin of the area is turning white, and the patient is shouting out in pain. What is the most appropriate initial action to take?
   a. Applying a cold compress to alleviate pain
   b. Flushing the affected area with water
   c. Applying a neutralizing agent to the area
   d. Removing any clothing or jewelry around the affected area

9. A five-year-old patient is being seen for possible asthma exacerbation. The patient's mother reports that the patient has used her rescue inhaler and nebulizer treatment but is still having difficulty breathing. Upon their arrival, the first responders find the patient tachypneic, wheezing, and using their accessory muscles. Without further intervention, the patient's breathing begins to slow to a normal rate and appears less labored. What should the EMT do first?
   a. Determine that the patient has improved and decide that it is safe to leave for a new call.
   b. Listen to breath sounds.
   c. Suction the patient's airway.
   d. Dispatch ALS response.

10. Which of the following signs is indicative of chest pain?
   a. Kernig's sign
   b. Brudzinski's sign
   c. Levine's sign
   d. Kehr's sign

11. After providing supplemental oxygenation by NRB at 15 LPM, you note the patient's end-tidal CO2 has risen to 70 mmHg, and the patient starts to become unresponsive. How would you describe the patient's condition?
   a. Respiratory distress
   b. Respiratory failure
   c. Respiratory arrest
   d. Respiratory compromise

12. A six-year-old male patient presents with hives and facial swelling after eating a cookie with peanuts at school. The patient is awake and alert but states that their throat is starting to feel tight, and they are having trouble breathing. What should you do first?
   a. Administer 0.15 mg subcutaneous/intramuscular epinephrine via Epi-Pen.
   b. Administer 0.15 mg IV epinephrine via Epi-Pen.
   c. Administer 1.5 mg subcutaneous/intramuscular epinephrine via Epi-Pen.
   d. Administer 0.30 mg subcutaneous/intramuscular epinephrine via Epi-Pen.

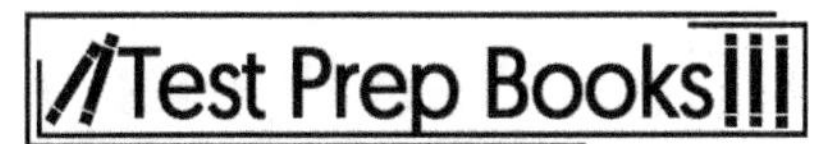

13. A patient who had an MI that led to cardiac arrest should be transported to which kind of facility?
    a. Stroke center
    b. PCI capable facility
    c. Level 3 trauma center
    d. Emergency room

14. The EMT is transporting a patient with MRSA and is told that the patient is in contact isolation. What protection is required in this situation?
    a. Gloves and disposable gown
    b. Gloves, surgical mask, and gown
    c. Gloves, surgical mask, gown, and eye protection
    d. Gloves, N95 respirator, and gown

15. You are on scene with a 12-year-old patient who was hit in the chest with a baseball bat and then went unconscious. After being unable to palpate a pulse, you place the defibrillator pads on the patient and see a waveform, but you are advised not to shock. Which of the following rhythms would a provider not defibrillate?
    a. PEA
    b. V-TACH
    c. Pulseless V-TACH
    d. V-FIB

16. After a call in a busy EMS system, an EMT notes that they have run out of non-rebreather masks. Dispatch informs them that there is a respiratory emergency call coming through. Which of the following actions is most appropriate?
    a. Informing dispatch that there will need to be a resupply before being dispatched to another call
    b. Taking the call and modifying equipment to meet patient needs
    c. Calling medical control to change protocols to meet patient needs
    d. Radioing another rig and asking them to respond to the patient

17. An EMT is dispatched to an adult male patient who is concerned as there is blood in his abdominal ostomy bag. He recently had an ileostomy due to cancer and is not sure what to do. He is unsure if the blood is coming from his stoma or intestines. What should the EMT's initial intervention be?
    a. To not touch the stoma but keep everything the way it is and transport the patient immediately
    b. To clean the area with alcohol-based disinfectant and then apply an occlusive dressing
    c. To moisten gauze with normal saline, apply it to the affected area, and hold it in place with bandages
    d. To apply direct pressure with clean, dry sterile gauze

18. Which of the following is NOT a type of stroke?
    a. Ischemic stroke
    b. Medullar stroke
    c. Hemorrhagic stroke
    d. TIA

19. You arrive on scene to a patient unable to breathe on his own. As you grab the BVM and return to the patient, you notice the patient has a beard. When you attempt to get a good seal with the mask, you hear air leaking out of the side of the mask. What is an appropriate way to attain a good seal?
    a. Using a pediatric mask over just the nose and close the mouth
    b. Taping the edges of the BVM mask to stop the air leak
    c. Placing Tegaderm over the patient's beard with a hole for the mouth
    d. Placing the patient in recovery position and attempt to ventilate from the side

20. An adult female is experiencing a vaso-occlusive event (VOE) secondary to sickle cell disease (SCD). She is complaining of chest pain that radiates to the back and a throbbing headache. She is alert and oriented but anxious. Her breathing is rapid and shallow. What should the EMT do next?
    a. Apply high-flow oxygen via non-rebreather mask, ask the patient to hold a baby aspirin under her tongue, and assist with nitro.
    b. Apply supplemental oxygen via nasal cannula, assess the patient's facial nerves, and look for equal strength in hands and feet to check for possible CVA.
    c. Apply high-flow oxygen via non-rebreather mask, ask the patient to hold a baby aspirin under her tongue, assess patient's facial nerves, and look for equal strength in hands and feet to check for possible CVA.
    d. Apply high-flow oxygen via non-rebreather mask, apply warm compresses to the chest and back for pain relief, and obtain medication history.

21. The EMT arrives on scene where the fire department has started compressions and ventilations on a patient in cardiac arrest. The EMT retrieves the AED and notes that the patient has a pacemaker underneath the skin on his left anterior chest. What should the EMT do next for this patient's care?
    a. Continue CPR without the use of an AED.
    b. Place the pads adjacent to the pacemaker and proceed.
    c. Allow the pacemaker to perform defibrillation.
    d. Use pediatric pads to circumvent the pacemaker.

22. A patient involved in a motor vehicle collision has a deformity of the lower leg with an open wound. Bone is visible from the wound, and there is moderate bleeding. What is the care of the open wound and visible bone fragments?
    a. Immobilizing the affected limb in the position found and controlling the bleeding with direct pressure; do not try to put the bone back into the wound
    b. Applying a traction splint to allow the exposed bone to be pulled back into the wound and using the straps on the splint to hold the gauze onto the wound to control the bleeding
    c. Attempting to manually align the limb in its anatomical position to see if it will pull the bone back into the wound and controlling the bleeding with direct pressure
    d. Leaving the exposed bone alone and attempting to immobilize and control the bleeding with the use of an air splint

23. Which of the following patients should a crew run "Code 3" or with lights and sirens when transporting?
    a. A patient complaining of tinnitus
    b. A patient who has vomited three times in the past hour
    c. A patient whose blood pressure reads 60/40
    d. A patient with a broken thumb

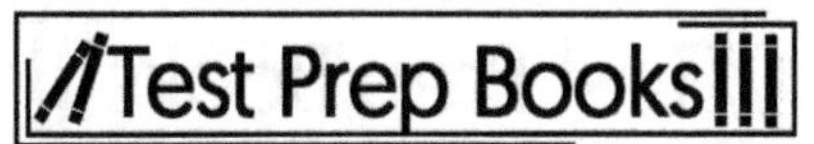

24. You are dispatched to an adult female with an altered mental state. Upon your arrival, you see the woman seated. She is conscious but is slurring her speech. She feels very warm to the touch, is tachypneic and tachycardic, and has elevated blood pressure. Her husband says she takes thyroid medication but has been out the past couple of days. What do you suspect and what care do you provide?
    a. The patient is experiencing hypothyroidism; restrict oral intake, apply high-flow oxygen, and check blood glucose levels.
    b. The patient is experiencing hyperthyroidism; monitor LOC and airway, apply supplemental oxygen if needed, and attempt to cool the patient with cool compresses.
    c. The patient is experiencing hyperthyroidism; apply high-flow oxygen, warm the patient with blankets, and check blood glucose levels.
    d. The patient is experiencing hypothyroidism; monitor LOC and airway, apply high-flow oxygen, and warm the patient with blankets.

25. You and your partner are providing PPV, or positive pressure ventilations, with supplemental oxygen to a patient with COPD. Which of the following examples is NOT correct for this scenario?
    a. Only ventilating with as much tidal volume to cause the chest to rise
    b. Stopping supplemental oxygen, as it may stop this patient's hypoxic drive
    c. Maintaining a good mask seal by using "C and E" hand positioning
    d. Placing an NPA if the patient becomes altered or unconscious

26. You arrive on scene to a patient who was found down but is now conscious. The patient claims that she was recently released from the hospital due to a UTI. You analyze the patient's vitals and note that the patient is hypotensive, tachycardic, and febrile. Which type of shock is this patient most likely suffering from?
    a. Hypovolemic shock
    b. Neurogenic shock
    c. Septic shock
    d. Cardiogenic shock

27. An EMT is presented with a patient who has suffered multiple traumatic injuries to more than one body system. What should they expect when providing the patient with emergency care?
    a. To immediately begin interventions on what the patient complains the most about
    b. To immediately treat critical injuries and be prepared for more complex issues to potentially arise
    c. To request an ALS unit as multisystem trauma is outside the scope of EMT care
    d. To immediately transport to the nearest hospital

28. An adult male is complaining of excruciating LRQ abdominal pain with nausea and vomiting. He states that he awoke in the middle of the night and the pain was a burning epigastric pain. He awoke in the morning to the pain moving to his LRQ and increasing in severity. What is the EMT's care for this patient?
    a. Asking the patient if there was any blood in his urine and applying ice packs to the affected area
    b. Gently palpating the LRQ, looking for point tenderness, and applying a heat pack to the affected area
    c. Auscultating bowel sounds as the patient drinks water to rule out bowel obstruction
    d. Encouraging the patient to take a stool softener with copious amounts of water

29. You respond to a home of an adult male who has been in bed for the last six days. His wife reports that he has a history of depression and recently lost his job. She isn't sure if he has been taking his medication. She called his doctor, who requested she bring him into the ER. She denies that he has threatened himself or anyone else, but she isn't sure how to get him to the hospital. How can you attempt to get the patient to agree to transport?
    a. By telling him that his doctor has requested he be seen and informing him that he can either go in the ambulance or that the police will be called to take him
    b. By not trying to reason with the patient but calling law enforcement and having them explain that he must go in for evaluation or they will take him into custody
    c. By respecting the patient's boundaries, empathizing with the patient, and attempting to gently reason that it would be best if he went in
    d. By telling the patient that he is being taken his doctor's appointment, then transporting him to the ER, per the doctor's request

30. A one-year-old patient presents unable to breathe with a suspected foreign body stuck in her upper airway. The first responders have performed the pediatric Heimlich maneuver, and the foreign body remains in place. The patient suddenly loses consciousness. What should the EMT do next?
    a. Sweep the mouth for the foreign body.
    b. Continue the pediatric Heimlich.
    c. Start CPR.
    d. Place an OPA.

31. In a patient with suspected traumatic brain injury, what intervention can be taken to alleviate intercranial pressure?
    a. Transporting the patient prone, as this will help drain excess fluid through the nasal sinuses
    b. Transporting the patient supine to prevent any movement which can cause further injury
    c. Transporting the patient on their side to help relieve pressure on at least one side of their brain
    d. Transporting the patient on their back with their head elevated 30 degrees to help alleviate pressure

32. The EMT arrives at the scene of a woman in active labor. Upon examination, the baby's head is crowning, and delivery is imminent. Which action should the EMT take next?
    a. Slightly elevate her pelvis and, with a sterile gloved hand, place gentle pressure on the baby's head to prevent expulsion.
    b. Instruct the woman to breathe rapidly and push hard at every contraction.
    c. Place the woman on the stretcher and immediately transport to the nearest hospital.
    d. Gently push the baby's head back inside of the birth canal until arrival at the hospital.

33. You arrive on scene where a pediatric patient is experiencing a racing heartbeat. Upon assessment, the paramedic on your truck claims that the patient is in SVT, and he is going to attempt to "vagal" the patient. Vagal maneuvers can convert a patient in SVT by doing what?
    a. Slowing conduction through the AV node
    b. Increasing the patient's cardiac output
    c. Causing systemic vasodilation
    d. Creating backwards pressure in the aorta

34. Upon arrival at the bedside at a small urgent clinic, the nurse tells you that the patient was showing signs of respiratory distress and needed to be taken to a regional hospital. When you evaluate the patient, you notice he is unresponsive but has a pulse. He has snoring respirations, and his oxygen saturation is at 85% with a nasal cannula in place running at 4 LPM. Which of the following should be your initial intervention?

a. Opening the patient's airway using head-tilt/chin-lift
b. Increasing his oxygen rate to 6 LPM
c. Placing an oropharyngeal airway
d. Administering the patient's prescribed inhaler

35. An adult male patient is found lying prone on the floor and is unresponsive to painful stimuli. There are no signs of trauma, and the patient has a pulse. The patient is breathing slowly and has an oxygen saturation of 92% on room air. The scene suggests a potential drug overdose, as paraphernalia is strewn about and friends are evasive. What should the EMT do?

a. Immediately request the police respond to illegal drug use.
b. Administer 0.4 mg Narcan intramuscularly via autoinjector and repeat after 2–3 minutes if there's no improvement.
c. Administer activated charcoal orally and provide an emesis basin for potential emesis.
d. Immediately transport the patient.

36. When presented with a patient with multiple traumatic injuries, what would be an indication that the patient is a high priority, critical transport patient?

a. The patient has a blood pressure of 170/110.
b. The patient complains of nausea.
c. The patient complains of loss of sensation and movement of extremities.
d. The patient appears confused and cannot answer basic questions.

37. If a patient has an altered level of consciousness and presents with stroke-like symptoms, which of the following procedures should be done prior to arriving at the hospital?

a. Administration of oxygen by NRB
b. Defibrillation
c. Blood glucose test
d. 4-lead ECG

38. How can CHF, or congestive heart failure, cause pulmonary distress?

a. The heart is unable to overcome the pressure of the aorta, which causes hypoxia.
b. The heart is unable to pump effectively, causing a backup of fluid into the lungs.
c. The lungs are unable to properly expand and contract.
d. The returning circulation causes tachycardia, which doesn't allow for hemoglobin loading.

39. A 60-year-old male patient presents with hypertension, tachycardia, and pain and distention in his abdomen. He seems confused and disoriented. The man reports that he hasn't urinated in two days despite drinking lots of water, and he doesn't have a history of kidney issues. How should the EMT care for this patient?

a. Check the patient's blood glucose levels and intervene as necessary.
b. Have the patient collect urine to check for kidney stones.
c. Encourage the patient to drink more water.
d. Apply warm a compress to the affected area, restrict oral intake, and place the patient in a position of comfort.

40. Upon arrival at the scene of an MVA, you note that the fire department is performing chest compressions on a pediatric patient in cardiac arrest. You note a deformity to the dashboard in front of where the 14-year-old was sitting, and the patient's anterior chest has a bruise across it. No other bleeding or injuries are found. What do you suspect is the cause of the arrest?
   a. Cardiac tamponade
   b. Liver insult
   c. Pericarditis
   d. Diaphragmatic hernia

41. An EMT arrives on the scene to find an adult male victim of a knife attack. The patient has an approximately 10-inch laceration across his abdomen just below the navel. The patient is alert and oriented and does not complain of any difficulty breathing. The EMT notes some of the intestines are protruding from the wound. What care should be taken for the abdomen?
   a. Carefully pushing the intestines back into the wound and covering the wound with an occlusive dressing
   b. Carefully pushing the intestines back into the wound and covering with some sterile gauze and bandages irrigated with saline
   c. Carefully draping some sterile gauze and bandages irrigated with saline over the wound, taking caution to leave the intestines in place
   d. Carefully draping some dry sterile gauze and bandages over the wound, taking caution to leave the intestines in place

42. A 47-year-old male patient with a history of asthma is experiencing chest tightness and shortness of breath. He is also in a tripod position. He used his prescribed albuterol inhaler but is not experiencing relief. What is the first action the EMT should take?
   a. Perform a lung assessment.
   b. Help the patient take another dose of their albuterol inhaler.
   c. Administer supplemental oxygen via nasal cannula.
   d. Initiate high-flow nebulizer albuterol treatment.

43. Which of the following is NOT a form of shock?
   a. Distributive shock
   b. Cardiogenic shock
   c. Hypovolemic shock
   d. Neurotrophic shock

44. Upon arrival at a residential address, there is a woman with endometriosis who is in significant distress due to severe pelvic pain. The woman rates her pain as a 10/10 and states that she has no relief from taking her prescribed pain medication. What should you do next?
   a. Transport the woman to the hospital and apply a warm compress to the pelvic area.
   b. Administer a higher dose of the patient's prescribed pain medication.
   c. Transport the patient on her right side covered with warm blankets.
   d. Have the patient follow up with her primary care provider.

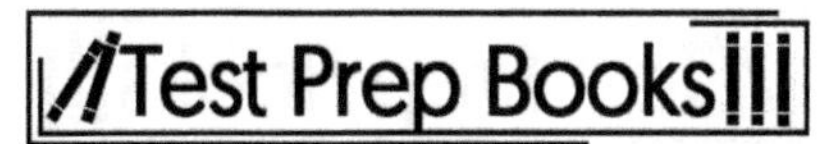

45. A 45-year-old male was a victim of blunt trauma to the chest. He is conscious but appears anxious and is complaining of difficulty breathing. The EMT performs a physical examination and does not see any visible trauma to the chest. From the signs and symptoms, they suspect a tension pneumothorax. What diagnostic tool would the EMT use to confirm their suspected diagnosis?
   a. When they auscultate breath sounds, they're present on one side but absent on the other.
   b. When they auscultate breath sounds, they hear a bubbling sound bilaterally.
   c. When they auscultate the heart, they hear the beats, but the beats seem to be muffled and not as distinct as normal.
   d. When they observe the patient's breathing, they see a section of chest that appears to move in the opposite direction than the majority of the chest.

46. An EMT is dispatched to respond to a call for a newborn baby that has just been delivered in a car. The baby is experiencing cyanosis and difficulty breathing. Upon further assessment, the EMT determines the baby's heart rate to be 120 beats per minute and notes that their respiratory rate is rapid. You suspect meconium aspiration syndrome. What steps should you take first?
   a. Obtain rectal temperature and apply supplemental oxygen.
   b. Auscultate breath sounds and apply high-flow oxygen.
   c. Suction newborn's mouth and airway and apply high-flow oxygen.
   d. Auscultate heart sounds and apply supplemental oxygen.

47. When performing CPR on a patient in cardiac arrest, what is the maximum amount of time that a provider should be "off the chest" when doing compressions?
   a. 20 seconds
   b. 3 seconds
   c. 30 seconds
   d. 10 seconds

48. While on scene, you note a 48-year-old male that is lying on the ground unresponsive. How should you check the patient's breathing?
   a. Using a pulse ox
   b. Noting cyanosis
   c. Looking for chest rise-and-fall
   d. Checking end-tidal CO2

49. You respond to an individual who appears to be intoxicated in his garage. The patient's wife states he has been depressed since losing his job, but she states that he doesn't drink alcohol. You notice a glass jar with a bright green fluid in it that you discover is antifreeze. You ask the patient if they had taken it, and he nods in the affirmative. What do you do next?
   a. Immediately contact poison control and transport as soon as possible.
   b. Check blood glucose levels to rule out hypoglycemia.
   c. Administer ipecac to induce vomiting.
   d. Have the patient drink water to dilute the antifreeze.

50. At the scene of a car accident, an EMT comes across the driver trapped inside their vehicle. The driver was restrained and denies loss of consciousness but is complaining of some neck pain. What is the first course of action for the patient?

a. Performing a neurological assessment of the driver to determine the potential for spinal injury
b. Finding a door that can be opened, then assisting the driver in safely exiting the vehicle as soon as possible
c. Applying a cold compress to the neck area to reduce pain and swelling
d. Immobilizing the driver's head and neck with a C-collar and extricating the patient using a Kendrick extrication device

51. Which of the following is caused by bleeding into the brain and cranial vault due to a ruptured blood vessel?

a. Ischemic stroke
b. Aneurysm
c. Cushing's triad
d. Hemorrhagic stroke

52. While responding to a call on a dual EMT ambulance, when should EMTs decide who will be the leader on the scene of an emergency?

a. There does not need to be a leader at the scene.
b. Whoever drives to the scene is automatically the leader.
c. The leader should be determined prior to arrival at the scene.
d. The passenger EMT is always the designated leader at a scene.

53. While attending a casualty collection point during a natural disaster, a supervisor asks an EMT to conduct triage duty. Which of the following accurately describes triage?

a. An approach to sorting patients depending on the nature of their injuries
b. Performing duties within an EMT's scope of practice
c. A method of running Code 3 to the hospital
d. A way to apply a pressure bandage

54. Maya, an EMT, is at a scene where an eight-year-old pediatric patient is in respiratory distress. The patient needs an emergency airway. How should she measure the appropriate OPA?

a. Nare of the nose to the ear lobe
b. Nare of the nose to the corner of the mouth
c. Corner of the mouth to the jaw line
d. Corner of the mouth to the ear lobe

55. An EMT responds to a call for an individual who reports being sexually assaulted by a stranger in the park. She is visibly distressed and states that she is ashamed and embarrassed. Other than that, she is reluctant to provide further details. The EMT should:

a. Conduct a detailed physical examination for legal purposes.
b. Assist the patient in reporting the incident to law enforcement immediately.
c. Avoid discussing the incident and focus on any injuries the patient may have.
d. Provide a supportive environment.

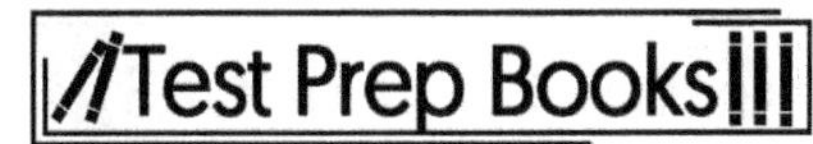

56. Hypertension can lead to all of the following diagnoses EXCEPT:
    a. Shock
    b. MI
    c. Renal disease
    d. Stroke

57. An EMT is dispatched to a residential address for a landscaper who has been struck in the eye by flying debris. Upon arrival, they notice an adult male with a wood splinter impaled in his right eye. The patient denies any blunt head trauma but is in a lot of pain. How should the EMT care for the patient?
    a. Stabilize the splinter to prevent further movement, control any bleeding with direct pressure, cover both eyes, and transport.
    b. Remove the splinter from the patient's eye, instruct the patient to tilt their head back while the EMT applies direct pressure to prevent fluid leakage, cover the affected eye, and transport.
    c. Stabilize the splinter to prevent further movement, control any bleeding with direct pressure, cover the affected eye, and transport.
    d. Irrigate the eye to see if the splinter can be dislodged; if not, cover the eye with a moist sterile dressing and transport.

58. What type of precautions should the EMT take for a patient who has a confirmed case of active tuberculosis?
    a. Contact
    b. Airborne
    c. Droplet
    d. Neutropenic

59. You respond to the local grade school for an adolescent female who has become ill during gym class. She is seated and appears confused. Her skin is cold and clammy, but her vital signs are stable. Her gym teacher reports she is a diabetic, but they do not know when her last meal or injection was. You check her blood glucose, and it reads 45 mg/dL. What is your course of action?
    a. Have the patient drink a glass of orange juice with a tablespoon of sugar dissolved in it or eat a small snack, or administer oral glucose.
    b. Assist the student with administering her prescribed insulin.
    c. Restrict oral intake and apply high-flow oxygen via non-rebreather mask.
    d. Encourage copious amounts of water and do blood glucose checks every five minutes.

60. You arrive on scene to a patient complaining of shortness of breath for one hour. Upon assessment, the patient is female, has no known medical history, and claims that this is the first time she has ever felt short of breath. After putting her on supplemental oxygen, you are still unable to get her O2 saturation up from 88%. While gathering history, you note she takes birth control. What disease or disorder do you suspect the patient of having?
    a. Pneumonia
    b. ARDS
    c. Atelectasis
    d. Pulmonary embolism

61. While performing EMS duties during a sporting event, an EMT and their partner are approached by a local TV station, and they are asked why response times have taken so long recently. Which of the following is the most appropriate response to the inquiry?
   a. "We are trying the best we can and are understaffed."
   b. "People need to be washing their hands more frequently."
   c. "Please refer to our media consultant for questions."
   d. "People aren't as tough as they used to be and overburden dispatch with irrelevant calls."

62. An adult female reports that she was having severe pelvic pain, and when she went to the bathroom, she noticed a lot of bleeding and what looks like tissue in the toilet bowl. She says her feminine pads have not stopped the bleeding. How should the EMT care for this patient?
   a. Request that law enforcement be dispatched to the scene for a potential sexual assault.
   b. Elevate the patient's pelvis to drain blood away and apply occlusive dressing.
   c. Conduct a vaginal exam and use hemostatic dressing.
   d. Have the patient apply bulky sterile dressing with direct pressure to the vaginal area.

63. Emergent care of a patient who is not appropriately breathing but has a palpable pulse includes all but which of the following actions?
   a. Supplemental O2
   b. Ventilatory support with a BVM
   c. Adequate airway management
   d. Cardiopulmonary resuscitation

64. When a patient is in a complete third-degree heart block, which of the following will NOT help?
   a. Epinephrine
   b. Atropine
   c. Pacing
   d. Dopamine

65. Which of the following can supplement administrative support and provide better patient outcomes in the prehospital environment?
   a. Constructive feedback about current policies that are out of date
   b. Quality reviews from superiors about all transfers
   c. Critical thinking meetings to expand on the station's medical knowledge
   d. Integration of multi-agency meetings into the weekly task log

66. You arrive to a 12-year-old female child who has been stung by a bee. The patient is complaining of pain, and you can see that her arm is swollen and that part of the stinger is visible. What care should you provide?
   a. Leave the stinger in place for identification and wrap the affected arm tightly with compression bandages.
   b. Use a pair of tweezers or hemostats to firmly grasp the stinger and gently remove it and then apply sterile gauze and ice to the affected area and wrap loosely.
   c. Use a pair of tweezers or hemostats to firmly grasp the stinger and gently remove it and then wrap the affected arm tightly with compression bandages.
   d. Attempt to remove the stinger using only the fingertip and if it can't be removed, leave it in place and apply sterile gauze and ice to the affected area and wrap loosely.

67. Which of the following is the best reason for EMTs to continually improve their craft and conduct professional development in the context of continuing education?
   a. To treat patients more effectively and efficiently
   b. To recertify their NREMT-B
   c. To further their career
   d. To get better credentials

68. In the context of EMS operations, what is the primary goal of the triage process during a mass casualty incident?
   a. To determine the severity of the incident
   b. To rank patients by injury severity and treatment urgency
   c. To identify the resources required at the scene
   d. To delegate responsibilities to EMS providers onsite

69. You are transporting an adult female with cerebral palsy. What care must be taken when moving and transporting this patient?
   a. Cerebral palsy patients are ventilator dependent, so airway management is a challenge.
   b. Cerebral palsy patients are non-verbal, so you must pay attention to visual clues.
   c. Cerebral palsy patients lack the ability to control motor movement, so the risk of injury is elevated.
   d. Cerebral palsy patients commonly need multiple medical devices, making moving and transport difficult.

70. After arriving on scene, you note a man face down beside his bed. The patient looks cyanotic. Which of the following actions should you initiate?
   a. Start providing bag-mask ventilations.
   b. Gather a history from family members.
   c. Check for responsiveness and a pulse.
   d. Check for possible medications on which he may have overdosed.

71. An 11-year-old child was playing baseball and knocked out a permanent tooth. Upon arrival at the scene, the parent has the tooth, and it is intact. Which of the following is the most appropriate action to take?
   a. Administering pain medication to the child
   b. Applying direct pressure to the area to control the bleeding
   c. Rinsing the tooth with water and reinserting it into the socket
   d. Storing the tooth in a container with milk or saline solution

72. While ventilating a patient, you note that the patient has an erythematous temporomandibular joint/neck, a swollen tongue on the same side, and is hard to ventilate. The most likely disease process this patient has is:
   a. Ludwig's angina
   b. RSV
   c. Pneumonia
   d. Epiglottitis

73. Several individuals have been exposed to a hazardous substance. When the EMT arrives at the scene, what should be the first step taken in the decontamination process?
    a. Identifying and managing any life-threatening injuries
    b. Administering antidotes or medications to counteract the exposure
    c. Transporting the patients to the nearest emergency room
    d. Removing the patients' clothing and belongings

74. A junior in high school playing organized football is tackled in a non-descript play after catching a pass. A couple of plays later he takes himself out of the game and is complaining of flank and upper back pain along his lower rib. He denies any head trauma, and there does not appear to be any respiratory distress. He reports some tenderness in the back area, and you observe a large dark bruise and swelling. What actions do you take?
    a. Check the patient's blood glucose levels and take appropriate intervention for hypo/hyperglycemia.
    b. Listen for breath and heart sounds, apply supplemental oxygen, and immobilize with a sling or swathe.
    c. Gently palpate the back and flank to look for further bleeding and if the patient can urinate, check for blood in the urine, and then apply ice to affected area.
    d. Listen for breath and heart sounds and gently palpate the back and flank to look for further bleeding, and then apply heat to the affected area.

75. What bloodborne pathogen could you become exposed to that you should be immunized against and checked for periodically?
    a. Human immunodeficiency virus (HIV)
    b. Severe acute respiratory syndrome (SARS)
    c. Hepatitis B virus (HBV)
    d. Influenza A

76. While you wait for your partner to grab the BVM and hook it to supplemental O2, you pull out a CPR mask and begin ventilating the patient with mouth-to-mask ventilations. Your partner returns and asks why it's imperative to place the patient on supplemental oxygen while ventilating a patient in respiratory arrest. You respond that mouth-to-mask ventilations only provide a low level of oxygenation to a patient. What percentage of oxygen does a patient receive through mouth-to-mask ventilation?
    a. 12%
    b. 17%
    c. 21%
    d. 50%

77. Which of the following persons are responsible for the inspection of the ambulance?
    a. The person who replaces inventory
    b. The shift supervisor
    c. The off-coming crew
    d. The oncoming crew

78. After getting return of spontaneous circulation on a patient who was in cardiac arrest, what end-tidal capnography should a provider attempt to attain?

a. 35-45
b. 30-40
c. 25-50
d. 15-25

79. An adult female was riding her bike when she fell. She cannot recall if she hit her head or had any loss of consciousness. She appears confused, and her speech is slurred and labored. The EMT notices a blood-tinged fluid draining from her ears. What is the immediate concern?

a. The patient suffered a potential skull fracture near her ear and is bleeding from the ears. The patient would require C-spine immobilization and rapid transport.
b. The patient suffered a minor head wound that the patient is superficially bleeding from near her ear. The patient would require C-spine immobilization and transport after a physical assessment.
c. The patient suffered a potential skull fracture with the presence of cerebrospinal fluid draining from her ear. The patient would require C-spine immobilization and rapid transport.
d. The patient suffered a cervical spine fracture and is bleeding from her ears. The patient would require C-spine immobilization and rapid transport.

80. A female patient is having vaginal bleeding and lower abdominal discomfort. She appears uncomfortable and slightly confused, and is hypotensive. She states that she does not feel comfortable with a male EMT and requests a female. What action should the male EMT take?

a. Request a female EMT to provide care for the patient.
b. Notify the patient that he is the only available EMT.
c. Continue with care for the patient's overall well-being.
d. Explain to the patient that she needs immediate care and cannot wait for a female EMT.

81. A severely depressed male ingested more than the prescribed amount of his psychotropic medications with the intent to end his life. Now, he has changed his mind and complains that he feels very sleepy and that his stomach hurts. What should the EMT immediately do?

a. Keep the patient awake and encourage vomiting by administering activated charcoal and ipecac.
b. Contact poison control or the pharmacy listed on the bottle(s) for instructions for a potential overdose.
c. Allow the patient to "sleep off" the medication's effects and monitor their airway.
d. Request police backup for a potential suicide attempt.

82. EMT Donnie arrives at the scene of a respiratory emergency. He notices that the environment is safe and attends to a patient who is lying on the floor. The patient appears to be middle-aged, and his face looks anxious and drawn. Donnie asks if the patient can say his name. The patient tries, but no sound comes out. He opens and closes his mouth a few times and begins gasping. Donnie has quickly assessed what about the patient?

a. The patient's WOB
b. The patient's PAT
c. The patient's heart rhythm
d. The patient's GCS

83. You respond to an adult female in the third trimester who is in active labor. She reports that her water broke, and her contractions are about 30 seconds apart. You notice the prolapsed cord. What do you do next?
    a. Cover the cord with warm wet dressings.
    b. Attempt to push the cord back.
    c. Encourage the mother to push.
    d. Check for a pulse in the cord.

84. You are transporting a patient post-cardiac arrest. To which level of hospital should the patient be transported?
    a. Level 1
    b. Level 3
    c. Level 4
    d. Level 5

85. What would be the next intervention after direct pressure for uncontrolled bleeding in the wrist/hand area for an infant?
    a. Using the brachial pressure point
    b. Placing a tourniquet close to the heart
    c. Using an air splint to increase the direct pressure
    d. Using the antecubital pressure point

86. An EMT arrives on-scene to a hazardous material storehouse for a call where a patient was found down and unresponsive. Which of the following should be used to reference the initial response to this incident?
    a. Medical control
    b. SDS or Safety Data Sheet
    c. Department of Transportation Emergency Response Guide
    d. Documentation from the transportation of the materials

87. An 18-year-old female is found lying prone and unresponsive. After rolling her to her back, you perform a head-tilt/chin-lift maneuver and notice she is apneic, hypoxic, and bradycardic. You attempt to give ventilations with a BVM, but her chest does not rise with inspiration. What is the next thing you should do?
    a. Check to see if the patient has a carotid pulse.
    b. Reattempt the head-tilt/chin-lift to attain a better airway.
    c. Start cardiopulmonary resuscitation, beginning with chest compressions.
    d. Forcefully ventilate the patient to note if air can be passed down.

88. You respond to an adult female who is feeling weak and unusually tired. She also complains of blurry vision and being extremely thirsty. She states that she is a newly diagnosed diabetic and is not certain if she took her medications correctly. You check her blood glucose levels and they read 135 mg/dL. What should you do for this patient?
    a. Encourage fluids to help dilute the amount of sugar in the blood.
    b. Have the patient drink a glass of orange juice with a tablespoon of sugar in it to get blood sugar levels within normal limits.
    c. Maintain airway and conduct periodic blood glucose checks.
    d. Administer 50 units of subcutaneous insulin.

89. You arrive to an adult female in active labor, and you notice the baby's arm presenting. What should you do next?
    a. Attempt to continue the delivery by guiding the shoulder out and then the head.
    b. Attempt to push the arm back so the baby may rotate for a normal delivery.
    c. Keep the limb warm and immediately transport.
    d. Check the presenting limb for a pulse, and if there is no pulse, apply high-flow oxygen to the mother.

90. An EMT arrives to see a patient with a kitchen knife protruding from the RUQ of the abdomen. The knife is impaled all the way to the hilt on an approximately 3-inch blade. The EMT is concerned that the liver or spleen could be lacerated. The abdomen is soft, and the only pain is at the wound site. What are the interventions for the wound?
    a. Removing the object and controlling the bleeding with direct pressure
    b. Leaving the object in place and immobilizing the object with sterile gauze to ensure that there is no further movement of the object while transporting
    c. Removing the object and controlling the bleeding with an occlusive dressing
    d. Leaving the object in place and controlling the bleeding with a hemostatic dressing

91. A 49-year-old male begins vomiting while you are en route to the hospital. You rolled him on his side, but he continues to have vomitus in his airway. How long should you perform suctioning on an adult patient?
    a. 45 seconds
    b. 20 seconds
    c. 10 seconds
    d. Until the airway is clear

92. You are dispatched to a call for a 51-year-old female with abdominal pain and shortness of breath. What should be considered as a differential diagnosis?
    a. COPD
    b. PE
    c. MI
    d. Stroke

93. An EMT is called to a shopping mall where an adult female is experiencing a seizure. Upon arrival, the seizure has stopped, but the patient is unresponsive. The immediate action for you to take is to:
    a. Keep the airway open, supply supplemental O2 if needed, and monitor the level of consciousness.
    b. Insert a rigid oral airway to maintain airway patency and check blood glucose levels.
    c. Check for a pulse and initiate CPR if needed.
    d. Immobilize the patient's head/spine, then check for an open airway, opening with the jaw thrust technique if needed.

94. A construction worker fell from a ladder on the job site. He landed on his outstretched hands. He complains of excruciating pain in the right wrist, which is swollen and bruised. The patient has good motor and neurological function distal to the wrist. What is the initial management of this injury?
    a. Administering pain medication to alleviate the discomfort
    b. Applying a cold compress to the area
    c. Immobilizing the right wrist with a splint
    d. Performing a mobility assessment of the right wrist

95. While on scene of a cardiac arrest, you and your EMT partner have been doing compressions when you notice a spike in ETCO2. You palpate for a pulse and are able to feel a carotid pulse. The patient is presenting bradycardic and still unable to respirate on their own. What is the most appropriate next step?
   a. Continue CPR at 100 to 120 compressions per minute.
   b. Perform defibrillation.
   c. Activate ALS to meet you en route to the hospital.
   d. Call a level 4 trauma center and request that an open bed be made ready.

96. An adult woman in her third trimester is in active labor. She has a history of three cesarean sections and is experiencing pressure in her abdomen with regular contractions. The EMT should:
   a. Assist the woman to a low Fowler's position to reduce uterine pressure.
   b. Encourage the woman to push during contractions.
   c. Transport the woman to the nearest hospital immediately.
   d. Prepare the woman for an emergency cesarean section.

97. You arrive on scene to a patient complaining of a racing heartbeat. As you are acquiring the patient's history, you note that she takes metoprolol. What classification of medication does this fall into?
   a. Sympathomimetic
   b. Anticholinergic
   c. Opiate
   d. Beta blocker

98. At the scene of a rollover, your patient was ejected from her vehicle. Upon arriving at the patient's side, you note the patient is not breathing. You open the patient's mouth and see broken teeth behind the patient's tongue. The patient also appears cyanotic and presents with an oxygen saturation of 76%. What should you do first?
   a. Suction the patient's airway for no more than 15 seconds.
   b. Attempt to ventilate the patient with a BVM.
   c. Place an NPA to help maintain the patient's airway.
   d. Call for ALS support to intubate the patient.

99. An adult female presents with altered mental status and lethargy. Her blood pressure is 110/50, pulse is 127, and respirations are 18 breaths per minute, but she says she finds herself breathing harder on exertion. Her skin is warm and dry. What should you do next?
   a. Apply supplemental oxygen via nasal catheter, check for external bleeding, and obtain detailed medical history.
   b. Apply high-flow oxygen via non-rebreather mask and check oxygen saturation and blood glucose levels.
   c. Check blood glucose and oxygen saturation levels, then encourage the patient to take small sips of water.
   d. Have the patient drink a glass of orange juice with a tablespoon of sugar dissolved in it or eat a small snack, or administer oral glucose.

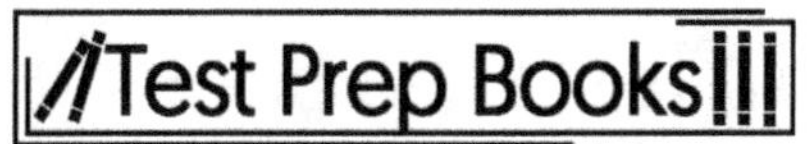

100. An EMT arrives on the scene where a gunfight occurred. A teenage female bystander was hit by two bullets. One bullet hit the patient in the chest and exited through her back; bright red blood is spurting from the wound. The other bullet hit her near her hip, but no exit wound can be found. From the location of the entrance wound, it is possible it may be lodged in or near the patient's spine. What would be appropriate for the first course of action?

a. Stabilizing the open chest wound with an occlusive dressing and sterile bandages
b. Immobilizing the patient on a longboard and checking for possible spinal cord injury by assessing motor/neurological function below the level of possible damage
c. Ensuring an open airway using the jaw-thrust method and supplying high flow oxygen via a non-rebreather mask
d. Immobilizing the patient's lumbar spine using a Kendrick extrication device

101. You are on scene of a patient who was found in a pool. The patient has a pulse but is not breathing, so you and your partner decided to ventilate the patient with a BVM. While performing rescue breathing, what indicators should you observe to ensure proper ventilation?

a. Proper end tidal reading
b. Chest rise-and-fall
c. Complete deflation of the BVM upon ventilating
d. Adequate pulse oximetry reading

102. Police have requested that the EMT transport an adult male who is reporting that he is hearing voices in his head telling him to harm himself. He is also reporting visual hallucinations. He is alert and oriented, and vitals are stable. During transport, he starts asking the EMT whether they see the other people in the squad and hear them talking. How should the EMT respond?

a. By repeating sternly that there are no other people and nobody else is talking
b. By agreeing that they see and hear other people, but that the EMT will keep the patient safe
c. By immediately requesting the police officers to place the patient in restraints
d. By reassuring the patient that there are no other people in the squad and that he is safe

103. An EMT is dispatched to a patient with chest discomfort and respiratory distress. The paramedic partner has acquired a 12-lead ECG and notes that he sees a STEMI in the inferior leads. He tells the EMT that this is a right-sided heart attack. Which of the following may prove hazardous for administration in a right-sided MI?

a. Oxygen
b. Normal saline
c. Aspirin
d. Nitroglycerin

104. An EMT responds to a 13-year-old female who is complaining of abdominal pain, cramping, and nausea. The parents tell the EMT the patient has been constipated for the past couple of days. The EMT notices the abdomen is swollen and doesn't hear bowel sounds in the left lower quadrant (LLQ) of the abdomen. What should the EMT suspect and do?

a. The patient has a potential bowel obstruction, so the EMT should restrict oral intake and transport in a position of comfort.
b. The patient is experiencing severe menstrual cramping, so the EMT should apply warm compresses to the affected area and transport the patient with her knees flexed.
c. The patient is suffering from peritonitis, which is potentially life threatening, and the patient requires immediate transport.
d. The patient has a potential bowel obstruction, so the EMT should encourage high fiber oral intake and lots of water to clear blockage and then transport the patient on her side with her knees flexed.

105. A 54-year-old patient has sustained a partial thickness burn from hot oil while cooking dinner for her family. Upon inspection, the patient is burned on the back of her hand and a third of the way up her forearm. The area appears red with some swelling, and small blisters cover most of the area. What action should the EMT take immediately?

a. Place a cool, moist cloth over the burn, taking care not to puncture the blisters.
b. Apply a thick layer of petroleum jelly over the burned area to prevent the blisters from breaking.
c. Pierce the blisters to release the fluid and reduce swelling, then cover the burn with a dry, sterile dressing.
d. Pierce the blisters to release the fluid and reduce swelling, then cover with a cool, moist dressing.

Answer Explanations #2

1. B: A partial avulsion is a wound where a flap of skin that has been cut remains attached. Care should be taken to keep this flap intact and attached. After cleansing the wound, the flap should be placed back to cover the wound, and then direct pressure should be applied with sterile bandages to control the bleeding. Choice *A* is incorrect as the flap should remain attached. Choice *C* is incorrect as tourniquets are indicated for bleeding that cannot be controlled with direct pressure. Choice *D* is incorrect as a hemostatic dressing would not be indicated in this situation.

2. D: The normal respiratory rate for an adult patient is 12 to 20 breaths per minute. The normal pediatric respiratory rate is 20 to 30 breaths per minute. The normal neonate respiratory rate is 30 to 50 breaths per minute. Knowing these rates allows a clinician to assess for respiratory distress and provide the correct ventilatory rate when using a BVM.

3. C: The Glasgow Coma Scale (GCS) assesses three components of neurological function: eye opening, verbal response, and motor response. Each component is assigned a score, and the total GCS score is calculated by adding the scores from all three components. The GCS score ranges from 3 to 15, with lower scores indicating a more severe impairment of consciousness. In this scenario, the patient would be rated as follows:

- Eye opening: The patient is unconscious, which corresponds to a GCS score of 1.
- Verbal response: The patient makes incomprehensible sounds, indicating a GCS score of 2.
- Motor response: The patient withdraws from painful stimuli, indicating a GCS score of 4.
- To calculate the total GCS score, add the scores from each component: 1 (eye opening) + 2 (verbal response) + 4 (motor response) = 7.

4. C: The initial intervention for any patient who has lost a pulse is to start CPR. Administering naloxone may be helpful if opiate overdose is a suspected cause of cardiac arrest, but CPR takes priority. Defibrillation should not be conducted until a compatible rhythm (pulseless ventricular tachycardia or ventricular fibrillation) is confirmed on the cardiac monitor. ALS should be dispatched, but CPR should be prioritized.

5. A: When direct pressure fails to control active arterial bleeding, applying a tourniquet above the wound is the next appropriate step. It effectively compresses the blood vessels, which halts the arterial bleeding. Applying a hemostatic dressing, Choice *B*, may be considered, but it is not the primary intervention when direct pressure fails. Administering IV fluids, Choice *C*, is important for maintaining blood pressure, but it does not directly address the bleeding. Transporting immediately without further attempts to control the bleeding, Choice *D*, is incorrect. Transporting is necessary but not before attempts are made to control the bleeding. Uncontrolled arterial bleeding will be fatal without intervention.

6. A: The Cincinnati Stroke Scale is the scale that prehospital clinicians use to assess whether a patient has had a stroke. The scale deals with arm drift, facial droop, and speech. If a patient is experiencing deficits in these areas, a provider should call a stroke alert to the hospital and transport expeditiously because there is a time limit for thrombolytic use.

7. A: It is common for heavily intoxicated patients to have upper airway obstruction from secretions or tongue positioning. This patient is showing signs of this obstruction with their snoring respirations. Because of this, an NPA should be placed to help the patient maintain their airway patency. An oropharyngeal airway would be appropriate if the patient did not have a gag reflex. This patient may benefit from supplemental oxygen (such as through a non-rebreather), but this would not be effective until the airway obstruction is resolved. Naloxone administration may be beneficial to ensure that the patient is not struggling to breathe due to an opiate overdose, but maintaining their airway takes priority.

8. B: When chemical exposure occurs, it is important to flush the affected area with copious amounts of water to help remove the chemical and reduce tissue damage. Applying a cold compress to alleviate pain, Choice *A,* is a helpful action to take to temporarily relieve pain but should not be done before flushing the affected area with water. Applying a neutralizing agent to the area, Choice *C,* without knowing what the chemical is or what it is composed of can worsen the burn or cause a chemical reaction and should not be done. Choice *D*, removing clothing and jewelry around the affected area, is important to prevent even further chemical contact but should be done after water flushing has begun.

9. D: In pediatric patients, a sudden change in respirations from tachypneic to unlabored is a sign of respiratory exhaustion and impending respiratory arrest. The first responders should dispatch ALS for advanced support and prepare for the potential need to administer rescue breaths and start CPR. It would be inappropriate to leave this patient without further medical evaluation. Listening to the patient's breath sounds may provide useful assessment data, but it is not as much of a priority as getting the patient advanced medical treatment. Currently, suctioning the patient's airway does not seem to be indicated.

10. C: Levine's sign is a universal sign of chest pain. The common presentation of this sign is a clenched fist over the chest. Kernig's and Brudzinski's signs are indicative of meningitis, and Kehr's sign is indicative of splenic rupture.

11. B: Respiratory failure is defined as having too little oxygen within the tissues of your body and too much CO2 in your blood. Respiratory distress shows as a notable decrease in the patient's ability to oxygenate. Respiratory arrest is the cessation of breathing. Respiratory compromise is not recognized terminology.

12. A: This patient is showing signs of anaphylaxis with impending closure of their airway. Administration of emergent intramuscular epinephrine should be the first responder's priority to prevent airway obstruction and reverse the effects of the allergic reaction. Choice *B* is incorrect, as you would not administer an Epi-Pen IV. Choices *C* and *D* are incorrect pediatric doses.

13. B: A patient who arrested due to a myocardial infarction will be at a higher risk of re-entering cardiac arrest if the MI is not addressed. Patients who have had a myocardial infarction need a facility capable of PCI, or percutaneous coronary intervention.

14. C: A patient with MRSA can spread the disease if any of their bodily fluid encounters a person's mucous membranes (eyes, nose, mouth). This patient will require that the EMT protects their entire body and especially mucous membranes. This will require eye protection in addition to other precautions. Choices *A*, *B*, and *D* do not protect the eyes, making them all incorrect.

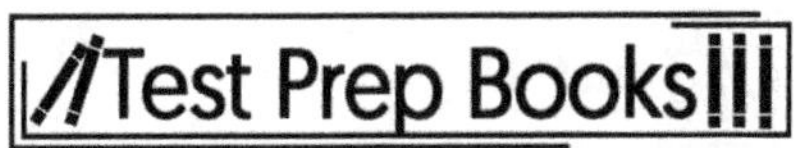

15. A: Two unshockable rhythms denoted by the AHA and ARC are PEA and asystole. The purpose in defibrillation is to allow the heart's pacemaker to "start over." If the patient is experiencing electromechanical dissociation, defibrillation will have no effect. Choices *B, C,* and *D* are all shockable rhythms.

16. A: Responding quickly to calls is imperative for EMTs, but it is not appropriate to respond to calls when deficient in supplies. An EMT crew should notify dispatch that resupply or restocking is needed in order to effectively treat and transport patients.

17. D: Often patients who have a newly placed ostomy will have some bleeding for days afterwards. Most bleeding in a patient's ostomy bag is not life threatening and can often be controlled by direct pressure. For minor bleeding, there is no special care that needs to be taken, but the patient should be transported for further evaluation. Left untreated, bleeding can become life threatening. Choice *A* is incorrect because it is not an urgent transport situation, and you can touch the stoma if you are gloved and the gauze is sterile. Choices *B* and *C* are incorrect, as these types of dressings would not be used in this situation.

18. B: The three types of recognized stroke are ischemic, hemorrhagic, and TIA. Ischemic strokes are caused by a clot or thrombus in the vasculature of the brain, causing tissue death. Hemorrhagic strokes are caused by aneurysm or bleeding within the brain. TIAs, or transient ischemic attacks, are "mini-strokes" that typically resolve by themselves.

19. C: If the patient has a beard and you are unable to create a good seal around the mask, a common technique is to cut a hole in the center of the Tegaderm and apply it over the patients' beard, Choice *C*. The other choices should not be performed, as they would not allow for proper ventilation.

20. D: A patient with SCD can experience mild pain from damaged blood cells in their circulatory system. Often the pain can be controlled at home and is not an emergency, but a buildup of damaged blood cells and other cells trying to remove debris can cause a narrowing or total occlusion of a larger blood vessel. This patient presents with signs and symptoms that could either be cardiac or CVA, but the patient's history along with symptoms indicate VOE. Oxygen should be high flow to prevent any hypoxia, and warm compresses to the chest and back can help with pain relief. The patient is not suffering from a cardiac event or CVA, making Choices *A*, *B*, and *C* incorrect.

21. B: A patient in cardiac arrest with a shockable rhythm needs immediate defibrillation. To perform defibrillation on a patient who has an internal pacemaker, an EMT should place the pads adjacent to the pacemaker—at least 3 cm away but in the same anatomical area. A pacemaker does not produce enough electricity to defibrillate the heart and cannot be accessed in the prehospital setting.

22. A: Attempting to get the exposed bone back into the wound is never indicated for the patient. The limb needs to be immobilized to prevent any further injury to the site. This would rule out Choices *B* and *C*. Choice *D* is correct to leave the bone alone, but attempting to immobilize with an air splint is not appropriate as the exposed bone could easily puncture the splint, thus defeating the purpose. In addition, it would put pressure on the exposed bone, pushing it back into the wound.

23. C: Code 3, or the combined use of lights and sirens, is reserved for responses to calls in which a crew needs to reduce response time to ensure a patient does not decompensate or when there is a greater risk for mortality. Common terms include *life*, *limb*, or *eyesight*. Each department can vary on when the use of Code 3 is warranted.

24. B: The patient has been without her hyperthyroid medication. Without it, the thyroid constantly secretes the hormone that the medication usually keeps under control, causing an increase in heart rate, blood pressure, and respiration. In addition, the patient will be very warm to the touch and could be hyperthermic. You are limited to maintaining airway and cooling the patient if needed. Choices *A* and *D* are incorrect, as the patient is not experiencing hypothyroidism. Choice *C* is incorrect, as the patient is not in need of high-flow oxygen, and warming the patient would exacerbate hyperthermia.

25. B: It was previously taught to withhold oxygen from a patient with COPD, as this may slow or stop their respiratory drive. Any patient who shows signs of hypoxia or has an oxygen saturation below 90% should be given supplemental oxygen.

26. C: When a patient is in shock, it is important to determine the type of shock so that the EMT may relay this information to the receiving hospital. Since this patient had a recent infection, the patient's most likely form of shock is septic. Hypovolemic shock would entail the patient losing intravascular fluid. Neurogenic shock would originate from some type of neurologic insult or injury. Cardiogenic shock would have cardiac complications surrounding shock, such as a myocardial infarction or CHF.

27. B: The care of the multisystem patient begins the same as any other patient; airway, breathing, and circulation assessments are immediately done, and interventions are taken as needed. With multisystem trauma, the extent of the injuries is not always apparent, so an EMT must look at the big picture and be prepared for more complex issues to arise. Choice *A* may be helpful for the patient's comfort, but the EMT must ascertain if there are any critical issues. Choice *C* may be needed if the patient's condition warrants, but a multisystem trauma patient can be cared for within the scope of the EMT. Choice *D* is partially correct—the patient should be transported to the nearest facility, but not until the patient has been stabilized for transport (unless they are considered a high-priority, critical transport patient).

28. B: Pain that starts in the epigastric region and "migrates" to the LRQ is indicative of an inflamed appendix. This vestigial organ at the beginning of the large intestine is usually ignored until there is a problem. Gentle palpation will show point tenderness, and the patient may guard the area. Heat packs can help alleviate some of the pain. Blood in the urine is not a sign of an inflamed appendix, making Choice *A* incorrect. Bowel sounds won't reveal any pertinent information, and oral intake should be restricted, making Choice *C* incorrect. While located in the large intestine, the appendix does not prevent a patient from having a bowel movement, so Choice *D* would be incorrect.

29. C: The events of job loss and not taking medication can cause some patients to fall into a deeper depression. Depression isn't always crying and sadness. It can be just the lost desire to do things that were once enjoyable. Left untreated, the patient can develop suicidal ideation. The information that the patient is on psychotropic medications should be a clue that there may have been past psychological emergencies. Choice *A* is incorrect, as threatening a patient is inappropriate. The patient is not a threat, and the introduction of law enforcement could make matters worse, making Choice *B* incorrect. Choice *D* is incorrect, as being deceitful with the patient is inappropriate.

30. C: If a pediatric patient loses consciousness due to inability to breathe, the first responder should start chest compressions immediately. Pediatric patients can go into cardiac arrest quickly from respiratory distress. Sweeping the mouth for the foreign body can be dangerous to the first responder and potentially push the foreign body deeper into the airway. This should not be done if the foreign body is not easily seen and not determined to be easily removed. Continuing the Heimlich will not assist the patient who is showing signs of going into cardiac or respiratory arrest. Placing an OPA may lodge the foreign body deeper into the airway and is not recommended.

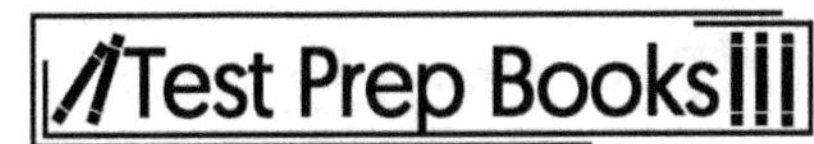

31. D: The EMT is limited on interventions to alleviate intercranial pressure. One that is quite simple and easy to transport is with the head slightly elevated. The elevation will allow gravity to decrease some of the pressure around the top of the brain. Choices *A*, *B*, and *C* provide no alleviation of pressure and could increase the risk of potential injury.

32. A: Delivery is imminent once a baby's head is visibly crowning. The EMT should assist the mother to elevate her pelvis slightly and place gentle pressure on the baby's head to prevent an explosive delivery. Instructing the mother to push is inappropriate; the baby's head is already crowning, and the body will naturally expel the baby. Pushing could lead to tearing or other complications, making Choice *B* incorrect. An uncomplicated delivery is not a life-threatening situation and does not require immediate transport. In addition, the delivery en route would be more difficult, making Choice *C* incorrect. Pushing the baby's head back into the birth canal until arrival at the hospital is not safe. Delivery is imminent at this point and should not be delayed, making Choice *D* incorrect.

33. A: SVT, or sinoatrial ventricular tachycardia, is a dysrhythmia that is typically over 180 bpm. The ECG will show a narrow complex QRS and, typically, hidden p-waves. By performing vagal maneuvers such as blowing into a syringe, placing a cold compress on the patient's head, or having the patient bare-down, the patient's autonomic nervous system causes the electrical conduction through the AV node to slow or stop. This can "convert" a patient back into a sinus rhythm.

34. A: After you conduct your initial impression, if there hasn't been any possibility of cervical trauma, the most appropriate intervention is to open the patient's airway by performing a head-tilt/chin-lift. EMTs should start with the most basic intervention to provide patient care. The nasal cannula is not helping the patient's oxygenation because the oxygen is not able to move into the patient's lungs. Further down the algorithm, placing an OPA may be the solution, but the immediate action should be to open the patient's airway and assess if he is breathing without help.

35. B: Administering naloxone, or Narcan, can reverse the effects of opiate overdose and allow the patient to improve rapidly. While determining if it is effective, the EMT should administer supplemental oxygen and potentially provide rescue breaths with a BVM. In this instance, the patient's O2 saturation is low, but the Narcan needs to be administered as quickly as possible. Choice *A* is incorrect, as the patient is the priority, not the suspected drug use. Choice *C* is incorrect, as you do not know the drug taken or the route. Activated charcoal would not be of use if the drug was taken intravenously. Choice *D* is incorrect, as the administration of Narcan should not be delayed. The patient can be prepped for transport while assessing the effectiveness of the initial dose.

36. D: A patient who presents with an altered mental status after suffering a traumatic injury should be considered to have suffered a head injury, and the necessary precautions to stabilize the patient should be taken. The patient can quickly become unresponsive, and immediate transport is necessary. Choices *A, B,* and *C* are all symptoms to pay attention to but do not require immediate transport.

37. C: Hypoglycemia can cause an altered level of consciousness and possibly even present as stroke-like symptoms such as aphasia. Blood glucose should be checked on all patients presenting with any level of altered mentation to rule out hypoglycemia.

38. B: In patients with CHF, the heart is unable to pump and eject blood effectively. This causes back pressure into the lungs, which in turn pushes fluid into the alveoli, increasing pulmonary pressure and edema.

39. D: The most telling aspects of this man's condition is that he hasn't urinated in two days, which is indicative of some sort of renal condition, and that he doesn't have a previous history of kidney function loss. Hypertension, tachycardia, and distention of the abdomen imply that urine cannot be formed, increasing blood pressure and causing edema. Acute renal failure is characterized by a sudden decrease in filtration through the glomeruli of the nephron, which causes all these symptoms—as well as anuria, the complete cessation of urine production—to occur over a period of days or weeks, meaning that the care in the field is limited. With any urinary issue, the EMT will want to restrict oral intake. Warm compresses may help alleviate pain, and the patient should be transported in the position that is most comfortable, making Choice *D* the correct answer. Choice *A* is incorrect because the patient's blood glucose levels will provide little useful information. A patient with acute renal failure may have normal blood glucose readings. Damage to the kidneys does not cause hyperglycemia; in fact, the opposite is true: uncontrolled hyperglycemia will cause kidney damage. The patient is experiencing no urine production, and a kidney stone is unlikely with a distended abdomen, so Choice *B* is incorrect. Choice *C* is incorrect because this will exacerbate the inability to urinate.

40. A: Cardiac tamponade is a condition where there is excess fluid/blood in between the pericardium and epicardium, preventing the heart from filling due to excessive pressure. Cardiac tamponade is one of the "Hs and Ts," which are the causes of cardiac arrest. While liver insult and diaphragmatic injury are possible in a collision involving the dashboard, neither of these choices would be a sole cause for cardiac arrest. If a heart is constricted by excess fluid/blood around it, that is a good determinant of cardiac arrest.

41. C: Exposed intestines due to evisceration must be left in place, and it is important to keep them moist. It should never be attempted to push the intestines back into place. Sterile gauze and bandages that are moist will help control the bleeding and keep the exposed intestines moist. Choices *A* and *B* involve pushing the intestines and should never be done. Choice *D* is incorrect because if dry bandages are used, they can become adhered to the intestine, making removal difficult and painful.

42. C: The first action the EMT should take is to administer supplemental oxygen via nasal cannula. Since the patient has a history of asthma and is experiencing chest tightness and shortness of breath in a tripod position, he needs increased oxygenation. If the EMT administers oxygen, the patient's respiratory distress will be relieved, and his oxygen levels will increase, which in turn will allow for increased oxygenation to vital organs. Although a lung assessment is important, delaying supplemental oxygen treatment can be detrimental, so Choice *A* is incorrect. Choices *B* and *D* may be necessary depending on the patient's response and the severity of his symptoms, but in this case, they are not the immediate actions to take.

43. D: The three main forms of shock are distributive, cardiogenic, and hypovolemic. Distributive shock indicates that the vessels are dilated; cardiogenic shock indicates that the heart is unable to pump appropriately or efficiently; and hypovolemic shock indicates that there isn't enough fluid/blood in the vasculature. All forms of shock indicate inadequate perfusion to the tissues of the body.

44. A: In cases of severe pain that is not responding to prescribed pain medication, especially in a patient with a known history of endometriosis, it is important to transport the individual to the hospital for further evaluation and pain management. Applying a heat pack to the pelvic area may be helpful. Choice *B* is incorrect; this would be illegal, as there is no doctor's order present. Additionally, many endometriosis pain medications are not allowed to be given by EMTs. While immediate transport is correct, transporting on the right side is not indicated in this situation, making Choice *C* incorrect. Choice *D* is incorrect because this does not address the patient's current distress.

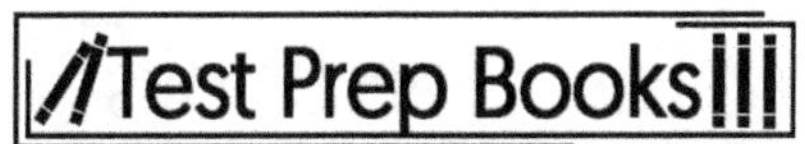

45. A: Tension pneumothorax is a life-threatening condition that occurs when air enters the pleural space (the space between the lungs and the chest wall) and becomes trapped, causing the affected lung to collapse. It can often occur when there is no visible trauma to the chest. Choice *B* would be indicative of a fluid buildup in the lungs. This can be caused by either disease (pneumonia) or trauma. Choice *C* describes the cardiac sounds for cardiac tamponade. The sac surrounding the heart is filling with blood and putting pressure on the heart, making contraction difficult. While it can be caused by trauma, the sign of difficulty breathing is not normally the presenting symptom. Choice *D* describes a flail chest. Three or more ribs are broken in two or more places. While commonly due to trauma, this is usually observed on the physical examination.

46. C: The baby's symptoms align with meconium aspiration syndrome. This occurs when the baby inhales their meconium, or first stool, during delivery. This can lead to respiratory issues. It causes respiratory distress and cyanosis, but the heart rate is within the normal limit of 120–160 bpm for neonates. The patient's airway must be cleared using flexible suction only into the airway as far as you can see and high-flow oxygen. Choice *A* is incorrect because the patient's body temperature is not pertinent to this situation, and the patient requires high-flow oxygen. Choice *B* is incorrect because when you suspect aspiration, the patient requires immediate suction. Breath sounds can be checked after interventions for the difficulty breathing are done. Choice *D* is incorrect, as heart sounds will provide little useful information, and the patient requires high-flow oxygen.

47. D: Studies have shown that the longer a provider is off the chest when performing compressions, the less augmentation the patient's cardiac output will have. This inhibits perfusion to vital organs and increases the mortality rate. Ten seconds is the maximum amount of time to check for pulses and perform rescue breathing.

48. C: While all options here should be considered, the first and foremost sign of respiration is noting chest rise-and-fall, or Choice *C*. If no rise-and-fall is noted, ventilating the patient with a BVM with supplemental oxygen is warranted, followed by pulse oximetry and end-tidal CO2 measurements.

49. A: Accidental or intentional ingestion of antifreeze is uncommon, but not unheard of. The signs of antifreeze ingestion mimic alcohol intoxication. Poison control will be your quickest resource for the type of antifreeze the patient took. Then, immediately transport because the systemic effects of antifreeze are life threatening. Choice *B* is incorrect because the patient confirmed drinking the antifreeze. You do not want to induce vomiting or give the patient anything to eat or drink unless directed by poison control, making Choices *C* and *D* incorrect.

50. D: Since the driver has complaints of neck pain, there is a potential for cervical spine injury. The EMT must immobilize the head and neck to prevent further movement and spinal cord damage during the removal of the patient from the vehicle. Once the driver's head and neck are immobilized, the EMT can perform a neurological assessment, Choice *A*. The driver should not be removed from the vehicle until their injury is stabilized, making Choice *B* incorrect. Choice *C* is incorrect because applying cold therapy to the injury without adequate immobilization can potentially make the injury worse and lead to complications.

51. D: There are two main classifications of stroke: ischemic and hemorrhagic. A hemorrhagic stroke is loss of perfusion to brain tissue due to bleeding or a ruptured vessel in the cranial vault. It is important to differentiate which type of stroke a patient is having due to contraindications of possible thrombolytic therapy that may be given once the patient reaches the hospital.

52. C: The leader should be determined prior to arrival at the scene to minimize confusion or chaos while allowing for efficiency and effective management of an emergency. Organizations may have rules or policies in place for determining leaders, but the person driving or riding in the passenger seat is not necessarily the leader at the scene.

53. A: To perform triage is to sort patients according to their respective injuries. Triage is used during mass casualty events to ensure that the patients with the most life-threatening injuries are treated first and accordingly.

54. D: Sizing a patient's OPA is an important part of maintaining a proper airway. The correct way to measure an OPA is from the corner of the mouth to the ear lobe. All of the other answer choices would not correctly give you the size needed for the pediatric patient and could cause obstruction if placed.

55. D: The most important action the EMT should take in this case is to ensure the patient's emotional and physical well-being. It is essential to provide a compassionate and supportive environment and allow the patient to disclose information on their own terms. Conducting a detailed physical examination is not within the scope of practice for EMTs, making Choice *A* incorrect. Although reporting the incident to law enforcement is important, making the patient report the incident without providing emotional support can cause further trauma, making Choice *B* incorrect. Choice *C* is also incorrect as this may cause the patient to feel isolated and unsupported during this time.

56. A: Hypertension, if left untreated, can lead to MIs, renal disease, and strokes. A patient in shock would be hypotensive. Hypertension affects up to 50% of the population in the United States. A large percentage of people in the US are unaware that they are hypertensive.

57. A: As with any impaled object, it should never be removed. Stabilize to prevent further movement and use direct pressure to control any bleeding. Both eyes need to be covered to prevent further movement. If the patient's other eye is not covered, they will attempt to move their "good" eye, but this will cause the affected eye to move. This could cause further injury. Choice *B* is incorrect for the stated reason that an impaled object should not be removed. The risk of further injury by movement of the unaffected eye is why Choice *C* is not correct. Choice *D* is not correct; as previously stated, the EMT should not try to remove impaled objects.

58. B: Tuberculosis is an airborne-transmitted infectious disease. The EMT should utilize airborne precautions, which include gloves, gowns, and N95 respirators. Choice *A* is incorrect as contact precautions are utilized when a patient is infected with microorganisms that can be spread through direct contact. Contact precautions include gloves and gowns. An individual would use contact precautions in patients with diseases such as MRSA or VRE. Choice *C* is incorrect as droplet precautions are used when patients have infectious diseases that can be spread through respiratory droplets. This occurs when the person coughs, sneezes, and talks. Droplet precautions would be used for diseases such as COVID-19 or influenza. Finally, Choice *D,* neutropenic precautions, are used for patients that have compromised immune systems. In this case, healthcare providers wear gowns, gloves, and masks to prevent pathogens from invading the immunocompromised individual.

59. A: The patient is experiencing acute hypoglycemia. If a diabetic patient misses a meal or exerts themselves physically without adequate food intake, they will become confused and lethargic and will sweat profusely. The patient's blood glucose levels are not too far below normal, and this can usually be corrected with ingestion of simple sugar. The recovery can be quite rapid. If this doesn't work, then transport the patient, as hypoglycemia can become life threatening if left untreated. Choices *B* and *C* are

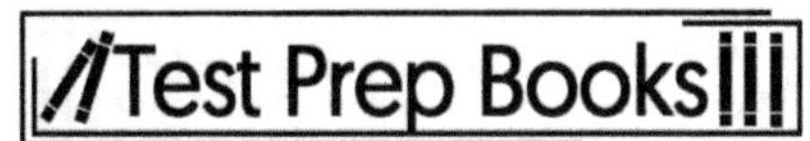

incorrect, as the patient needs more sugar in their blood and insulin would decrease it further, and restricting food would not be beneficial. Choice *D* is incorrect, as water is not going to help raise blood glucose levels.

60. D: When a patient has respiratory distress without any prior medical history, a pulmonary embolism should be in a clinician's differential diagnosis. Females taking birth control are at a higher risk of embolisms due to the medication. This information should be quickly transmitted to the receiving ER to facilitate the appropriate steps upon arrival.

61. C: Speaking to the press can often result in more problems if an EMT hasn't been instructed on what to respond to. The best course of action is to direct the press to speak to their company's representative in order to not hurt community relations.

62. D. Vaginal bleeding can be profuse, and direct pressure can take time to stem the bleeding, but there is no other effective way to control the bleeding. The patient should apply direct pressure to avoid the EMT having to touch the genitalia. Choice *A* would be inappropriate, as there is no evidence of a crime. Choices *B* and *C* call for an inappropriate dressing for vaginal bleeding.

63. D: If a patient has a pulse, a clinician should not perform CPR, or cardiopulmonary resuscitation. The point of CPR is to move blood to perfuse the organs if the heart has stopped. Adequate airway management, oxygen, and ventilation should be provided for patients who are no longer breathing.

64. B: When the patient is in a third-degree heart block, atropine will have no effect on the heart rate since it acts on the AV node. In a high degree heart block, the AV node is where the electrical disconnect is, which is why the atria and ventricles are not beating in rhythm.

65. A: EMS systems and leadership may ask which treatments or procedures are working in the current prehospital setting. When a protocol or standing order is no longer effective, it is important to provide feedback to leadership to ensure the best possible care for patients in the future.

66. D: The patient is experiencing an allergic reaction to the sting of the bee. Presently the reaction is localized to the arm, and the patient does not exhibit any signs of anaphylaxis. If you can easily remove the stinger with the tips of your fingers, you may attempt. If unable, leave the stinger in place. Ice may help with local swelling. Choices *A*, *B*, and *C* are incorrect, as the increased pressure they would put on the local area could push into a systemic issue.

67. A: Continuing education is a big part of working in EMS. Practices, standards, and treatments can be updated often. Continuing education allows EMTs to ensure they are giving the most up-to-date treatments and reduces mortality for the patients they serve.

68. B: Triage is a vital concept in EMS, especially during mass casualty incidents. The primary purpose of triage is to assess and categorize patients based on the severity of their injuries. This ensures that those with the most critical needs receive medical attention first. While triage can give insight into the overall severity of an incident, Choice *A*, its primary purpose is to prioritize individual patient care rather than assess the situation's overall magnitude. While the triage process can indirectly provide information about resource needs, its direct aim is not resource identification; therefore, Choice *C* is incorrect. Choice *D* is also not the central purpose of the triage process.

69. C: Cerebral palsy is a movement disorder that usually appears in early childhood. Signs and symptoms include poor coordination, stiff and weak muscles, and tremors. The patient has no control over these movements, so care needs to be taken so that the patient doesn't injure themselves during movement and transport. The patient with cerebral palsy may be ventilator dependent and non-verbal and may use multiple medical devices, but this would be because of other comorbidities and not the disease itself, making Choices *A*, *B* and *D* incorrect.

70. C: After getting an initial impression, you should check for breathing and a pulse while assessing responsiveness. Since this patient is cyanotic, you should expect that the patient is not breathing or perfusing. If the patient did not have a pulse, CPR should begin.

71. B: Since the injury has not caused an airway obstruction or difficulty breathing, the next step is to control the bleeding. This is easily accomplished by packing the area with sterile gauze and instructing the patient to bite down to maintain pressure. Choice *A,* administering pain medication to the child, is out of the EMT scope of practice. Choice *C*, reinserting the tooth, is ultimately desirable but should only be performed by a dentist. The EMT's responsibility is to provide first aid and adequate storage of the tooth. While Choice *D* is important to maintain the viability of the tooth until it can be properly implanted by a dentist, this can be done after the bleeding has been addressed. The best way to preserve the tooth is to place it in a container with milk or saline solution.

72. A: Ludwig's angina is an acute form of cellulitis that affects the soft tissue of the mouth and neck. The infection spreads quickly and can lead to ventilatory or respiratory problems due to its obstruction of the airway.

73. D: When someone is exposed to a hazardous substance, it is important to remove clothing and belongings to reduce the risk of continued exposure. This also helps protect emergency personnel from being exposed to the substance. Although identifying and managing life-threatening injuries is important, the first step in the decontamination process is to remove the patients' clothing and belongings to prevent the spread of the hazardous material. This makes Choice *A* incorrect. Administering antidotes or medications to counteract the exposure may be necessary, but this is not the first step in the decontamination process, making Choice *B* incorrect. Choice *C* is also incorrect because immediately transporting the patients to a hospital can cause the hazardous substance to spread to other areas.

74. C: From the signs and symptoms and mechanism of injury, it appears the player may have suffered a lacerated kidney. An acute laceration can present with similar signs and symptoms to other kidney issues, and blood in the urine is indicative of an injury to the urinary system. Gently check the back for any further injury and apply ice to help reduce swelling. The patient is not experiencing hypo/hyperglycemia, so checking blood glucose levels will not provide any useful information, making Choice *A* incorrect. The patient did not suffer a chest injury and does not require a sling or swathe, and breath and hearts sounds will give little useful data, making Choice *B* incorrect. Choice *D* is incorrect, as breath and heart sounds will yield little information, and heat to the affected area will provide little benefit to the patient.

75. C: Hepatitis is a potential risk for any healthcare provider. Every day, you will encounter patients who are bleeding or have open sores. Since hepatitis patients feel fine until the condition is chronic, they may not be able to warn you about potential exposure. You may be required to be immunized against HBV, and you should have periodic blood draws to ensure therapeutic levels. While HIV is also a potential risk, there currently is no vaccine for HIV, making Choice *A* incorrect. Choices *B* and *D* are incorrect, as neither is a bloodborne pathogen.

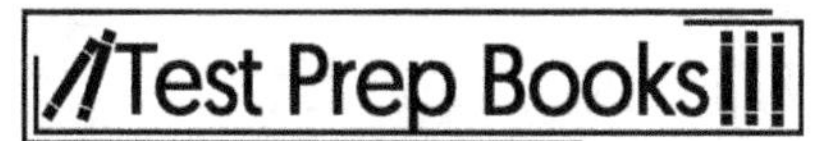

76. B: Normal inhaled air contains 21% oxygen along with all other gases. While performing mouth-to-mask ventilation, the patient is also inhaling the CO2 that you are ventilating with. This should be kept in mind as to why supplemental oxygen, along with a BVM, allows for better oxygenation of a patient since a patient in respiratory arrest already has an oxygen deficit.

77. D: Each service can have its own standards regarding cleaning and the replacement of supplies. It is the oncoming crew's responsibility to ensure the ambulance is ready to be used during their shift. Inventory, minor maintenance, and cleaning are common responsibilities for oncoming crewmembers.

78. A: Normal end-tidal capnography for patients should be titrated to 35-45. The way to modulate a patient's end-tidal is to increase ventilatory rate so as to facilitate the exchange of CO2 for oxygen. Patients post-ROSC will typically present with a higher ETCO2 since they were unable to correctly exchange CO2 when not respirating.

79. C: Cerebrospinal fluid leaking from the ears and/or nose is indicative of a skull fracture. While the fluid may be blood-tinged, it is not bleeding. This and the patient's level of consciousness would indicate that this patient requires C-spine immobilization and rapid transport. Choices *A, B,* and *D* are all incorrect as the fluid is not blood but cerebrospinal fluid.

80. A: The EMT should respect the patient's wishes and allow her to receive care from a female EMT. Patients have the right to refuse care if they are uncomfortable. Choice *B* is incorrect; female EMTs can be called to respond to the scene, and the scenario does not indicate that this is not possible. Choice *C* is incorrect, as the patient has voiced that she is uncomfortable. The EMT should only proceed if the woman is unconscious, where the principle of implied consent applies. Choice *D* is also incorrect for the same reason of consent.

81. B: There are a myriad of psychotropic medications with each having its own precautions regarding an overdose—far too many for you to remember. The first action is to obtain the medication containers or have the patient list the medications and then contact appropriate resources for guidance. Choice *A* is incorrect, as the EMT should not induce vomiting without proper guidance. While the airway will always be monitored, Choice *C* is incorrect, as the patient should be kept as alert as possible. Choice *D* is incorrect, as the patient is not violent. Notification (if applicable) can be done after patient care is completed.

82. A: WOB stands for work of breath, which refers to how hard the patient is laboring to breathe. In this case, Donnie is able to assess that the patient is laboring to breathe. PAT is the pediatric assessment triangle. From this initial visual encounter, Donnie isn't able to gather accurate information about the patient's heart or kidneys.

83. D: When the chord presents first, the baby continues and puts pressure on the cord, which could stop blood flow from the placenta. This can be life threatening, and your first action is to check for a pulsating cord. If you detect a pulse, place mother in knee-chest position to take pressure off the cord and cover it with a sterile cloth. The baby can lose body heat through the cord exposed to the outside air. If there is no pulse, with a sterile gloved hand, gently place a hand in the vagina to lift the baby's head off the cord to maintain circulation. Choices *A*, *B*, and *C* would not relieve the pressure on the cord and could exacerbate the situation.

84. A: Patients who have arrested and had ROSC need extensive post-cardiac arrest care. Many causes of cardiac arrest require high-level interventions—which can be performed at Level 1 hospitals—from specialists to ensure that the patient does not re-enter cardiac arrest.

85. A: The next step when direct pressure is not controlling the bleeding in an infant is the use of pressure points. The preferred spot for a lower arm injury is the brachial pressure point, which is the same point that is used to check for a pulse on an unresponsive infant. Choice *B* is incorrect as tourniquets are not indicated for infants. Choice *C* is incorrect as an air splint is not indicated for infant use. Choice *D* is incorrect as the antecubital pressure point can be difficult to locate and maintain pressure.

86. C: The Department of Transportation Emergency Response Guide is a guidebook that helps responders in a HazMat context. This guidebook carries information about different hazardous materials, which allows responders to approach appropriately and safely, so as not to become patients themselves.

87. B: If you are unable to successfully ventilate a patient, the problem typically lies with the airway not being anatomically correct to allow the air to pass down into the lungs. You should reposition the airway and attempt to give ventilations again. If this fails, consider an airway adjunct device to facilitate the ventilations.

88. C: The patient's blood glucose reading indicates that the patient is in hyperglycemia, which is not uncommon for newly diagnosed patients. The patient's current levels are high, but not to the life-threatening range—but that can change. Your care is limited to airway management and periodic blood glucose checks. While fluids are needed to lower the blood sugar levels, oral intake would not be sufficient, and you do not want to induce vomiting, making Choice *A* incorrect. Choice *B* would further exacerbate hyperglycemia, and you do not want to administer the patient's insulin, as that is not within your scope of care.

89. C: A limb presentation birth is a non-deliverable situation. Cover the limb with a sterile cloth and transport immediately. As mentioned, this is a non-deliverable situation, making Choice *A* incorrect. You should never attempt to push any part of the delivery back into the mother, making Choice *B* incorrect. Checking the limb for a pulse and high-flow oxygen for the mother are not indicated in this situation, making Choice *D* incorrect.

90. B: An impaled object should always be left in place. The object should be stabilized and the bleeding controlled with sterile gauze. Choices *A* and *C* state to remove the object, which should never be done, and Choice *D* would not be appropriate as a hemostatic dressing would not be indicated in an instance like this.

91. C: The maximum time a clinician should suction a patient's airway is fifteen seconds. While suctioning, the patient is unable to oxygenate. If the patient's airway becomes blocked again, the procedure can be reattempted after re-oxygenating the patient.

92. C: If a clinician is dispatched for any abdominal pain, there should always be a high suspicion of cardiac involvement. Myocardial infarctions can manifest as abdominal pain due to dermatome pathways. For this reason, transporting these patients to a facility with cardiac catheterization capabilities is imperative.

93. A: The most important action in this scenario is to open and maintain the patient's airway. When a patient is unresponsive after a seizure, ensuring their airway is the priority. Patients are at an increased risk for ineffective airway clearance because of neuromuscular impairment post-seizure. The tongue may obstruct the patient's airway, or the patient may aspirate saliva or emesis. Choice *B* is incorrect, as the patient may have an intact gag reflex, and the blood glucose level would reveal little beneficial information at the present. Checking for a pulse and initiating CPR would be the next step if the patient is pulseless and not breathing, making Choice *C* incorrect. There is no evidence of head or neck trauma, so there is no need for immobilization, making Choice *D* incorrect.

94. C: The initial management of this injury is to immobilize the right wrist with a splint. Immobilization allows for stability, prevents further movement, and minimizes the risk of worsening the injury until it can be assessed by a physician. Choice *A* is incorrect as pain medication should only be administered under the direction of a physician. Choice *B*, applying a cold compress, can reduce swelling to the affected area and provide some comfort; however, immobilization of the injury takes priority, making Choice *B* incorrect. Choice *D* is incorrect as a mobility assessment can further aggravate the injury and could cause potential complications.

95. C: Post-arrest patients require ALS intervention to ensure that they do not re-enter cardiac arrest. An ALS team can bring some aspects of critical care to a patient post-ROSC, such as pressors, pacing, and other interventions.

96. C: The EMT should transport the woman to the nearest hospital immediately. Women in active labor with a history of cesarean sections are considered high risk due to possible adhesions in the abdominal cavity or uterine rupture. Choice *A,* assisting the woman to a low Fowler's position, is not appropriate. This may impede the delivery process and make the situation dangerous for both her and the baby, who is most likely moving through the birth canal. The EMT should not encourage the woman to push through contractions; pushing is not advised until a healthcare provider evaluates her cervix to determine full dilation. This makes Choice *B* incorrect. Choice *D,* preparing the woman for an emergency cesarean section, is not appropriate for the EMT to determine. The focus of the EMT is to transport the woman to receive an immediate evaluation to prevent complications.

97. D: Any medication that ends in "lol" should be considered a beta blocker. Beta blockers help slow the heart rate down and lower the patient's cardiac output. These medications are typically prescribed to patients with hypertension.

98. A: The patient's airway is obstructed by the broken teeth. Attempting to ventilate the patient without clearing the airway can cause further obstruction and could also cause pneumonia in their later care. The appropriate action is to suction the airway for no more than 15 seconds, then attempt to ventilate for the patient.

99. A: Anemia is a condition in which there aren't enough healthy red blood cells to carry oxygen to the body's tissues. Anemia can be an acute or chronic condition, and there are many causes. Blood loss is a common cause of acute anemia, though it may not be visible (i.e., it's internal). The patient's vital signs point to mild hypoperfusion issues, so supplemental oxygen will be beneficial and may stabilize vitals. Checking for an external bleeding source and obtaining a detailed medical history would be your next step. Choice *B* is incorrect, as the patient does not require high-flow oxygen now, and blood glucose levels will not provide any beneficial information. Choice *C* is incorrect, as, again, blood glucose levels will not provide any beneficial information, and oral intake should be restricted, which would also make Choice *D* incorrect.

100. A: The chest wound is the most critical injury in this case. Spurting bright red blood is indicative of an arterial bleed. The patient could bleed out within minutes. Choice *B* is incorrect; there is no indication that immobilization would be beneficial as the primary course of action. Likewise, Choice *C* would be of no benefit to the patient—there is no indication that the airway is obstructed. Choice *D* is also incorrect; gunshot victims would not be immobilized in the Kendrick extrication device.

101. B: Choice *B*, chest rise-and-fall, is the primary indicator of proper ventilation. While Choices *A* and *D* could be beneficial to confirm the patient is receiving adequate oxygen exchange, you should watch the patient's chest rise and fall to ensure your rescue breaths are making it down into the lungs. If you squeeze the BVM with too much pressure, as Choice *C* indicates, you could cause barotrauma to the patient.

102. D: A patient with auditory and visual hallucinations is having a break from reality and is having trouble determining what is real. This can lead to agitation and a further escalation of the emergency. The patient doesn't appear to presently be a threat, and the interventions are limited. Gently reassuring the patient of what is real and that they are safe is the best option. Sternly correcting the patient will exacerbate the issue, making Choice *A* incorrect. The EMT should not agree that they see and hear the patient's hallucinations, as this will make distinguishing what is real or fake harder for the patient, making Choice *B* incorrect. Choice *C* is incorrect, as the patient is not posing a threat. Not all patients suffering a reality break are violent, and restraints are the means of last resort.

103. D: The heart is perfused through two main coronary arteries. The right side of the heart is preload dependent, which means that if there isn't enough preload, the heart can't output enough blood to the rest of the body. Nitroglycerin will reduce preload due to vasodilation. In a right-sided MI, nitroglycerin is contraindicated unless the blood pressure is high enough to offset the vasodilatory effect of nitro.

104. A: The signs of constipation, vomiting, and the absence of bowel sounds point to bowel obstruction. While not life threatening now, a prolonged blockage can lead to peritonitis, which is life threatening. Choice *B* is incorrect, as menstrual cramping would not present with absence of bowel sounds. While Choice *C* is life threatening and could result from a bowel obstruction, a patient with peritonitis presents with severe pain, abdominal rigidity, and a very high fever. Choice *D* is incorrect, as increasing oral intake will exacerbate the obstruction.

105. A: Because the burn is red and blistered, it is important to take care not to break the blisters. With a partial thickness burn, keeping the area clean with a moist healing environment is ideal. The cool dressing will help arrest the burning. Petroleum jelly is used for superficial burns where the integrity of the skin is intact, making Choice *B* incorrect. The blisters should never be broken, as this can lead to infection and increased healing time, so Choices *C* and *D* are incorrect.

EMT Practice Test #3

1. While on scene, your paramedic partner is performing a 12-lead ECG. Upon printing the strip, your partner notes that the patient is presenting with a STEMI. Which of the following is the correct breakdown of the STEMI acronym?
   a. Systemic Troponin Esophageal Myocardial Infarction
   b. ST Elevation Myocardial Infarction
   c. Sonogram Topography Eosinophil Myocardial Infarction
   d. ST Erroneous Myosin Inflammation

2. An EMT is called to the scene of an older female patient lying on the ground, clutching her thigh at a spot from where blood is flowing heavily. She seems confused, pale, and is breathing heavily. Her eyes are fluttering as if they are about to close, and she is unable to respond when a rescuer calls her. A quick blood pressure assessment shows a reading of 100/65. What would be the next step?
   a. Attempting to keep the patient awake with verbal or painful stimuli
   b. Applying high-flow oxygen and beginning attempts to control the bleeding from the thigh wound
   c. Beginning motor/neuro checks to ascertain whether the patient suffered a cerebrovascular accident
   d. Applying high-flow oxygen, administering low-dose aspirin sublingual, and assisting the patient with nitroglycerin if they have it

3. You are dispatched to a residence. Upon arrival you find a 19-year-old patient who appears to be attempting to talk without making any sound and is grabbing their neck. You note the patient isn't breathing. Which of the following emergency actions would you perform on the patient?
   a. Suction the patient's mouth.
   b. Perform abdominal thrusts.
   c. Insert an NPA.
   d. Apply a nasal cannula.

4. You arrive on scene to a teenage female who was witnessed to have experienced a seizure on a playground. Witnesses say that while she was playing, she grabbed her head and sat down. She then slumped to the floor and began seizing uncontrollably. You come upon her lying supine. She is unresponsive to verbal stimuli but responds to pain. She is breathing normally but sounds like she is snoring. She is extremely moist from profuse sweating, and it appears she has lost bladder control. Witnesses deny any trauma prior to seizures. What actions should you take next?
   a. Immobilize the patient's head and C-spine, maintain the airway with the jaw-thrust method, and apply high-flow oxygen.
   b. Open the patient's airway with the head tilt-chin lift technique, insert an oral airway, and apply oxygen via nasal cannula.
   c. Maintain the patient's airway as found, but insert a nasal airway if it cannot be maintained by manual techniques, and apply a cervical collar to keep the patient's head still.
   d. Maintain the patient's airway as found, but insert a nasal airway if it cannot be maintained by manual techniques, and cover the patient with a dry sheet or blanket.

5. While attempting to suction a patient's airway, you note that you should not continuously touch the back of the throat. Why should this action be avoided?
   a. It can cause the epiglottis to spasm and close off.
   b. It can cause an increased risk of airway infection.
   c. It can cause a vagal response.
   d. It can cause a patient to vomit.

6. You are on scene with your paramedic partner to transport a patient with a racing heart and respiratory distress. You partner places the 4-lead on the patient and notes a tachycardic rhythm. You note that the patient is diaphoretic and confused when interacting with you, which leads you to determine that he has a cardiac dysrhythmia. Which of the following rhythms is NOT a perfusing rhythm?
   a. Sinus tachycardia
   b. Sinus bradycardia
   c. V-TACH
   d. STEMI

7. Which of the following places is the most common area for ambulances to be involved in a collision?
   a. Close to the station
   b. On an interstate
   c. At an intersection
   d. At the scene of a call

8. An EMT is dispatched to a skilled nursing facility for a geriatric male patient with an altered level of consciousness who is being non-compliant with staff. The patient has Parkinson's disease, is experiencing visual and auditory hallucinations, and is quite anxious. Upon meeting, the patient wants to know if the EMT is his son and if he is there to take him home. He says the staff are vampires and the food is poisoned. What should the EMT do next?
   a. Tell the patient that yes, he is his son and that he is there to take him home.
   b. Reassure the patient that he is not his son, that he is there to help, and that the patient is safe.
   c. Ask the facility to request law enforcement to respond and place the patient on a psychiatric hold.
   d. Reassure the patient that he is a vampire hunter and that he will tell the police about the poisoned food.

9. Hypotension in septic shock is caused by which of the following?
   a. Dilated and leaky vessels
   b. Constricted and leaky vessels
   c. Increased diuresis
   d. Antigen and macrophage response

10. While attempting to ventilate a two-year-old pediatric patient, you note minimal chest rise-and-fall. You reposition the mask and have asked your partner to assist you, to no avail. Which of the following choices should be considered when providing bag-valve-mask ventilations on a pediatric patient?
   a. Pediatric patients have a more difficult time with oxygenation due to congenital heart defects.
   b. Pediatric patients have larger heads, which requires padding under the shoulders.
   c. Most pediatric patients have less compliance when ventilating.
   d. Pediatric patients require earlier airway management if becoming hypoxic.

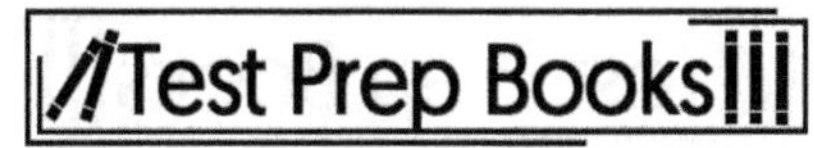

11. When caring for a patient with advanced Parkinson's disease, what special care must be taken?
    a. Parkinson's patients are always ventilator dependent, so prepare to provide suction.
    b. Parkinson's patients have rhythmic body tremors, ticks, and contractions that make maintaining an airway without an artificial airway extremely difficult.
    c. Parkinson's patients have uncontrollable body tremors, ticks, and contractions that can inadvertently injure the patient and can make taking vital signs challenging.
    d. Parkinson's patients are asymptomatic and don't require any special care.

12. What is the primary cause of pediatric cardiac arrest?
    a. Infection
    b. Hypoxia
    c. Hypovolemia
    d. Congenital heart defects

13. An EMT arrives on scene to find an elderly female lying supine on her bedroom floor. Her husband reports that she fell on her way back from the bathroom. She denies any head trauma or loss of consciousness but complains of hip pain. The EMT's physical exam notes some bruising and swelling in the upper thigh and that one leg is shorter than the other and its foot is turned outward. The layout of the room makes moving the patient difficult. What would be the best method for moving the patient while keeping the hip stable?
    a. Applying a vacuum splint to the affected area then securing the patient to a longboard
    b. Applying a traction splint to the affected limb and securing the splint and the patient to a longboard
    c. Positioning the hip in the most comfortable position and carefully logrolling the patient to the longboard
    d. Positioning the hip in the most comfortable position and carefully using a scoop stretcher to maintain their position and facilitate moving the patient

14. What precaution must be taken when caring for and transporting a patient with hemophilia?
    a. Patients with hemophilia have deformed blood cells and require supplemental oxygen.
    b. Patients with hemophilia have trouble stopping bleeding, so extra care needs to be taken for minimal bleeding.
    c. Patients with hemophilia have difficulty regulating body temperature and are at risk of hypothermia, so you must warm the patient with blankets.
    d. Patients with hemophilia often have hypoglycemia, so you must administer oral glucagon.

15. Upon arriving at the scene of a patient in respiratory distress, the EMT finds a 22-year-old male patient in respiratory distress and only responsive to pain. The patient's vitals are 48 HR, 70/60 BP, 4 RR, and 86% SpO2 on room air. What should the EMT do first?
    a. Apply the automated external defibrillator and prepare to perform CPR.
    b. Assist the patient's respirations with ventilatory support using a BVM.
    c. Administer a dose of epinephrine from an EpiPen.
    d. Administer supplemental oxygen via NC at 6 LPM.

16. You respond to a patient who is unconscious but respirating on their own. The patient's blood pressure is 70/50. Upon assessment, the patient has angioedema, hives, and has an epi-pen in his hand. Which type of shock do you suspect that this patient is experiencing?
    a. Cardiogenic
    b. Hypovolemic
    c. Anaphylactic
    d. Neurogenic

17. Which of the following sets of medications should be given if a patient complains of chest discomfort, left arm pain, and respiratory distress?
    a. Metoprolol and ketamine
    b. Tylenol and oxygen
    c. ACE inhibitor and heparin
    d. Aspirin and nitroglycerin

18. An EMT responds to a motorcycle collision where the rider was not wearing a helmet. He appears alert and oriented with some scalp lacerations that are bleeding profusely. The EMT detects bleeding from his nose and ears, so they believe he may have suffered a basilar skull fracture. Along with head/C-spine immobilization, what precaution needs to be taken with this particular concern?
    a. Extreme care needs to be taken when using direct pressure to control scalp lacerations.
    b. Basilar skull fractures often lead to concussions, so the EMT must be prepared to assist with airway management.
    c. A basilar skull fracture can lead to respiratory arrest, so the EMT must be prepared to assist with respirations.
    d. A basilar skull fracture can lead to mandible paralysis, so the EMT must be prepared to assist with airway management.

19. The EMT arrives at a residence for an adult male who is home from laparoscopic abdominal surgery four days ago. He is now complaining of abdominal pain rated at 8/10 and nausea. He denies any vomiting and states he last ate breakfast this morning. His incisions are oozing a little through the dressings. How should the EMT care for this patient?
    a. Restrict oral intake, apply warm compresses to affected area, and transport the patient in position of comfort.
    b. Administer OTC antacid and encourage clear fluid intake, then apply cold compresses to the affected area and transport patient in recovery position.
    c. Remove the patient's incisional dressings, check for signs and symptoms of infection, and take oral temperature. Clean and reapply with new dressings.
    d. Check the patient's blood glucose levels and take necessary intervention for hyper/hypoglycemia.

20. Your patient is complaining of heart palpitations while seated in a chair. Upon assessment, the patient's blood pressure is 100/90, heart rate is 184 bpm, SpO2 is 84% on room air, and respiratory rate is 30 breaths a minute. What should you do first?
    a. Administer nitroglycerin.
    b. Administer supplemental oxygen.
    c. Place patient in left lateral recumbent position.
    d. Attach AED pads.

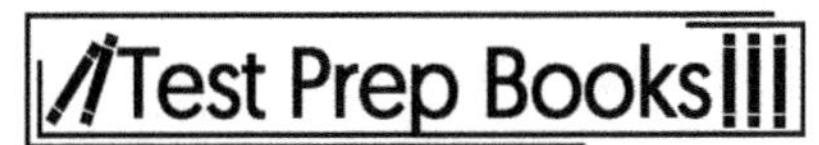

21. A 67-year-old facial trauma patient is in respiratory arrest, unconscious, and unable to respirate on her own. During ventilations, you do not note chest rise-and-fall. After repositioning the BVM and ensuring a good face-mask seal, what would be the next best course of action?
   a. Inserting an NPA
   b. Starting waveform capnography
   c. Assessing her Sp02
   d. Inserting an OPA

22. An EMT responds to a parent who states that after her 11-year-old daughter walked in the woods, her arms swelled up and there appear to be small blisters on her arms. She complains of a burning sensation and intense itching. She is breathing rapidly, but that appears to be from the commotion. What should the EMT do next?
   a. Administer 0.15 mg epinephrine subcutaneous/intramuscular via EpiPen.
   b. Break the blisters on the forearms, then clean the area and cover with sterile gauze and bandages.
   c. Leave the blisters intact and apply a cold compress to the affected area.
   d. Leave the blisters intact and tightly wrap the arm in a compression bandage.

23. A patient presents with what appears to be a small puncture wound to the right chest. The patient is struggling to breathe and has decreased breath sounds on the right. What should the EMT do first?
   a. Place the patient on CPAP to assist with respirations.
   b. Place the patient supine and begin CPR.
   c. Place the patient in a position of comfort but anticipate intubation.
   d. Place a sterile dressing on the wound.

24. You arrive at a skilled nursing facility for an elderly female with an altered level of consciousness. Staff reports that normally the patient is quite alert and oriented for her age, but this morning she awoke and was confused and somewhat agitated. You see that she is breathing normally and has a steady pulse and feels warm to the touch. Staff have reported that everything has been fine lately other than some random episodes of urinary incontinence. What is your next step?
   a. Take an oral temp, and if it's elevated, ask the staff to administer 650 mg of Tylenol.
   b. Take an oral temp, note if elevated, provide support, and attempt to collect urine if able.
   c. Check blood glucose levels and intervene as necessary.
   d. Check oxygen saturation levels and intervene as necessary.

25. After the application of splinting materials, it can be difficult to assess circulatory function distal to the affected area. What is one method that can be used to ensure good circulation?
   a. Feeling the patient's distal digits for warmth
   b. Asking the patient to move the distal digits
   c. Asking the patient if they can feel a small prick on digit tips
   d. Pressing on the patient's nail bed and looking for blanching to return to pink

26. Where in the heart does the cardiac rhythm originate?
   a. The ventricles
   b. The bundle of His
   c. The aorta
   d. The atria

27. Your 20-year-old patient is in respiratory arrest and not currently breathing after falling off their house, which is 10 feet tall. The patient has a bradycardic pulse. Which is the most appropriate treatment?
    a. Performing a jaw thrust and administering one breath every five to six seconds
    b. Applying a cervical collar and inserting an oropharyngeal airway
    c. Applying AED pads and preparing to start chest compressions
    d. Inserting an NPA and assessing for a spinal injury

28. You are transporting a patient with stroke-like symptoms and have activated the stroke protocol by contacting the hospital. Which drug used to break down clots may the hospital administer?
    a. PPD
    b. Fibrinolytics
    c. Aspirin
    d. TPA

29. An EMT responds to a two-vehicle MVA. They come to a child who was a restrained passenger in the passenger rear seat who is complaining of LLQ abdominal pain. There are no physical signs of trauma present. What are the steps to assess the patient's abdomen?
    a. Visually examine the entire abdomen, looking for distention and/or bruising; gently palpate the abdomen, checking for rigidity and/or tenderness; and auscultate bowel sounds for a potential blockage or perforation.
    b. Auscultate bowel sounds to determine any blockage or perforation, gently tap the abdomen and listen for the differences between solid (liver) and hollow (stomach) organs, and note any abnormalities.
    c. Gently palpate the abdomen using both hands, comparing any differences; auscultate bowel sounds, noting any abnormalities; and transport immediately.
    d. Visually examine the entire abdomen, looking for distention and/or bruising; gently tap the abdomen, listening for the differences between solid (liver) and hollow (stomach) organs and noting any abnormalities; and auscultate bowel sounds for potential blockage or perforation.

30. You arrive on the scene to a 22-year-old male in respiratory distress. Upon evaluation, you find the patient has a known history of asthma and is prescribed an inhaler. Which receptor does albuterol effect?
    a. Alpha-1
    b. Alpha-2
    c. Beta-1
    d. Beta-2

31. You are on scene with a patient complaining of chest pain. The patient claims that he was prescribed nitroglycerin. What is the correct single dose of nitroglycerin?
    a. 4 mg
    b. 0.04 mcg
    c. 4 mcg
    d. 0.4 mg

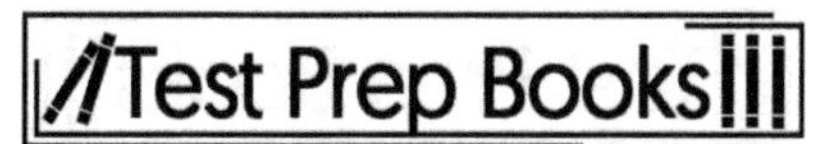

32. You arrive at the scene of an adult male who, according to his parents, suffers from bipolar disorder. They say that lately he has been very upbeat—almost hyper—and has been spending his money freely, but recently that has all changed. Today he has cut his wrist and said that he wants to kill himself. He is not armed, but he is bleeding from a cut on his right wrist. The bleed does not appear to be arterial, and he is alert and agitated. He denies that he wants to harm anyone else and agrees to let you look at this arm. He repeats his desire to kill himself but won't do it at his parents' home. He refuses transport and says he is willing to sign a paper saying so. What is your next step?
   a. The patient is an adult and can refuse transport. Have him sign the release and tell the parents to call if there are any further problems.
   b. Back away from the patient but try to keep him in sight and request law enforcement to intervene.
   c. Have the patient sign paperwork that states he is refusing transportation to a healthcare facility but will go via his parents' vehicle.
   d. Explain to the patient that he has verbally voiced a desire to harm himself and has tried to do so. He can either go voluntarily in the ambulance to the hospital or law enforcement will need to be informed.

33. An EMT arrives on the scene of a motor vehicle accident and finds a patient who exhibits significant neck pain, difficulty moving his head, and trouble swallowing, suggesting a possible hangman's fracture. Due to the location of the fracture, what care needs to be taken?
   a. The patient requires total head and spinal immobilization.
   b. The patient requires head and cervical spine immobilization.
   c. The patient requires cervical and thoracic spine immobilization.
   d. The patient requires thoracic and lumbar spine immobilization.

34. When ventilating a patient, why is it important to NOT hyperventilate?
   a. Hyperventilation can cause the hemoglobin to become too saturated to perfuse the patient.
   b. Hyperventilation can cause respiratory alkalosis.
   c. Hyperventilation can cause hypercapnia.
   d. Hyperventilation can induce thrombocytopenia.

35. While running Code 3 on the way to a scene, an EMT is approaching a busy four-way intersection. How should they proceed in this situation?
   a. Proceed only after ensuring the intersection is clear.
   b. Slow down to 10 mph and only pass through yellow lights.
   c. Continuously use the siren and horn to ensure the path is clear.
   d. Wait for a police escort to go through red lights.

36. When treating a patient with hepatitis C, what precautions will you take for you and the patient?
   a. Standard body substance isolation precautions
   b. Gloves, surgical mask, and eye protection
   c. Gloves, eye protection, and a surgical mask for both you and the patient
   d. Gloves, surgical mask, eye protection, and gown

37. Upon arrival at a residential address, an EMT receives a report that a man has been shocked while using faulty electrical equipment. The faulty equipment has been de-energized and removed. The patient is alert and oriented. He denies any physical injuries but reports pain and tingling in the arm that was exposed to the electricity. The physical assessment does not reveal any apparent trauma, but the EMT suspects compartment syndrome. What should be done for the patient?
   a. Remove any jewelry or constricting items from the affected arm.
   b. Apply a cold pack to the area to reduce pain and swelling.
   c. Immerse the man's arm in warm water.
   d. Immediately transport the man to the nearest emergency department.

38. You arrive on scene to find a patient slumped over his steering wheel and not breathing. Upon administering ventilations via a BVM, your partner notes the patient's pupils are pinpoint and unreactive. Which of the following treatments could bring this patient's respiratory drive back?
   a. Precordial thump
   b. Defibrillation with an AED
   c. Nasal naloxone
   d. Inserting a King LT

39. Which of the following disorders refers to death to brain tissue due to deprivation of oxygen?
   a. Myocardial infarction
   b. Stroke
   c. Supine hypotensive syndrome
   d. COPD

40. You respond to a grocery store where an adult female states that she suddenly felt very tired and weak. She began to sweat and stagger in line before those around her helped her to the floor, and she doesn't remember anything until you arrived. She is alert and oriented, BP 84/50, with a pulse of 80, respirations of 18, and some mild lower abdominal tenderness. She reports that she had some pelvic cramping and some vaginal spotting. She doesn't remember when her last period was and denies any pain or burning on urination. What do you suspect, and what care do you provide?
   a. The patient is suffering from an inflamed appendix. Restrict oral intake and apply a warm compress to the affected area.
   b. The patient could be having an ectopic pregnancy. This is potentially life threatening, and the patient should be transported immediately.
   c. The patient is suffering from placenta previa. Control vaginal bleeding with bulky dressings and elevate the patient's legs.
   d. The patient is experiencing hypoglycemia. Check blood glucose levels and administer oral glucagon.

41. You and your partner have attained ROSC on a pediatric patient. At which of the following respiratory rates should you ventilate them if they still are unable to respirate on their own?
   a. One breath every two to three seconds
   b. One breath every five to six seconds
   c. Two breaths every two to three seconds
   d. At least 50 times per minute

42. A middle-aged woman is found unconscious in her home. She is breathing rapidly, and you notice a fruity odor in the air. Her skin is warm and flushed. Which action should the EMT take?
   a. Perform a blood glucose test and monitor her airway.
   b. Insert an oral airway and check blood glucose levels.
   c. Administer glucagon and monitor her airway.
   d. Insert a nasal airway and check blood glucose levels.

43. You arrive on scene to find an unconscious patient beside a ladder. Upon assessment, you note snoring respirations and find CSF upon completion of a halo test from the fluid draining from the patient's ear. Which of the following airway adjuncts is contraindicated in this patient?
   a. NPA
   b. OPA
   c. ET tube
   d. King LT

44. Which of the following choices most correctly matches the description of hypovolemic shock?
   a. A condition where there is a depletion of intravascular fluid or blood
   b. A condition where the vessels are dilated and cause third spacing of fluid
   c. A condition where the heart is unable to pump blood effectively or efficiently
   d. A condition where the kidneys filter out too much plasma from the blood

45. What is the best means of extrication for a driver with non-life-threatening head, neck, and chest injuries?
   a. While maintaining manual stabilization of the head and neck, carefully transfer and secure the patient to the longboard.
   b. Roll a large blanket and place it around the patient's head/neck. Grab the length furthest away from behind the patient's back. Using both ends with equal pressure, pull the patient from the vehicle to a longboard.
   c. Start with manual stabilization of head and neck until a rigid C-collar can be put on the patient. Then, use a Kendrick extrication device to maintain head, cervical, and thoracic spine alignment to transfer the patient to a longboard.
   d. Start with manual stabilization of the head and neck until a rigid C-collar can be put on the patient. Then, carefully transfer the patient and secure them to a longboard.

46. While on a welfare check, you find your patient in respiratory distress. The patient has a rotund abdomen, a productive cough, and a temperature of 97.9 degrees Fahrenheit. They appear cyanotic and are wheezing. Which of the following conditions do you suspect the patient to have?
   a. Chronic bronchitis
   b. Emphysema
   c. Pneumonia
   d. Pneumothorax

47. Your patient had previously arrested, and it is five minutes post-ROSC. It was determined that the patient arrested due to a myocardial infarction. Which of the following treatments should be followed to ensure that the patient does not re-enter cardiac arrest?
   a. Ensure that the patient does not take anything by mouth.
   b. Provide ventilations at a rate of 25 bpm.
   c. Provide supplemental oxygenation to achieve 94% saturation.
   d. Defibrillate patient at 200 joules with a biphasic monitor.

48. An EMT arrives at a scene call and begins resuscitation on a pulseless patient when a medical doctor arrives on the scene. The doctor states that he is a podiatrist but is still a doctor and wants to take the lead on patient care. How should an EMT proceed?
   a. Call medical control.
   b. Allow the doctor to treat and assist in transport.
   c. Advise the doctor to not help in patient care.
   d. Call for police assistance.

49. A 65-year-old man has called 911 complaining of worsening shortness of breath. The first responders find him in the tripod position with pursed lip breathing. The patient is audibly wheezing and struggling to speak in full sentences. The patient is tachypneic with an oxygen saturation of 90% on his baseline two liters supplemental oxygen. What should the EMT do first?
   a. Increase the patient's oxygen until his pulse oximeter reads 100%.
   b. Assist the patient's ventilation with a BVM.
   c. Assist the patient to use his home nebulizer.
   d. Administer emergent intramuscular epinephrine.

50. You are transporting a patient with a possible ischemic stroke. Which of the following is the most important when dealing with strokes?
   a. Ensuring proper documentation of the patient's insurance information
   b. Placing the patient in a position of comfort
   c. Determining the patient's medical history
   d. Transportation to a stroke facility

51. While staging during a mass casualty event due to a tornado, an EMT's partner asks how multiple agencies can seamlessly integrate together in order to facilitate emergency response. Which of the following acronyms describes a "standardized" approach to command and coordination of the emergency response hierarchy during multi-agency response?
   a. FEMA
   b. ICS
   c. MCI
   d. MVC

52. You are called to a residence for an adult female with RUQ abdominal pain of 8/10. She states that her last oral intake was approximately two hours ago, and she denies any bladder or bowel issues. There is no distention or bruising, but there is some rebound pain in the RUQ when palpated. She states that her last period was a little over four weeks ago and was normal. She denies any chance of pregnancy. What step is next?
   a. Restrict oral intake, listen to bowel sounds, and transport the patient with knees flexed.
   b. Check the patient's blood glucose levels, intervene as necessary, and transport the patient in Fowler's position.
   c. Encourage the patient to take small sips of water while listening to bowel sounds and transport the patient on her side with knees flexed.
   d. Restrict oral intake, listen to bowel sounds, and transport in Trendelenburg position.

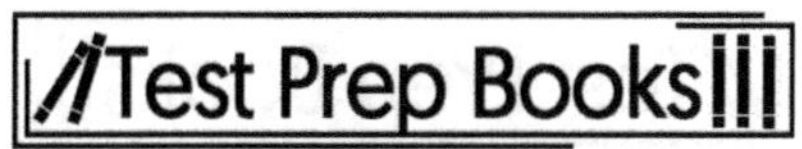

53. A young adult female complains of abdominal pain after suffering a blunt force injury to her abdomen. Upon a visual examination, the EMT notes some discoloration of the LLQ, and the patient is guarding when the area is gently palpated. Bowel sounds are absent in the LLQ. Based on this information, what will be the care for the patient?

a. Immobilize the patient's lumbar spine using KED device, secure the patient to a longboard, and have the patient hold an ice pack over the affected area.
b. Offer the patient small sips of water or ice chips, apply a heat compress to the affected area, and transport the patient prone to relieve pressure.
c. Transport the patient seated with her knees flexed to relieve the pain, give nothing by mouth, and apply an ice pack.
d. Gently wrap sterile bandages around the patient's abdomen with as much pressure as she can tolerate and transport seated with her knees flexed.

54. You are attempting to gather information from an adolescent female patient who is deaf. She has a family member who is willing to interpret for you. What do you do?

a. Kindly refuse the family member and explain that official translators must be used and that notes can be passed until one arrives.
b. Ask the questions directly to the family member and then look to the interpreter for a response to the questions.
c. Ask the questions directly to the patient and look at the patient when hearing the responses. Look at the interpreter when addressing them.
d. Do not rely on an interpreter. Written communication can be passed back and forth, even though it may take longer.

55. A patient with COPD may enter respiratory failure due to:

a. Slow respiratory rate
b. Pulmonary stenosis
c. Bronchospasms of the bronchus
d. Inadequate elimination of CO2

56. You respond for an adult female who is currently seizing at her place of work. When you arrive, you see the patient with active seizure motions, and it appears there is blood coming from her mouth. What steps do you take?

a. Attempt to gently restrain the patient so she doesn't hurt herself further and place a tongue depressor between her teeth to prevent further oral injury.
b. Protect the patient from further harm by guarding the area around her; attempt to protect her head if possible; and after seizing ends, clear the airway of blood in the mouth and assess for an oral injury.
c. Protect the patient from further harm by guarding the area around her; attempt to protect the head if possible; and after seizing ends, insert an oral airway and provide high-flow oxygen.
d. Move the patient to a soft surface and do not interfere with seizure activity, and after seizing ends, clear the airway of blood in the mouth, assess for an oral injury, and then insert an oral airway.

57. You respond to an adolescent male who is reported to have multiple lacerations on his arm. You arrive, and his parents tell you he suffers from depression and that he occasionally cuts himself "to relieve the pain." Today there are more cuts than usual, and the parents are concerned. You approach and see an agitated male with numerous superficial horizontal lacerations on his right forearm. He said he uses his fingernails to draw blood. He denies being suicidal, and he keeps telling you that usually the cutting helps the pain, but it didn't today. What is your initial step?

a. Cleaning and treating the arm wounds and controlling the bleeding with sterile gauze and direct pressure
b. Keeping the patient within sight while law enforcement arrives to secure the scene
c. Quickly approaching the patient and, with the help of a partner, maintaining control of the patient's upper extremities
d. Asking the patient to keep his hands raised while approaching him and gently restraining his arms while a partner secures the scene

58. While in a small clinic, a patient complains of palpitations. Upon assessment, your paramedic partner claims that the patient is in V-TACH. From where does the rhythm originate when a patient is in V-TACH?

a. The ventricles
b. The atria
c. The Purkinje fibers
d. The bundle of His

59. You respond to a residential address to find an adult male in his bathroom with the door barely open. You can hear he is agitated, and his roommate says that he has been talking about killing himself. You ask if there is access to firearms and the roommate says yes. What is your next step?

a. Carefully approach the bathroom after announcing yourself and gently push the door open to see if the man is armed; if he's not, begin talking with him.
b. Ask the roommate the location of the firearms and back out. Request law enforcement to secure the scene before proceeding.
c. Ask the man if he is armed. If he replies no, then ask him to come out of the bathroom so that you can talk.
d. Ask the roommate to go secure all the firearms. After they are secured, carefully approach the door and engage in conversation.

60. After arriving at the scene of a woman in active labor, she delivers a stillborn baby. How should the EMT proceed?

a. Offer grieving resources.
b. Take the baby for medical evaluation.
c. Avoid discussing the baby and focus on the mother's care.
d. Provide emotional support.

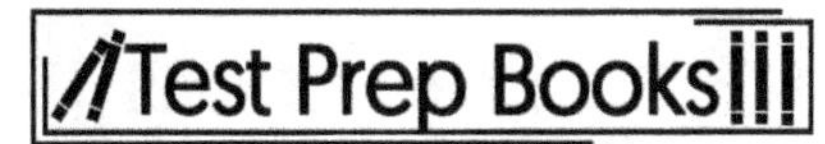

61. You arrive to a home of an adult male who is unresponsive. His wife states he hasn't been feeling well for the past couple of days and he went to take a nap. When she went to check on him, he wouldn't wake up. He is breathing and has a strong, steady pulse. His wife states that he has a history of Addison's disease. What would be your care for this patient?
   a. Maintaining the patient's airway, being prepared to manually open it if needed, checking blood glucose levels, and monitoring blood pressure
   b. Maintaining an open airway and administering oral glucagon to counteract hypoglycemia
   c. Addison's disease is a life-threatening condition that requires invasive measures, requiring ALS response.
   d. Placing the patient in recovery position, inserting an oral airway, and applying supplemental oxygen and monitoring oxygen saturation

62. A mother calls 911 reporting that her unvaccinated two-year-old daughter has been having trouble swallowing and has been fussy. First responders find that the patient is febrile, drooling, and appears to be in pain when she attempts to speak. The patient currently appears to be in no respiratory distress. What should the EMT do first?
   a. Inspect the patient's airway.
   b. Encourage the mother to keep the patient calm and comfortable.
   c. Encourage the mother to feed the patient.
   d. Educate the mother on the need to vaccinate her child.

63. An EMT responds to a school playground where a young girl has fallen with her arm outstretched and is now complaining of pain in her shoulder area. She is seated, cradling her affected arm in her good arm. She can move her fingers and has a good distal pulse. What steps should be taken for the injured limb?
   a. Attempt to return the limb to its natural position, immobilize the arm extended with a rigid or air splint, and transport.
   b. Leave the limb in the position found, have the patient maintain its position, apply ice to the affected area, and transport.
   c. Leave the limb in the position found, maintain its position and immobilize the shoulder joint with a sling and swath, apply ice to the affected area, and transport.
   d. Attempt to return the limb to its natural position, have the patient maintain its position or use rigid splints, apply ice to the affected area, and transport.

64. Which of the following disorders can mimic stroke-like symptoms and should be ruled out prior to calling the hospital to start the stroke protocol?
   a. Myocardial infarction
   b. Aortic aneurysm
   c. Hypoglycemia
   d. Anaphylaxis

65. An EMT responds to a structure fire for an injured firefighter. He was injured when a beam fell on his back, knocking him over. He was found with his mask off, saying his arm and back were hurt. He was able to ambulate out under his own power. After removing his gear, the EMT notes some superficial burns on his back and some deformity of his right shoulder. What are the priorities for this patient?

a. Treating the burns first with ice or cold compresses, applying ice to the deformed joint and then immobilizing it with a sling and swath, assessing the airway for smoke inhalation, and providing oxygen as necessary
b. Assessing the airway for smoke inhalation, providing oxygen, applying ice to the deformed joint and then immobilizing it with a sling and swath, and treating the burns with ice or cold compresses
c. Assessing the airway for smoke inhalation, providing oxygen, treating the burns with ice or cold compresses, and applying ice to the deformed joint and then immobilizing it with a sling and swath
d. Treating the burns first with ice or cold compresses, assessing the airway for smoke inhalation, providing oxygen, and applying ice to the deformed joint and then immobilizing it with a sling and swath

66. Your patient is a 67-year-old male. His caregivers claim his initial symptoms began one day ago and started with a cough. He now is acting different and has had ample secretions. Upon assessment, your patient has a temperature of 103.4 degrees Fahrenheit, an 87% oxygen saturation, and appears lethargic. Which of the following diseases do you suspect the patient to have?

a. Pneumonia
b. ARDS
c. Anaphylaxis
d. COPD

67. What type of force may an EMT use to prevent a patient from harming themselves?

a. Lawful force
b. Reserved force
c. Reasonable force
d. Force with justification

68. You arrive on scene to an adult male who is unresponsive to verbal and painful stimuli. He is breathing, but it is shallow. He appears pale, cool, and clammy. His pulse is rapid and bounding. You notice around his wrist is a Life Alert bracelet that informs you that the patient is a diabetic. You take his blood glucose levels, and they read 30 mg/dL. What are your next steps?

a. Immediately administering oral glucagon in the patient's cheek, monitoring airway, and rechecking blood glucose levels every three minutes until they are within normal limits
b. Immediately administering 50 units of the patient's insulin and rechecking blood glucose levels every three minutes until they are within normal limits
c. Maintaining the patient's airway, applying high-flow oxygen via non-rebreather mask, and transporting immediately
d. Manually opening the airway, inserting an oral airway, applying high-flow oxygen via non-rebreather mask, and transporting immediately

69. During CPR, what is the proper ratio of compressions to breaths with a BVM to administer to an adult patient when two first responders are present?
   a. 60:2
   b. 15:2
   c. 30:2
   d. 10:2

70. When treating any infant trauma patient, what unique characteristic must EMTs always remember?
   a. Infants are pliable and often suffer fewer traumatic injuries than adults.
   b. The signs of shock can be very hard to see. Infants compensate for any apparent injury, but decompensation is quick and severe compared to adults.
   c. Infants often don't provide sufficient signs, so EMTs must be prepared for anything.
   d. Most infant injuries are the result of abuse and neglect.

71. What should you do if you experience an accidental needlestick?
   a. Immediately wash the area with soap and water and, if able, "milk" the area to push any blood out. Notify your supervisor and seek medical attention.
   b. Immediately wash the area with soap and water, then apply alcohol-based disinfectant to the area. Cover the area with sterile dressing and seek medical attention.
   c. Immediately wash the area with soap and water, apply constant and steady pressure above the needlestick site with a BP cuff, and seek medical attention.
   d. Immediately wash the area with soap and water, and if the stick is minor, keep the area covered. Notify your supervisor and seek medical attention if symptoms are present.

72. Which of the following patients is CPAP contraindicated for?
   a. A pediatric patient with RSV
   b. A geriatric patient with bilateral pneumonia
   c. An adult patient in anaphylaxis
   d. A geriatric patient with altered mental status

73. An adult female has successfully delivered a newborn female baby. The baby is breathing on its own and is pink. You have dried and wrapped the baby. How do you cut the umbilical cord?
   a. Immediately clamp the cord, cut between the clamps, and leave the clamps in place.
   b. After the cord stops pulsing, clamp the cord, cut between the clamps, and leave the clamps in place.
   c. Wait until the placenta is delivered, then clamp the cord, cut between the clamps, and then remove the clamps.
   d. Wait until the cord stops pulsing, then clamp the cord, cut between the clamps, and remove the clamps.

74. Which of the following outreach programs allows EMS to foster a community and provide a service that is often overlooked?
   a. Conducting tire pressure checks at their crew house for the community
   b. Holding a forum for the community to allow them to speak about discrepancies and response times
   c. Providing EMT instructor courses for families
   d. Conducting first aid classes for the community

75. You receive a report from a caregiver that an elderly male patient with end-stage renal disease (ESRD) is now having some difficulty breathing when lying down. What steps would you take?
   a. Listen to breath sounds and check for pedal edema, then apply supplemental oxygen.
   b. Listen to breath sounds and check oral temperature, then administer Tylenol for fever control.
   c. Listen to breath sounds and check upper extremity edema, then apply supplemental oxygen.
   d. Listen to breath sounds and check for pedal edema. Apply high-flow oxygen.

76. Which of the following can an EMT do in order to provide administrative support and ensure the company functions appropriately with the correct budget?
   a. Properly document patients' insurance information.
   b. Use fewer supplies to ensure there is not fraud, waste, or abuse.
   c. Attend fundraisers for their EMS system.
   d. Cut back on non-vital medical products for transport.

77. Which of the following selections supports quality assurance in EMS to ensure the highest standard and quality of care for patients?
   a. Reviewing all patient care reports
   b. Providing feedback to police who arrive at the scene before the EMS crew
   c. Modulating protocols to fit patient needs
   d. Using open-loop communication during debriefs

78. You are providing ventilations on an adult patient post-resuscitation with a bag valve mask. Which of the following tidal volume ranges should be targeted in order to ensure adequate post-ROSC respiration?
   a. 6-8 mL/kg
   b. 4-6 mL/kg
   c. 2-4 mL/kg
   d. 8-10 mL/kg

79. While treating a patient at a residence, the patient's husband begins to have a generalized seizure. As you approach the male subject, you note that the patient has vomited, and you can hear audible gurgling. What is the maximum time for suctioning of the adult patient?
   a. Five seconds
   b. Ten seconds
   c. Fifteen seconds
   d. Seven seconds

80. What is the greatest immediate concern in a patient with signs of facial burns?
   a. Infection from open wounds of the head and face
   b. Scarring from damaged skin around the eyes, nose, and mouth
   c. Treatment of the intense pain the patient may be experiencing
   d. Airway obstruction from swelling in the upper airway

81. You arrive at a small health clinic where the staff is performing CPR on a 12-year-old pediatric patient. At what rate should a provider provide compressions?
   a. 60-100 bpm
   b. 90-100 bpm
   c. 100-120 bpm
   d. 120-140 bpm

82. A mother tells you that her two-year-old son came running to the house crying loudly. She noticed that his forehead had begun to swell, and it caused pain if she tried to touch it. There is some scant bleeding from a small circular wound on the forehead. What are your next steps for the child?

a. Place the patient in a soft cervical collar, as the child has suffered a head injury. Maintain airway and immobilize C-spine.
b. Check for a stinger, as the child has been stung by an unknown animal. Monitor airway for respiratory distress and apply a cold compress to the affected area.
c. Assess for cranial nerve function, as the patient has suffered head trauma. Monitor his level of consciousness and control bleeding.
d. The child is having an allergic reaction to an unknown animal bite. Administer 0.15 mg subcutaneous/intramuscular epinephrine via EpiPen.

83. If an EMT is in the first responding unit to arrive at the scene of a motor vehicle accident, where should their crew position the ambulance?

a. Adjacent to the crash to ensure the rig is not hit inadvertently
b. The opposite side of the road
c. On the opposite side of the crash
d. Between the traffic and the crash

84. A pregnant woman in her mid-twenties has fallen. She is alert and conscious, but she has complaints of abdominal pain. There is noticeable vaginal bleeding. What should you do in this scenario?

a. Immediately transport the woman to the nearest hospital.
b. Encourage the patient to take small sips of water to stay hydrated.
c. Elevate the woman's legs to promote blood flow to the placenta and baby.
d. Obtain vital signs and assess the extent of bleeding.

85. An EMT is called to a residence for a trauma involving a kitchen knife. After ensuring the area is safe, they approach the patient and note that he has a three-inch laceration on the lateral aspect of his neck. After bandaging it, the patient claims that he does not wish to be taken to the hospital. Which of the following is the most correct course of action next?

a. Ask police the restrain the patient to allow the crew to transfer him.
b. Explain the risks and possible complications of not being seen by a doctor.
c. Chemically sedate the patient.
d. Have the patient sign the refusal and immediately leave.

86. An EMT is on scene to an adult male complaining of left-sided chest pain after being struck with a baseball. He is complaining of left-sided tenderness and pain that is increased on inspiration. The EMT's physical exam detects some deformity laterally of ribs 6 and 7. Breath sounds are normal bilateral, and the EMT suspects a rib fracture. How would they splint the injury?

a. Splint the patient's arm to the affected side of the chest.
b. Apply a rigid splint from the patient's armpit to his waistline.
c. Place sandbags on the affected ribs and transport the patient on his unaffected side.
d. Apply a thoracic air splint to the patient's chest and inflate until the patient can inhale without pain.

87. You are attempting to ventilate a patient with an OPA in place and a BVM. Which of the following is within the appropriate range of tidal volume for an adult patient per breath?
    a. 1,000–2,000 mL
    b. 100–200 mL
    c. 800–1,000 mL
    d. 500–600 mL

88. After the acquisition of the NREMT-B certification, what else must an EMT receive in order to practice in their respective area?
    a. State license
    b. Advance Life Support certification
    c. Prehospital Trauma Life Support certification
    d. ECG interpretation certification

89. A congenital blood disorder that causes red blood cells to become crescent shaped and can lead to clots within the circulatory system is indicative of what?
    a. Insulin-dependent diabetes (Type I)
    b. Human immunodeficiency virus (HIV)
    c. Sickle cell disease (SCD)
    d. Hepatitis B virus (HBV)

90. Which of the following patients would be categorized as "RED" (immediate) when triaging during a mass casualty incident?
    a. A patient requiring 12 LPM VIA NRB
    b. A patient with controlled arterial bleeding
    c. A patient with a femur fracture
    d. A patient with a tension pneumothorax

91. Using the rule of nines chart, what is one unique characteristic of children in comparison to adults?
    a. Children are 4.5% for every area of 9% on an adult.
    b. Children are 18% for every area of 9% on an adult.
    c. A child's head is 4.5% of their surface area in comparison to 9% for an adult.
    d. A child's head is 18% of their surface area in comparison to 9% for an adult.

92. After a successful full-term delivery of a male baby, you have tended to the infant and mother and cut the umbilical cord. What do you do to assist in delivery of the placenta?
    a. Perform a fundal massage to stimulate uterine contractions.
    b. Pull on the umbilical cord to assist separation from the uterus.
    c. Wait for the placenta to be delivered naturally, check for any missing or torn tissue, and collect it in a plastic bag for further examination.
    d. Wait for the placenta to be delivered naturally, check for any missing or torn tissue, and dispose of it in a biohazard bag.

93. A postpartum woman delivered twins two weeks ago. She is experiencing heavy bleeding, elevated heart rate, and decreased blood pressure. What is the most appropriate action you to take?
    a. Manually massage the woman's uterus to stimulate uterine contractions.
    b. Have the mother breastfeed to stimulate uterine contractions.
    c. Place the mother in the Trendelenburg position to improve blood flow.
    d. Administer pain medication to the mother.

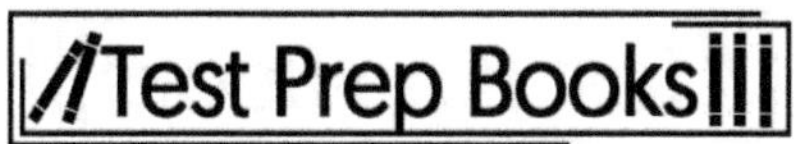

94.When treating a patient with respiratory complications, which of the following signs indicates the patient is in respiratory failure?

a. End-tidal CO2 of 55
b. BP of 70/60
c. HR of 26
d. SpO2 of 90%

95. You respond to a restaurant for an adult male who is complaining of intense heartburn. The patient is diaphoretic and slightly warm to the touch. He states the pain came on after a dinner of all-you-can-eat fried fish. He denies any past medical history other than being overweight. His blood pressure is 160/90, pulse is 90, and respirations are 14 breaths per minute. What actions do you take?

a. Apply high-flow oxygen, attach AED for precautionary measures, and request ALS response.
b. Listen for bowel sounds, check the patient's blood glucose levels, and take necessary intervention for hyper/hypoglycemia.
c. Maintain airway and take precautions for emesis and transport the patient with their knees flexed.
d. Apply supplemental oxygen, administer activated charcoal, and encourage emesis.

96. Which of the following is the correct option for treatment if a patient is in PEA?

a. CPR
b. 200-joule biphasic defibrillation
c. Placement of an airway
d. Stop resuscitation

97. You have successfully delivered a newborn male baby. You suctioned the nose and mouth with the bulb syringe and clamped the umbilical cord. You begin to dry the baby and note that he still has not taken any breaths and is turning blue. What is your next step?

a. Measure a flexible suction catheter from ear to mid-sternum and suction the baby's airway, give rescue breaths, and check for a brachial pulse.
b. Attempt tactile stimulation if the baby has not taken a breath within 60 seconds, give rescue breaths, and check brachial pulse.
c. Using rigid suction, clear the mouth only to a level that you can visualize, give rescue breaths, and check for carotid pulse.
d. Suction the baby with bulb syringe again, give rescue breaths, and check for carotid pulse.

98. An EMT arrives at the scene of a structure fire where an infant has significant partial thickness burns over 25% of their body. The EMT intends to use a sterile wet sheet to drape over most of the patient's body. What is one unique factor they must pay attention to?

a. Hypoxia
b. Hypovolemia
c. Hypothermia
d. Hypoperfusion

99. When a patient is in respiratory distress, what is the term for oxygen deficiency in the blood?

a. Hypocarbia
b. Hypoxia
c. Hypoxemia
d. Hypercapnia

100. You respond to the report of a 15-year-old female who is unresponsive. You arrive, and the mother tells you that she suffers from anxiety and depression. She states that her daughter has had a tough time at school and that today her daughter would not wake up. You see that she is lying in bed. She is unresponsive to verbal stimuli, but she responds to painful stimuli. She is breathing and has a strong, steady pulse. Her mother hands you a bottle of pills, thinking she may have taken too many, as it was just filled yesterday and now it is almost empty. You recognize the medication as benzodiazepines. What is your care for this patient?

a. Insert an oral airway, monitor respirations, and contact the pharmacy for instructions for potential overdose.
b. Maintain the patient's airway manually, monitor respirations, and contact the pharmacy for instructions for potential overdose.
c. Arouse the patient enough to administer activated charcoal to counteract the effects of the medication.
d. Administer 0.4 mg Narcan IM via autoinjector and repeat after two to three minutes if there is no improvement.

101. While transporting a patient that you and your partner achieved ROSC on, your partner notes that the patient's blood sugar is low. Which of the following answers is the appropriate range for blood glucose?

a. 50-90 mmol/L
b. 200-300 mmol/L
c. 70-110 mmol/L
d. 25-50 mmol/L

102. An EMT has attempted to stop bleeding using direct pressure and pressure points for a patient who has suffered a traumatic amputation and is bleeding heavily. What is the next intervention?

a. Apply a tourniquet distal to the amputation site and begin to tighten until the bleeding stops. After a few minutes, loosen the tourniquet to determine if the bleeding continues.
b. Apply a tourniquet as far proximally as possible and begin to tighten until the bleeding stops. Document the time of application and mark the patient's forehead with a capital T and the time of the tourniquet application.
c. Apply a tourniquet proximally across the closest joint to the amputation site. Begin to tighten the tourniquet until the bleeding stops. Document the time of application.
d. Apply a tourniquet as close to the amputation site as possible. Begin to tighten the tourniquet until the bleeding stops. Document the time of application.

103. A frantic parent walks over to your ambulance and claims her child is having trouble breathing. Upon assessment, you find a three-year-old male pediatric patient with stridor, very warm to touch, and a "seal-like" bark when he coughs. Which of the following diseases could be the cause of his symptoms?

a. Strep
b. Seasonal cold
c. Pneumonia
d. Croup

104. What are the two quickest methods you can use to check for cranial nerve damage from a suspected cerebrovascular accident (CVA) patient?

a. Gently palpating the patient's skull, including facial bones, and feeling for deformations and asking the patient if they can feel the touch
b. Having the patient rotate their head in all directions and asking if they experience any pain or numbness when they do that
c. Checking the patient's pupils for equal reactivity and then having the patient follow the penlight with just their eyes
d. Asking the patient to smile and raise their eyebrows

105. You arrive on scene to a patient complaining of chest pain for 12 hours. The patient claims that his only pain relief comes from leaning forward. The patient also claims that he has recently used IV drugs. Which of the following conditions do you suspect?

a. Pericarditis
b. CHF
c. Cor pulmonale
d. Stroke

Answer Explanations #3

1. B: The STEMI acronym is used to identify myocardial infarctions. On an ECG, an MI will present as an ST segment that is elevated over the baseline of the rhythm. When the STEMI acronym is combined with the lead interpretation, a provider can diagnose a STEMI with an ECG.

2. B: Confusion, pale skin, shortness of breath, loss of consciousness, and low blood pressure are all indicators of hypovolemic shock. The detail about the patient's leg bleeding indicates a possible femoral artery blow, which would lead to a large amount of blood loss. This is a common precursor to hypovolemic shock. In this scenario, the patient's airway is patent, and high flow oxygen is indicated with the signs of hypovolemia visible. The next priority is managing blood loss from the thigh wound. Choices *A, C,* and *D* are incorrect for this situation.

3. B: The correct course of action for a chocking patient is Choice *B,* perform abdominal thrusts. Performing tracheal suctioning could cause the object to be inserted deeper into the airway. Inserting an NPA would not allow for ventilation or respiration. Applying a nasal cannula might be the next course of action, but only after getting the patient's airway back.

4. D: The patient most likely is postictal to a seizure. In this state, the patient appears to be soundly asleep and will not often be aroused by verbal stimuli. As found, her airway appears open, but it could become blocked by tissue that was bitten from inside the mouth during the seizure. Manual techniques are often enough to maintain the airway, but a nasal airway may be necessary. In addition, profuse sweating can cause the patient to become hypothermic from the cooling effect of sweating. Loss of bowel or bladder control is common during a seizure, and the patient should be covered to protect modesty. There is no evidence of head or neck trauma, so Choice *A* is incorrect. The patient responds to painful stimuli, so an oral airway would encounter the gag reflex, making Choice *B* incorrect. Choice *C* is incorrect, as the patient does not require a C-collar.

5. C: The vagus nerve innervates from the head to the duodenum. The vagus nerve is responsible for activating the parasympathetic response, which can cause a patient's heart rate to drop or lower. Limit contact with the back of the throat to ensure this nerve is not innervated.

6. C: Ventricular tachycardia is a rhythm that only comes from the ventricles of the heart. Often, V-TACH will present pulseless or unconscious and requires defibrillation/cardioversion to correct.

7. C: The most common area for an ambulance traffic collision to occur is at an intersection. It is imperative that responders enter intersections carefully and ensure that all other traffic has come to a halt before proceeding.

8. B: Parkinson's patients often suffer from a side effect from long-term use of medications to control the symptoms. This produces hallucinations, anxiety, and potential combativeness. In this instance, the patient is anxious and fearful of the staff and food. Gentle reassurance and the EMTs presence as a figure of authority can help ease the tension to allow an exam to proceed. It is inappropriate to lie to a patient to coerce them to consent to anything, making Choices *A* and *D* incorrect. The patient is anxious but is not a threat to himself nor anyone else, and the presence of law enforcement could exacerbate the situation, making Choice *C* incorrect.

9. A: Hypotension in septic shock is caused by dilated and leaky vessels. When infection occurs in the body, the immune response causes histamines to respond to the area. Histamines cause vessels to dilate. When these vessels dilate, fluid is able to exchange into the surrounding tissues, causing a decrease in intravascular fluid. This causes hypotension when done on a systemic level.

10. B: To best facilitate the movement of oxygen into the lungs, providers should pad underneath the pediatric patient's shoulders to obtain a neutral position. This is because pediatric patients have larger heads. When they are supine, this causes misalignment of the airway. While Choice *D* is technically correct, the primary way to allow for proper ventilation is to pad the shoulders.

11. C: Parkinson's is a progressive neuro-motor disease that causes the patients to have tremors and ticks that can range from barely noticeable to the point that the patient is constantly moving. You will not be able to prepare for the patient's movements, so care needs to be taken when assessing and transporting the patient to prevent further injury. In addition, it can make taking vitals difficult. You may need to listen to the heart for pulse and take pedal blood pressure. Some patients are ventilator dependent, but it is not the norm for a Parkinson's patient to be on a ventilator, making Choice *A* incorrect. Choice *B* is incorrect, as there is no rhythm to the body tremors, and a Parkinson's patient doesn't normally present with airway management issues. Parkinson's patients are usually symptomatic to a varying degree, but it is extremely rare for a patient to be asymptomatic, making Choice *D* incorrect.

12. B: The primary cause of pediatric cardiac arrest is hypoxia. Hypoxia should be aggressively treated with supplemental oxygen and ventilatory support if identified.

13. D: Often, elderly patients will suffer a hip fracture from a fall. This fracture is usually high on the femur near the head or greater trochanter. Movement often causes the patient more pain and can cause further injury. The best approach is to keep the patient in the most comfortable position and maintain that until surgical reduction can be completed. A scoop stretcher allows for the stretcher to slide under the patient, causing minimal movement. Patients can be quickly picked up and loaded for transport. Choice *A* would be a possibility, but the amount of time and resources it takes to use such a device would far outweigh the benefits of quick transport of the scoop stretcher. Choice *B* would be indicated for a mid-femur fracture and not for one as high up as the signs suggest. Choice *C* would require considerable manipulation of the affected limb to make it a viable choice.

14. B: Hemophilia is a disorder in which the patient has trouble producing blood clots like a healthy individual. Extra care needs to be taken because a slight cut can bleed profusely and may require more than direct pressure. Choices *A*, *C*, and *D* are all incorrect, as a patient with hemophilia does not suffer from any of those conditions.

15. B: This patient is in respiratory failure and is unable to perfuse his brain, as noted by the AVPU scale of pain. The correct next step in the algorithm is to assist this patient by providing ventilation. Supplemental O2 with a nasal cannula would only help if the patient was breathing in the correct range of 12-20 BPM. From the scenario, the patient has a pulse, so CPR would not be warranted.

16. C: Upon assessment, the patient had signs of anaphylaxis. The patient was unconscious and had a hypotensive blood pressure, indicating that anaphylaxis caused the shock.

17. D: While staying within an EMT's scope of practice, two medications that should be administered to a patient with a possible myocardial infarction are nitroglycerin and aspirin. Aspirin will prevent the clot from growing, and nitroglycerin will reduce preload to the heart while relaxing the coronary arteries to allow for more perfusion.

18. A: A basilar skull fracture is in the occipital region of the skull and often presents with bleeding from the ears/nose. While immobilization of the head and C-spine is necessary, as is bleeding control, care needs to be taken to ensure that any potential bone fragments are not pushed into the skull cavity. The mechanism of injury suggests that any of Choices *B, C,* and *D* may be possible and care should be taken in all of these, but the presence of scalp lacerations and the need to immobilize the head/C-spine require extra care be taken when treating the head.

19. A: Abdominal adhesions are a potential adverse event of any abdominal surgery. Adhesions form when there are breaches in the exterior mucous lining of the intestine. If the intestines come in contact, they will begin to fuse together. This can cause intense abdominal pain and, if left untreated, can form a bowl obstruction. As with any abdominal issue, you should restrict oral intake. Warm compresses may alleviate some of the pain. Having the patient transported in a position that is most comfortable can also help alleviate pain. As mentioned, oral intake is to be restricted, making Choice *B* incorrect. There is no indication of an issue with the patient's incisions other than some minor oozing, which could be expected post-surgery, so Choice *C* would be incorrect. The patient is not indicating any signs of hypo/hyperglycemia, and there is no indication that the patient is diabetic.

20. B: This patient is stable SVT. This is a perfusing rhythm as noted by his blood pressure and mental status. The patient's SpO2 is low and needs supplemental oxygen, most likely administered by a non-rebreather mask to increase his oxygen saturation.

21. D: While all options would be indicated clinically, the most appropriate next action would be to insert an airway adjunct to facilitate the movement of air into the lungs. NPAs are contraindicated when dealing with a patient with facial trauma, as they may migrate into the cranial vault.

22. C: The patient appears to have encountered some sort of plant that is causing a histamine reaction. The blisters and swelling are the telltale signs of a histamine reaction. The EMT should not break the blisters, as this opens a pathway for potential infection. Cold compresses to the area will help reduce swelling and may alleviate the pain. Covering the area is not necessary unless there is active bleeding. While it may look severe, the patient is having a localized histamine reaction, and epinephrine would be indicated for anaphylactic shock, making Choice *A* incorrect. As mentioned, the EMT should not break the blisters, and covering is not necessary in this scenario, making Choice *B* incorrect. Wrapping the area tightly could cause increased pain and could break the blisters inadvertently, making Choice *D* incorrect.

23. D: Placing a bandage on the puncture wound is meant to both reduce blood loss and maintain the pressure within the lungs. CPAP would not be appropriate, as it may cause additional trauma to the injured lung. CPR and intubation are not indicated as there is no indication that the patient has lost their pulse, and they are breathing on their own.

24. B: Due to a shorter urethral channel, females are more prone to urinary tract infections than men. In elderly females, a UTI will often manifest itself with a low-grade fever and altered mental status. In this instance, there is no past medical history to point to other conditions, so the temperature of the skin should be your clue to check for a fever. Asking the staff to administer Tylenol would be inappropriate, making Choice *A* incorrect. While blood glucose could be checked, there is nothing to indicate a change in blood sugar levels, and warm skin points to fever, making Choice *C* incorrect. Oxygen saturation could be checked, but again, the signs and symptoms don't point to hypoxia, so Choice *D* would be incorrect.

25. D: Capillary bed refill is a quick and reliable check for circulation. The pressure on the nail beds will turn them white. With good perfusion, they should return to pink quickly. Choice *A* would not be a good

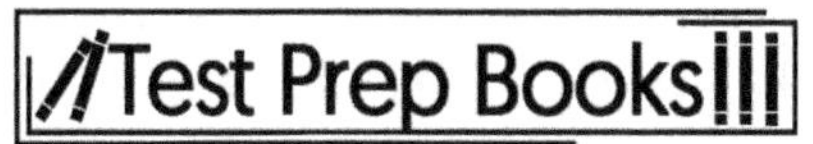

indicator, as environmental conditions could play a role. Choice *B* would be a good indicator of motor function, and Choice *C* would be a good indicator of sensory function.

26. D: The cardiac rhythm originates from the atria. The right atrium is where the SA node is located, which originates the electrical impulse that is sent throughout the heart to create mechanical contraction.

27. A: When a clinician notes the patient is not breathing while performing an initial assessment, the first course of action should be to ventilate the patient. Because this patient has fallen from a great height, the use of a jaw thrust is warranted. Always start with the least invasive measures to treat patients. This patient may be able to be ventilated with the BVM alone, without an airway adjunct.

28. D: TPA, or tissue plasminogen activator, is given at a hospital for acute stroke. TPA is a "clot-busting" medication. This allows for perfusion of the tissue distal to the clot and can help resolve stroke symptoms.

29. A: Most auto seat belts are meant for adult-sized passengers. This can create a situation where a child wearing the seat belt has it on incorrectly, draped above the arches of the hip bone. This can cause abdominal trauma from rapid deceleration. The first step is to visually examine the abdomen. Visual examination can identify any deformation, distention, or discoloration. Gently palpating the abdomen will reveal any rigidity or point tenderness, and bowel sounds can indicate a potential perforation. Choices *B* and *C* are incorrect because the first step is to visualize the abdomen. Choice *D* is incorrect because tapping the organs is not going to provide any pertinent information.

30. D: Albuterol is a bronchodilator that is typically prescribed for a patient diagnosed with asthma. Beta-2 agonists cause bronchodilation, which alleviates the restricted airway. Alpha-1 receptors cause vasoconstriction, and beta-1 receptors cause an increase in inotropy, chronotropy, and dromotropy for the heart.

31. D: The correct dose of nitroglycerin is 0.4 mg, which is to be administered sublingually. Nitroglycerin is a potent medication that, if misdosed, can cause extensive hypotension and possibly death.

32. D: This patient is displaying classic signs of bipolar disorder, such as hyperactivity, enthusiasm, and free spending. This is quickly followed by bouts of severe depression. You do not need to be forceful, but truthfully explaining the situation with the patient is the best method. If the patient continues to refuse transport, then you are required to contact law enforcement. While the patient is an adult and can refuse treatment or transport, he has verbally communicated a threat to harm himself. You are witness to an attempt on his life, so you cannot allow him to refuse transport, making Choice *A* incorrect. The patient isn't an active threat to you now, so backing away and requesting immediate law enforcement could exacerbate the situation, making Choice *B* incorrect. There is no paperwork that allows you to release the patient to the care of the parents, making Choice *C* incorrect.

33. B: A hangman's fracture refers specifically to a fracture of the second cervical vertebra, also known as C2. This type of fracture typically occurs due to extreme hyperextension of the head. Other vertebrae like C1, C7, or T1 can also be fractured during traumas, but the term *hangman's fracture* is not applied to fractures at those levels. Choice *A* is not required as the patient is not presenting symptoms that would indicate a lumbar or thoracic fracture. While the entire spine should be protected, excessive movement to immobilize the rest of the spine risks further injury to the cervical spine. Choice *C* is incorrect as there is no head immobilization, and Choice *D* is incorrect as there is no head or cervical immobilization.

34. B: There are two ways the body shifts its pH: through ventilation and through the renal system. If a clinician hyperventilates a patient, this can cause respiratory alkalosis. When the body is not in homeostasis, cellular processes do not function correctly, and cellular death can occur.

35. A: While some services are different when it comes to intersections, the most appropriate way for an EMS crew to go through a red light is to only proceed once they are sure that cross traffic has come to a stop.

36. B: Hepatitis is one of the most common bloodborne pathogens you may come in contact with. You must take care to protect any exposed mucous membranes, as these will be transmission routes. Extra care for any open sores that may be exposed should be covered in addition to the required PPE. Choices *A*, *C*, and *D* are inappropriate for this scenario.

37. A: Electric shocks can cause swelling and potential compartment syndrome. It is crucial to remove any constricting items (such as jewelry) from the affected area to prevent complications. Choice *B* (applying a cold pack to the area) is not the best action in this scenario, even though it will provide temporary relief of pain. The priority is to ensure the person's safety. Choice *C* is incorrect as warm water immersion would not address any underlying issues that occur with electric shock. Although immediately transporting the individual to the nearest emergency department may be necessary depending on the severity of the injury, the immediate action should be to remove restrictive items, making Choice *D* incorrect.

38. C: Fixed and constricted pupils are a common sign of opiate overdose. An overdose on an opiate will cause the patients respiratory drive to fail, which in turn causes hypoxia and hypoxemia. The intervention that will allow the patient to possibly breathe on his own again is administering naloxone, or Narcan, to counteract the opiate overdose.

39. B: A stroke is death to brain tissue due to a lack of perfusion. This can be caused by either an aneurysm or a blockage in an artery that supplies the brain with blood.

40. B: An ectopic pregnancy is where a fertilized egg implanted in the fallopian tubes rather than the uterus. As the fetus develops, pressure is put on the tube and rupture can occur. This is not a deliverable pregnancy. The patient's inability to recall her last period and the vaginal spotting are indicative of an ectopic pregnancy, and this is a life-threatening condition. If the fallopian tube were to rupture, peritonitis would follow. Rapid transport is required. The signs and symptoms do not point to any of the other conditions listed, making Choices *A*, *C*, and *D* incorrect.

41. A: After cardiac arrest, if a patient is still unable to respirate on their own, they should receive ventilatory support with a BVM. Pediatric patients should be ventilated at 20-30 breaths per minute, which is one breath every two to three seconds.

42. A: In this scenario, the patient is experiencing symptoms of diabetic ketoacidosis (DKA), which occurs when blood glucose levels are extremely high. The EMT should determine the patient's blood glucose level to determine the next action. Choice *B* is incorrect, as the patient may have a gag reflex, and blood glucose levels take priority. Choice *C* is incorrect, as glucagon is a medication used to treat low blood glucose levels (known as hypoglycemia), and the patient should not be given anything by mouth. Choice

D is incorrect, as the patient's respiratory function appears adequate, and blood sugar readings are a priority.

43. A: The patient has CSF noted from the halo test, which could indicate a basilar skull fracture. A contraindication for placement of an NPA is a basilar skull fracture, as it could cause deviation of the NPA into the cranial vault, so the correct answer is Choice *A*. Choices *B, C,* and *D* could all be used in this patient with this MOI.

44. A: Shock is a condition where perfusion demand is not being met throughout the body and vital organs. The three types of shock are distributive, cardiogenic, and hypovolemic. All other types of shock come from these main categories. Choice *B* refers to distributive shock. Choice *C* refers to cardiogenic shock. Choice *D* is not a form of shock.

45. C. Using the KED device to remove a patient with multiple potential injuries where spinal stabilization is required is the best choice in this situation. Choices *A, B,* and *D* would be inappropriate for the above situation.

46. A: Chronic bronchitis patients can present with cyanosis, productive coughs, hypoxia, and appear barrel chested. Emphysema patients will present as the "pink puffers" who have pursed lips to auto-PEEP and are without cyanosis. Pneumonia patients present with a fever. A pneumothorax is air between the visceral and parietal pleura and does not fit this presentation.

47. C: Patients who have recently been in cardiac arrest should be closely monitored because it is very possible that the arrest could happen again. Providing supplemental oxygenation to achieve a saturation of 94% is the AHA guideline for myocardial infarction.

48. A: If a provider or any other healthcare providers arrive on the scene and begin to dictate patient care, an EMT should call medical control and follow their guidance. Medical control has the final say on patient care and transportation.

49. C: This patient is presenting with signs of COPD exacerbation. The first treatment for this condition is administration of either a rescue inhaler or nebulizer to decrease the bronchospasms that are causing the condition. COPD patients will often have a slightly lower-than-average oxygen saturation, and increasing the patient's oxygen to read 100% can actually be dangerous for some COPD patients. This does not mean you should ever withhold oxygen from a COPD patient, though. Use of a BVM (bag valve mask) is not indicated, as the patient is breathing independently. Epinephrine is not indicated, as the patient is not showing signs of anaphylaxis.

50. D: The most important action for a provider to take with a patient having an ischemic stroke is to transport them to a stroke center. These centers provide crucial thrombolytic therapy to stroke patients. The quicker they are alerted and utilized, the more effectively they can save brain tissue.

51. B: ICS, or the Incident Command System, is a standardized hierarchy structure that allows multiple agencies to work together to establish command and control during more large-scale events such as tornadoes, CBRN, and other disasters. The model allows for multiple agencies to work together efficiently and effectively.

52. A: As with all abdominal issues, the patient's oral intake should be restricted. Listening to bowel sounds can help eliminate a digestive system problem. The scenario indicates that the patient could be suffering from an ovarian issue (e.g., fibroid tumors, cysts). Her being around the time of ovulation can exacerbate an ovarian issue. Hearing normal bowel sounds and there being a lack of back pain would indicate a potential ovarian issue. Your care is limited to providing support and treating any symptoms that may arise (e.g., respirations, pulse), and transporting with knees flexed may alleviate some of the pain. Choice *B* is incorrect, as nothing indicates the patient is experiencing a blood sugar issue. Choice *C* is incorrect because, as previously mentioned, the patient's oral intake needs to be restricted. Choice *D* is incorrect because transporting in Trendelenburg could exacerbate abdominal pain.

53. C: The interventions for an internal abdominal injury are limited, but transporting the patient seated with knees flexed will provide the most comfort and relieve pressure on the lower abdomen. In addition, ice may help with pain and swelling. Choice *A* is incorrect; there is nothing to indicate that the patient requires lumbar immobilization, and transporting supine would not be recommended. Choice *B* is incorrect as abdominal trauma patients should not be given anything to eat or drink. Choice *D* is incorrect as wrapping the patient's abdomen in sterile bandages will provide no benefit to the patient.

54. C: When dealing with a patient who is hearing impaired and uses a sign interpreter, always address the patient directly and do so as the response is given. This allows the patient to feel like they are part of the conversation, and it allows you to pick up on nonverbal cues. Address questions for the family member directly to them. Choices *A*, *B*, and *D* are all inappropriate responses for this scenario.

55. D: Patients with COPD have a chronic ventilation to perfusion mismatch. This V/Q mismatch causes the patient to be unable to offload CO2 correctly, creating a respiratory acidotic state. This state causes inadequate oxygenation and hypercapnia, which leads to respiratory failure.

56. B: A patient that is actively seizing upon your arrival should be protected from the environment to the best of your abilities. Remove any objects that may injure the patient, and if possible, place padding near or under the patient, taking care to protect the head. After the patient becomes post-ictal, clear the airway of any blood or saliva that may have accumulated. Once cleared, assess the mouth for any injury that may hinder airway management. You should never attempt to restrain a patient that is actively seizing, but rather guard them. Also, you never want to attempt to put anything into a seizing patient's mouth; therefore, Choice *A* is incorrect. A postictal patient may appear unresponsive, but they will still have a gag reflex, so an oral airway would not be indicated, making Choice *C* incorrect. You do not want to attempt to move the patient unless it is necessary for the safety of the patient, and an oral airway would not be indicated in this instance, so Choice *D* is incorrect.

57. A: A depressed person can use cutting as a means of psychological pain relief. Nobody knows for certain why patients do this, but it is not an uncommon occurrence. Most cutting is not done to inflict permanent damage or strike an artery; the lacerations are usually superficial and easily controlled with direct pressure. The patient is non-violent, and most "cutters" do not display a suicidal ideation; the cutting is their release in the same way some may use alcohol or drugs, so law enforcement is not required unless there is a threat to others, making Choice *B* incorrect. There is no reason to rush the patient and/or restrain this patient, as he is not conveying a threat to himself, making Choices *C* and *D* incorrect.

58. A: When a patient is in V-TACH, the electrical signal originates in the ventricles. The ventricles must pump faster in order to compensate for the lack of preload to the heart since the atria are not contracting. This is why a patient in V-TACH will be tachycardic and typically not perfusing well.

59. B: Scene safety is your top priority. The roommate's mention of firearms means the scene is not safe. You must immediately back out and request law enforcement to secure the scene and determine

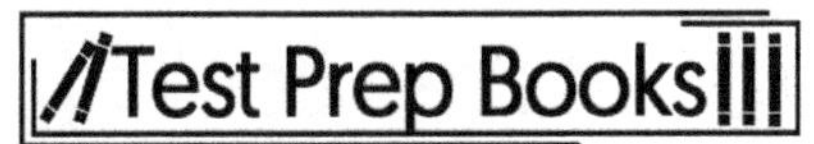

what approach to take with the man. Location information is beneficial to law enforcement upon arrival. Choices *A, C,* and *D* are all inappropriate for a potentially armed suicidal patient.

60. D: It is the EMT's responsibility to address the situation with sensitivity and understanding. In the case of a stillborn baby, the EMT should focus on the emotional well-being of the parents. Offering grieving resources at this time would be inappropriate as this scenario has just occurred. It is also the responsibility of the obstetrician and other medical providers, making Choice *A* incorrect. In the case of stillborn delivery, the baby should not be separated from the parents without their permission, making Choice *B* incorrect. Not acknowledging the baby is inappropriate; instead, acknowledge the stillbirth and the baby's existence and express condolences to the parents. It is important to use the baby's name if one is given. This makes Choice *C* incorrect.

61. A: Addison's is an autoimmune disease where the patient's own immune system attacks their adrenal glands, reducing production of necessary hormones (i.e., cortisol). This can cause fatigue, nausea, and hypoglycemia. Your priority is to maintain the airway, then check blood sugar levels. Your care is limited for a non-responsive patient. Choice *B* is incorrect because the patient is unresponsive, and administering anything oral is not indicated. Addison's is a chronic condition that patients usually manage with medications and other treatments. An acute flare-up of the condition is not life threatening unless airway management becomes difficult or hypoglycemia is severe, making Choice *C* incorrect. Choice *D* is incorrect, as the patient may have a gag reflex and an oral airway would not be indicated.

62. B: The patient is showing signs of epiglottitis, or swelling to the epiglottis, usually caused by a bacterial infection. If swelling worsens, it can lead to airway obstruction in the patient. Because of this, the mother should be encouraged to keep the patient calm and comfortable to reduce interactions that may further irritate the epiglottis (e.g., crying). As the patient appears to not be in respiratory distress, an airway inspection is not indicated and could actually cause the patient's condition to worsen, as it may agitate the airway. Feeding should be discouraged until the airway is secured after further medical intervention. Educating the mother on vaccinating her child should wait until after the emergency situation has been resolved.

63. C: Often when a person falls on an outstretched arm, the clavicle (collarbone) is fractured. This usually presents with the affected shoulder "sagging," and the most comfortable position that reduces the risk of further injury is supporting the affected shoulder with a sling and immobilizing the joint swathed against the patient's chest. Ice to the affected area can reduce swelling. Choice *A* is incorrect as the patient will usually experience considerable pain when trying to reposition their arm, and a rigid or air splint would not be indicated. Choice *B* is incorrect as the patient cannot maintain sufficient support. Choice *D* is incorrect for the same reasons as Choices *A* and *B*.

64. C: Patients who are hypoglycemic have signs that can mimic strokes. The most notable are dyscoordination, altered mental status, and slurred speech. A blood glucose check should be performed quickly to determine if the patient is hypoglycemic and to rule out stroke.

65. C: From the description, the firefighter was inside the fire with his mask off and is likely suffering from smoke inhalation, so ensure a patent airway and provide oxygen immediately. While only superficial, the integrity of the skin is at risk, so stopping the burning process with a cool compress on the back would be the next priority. From the mechanism of injury, it appears that the firefighter dislocated his shoulder, and this would be the next priority. Choices *A, B,* and *D* are all incorrect.

66. A: From the scenario, the patient has caregivers and would most likely have a sedentary lifestyle, which can contribute to pneumonia. This patient is febrile, which should lead the clinician to suspect an infection. Pneumonia, Choice *A*, is the only infection listed here that would cause a patient to be febrile.

67. C: There may be a time when patients require some degree of reasonable force to prevent them from unintentional harm to themselves and others. The remaining choices are not terms associated with the removal of a patient with the intention of reducing the risk of harm to self or others.

68. C: The patient's blood glucose level and the fact that he is unresponsive to verbal and painful stimuli indicate that the patient is experiencing diabetic coma. A diabetic coma can be the result of either severe hypo- or hyperglycemia. In this instance, the patient is in severe hypoglycemia, and his systems are starving for glucose. This is a life-threatening scenario. The patient requires high-flow oxygen and rapid transport, as invasive measures will need to be taken to restore blood glucose levels. Choice *A* is incorrect, as you would never try to administer anything to an unresponsive patient, and oral glucose will be insufficient to raise levels rapidly enough. Choice *B* is incorrect, as it is not within your scope of care, and adding insulin would lower blood glucose levels further. At present, the patient has a patent airway, so there isn't a need to open the airway, but if respiratory function worsens, then Choice *D* would be the next step.

69. C: The correct ratio of compressions to breaths while doing CPR on an adult patient is 30:2. A 15:2 ratio is correct for a pediatric patient with two first responders present. The patient would be hyperventilated with a 10:2 ratio and hypoventilated with a 60:2 ratio.

70. B: At first sight, infants can often appear to be very stable after a traumatic event because their systems are small and initial compensation is easy. The issue is that this compensation is very short-lived. While small, the systems are not developed and cannot sustain the needed perfusion. Once the decompensation begins, it is very rapid and, without immediate interventions, will often result in death. Choices *A, C,* and *D* are incorrect.

71. A: Accidental needlesticks are the most common method of transmission experienced by healthcare workers. They can happen for a multitude of reasons, and most do not result in infection of the healthcare worker, but each should be treated seriously and immediately. The first thing to do is wash the area with warm soapy water vigorously and for an extended time. If you are able, you will want to exert some pressure above the wound in a milking fashion to flush any superficial blood away and rewash the area. Immediately notify your supervisor and seek medical attention. Choice *B* is incorrect, as an alcohol disinfectant is not indicated for an accidental needle stick. You would not use constant pressure above the wound, as that will not prevent transmission of a bloodborne pathogen, making Choice *C* incorrect. Choice *D* is incorrect, as you should immediately notify your supervisor and seek medical attention, not wait for symptoms to present.

72. D: CPAP, or continuous positive airway pressure, helps oxygenate a patient by forcing alveoli open and increasing surface area during ventilation. A contraindication to CPAP is altered mental status or unconsciousness, as it does not breathe or ventilate for patients.

73. B: There is no rush to cut the cord. Care for the mother and newborn should be taken first and then attention to the cord can be taken. Ensure the cord has stopped pulsing before putting any clamps in place. Place the first clamp approximately 10 cm from the baby's umbilicus and the second clamp about 5 cm up from that. Cleanly cut between the clamps and leave them in place to prevent blood loss. Keep the cord warm and dry. Choice *A* is incorrect, as you do not want to put the clamps in place

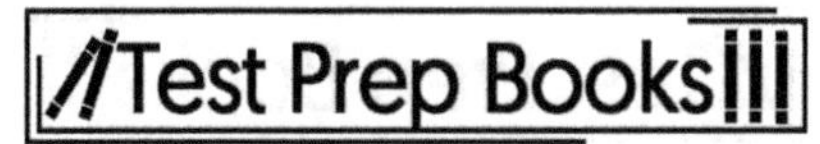

immediately. Tend to the infant and mother, then check for cord pulsing. Choice *C* is incorrect, as you do not need to await placental delivery. Choice *D* is incorrect, as you would not remove the clamps; doing so could lead to blood loss for both the infant and mother.

74. D: While every option would be helpful in a community, an EMT should only conduct programs that intertwine with their respective skillset. Conducting simple first aid classes shows the community that EMS cares and displays competency in necessary skills.

75. D: ESRD is chronic renal failure that has progressed to permanent and irreversible loss of renal function. The kidney maintains the correct fluid balance within the body, and in the case of ESRD, the kidney no longer provides that balance. Fluid overload is common, and when presented with difficulty breathing lying down, it indicates a backup of fluid. This can cause bubbling breath sounds in the lower lobes and shortness of breath when supine. The presence of swelling in the ankles and bubbling breath sounds are indicative of fluid backup and require high-flow oxygen. Choice *A* would not be correct, as the patient requires more than supplemental oxygen via nasal cannula. Choice *B* would be incorrect, as the presence of a fever will not alter your care, and administration of OTC medication is beyond your scope of care. A patient with difficulty breathing lying down will develop pedal edema due to the feet being the furthest away from the heart, i.e., where fluid will build up. Edema will not be present in the upper extremities.

76. A: In order for a system to get reimbursed for the transport, the patient's insurance should be documented by the EMS crew. There are many types of insurance, and people can have redundant names, which makes it harder for billing to receive payment for the transport and medical care. This can be alleviated by ensuring proper documentation during the call.

77. A: It is common practice for most EMS agencies to conduct QA, or quality assurance, audits on PCRs to ensure accuracy and correct medical practice. A QA process usually involves a senior member of the agency reading and providing feedback for PCRs to crews who transport patients. QA also allows for reflection and debriefs of complicated cases that can be used as an example for future calls.

78. A: Patients post-ROSC can present with a much higher ETCO2 due to being in anaerobic metabolism for so long. Both hypo- and hypercapnia are associated with increased mortality rates. The normal tidal volume range for adults is 6-8 milliliters per kilogram.

79. C: The maximum time oral suctioning should occur is 15 seconds, Choice *C*. If you suction too long, you increase the risk of hypoxia. While suctioning, you may also cause bradycardia due to vagal stimulation.

80. D: Patients with facial burns are at risk of upper airway obstruction caused by swelling. Choices *A, B,* and *C* may be concerns, but infection and scarring are issues that would not present themselves in the acute setting; although pain will be present, pain management interventions are limited for the EMT.

81. C: According to the American Heart Association, compressions on both adults and pediatric patients should be performed at a rate of 100-120 beats per minute. This allows for the best perfusion while a patient is in cardiac arrest.

82. B: Most likely, the patient has been stung by an insect and is having a localized reaction. Rapid swelling to the area is the body's way to wall off the toxin from other parts of the body. While this can look severe, it is not normally life threatening. It is a slightly more severe reaction than normal, so you want to be vigilant for anaphylactic shock. Applying cold compresses usually alleviates pain and swelling.

There is no indication of head injury or trauma. Since the patient ran to the house rather than being found injured, head or neck trauma can most likely be ruled out, making Choices *A* and *C* incorrect. While the child is having an elevated allergic reaction, his symptoms don't rise to the need for epinephrine, making Choice *D* incorrect.

83. D: The ambulance should be in between the crash and the traffic to provide protection for the crew and injured personnel. If a crew is not the first to arrive at the scene, police or fire may instruct the crew on where to park the ambulance.

84. D: The priority is to assess the woman's vital signs and bleeding, since her complaints of abdominal pain can indicate potential complications or injuries. Assessment of the woman's vitals and the amount of vaginal bleeding will allow you to determine the next actions to take and will help you notify the hospital of her current state. Choice *A,* transporting the woman to the nearest hospital, is necessary but is not the first step. The EMT should determine the woman's condition and then provide appropriate care during transport to the hospital. Choice *B* is incorrect because, as with any abdominal issue, the patient's oral intake should be restricted and will do very little to manage pain and bleeding. Choice *C,* elevating the legs, may worsen the bleeding if there are underlying injuries, making this choice also incorrect.

85. B: Patients have the right, if alert and oriented, to refuse to be transported. EMTs should tell the patient about the consequences that come from inappropriate care for a wound such as this. Along with education, the EMT should ensure the patient signs the agency's refusal form.

86. A: The quickest and most effective way to splint a potential rib fracture is to have the patient bring their upper arm against the affected area. The EMT would then bandage the arm in place and instruct the patient to press against the chest harder on inspiration. Choices *B, C,* and *D* are all inappropriate for the above scenario.

87. D: Choice *D* is within the correct range for tidal volumes for adults. Normal tidal volumes should be between 4 and 8 mL/kg each breath. Choices *A* and *C* are too high. Choice *B* is far too little when providing ventilation on a typical adult patient. Keep in mind that a BVM can ventilate up to 1.5 liters, so ensuring that you don't squeeze the bag too hard is important.

88. A: The NREMT is the nationally recognized certification for EMS workers, but in order to practice in their specific state, an EMT must apply for state licensure through their respective state EMS office.

89. C: Sickle cell disease (SCD) is a congenital disease where red blood cells are damaged and become crescent or sickle shaped. These cells can become lodged in smaller blood vessels, causing sickle cell crisis, where the patient can experience pain, especially in their lower back and extremities. Choice *A* is incorrect, as type I diabetes is a disease of the pancreas and is not blood related. HIV is a blood-related disease, but it is not congenital; it is a sexually transmitted infection, making choice *B* incorrect. Hepatitis B is a disease of the liver, not the blood, making Choice *D* incorrect.

90. D: The classification of immediate or "red" signifies that the patient's condition will deteriorate immediately if not definitively treated. A patient with a tension pneumothorax needs surgical correction by means of a chest tube in order to prevent obstructive shock, which may lead to death.

91. D: When assessing pediatric burn patients, EMTs must consider that a child's head accounts for more of their entire surface area compared to an adult. While there are some differences in other areas, none are as prominent as the head. Choices *A, B,* and *C* are not correct.

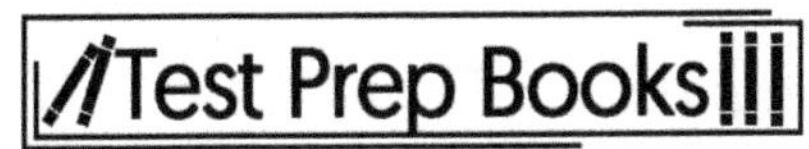

92. C: There is no rush for the placenta to be delivered. It can take as long as 30 minutes, time that can be used to transport the mother and the baby. The placenta will detach by itself from the uterus and will be delivered by the mother. You want to inspect the placenta to see if there appear to be any tears or areas where tissue is missing. You will want to collect the placenta for further examination. If the placenta is not delivered within 30 minutes, the mother will need care that is beyond your scope. Fundal massage has been reported to help alleviate uterine bleeding after the placenta is delivered, but it is not indicated for placental delivery stimulation, making Choice *A* incorrect. You never want to pull on the umbilical cord at any point of the placental delivery; doing so can cause a tear in the uterus and heavy bleeding, making Choice *B* incorrect. Choice *D* is incorrect, as you do not want to dispose of the placenta.

93. A: This woman is most likely experiencing a postpartum hemorrhage, which can occur up to 12 weeks after giving birth. The EMT should massage the uterus to aid contraction, which can potentially reduce bleeding. Although breastfeeding can assist with uterine contractions, it is not as effective in severe hemorrhage as fundal or uterine massage, making Choice *B* incorrect. Choice *C* is also incorrect, as the Trendelenburg position is no longer recommended in the management of shock—it can make the condition worse and does not address the hemorrhage itself. Choice *D*, administering pain medication, is not within your scope of care.

94. A: Patients in respiratory failure are unable to eliminate CO2 from their bodies. End-tidal CO2 reflects the amount of carbon dioxide being exhaled, or eliminated. Normal ranges for end-tidal CO2 are from 35 to 45. An end-tidal reading of 55 shows that the patient has far too much CO2 in the body and indicates respiratory failure.

95. C: The patient's admission to being overweight and just eating a large fried meal before symptom onset indicates potentially an inflamed gallbladder or pancreatitis. Both will present with pain after eating fried foods and are common in overweight people. While it initially sounds like a potential cardiac emergency since an MI can present with heartburn, the stable vital signs and onset of symptoms make Choice *A* incorrect. Listening to bowel sounds and taking blood glucose levels would not be correct, as it is expected that the patient's blood sugar would be elevated, but this would not warrant intervention as there is no indication of diabetes, making Choice *B* incorrect. As with any abdominal issue, the patient should not be given anything by mouth, making Choice *D* incorrect.

96. A: PEA is a condition during cardiac arrest that is defined by electrical activity without mechanical action. The heart relies on electricity to beat, but if that electrical component is not strong enough to cause mechanical contraction, the heart won't actually beat. The correct treatment during PEA is to continue CPR because defibrillation won't be effective.

97. B: Under most circumstances, a newborn will spontaneously begin breathing. If respirations do not begin within a minute of birth, they can often be stimulated tactically (e.g., drying of the neonate, flicking of heels). Your next step would be to provide rescue breaths and check for a pulse. The effectiveness of your breaths and presence of a pulse will determine if you need to begin CPR or assist with ventilation. Infants within the first minutes of birth should not be suctioned any more than the initial suctioning with a bulb syringe immediately post birth, making Choices *A*, *C*, and *D* incorrect.

98. C: Infants have poor thermoregulation, and the cooling effect of a wet sheet could cause the patient to suffer hypothermia. Choices *A*, *B*, and *D* are not correct.

99. C: Hypoxemia, Choice *C*, is the term for oxygen deficiency in the blood. *Hypoxia* means oxygen deficiency in the tissues of the body. *Hypercapnia* means excessive carbon dioxide in the blood. *Hypocarbia* is a decreased level of carbon dioxide in the blood.

100. B: Benzodiazepines are often prescribed for patients with severe anxiety. The come from the family that is known as "downers," and they do just that: they suppress the mood, but they also depress other bodily functions, including respiration. A patient who has taken more than prescribed will often be very sleepy and difficult to arouse. They will respond to painful stimuli unless the intoxication is severe. In this scenario, your main concern is to ensure a patent airway and assist if necessary. The pharmacy on the bottle may be able to provide any other interventions you could take. Choice *A* is incorrect, as the patient would have a gag reflex. A patient in this altered state should not be given anything by mouth, making Choice *C* incorrect. Narcan is only indicated for potential overdose of narcotics; it will have no effect on non-opiate medications, making Choice *D* incorrect.

101. C: Patients in post-resuscitation care are at a much greater risk of re-entering cardiac arrest if the body is not in homeostasis. Glucose is vital to cellular function and is essential for organs to work. The normal level of blood glucose when taken by a BGL is 70-110 mmol/L.

102. B: A tourniquet is only used for life-threatening bleeding. A tourniquet is applied proximally to the site as close to the heart as possible and can only be in place for two hours or long-term damage to the limb can occur. Marking the patient's head with a capital T and the time of application will aid in knowing the exact time of application, in case the person who applied it is no longer available. Choice *A* is incorrect as the tourniquet is applied proximally and as close to the heart as possible and should never be loosened to check the bleeding. Choice *C* is incorrect as tourniquet application should never be across joints, and Choice *D* is incorrect as the application would not be as close to the wound as possible.

103. D: One of the more common pediatric upper airway emergencies is croup, Choice *D*. The typical scenario is a patient between six months and three years of age. A patient with croup will often present with a "seal-like" bark and stridor. The infection causes narrowing of the upper airway, which creates difficulty breathing.

104. D: A CVA patient will often have paralysis to one cranial nerve but rarely both. The quickest way to observe it is to have the patient smile and raise their eyebrows. If one side reacts and the other doesn't, it is an indication of one-sided paralysis. Choice *A* would be how you would check for a potential skull fracture. Choice *B* will give you no indication of facial paralysis, and while Choice *C* would be a way to check optic nerve function, the time it takes is considerably longer than a simple verbal request that most people can comply with.

105. A: Pericarditis is inflammation of the pericardium surrounding the heart. One of the most infamous presentations of pericarditis is the relief of pain when a patient leans forward. IV drug use is the most typical way for a patient to get pericarditis.

Index

Abandonment, 114, 121, 122, 127, 128
ABCDE Approach, 55
Abrasion, 64, 73
Acquired Brain Injury (ABI), 70
Actual Consent, 123, 127, 128
Acute Pulmonary Edema, 28
Adrenal Gland, 93, 94
Afferent Arteriole, 100
Air Medical Service, 118
Airway, 13, 14, 15, 16, 17, 18, 19, 22, 23, 25, 26, 27, 28, 31, 32, 34, 36, 37, 38, 48, 52, 54, 55, 58, 67, 72, 73, 81, 107, 110, 111, 113, 117, 142, 158, 159
Aldosterone, 94, 100
Allergic Reaction, 89, 90
Altered Mental Status (AMS), 86
Amputation, 52, 53, 66, 80, 83
Anaphylaxis, 89, 90, 163
Aneurysms, 71
Angina Pectoralis, 42
Anuria, 102
Aortic Rupture, 59
Aortic Valve, 40
Aplastic Crisis, 97
Appendicular Skeleton, 60
Arrhythmias, 43, 44, 47, 48, 49, 55
Arterial Bleeding, 56
Arteries, 39, 40, 41, 42, 45, 56, 67, 71, 81
Arteriosclerosis, 42
Arteriovenous Malformation (AVM), 71
Ascending Nerve Tracts, 74
Assault, 105, 123, 126, 127, 128
Asthma, 19, 20, 21, 28, 29, 32, 58
Atelectasis, 58
Atherosclerosis, 42
Atrial Fibrillation, 44
Atrium, 39, 40, 43
Auscultation, 22, 58
Automated External Defibrillator (AED), 48, 90
Avulsion, 65
Axial Loading, 75
Axial Skeleton, 60
Azotemia, 102
Bacterial Vaginosis, 105
Bartholin Glands, 103
Basilar Fractures, 68, 69
Battery, 49, 112, 123, 127, 128
Bladder, 35, 60, 82, 88, 98, 100, 101, 102, 109
Bleeds, 55, 56
Blood Clotting, 63
Blood Pressure, 13, 20, 21, 22, 23, 27, 35, 36, 41, 46, 47, 49, 50, 51, 55, 56, 57, 67, 71, 75, 80, 81, 82, 85, 88, 90, 93, 95, 110, 190
Blow-by Technique, 31
Blowout Fracture, 73
Blowout Fractures, 73
Blunt Trauma, 57, 58, 72, 73, 76
Brachial Artery, 57
Bradycardia, 16, 41, 70, 94, 138, 157
Brain Hemorrhage, 69, 71
Brain Hypoxia, 70
Breathing, 13, 15, 17, 18, 19, 20, 21, 22, 23, 24, 27, 28, 30, 31, 37, 38, 46, 47, 55, 58, 59, 81, 89, 90, 91, 96, 97, 104, 106, 107, 147
Breech Delivery, 107
Bronchitis, 25, 26
Bronchopulmonary Dysplasia, 29
BVM, 14, 16, 17, 18, 19, 26, 28, 30, 31
Capillaries, 28, 39, 40, 63, 100
Capillary Bleeding, 56
Cardiac Arrest, 13, 15, 17, 26, 27, 28, 39, 41, 42, 44, 45, 46, 47, 48, 49, 51, 55, 71, 81, 96
Cardiac Ischemia, 42
Cardiogenic Shock, 47
Cardiology, 39
Cardiopulmonary Resuscitation (CPR), 47
Cardiovascular System, 20, 39, 47
Cerebral Contusion, 70
Cerebral Edema, 70, 95
Cerebral Hematoma, 71
Cerebrospinal Fluid Leakage, 69
Cervical Collars, 81, 111
Cervical Vertebrae, 74, 75, 77
Cervix, 103, 104
Cheek Bone, 72, 73
Cheloids, 64
Chest Trauma, 58
Chlamydia, 104, 105, 108

Chlamydia Trachomatis, 105
Cicatrix, 64
Circulation, 13, 20, 23, 37, 38, 39, 47, 55, 58, 65, 79, 80, 81
Closed Fractures, 61
Closed Pneumothorax, 59
Closed Wounds, 64
Clotting Disorder, 97
Coagulation, 63
Cold Zone, 117
Collagen, 63
Comminuted, 61
Communicable, 90, 111, 117
Compartment Syndrome, 66
Concussion, 67, 68, 76
Confidentiality, 115, 125
Consent, 105, 121, 122, 123, 124, 125, 127, 128
Contrecoup, 70
Contusion, 57, 59, 62, 67, 73
Contusions, 62, 64, 66, 70
Corneal Abrasion, 73
Coronary Artery Disease, 44, 49
Cortisol, 44, 94
Coup, 70
CPR, 14, 17, 18, 19, 47, 48, 49, 50, 51, 85, 106
Crackles, 58
Crepitus, 58, 72
Croup, 27, 32
Crush Injury, 65, 66
Crush Syndrome, 65
Cystic Fibrosis, 19, 27, 28, 30
Decreased Perfusion, 88
Deep Vein Thrombosis, 98
Degloving Injury, 65
Delta Pressure, 66
Depressed Fractures, 68
Dermis, 62, 63
Descending Nerve Tracts, 74
Diabetes, 30, 37, 64, 95, 138
Diabetic Ketoacidosis (DKA), 95
Diastolic Blood Pressure, 41, 66
Diffuse Injuries, 69
Diffuse Injury, 67
Direct Injury, 66
Disability, 23, 45, 55, 58, 66
Distal Convoluted Tubule, 100
Double Vision (Diplopia), 73
Dynamic Traction Splints, 79
Dyspnea, 20, 21, 25, 29, 30
Ecchymosis, 69, 72
Efferent Arteriole, 100
Emancipated Minor, 122, 123, 124, 127, 128
Emergency Medical Service (EMS), 115
Emergency Medical Technician (EMT), 41, 85
Endocrine System, 92, 93
Endotracheal Suctioning, 32
Environmental Emergencies, 54
Epidemics, 90, 92
Epidural Hematoma, 71, 83
Epiglottis, 16, 26
Epiphyseal Plates, 61
Epistaxis, 73, 74
Equilibrium, 63, 68
Evisceration, 60
Exposure, 23, 44, 54, 55, 58, 105, 116, 117, 127
Expressed Consent, 123, 127, 128
Exsanguination, 72
External Bleeding, 56
Extremity Splinting, 79, 83
Extrication, 74, 82
Fallopian Tubes, 98, 103, 104, 105
False Ribs, 58
FBAO, 26, 27
Febrile Seizure, 86
Femoral Artery, 57, 81
Femoral Injuries, 62
Field Delivery, 106
Flail Chest, 58
Flora, 102
Focal Injuries, 69, 70
Follicles, 103
Fractures, 52, 53, 58, 61, 62, 66, 68, 69, 71, 72, 73, 74, 75, 79
Generalized Tonic-Clonic Seizure, 86
Genital Herpes, 105
Genitourinary, 60, 98, 100, 102
Glasgow Coma Scale, 13, 52, 69
Glomerular (Bowman's) Capsule, 100
Glomerular Filtration Rate, 100
Glomerulus, 100
Golden Hour, 55
Gonorrhea, 105
Good Samaritan Laws, 124
Grade 1 Concussions, 67

Grade 2 Concussions, 67
Grade 3 Concussions, 67
Greenstick Fracture, 61
Grey Turner's Sign, 60
Gynecology, 85, 103, 110, 111
Hare Traction Splint, 79, 83, 84
Hazardous Materials, 115, 116, 117
Hazmat (Hazardous Material), 116
Head-Tilt/Chin-Lift, 14, 16
Heart, 13, 14, 17, 20, 23, 25, 27, 28, 30, 35, 38, 39, 40, 41, 42, 43, 44, 45, 46, 47, 49, 50, 51, 52, 53, 55, 56, 57, 58, 59, 66, 71, 86, 102, 106, 121, 161, 179, 195
Hematology, 97
Hematoma, 62, 66, 71
Hemoglobin, 29, 34, 35, 97
Hemolysis, 97
Hemophilia, 56, 98
Hemopneumothorax, 59
Hemorrhages, 55, 71, 81
Hemorrhagic, 59, 60, 65, 86
Hemostasis, 62, 63
Hemothorax, 59
Hemotympanum, 69
High-Efficiency Particulate Air Filter (HEPA) Mask, 117
Histamine, 63
Histamines, 89
Homeostasis, 63, 92
Hot Zone, 117
Hyperemia, 63
Hyperkalemia, 65, 94
Hyperphosphatemia, 65
Hypertensive, 46, 47, 71
Hypertrophic Scars, 64
Hyperuricemia, 65
Hyperventilation, 18, 19, 20, 21, 22, 23, 46, 86, 88
Hypocalcemia, 65
Hypoglycemia, 46, 94
Hypotension, 46, 47, 59, 94, 102, 138, 157
Hypothalamus, 92, 93
Hypovolemic Shock, 47, 56, 65
Hypoxemia, 21, 24
Hypoxia, 20, 21, 23, 31, 59, 97, 98, 160
Immunology, 89
Indirect Injury, 66
Infectious Disease, 90, 92
Inferior Vena Cava, 40
Inflammatory Response, 63
Inner Dermis, 62
Insulin, 46, 86, 93, 94, 95
Internal Bleeding, 57
Interstitial Fluid, 63
Intracerebral Hemorrhage, 71
Intracranial, 70, 71, 82
Intracranial Pressure (ICP), 70
Involuntary Consent, 123
Ischemia, 42, 53, 70, 73
Ischemic, 55, 65, 86, 88
Ischemic Chest Pain, 88
Jaw-Thrust, 14, 16
Keloids, 64
Kendrick Extrication Device, 78
Keratin, 62
Kidney Stones, 88, 102, 108, 109, 171
Kidneys, 37, 38, 57, 60, 65, 93, 98, 100, 109, 195
Lacerations, 54, 64, 69, 117
Lateral Bending, 75
Le Fort Fractures, 72
Le Fort I Fractures, 72
Le Fort II Fractures, 72
Le Fort III Fractures, 73
Leukocytes, 64
Leukotrienes, 89
Libel, 122, 126
Limb Presentation, 107
Linear Fractures, 68
Liver, 57, 60, 64, 88, 91, 94
Long Boards, 78
Loop of Henle, 100
Mechanical Patient Restraint, 79
Mechanism of Injury (MOI), 74
Medical Practice Act, 120
Melanin, 63
Melena, 57
Metabolic Acidosis, 65, 102
Military Anti-Shock Trousers (MAST)/Pneumatic Anti-Shock Garments (PASG), 80
Minors, 123, 124, 127, 128
Mitral Valve, 40
Moderate Diffuse Axonal Injury, 68
Multisystem Trauma, 52, 53, 84
Musculoskeletal Injuries, 62

Mydriasis, 73
Myocardial Contusion, 59
Myocardial Rupture, 59
Myxedema Coma, 94
Nasal Cannulas, 30, 32
Nasotracheal and Nasopharyngeal Suctioning, 32
National Association of Emergency Medical Technicians (NAEMT), 121
National Institute for Occupational Safety and Health (NIOSH), 111
Natural Disasters, 54
Neck, 16, 22, 27, 31, 32, 49, 52, 53, 55, 57, 66, 71, 72, 75, 77, 78, 81, 82, 91, 106
Negative Feedback Loops, 93
Negligence, 114, 121
Nephrons, 100, 102
Neural Processes (Axons), 67
Non-Rebreather Masks, 30
Nuchal Cord, 107
Oblique Fractures, 61
Obstetrics, 85, 103, 104, 110, 111
Occupational Safety and Health Administration (OSHA), 111
Oliguria, 102
One-Way Tricuspid Valve, 40
Open Fracture, 61, 79
Open Pneumothorax, 59
Open Vault Fractures, 69
Open Wounds, 64
Oropharyngeal Suctioning, 32
Orthostatic Hypotension, 47, 57
Osteoblasts, 62
Outer Epidermis, 62
Ovarian, 104, 105
Ovaries, 93, 98, 103, 104, 105
Ovum, 103
Pancreas, 60, 88, 93, 94
Pandemics, 90
Parathyroid Glands, 93
Parietal, 87, 108
Patient Safety Act, 120
Pediatric Patients, 13, 15, 16, 19, 23, 24, 25, 27, 29, 31, 34, 39, 41, 44, 47, 48, 50, 51, 52, 53, 55, 59, 61, 80, 83, 84, 98
Pelvic Inflammatory Disease, 104
Penetrating Trauma, 57, 75, 76
Pericardial Tamponade, 59
Peritoneum, 57, 60, 87, 88
Peritonitis, 56, 60, 88
Phalangeal, 62
Pineal Gland, 93
Pituitary Gland, 92, 93, 94, 100
Plasma, 63, 97
Platelet Plug, 63
Platelets, 63, 97, 100
Pleuritic (Respiratory) Issues, 88
Pneumatic Antishock Garment (PASG), 62
Pneumothorax, 34, 59
Podocytes, 100
Preeclampsia, 47
Pressure Points, 57
Primary Brain Injury, 69
Prolapse of the Umbilical Cord, 107
Proximal Convoluted Tubule, 100
Psychiatric Emergency, 96, 97
Pulmonary Embolism, 20, 29
Pulmonary Loop, 39
Puncture Wounds, 64
Radial Artery, 57
Rapid Extrication, 82
Referred Pain, 87, 108, 109
Reperfusion, 65
Respiratory Syncytial Virus, 29
Retroperitoneal Space, 60, 100, 109
Rhonchi, 58
Rotator Cuff Tendon Injuries, 61
Sacrum, 74
Sager Traction Splint, 79, 83, 84
Scar Tissue, 62, 64
Seated Spinal Immobilizations, 78
Secondary Assessment, 55, 58, 61
Secondary Brain Injury, 69
Seizure, 69, 80, 86
Septum, 39, 72
Severe Diffuse Axonal Injury, 68
Sexual Assault, 103, 105, 125
Shearing Forces, 60
Shock, 33, 47, 49, 52, 56, 58, 59, 60, 62, 65, 79, 81, 89, 104, 106, 108
Sickle Cell Disease, 34, 86, 97
Signs of Panic, 88
Silent Cardiac Ischemia, 42, 50, 51
Sinoatrial Node, 43, 144

Skin, 13, 19, 21, 22, 23, 34, 41, 47, 49, 50, 56, 57, 58, 60, 61, 62, 63, 64, 65, 66, 79, 89, 94, 95, 98, 108, 109
Slander, 122, 126
Sniffing Position, 14, 16, 17, 37, 140, 158
Soft Tissue Trauma, 62
Somatic) Pain, 87
Spinal Canal, 74, 75
Spinal Column, 55, 74, 79, 100
Spinal Cord, 52, 74, 75, 81
Spinal Immobilization, 66, 67, 74, 77, 83, 84
Spinal Injury, 31, 66, 68, 74, 75, 77, 78, 81, 82
Spiral Fracture, 61
Spleen, 57, 60, 87, 88, 97
Splenic Sequestration Crisis, 97
Splints, 61, 79, 111
Spontaneous Abortion, 107
Sternum, 14, 17, 19, 47, 58, 129
Strain, 61
Stridor, 19, 24, 58
Stroke, 27, 41, 45, 46, 47, 50, 57, 70, 71, 86, 108, 109
Subarachnoid Hematoma, 71
Subdural Hematoma, 71
Suctioning, 13, 15, 16, 32, 47
Superior Vena Cava, 40
Surface Trauma, 62, 63
Syncope, 57, 86
Systemic Loop, 39
Systolic Blood Pressure, 41, 52, 59
Tachycardia, 41, 59, 86, 94, 102, 171, 190
Tachypnea, 41
Temporal Artery, 57
Tension Pneumothorax, 59
Testes and Ovaries, 93
the Health Insurance Portability and Accountability Act (HIPAA), 125
the Institute of Hazardous Materials Management (IHMM), 115
Thrombin, 63
Thrombocytes, 63
Thrombophilia, 98
Thrombosis, 97
Thymus Gland, 93
Thyroid Gland, 93
Thyrotoxic Crisis, 94
Tissue Infarction, 42
Tourniquet, 57, 66, 80, 83, 108
Tourniquets, 57, 80, 83, 84
Toxic Inhalation, 25, 29
Traction Splint, 61, 79, 83
Traction Splints, 61, 79
Transverse Fracture, 61
Trauma, 14, 15, 19, 20, 22, 31, 32, 33, 34, 52, 53, 55, 58, 60, 61, 62, 64, 65, 66, 69, 71, 73, 74, 75, 76, 77, 78, 80, 82, 83, 84, 86, 96, 104, 106, 107
Traumatic Brain Injury (TBI), 69
Traumatic Hyphema, 73
True Ribs, 58
Tubo-Ovarian Abscess, 105
Type 1 (Insulin-Dependent), 95
Type 2 (Non-Insulin-Dependent), 95
Uremia, 86, 102
Ureters, 98, 100, 101
Urethra, 60, 98, 101, 102
Uterus, 88, 98, 103, 104
Utilizing the Semi-Fowler's Position, 14
Vagina, 98, 103, 105, 107
Vascular Response, 63
Vasoconstriction, 46, 63, 90
Vaso-Occlusive Crisis, 97
Veins, 39, 40, 71, 81
Venous Bleeding, 56
Ventilation, 13, 14, 16, 17, 18, 19, 23, 24, 26, 27, 28, 29, 30, 31, 32, 33, 34, 35, 37, 38, 45, 46, 47, 48, 49, 52, 54, 72, 81
Ventricle, 39, 40, 41, 44, 46, 144
Ventricular Fibrillation, 44, 48
Ventricular Tachycardia, 44, 48
Vertebral Foramen, 74
Visceral Pain, 87, 108, 109
Von Willebrand's Disease, 56
Warm Zone, 117
Wheezing, 13, 19, 21, 22, 23, 24, 25, 28, 58, 89
Withdraw Consent, 124
Wolff-Parkinson-White Syndrome, 43
Wound, 56, 58, 59, 60, 64, 66, 76, 78, 80, 81, 83, 110, 111
Zygoma, 73, 74
Zygomatic Fracture, 73

Dear EMT Test Taker,

Thank you again for purchasing this study guide for your EMT exam. We hope that we exceeded your expectations.

Our goal in creating this study guide was to cover all of the topics that you will see on the test. We also strove to make our practice questions as similar as possible to what you will encounter on test day. With that being said, if you found something that you feel was not up to your standards, please send us an email and let us know.

We would also like to let you know about other books in our catalog that may interest you.

ATI TEAS

This can be found on Amazon: amazon.com/dp/1628453109

HESI

amazon.com/dp/1637751214

We have study guides in a wide variety of fields. If the one you are looking for isn't listed above, then try searching for it on Amazon or send us an email.

Thanks Again and Happy Testing!
Product Development Team
info@studyguideteam.com

FREE Test Taking Tips Video/DVD Offer

To better serve you, we created videos covering test taking tips that we want to give you for FREE. **These videos cover world-class tips that will help you succeed on your test.**

We just ask that you send us feedback about this product. Please let us know what you thought about it—whether good, bad, or indifferent.

To get your **FREE videos**, you can use the QR code below or email freevideos@studyguideteam.com with "Free Videos" in the subject line and the following information in the body of the email:

a. The title of your product

b. Your product rating on a scale of 1-5, with 5 being the highest

c. Your feedback about the product

If you have any questions or concerns, please don't hesitate to contact us at info@studyguideteam.com.

Thank you!

Printed in the USA
CPSIA information can be obtained
at www.ICGtesting.com
LVHW061642040424
776438LV00006B/774